CONTENTS

Principles of Public International Law

Cavendish Publishing Limited

London • Sydney

Principles of Public International Law

Timothy Hillier, LLB, MA
Senior Lecturer in Law
De Montfort University
Leicester

Cavendish Publishing Limited

London • Sydney

First published in Great Britain 1995 by Cavendish Publishing Limited
The Glass House, Wharton Street, London WC1X 9PX, United Kingdom.
Telephone: +44 (0) 171 278 8000 Facsimile: +44 (0) 171 278 8080
e-mail: info@cavendishpublishing.com
Visit our Home Page on http://www.cavendishpublishing.com

This title was previously published under the Lecture Notes series.

First edition 1994
Second edition 1999

British Library Cataloguing in Publication Data

Hillier, Timothy
Principles of Public International Law – 2nd ed
1. International Law
I. Title II. Public International Law
341

ISBN 1 85941 461 3

Printed and bound in Great Britain

TABLE OF CASES

TABLE OF AUTHORITIES

TABLE OF TREATIES

TABLE OF ABBREVIATIONS

AJIL	American Journal of International Law
AMF	Arab Monetry Fund
Astronauts Treaty	Agreement on the Rescue of Astronauts, the Return of Astronauts and the Return of Objects Launched into Space 1968
BIICL	British Institute of International and Comparative Law
Bonn Convention	Convention on the Conservation of Migratory Species of Wild Animals 1980
BYIL	British Yearbook of International Law
CFC	Chlorofluorocarbon
CITES	Convention on International Trade in Endangered Species of Wild Fauna and Flora 1973
CLJ	Cambridge Law Journal
CRISTAL	Contract Regarding an Interim Supplement to Tanker Liability for Oil Pollution
CSC	Convention on the Continental Shelf 1958
ECHR	European Convention for the Protection of Human Rights and Fundamental Freedoms 1950
ECOSOC	Economic and Social Council
EEC	European Economic Union
EEZ	Exclusive Economic Zone
EJIL	European Journal of International Law
EU	European Union
FC	Convention on Fishing and the Conservation of the Living Resources of the High Seas 1958
FCN Treaties	Treaties of Friendship, Commerce and Navigation
GA	General Assembly
GATT	General Agreement on Tariffs and Trade 1947
GDR	German Democratic Republic
Hague Recueil	Recueil des Cours de l'Academie de Droit International
HSC	Convention on the High Seas 1958
IAEA	International Atomic Energy Agency
IATA	International Air Transport Association
IBRD	International Bank for Reconstruction and Development

ICAO	International Civil Aviation Organisation
ICESR	International Covenant on Economic, Social and Cultural Rights 1966
ICJ	International Court of Justice
ICLQ	International and Comparative Law Quarterly
ICPR	International Covenant on Civil and Political Rights 1966
ICRC	International Committee of the Red Cross
IDA	International Development Association
IFC	International Finance Corporation
ILC	International Law Commission
IMF	International Monetary Fund
IMO	International Maritime Organisation
INTELSAT	International Telecommunications Satellite Organisation
ITLOS	International Tribunal for the Law of the Sea
ITO	International Trade Organisation
ITU	International Telecommunications Union
London Dumping Convention	Convention for the Prevention of Marine Pollution by Dumping of Wastes and Other Matters 1972
LOSC	Law of the Sea Convention 1982
Liability Convention	Convention on International Liability for Damages Caused by Space Objects 1972
MARPOL	International Convention for the Prevention of Pollution by Ships 1973
MFA	Multifibre Agreement
MFN	Most-favoured-nation
MLR	Modern Law Review
MTO	Multilateral Trade Organisation
Moon Treaty	Agreement Governing Activities of States on the Moon and Other Celestial Bodies 1979
NIEO	New International Economic Order
OECD	Organisation for Economic Co-operation and Development
OEEC	Organisation for European Economic Co-operation
Oslo Dumping Convention	Convention for the Prevention of Marine Pollution by Dumping from Ships and Aircraft 1972
PCA	Permanent Court of Arbitration

PCIJ	Permanent Court of International Justice
PLO	Palestine Liberation Organisation
POW	Prisoner of war
Ramsar Convention	Convention on Wetlands of International Importance
SFRY	Socialist Federal Republic of Yugoslavia
SOLAS	International Convention for the Safety of Life at Sea 1974
Space Treaty	Treaty on Principles Governing the Activities of States in the Exploration and Use of Outer Space Including the Moon and Other Celestial Bodies 1967
Stockholm Declaration	Stockholm Declaration on the Human Environment 1972
SWAPO	South West African People's Organisation
TOVALOP	Tanker Owners' Voluntary Agreement Concerning Liability for Oil Pollution
TSC	Convention on the Territorial Sea and Contiguous Zone 1958
UDHR	Universal Declaration of Human Rights 1948
UN	United Nations
UNCITRAL	UN Commission on International Trade Law
UNCLOS I	UN Conference on the Law of the Sea 1958
UNCLOS II	UN Conference on the Law of the Sea 1960
UNCLOS III	UN Conference on the Law of the Sea 1973
UNCLOT	UN Conference on the Law of Treaties
UNCOPUOS	UN Committee on the Peaceful Use of Outer Space
UNCTAD	UN Conference on Trade and Development
UNEP	UN Environment Programme
UNESCO	UN Educational, Scientific and Cultural Organisation
UNIDO	UN Industrial Development Organisation
VCIO	Vienna Convention on the Law of Treaties between States and International Organisations or between International Organisations 1986
VCS	Vienna Convention on Succession of States in Respect of Treaties 1978
VCT	Vienna Convention on the Law of Treaties 1969
WCED	World Commission on Environment and Development

WHO	World Health Organisation
World Heritage Convention	Convention for the Protection of the World's Cultural and National Heritage 1972
WTO	World Trade Organisation
YBILC	Yearbook of the International Law Commission

CHAPTER 1

INTRODUCTION

1.1 Historical development

Throughout history, the world's resources have been the subject of conflict as the perceived need to acquire territory or spread influence has shaped civilisations. Where disputes have led to the use of force and to war, in the end, some agreement has had to be reached between conqueror and conquered. One of the oldest written agreements discovered dates back to 3100 BC and concluded a war between Eannatum, the ruler of the Mesopotamian city State of Lagash, and the representatives of Umma, another Mesopotamian State. During the period of the Roman Empire, two systems of law existed: *Jus Civile* was the law for Roman citizens and determined the rights and obligations between them; *Jus Gentium* was the law for those inhabitants of the Roman Empire who were not Roman citizens, and governed their relations with Roman citizens. Modern international law can trace some of its concepts (for example, *pacta sunt servanda* – treaties must be observed) from *Jus Gentium*. During the Middle Ages, Islamic law came to have an influence on a large part of Asia and North Africa, whilst, in Europe, the struggle for continental power was between the Holy Roman Emperor and the Pope. The presence of two universal legal systems, ecclesiastical and imperial, left little room for a system of international law to develop.

The modern system of international law is a product of the last 400 years and generally traces its origin to the Peace of Westphalia 1648, which is seen as the beginning of the system of nation States. The traditional Western view is that international law is founded essentially on consensus and has been created in two ways: by the practice of States (custom) and through agreements entered into by States (treaties). With the gradual break up of the Holy Roman Empire after 1648, States such as England, the Netherlands, France and Spain became strong and independent from any superior authority. Without the influence of Papal or Imperial laws, new rules to govern inter-national relations developed. These rules owed much to doctrines of canon law and Roman law. International law also bears witness to the jurists and writers of the 16th and 17th centuries who first formulated some of its most fundamental tenets – sovereignty, independence, and equality. Important theorists of this time were Bodin (1530–96), Hobbes (1588–1679), and Machiavelli (1469–1527). Following them, came the exponents of natural law, who were particularly interested in the laws of war. Two jurists writing at the end of the 16th century are often referred to as the founders of modern international law. They are Gentilis and Grotius, the latter completing his main work, *De Jure Belli et Pacis*, in 1625. The book, which was put on the papal list of banned books, where it remained for the next 300 years, dealt with ideas of just and unjust war, individual rights and duties and the emergence of the modern State system.

Modern international law developed from these European roots as treaties were formed and customs developed. As new nations came into existence, they sought to gain acceptance by the international community by abiding by the rules of international law. The Western emphasis on the role of the custom of States in creating rules of international law has not always met with complete acceptance. It should be noted that the newer nations have always put greater stress on treaties and international conventions as a source of law as compared to those rules of international custom, which predate the 20th century and which they had no part in creating.

During the twentieth century, international law has undergone considerable development, recognised in the distinction some writers draw between 'classical' international law and 'modern' or 'post-classical' international law. For these purposes, the dividing date is 1919. The end of the First World War and the emergence of the League of Nations resulted in a considerable change in the character of international law. One manifestation of the changes was the creation of an international court – the Permanent Court of International Justice. Further significant modifications took place in the wake of World War II. The establishing of the United Nations Organisation, in 1945, meant that it was no longer possible to argue that international law applied solely and exclusively to sovereign States – international organisations now had a status in the international legal system and the emerging body of human rights law gave rights and responsibilities to individuals on the international plane.

1.2 The nature of public international law

The subject matter of this book is public international law. For convenience, the terms 'public international law' and 'international law' will be used interchangeably. The subject has also been known as the law of nations and the law of war and peace. International law must be distinguished from municipal, internal or domestic law. As a starting point, international law can be said to apply only between those entities that can claim international personality, whilst municipal law is the internal law of States and regulates the conduct of individuals and other legal persons within the jurisdiction. Public international law should also be distinguished from private international law. Private international law, or the conflict of laws, is the term used to describe the body of rules of municipal law that regulates legal relations with a foreign element, such as contracts of sale between persons in different countries or marriages between persons from different legal systems.

A number of different categories of international law may usefully be identified. *Universal* international law, binding on all legal subjects, may be distinguished from *particular* international law, which is binding on a limited number of States only. *General* international law refers to the body of law which is binding on most, but not all, subjects. For example, an agreement between three States on the construction of a fighter plane would create *particular* international law; a convention to which one hundred and twenty States are party would be considered as creating rules of *general* international law; the prohibition on genocide is considered to be *universal* international law.

Legal theorists have devoted much time to the problem of defining 'law' and to the question of whether a definition is either possible or desirable. This book does not attempt to enter into a full debate about definitions of law in general or of international law in particular. Rather, the aim here is to introduce a number of formulations that have been offered over the years and to draw out the fundamental distinctions that exist between the various theories. One of the difficulties involved in any consideration of the nature of law is knowing exactly when to hold the discussion. It may be argued that a definition of the subject is fundamental and logically prior to discussion of the subject itself. On the other hand, it is difficult to define a subject without knowing anything of its contents. The choice has been made to refer to the various theories at the start of this book. It is important, however, to continue to have regard to the theoretical issues when considering the substantive rules of international law. It is not possible to do justice to the variety of theories about international law here and what follows is very much in the nature of a summary. Readers who wish to investigate the theoretical underpinnings of international law further are referred to the Further Reading section at the end of this book.

1.2.1 The traditional view

As has been already indicated at 1.1, the modern system of international law developed as a system of rules governing the relations between nation States. Traditional definitions reflect this by concentrating on the central and exclusive role of States. For example, WE Hall, in *A Treatise on International Law* (3rd edn, 1890, Oxford: Clarendon), wrote:

> International law consists in certain rules of conduct which modern civilised States regard as being binding on them in their relations with one another with a force comparable in nature and degree to that binding the conscientious person to obey the laws of the country, and which they also regard as being enforceable by appropriate means in case of infringement.

Four years later, Westlake, in *Chapters on the Principles of International Law* (1894, Cambridge: CUP), stated that 'International law is the body of rules prevailing between States'.

Oppenheim was even more explicit when he wrote, in *International Law* (1905, London: Longmans), 'States solely and exclusively are the subjects of international law.'

Traditional definitions also emphasise the point that international law owes its validity to the consent of equal, sovereign States, as expressed in custom and treaty. In 1927, the Permanent Court of International Justice (PCIJ) was called upon to decide a dispute between France and Turkey (the *Lotus* case (1927)). In the course of the judgment, the court found it necessary to set down the parameters of international law:

> International law governs relations between independent States. The rules of law binding upon States therefore emanate from their own free will as expressed in conventions or by usages generally accepted as expressing principles of law and established in order to regulate the relations between these co-existing independent communities or with a view to the achievement of common aims.

The traditional view is characterised by the fact that it considers international law to be a system of rules which confers rights and imposes obligations exclusively upon sovereign States, and which owes its validity to the consent of States. It may be doubted whether this view ever truly reflected the entirety of international law but it is certain that by the middle of this century the traditional definition was no longer adequate.

1.2.2 The modern view

Although international law may have developed as a system of rules governing the relations between sovereign States, it has developed beyond that. The establishment of the League of Nations after the First World War marked a shift in approach to international relations which received further impetus with the setting up of the United Nations Organisation in 1945. The Nuremberg War Crimes Tribunal in 1946 raised questions of the international obligations of individuals and the Universal Declaration of Human Rights 1948 suggested the possibility of individual international rights. In the wake of the United Nations, a number of other international organisations were established, all raising questions of their status within the community of nation States. In 1949, the International Court of Justice was asked by the General Assembly of the United Nations for its opinion on matters arising out of the assassination of a UN Representative in Jerusalem. In the course of its judgment in the *Reparation for Injuries Suffered in the Service of the United Nations* case (1949), the court stated:

> ... [the United Nations Organisation] is a subject of international law and capable of possessing international rights and duties, and ... has capacity to maintain its rights by bringing international claims.

It was becoming clear that it was no longer adequate to discuss international law in terms of a system of rules governing exclusively the relations between States. Later definitions, for example, that of C Jenks in *The Common Law of Mankind* (1958, London: Stevens), reflected this fact:

> International law can no longer be adequately or reasonably defined or described as the law governing the mutual relations of States, even if such a basic definition is accompanied by qualifications or exceptions designed to allow for modern developments; it represents the common law of mankind in an early stage of development, of which the law governing the relations between States is one, but only one, major division.

Some definitions continued to stress the primacy of States, for example, C Parry in *Manual of International Law* (Sorensen, M (ed), 1968, London: Macmillan):

> 'International law' is a strict term of art, connoting that system of law whose primary function it is to regulate the relations of States with one another. As States have formed organisations of themselves, it has come also to be concerned with international organisations and an increasing concern with them must follow from the trend which we are now witnessing towards the integration of the community of States. And because States are composed of individuals and exist primarily to serve the needs of individuals, international law has always had a certain concern with the relations of the individual, if not to his own State, at least to other States ... even the relations between the individual and his own State have come to involve questions of international law ... *Nevertheless, international law is and remains essentially a law for States* and thus stands in contrast to what international lawyers are accustomed to call municipal law ... [emphasis added]

Other definitions give greater acknowledgement to non-State entities, for example, that of Hersch Lauterpacht in *Collected Papers* (vol 1, 1970, Cambridge: CUP):

> International law is the body of rules of conduct, enforceable by external sanction, which confer rights and impose obligations primarily, though not exclusively, upon sovereign States and which owe their validity both to the consent of States as expressed in custom and treaties and to the fact of the existence of an international community of States and individuals. In that sense international law may be defined more briefly (though perhaps less usefully), as the law of the international community.

1.2.3 Contemporary theories

Although the early development of international law owes considerable debt to natural law concepts, much of the discussion about its nature over the last 100 years has been held within the broad church of legal positivism. Analysis of international law tended to concentrate on the activities of States and the identification of positive legal rules. Underlying the theories was a firm view that international law was based on the consensus of States to be bound. After the Second World War, world events increasingly undermined this view of law. The independence of former colonies raised the issue of the extent to which new States could be truly taken to consent to existing rules of international law. The onset of the Cold War and the dominance of the two superpowers brought into question the extent to which the behaviour of the US and the Soviet Union was guided by positive legal rules. In the 1950s, the American Realists turned their attention from analysing municipal legal systems to international law. They found that law was not determined by legal rules nor by precedents but that judicial decision making was an intuitive act motivated by a desire to do justice in a particular context. International law needs to be studied in the context of international society and not merely as a collection of legal rules capable of being understood on their own.

Another approach, often referred to as 'sociological jurisprudence', involved an attempt to move away from simple analysis of rules to consider international law as an integral part of the diplomatic and political process. Notable here is the work of Myres McDougal, whose policy orientated approach sees law as a process of decision making rather than a system of rules and obligations. McDougal has been criticised for minimising the legal content of the study of international law and later writers, such as Richard Falk, while adopting the general approach of McDougal, have sought to place greater emphasis on the importance of legal rules and structures.

More recently, and coinciding with the rise of the critical legal studies movement, there has been an increase in interest in international legal theory. Writers such as Anthony Carty, David Kennedy and Philip Allott have all made valuable contributions to this area of study by re-examining the nature of international law. A major reason for the increase in interest has been the perceived decline in the influence of the sovereign State, particularly in the light of events in the Balkans and elsewhere in Eastern Europe. Characteristic of the new approach is the view that the traditional ideal of international law is based on contradictory premises. Social conflict is resolved by political means and law is just one of the political weapons available. Such theorists argue that a universal definition of law is not possible and, instead, maintain that the study of law should involve analysis of the way in which States behave and the way in which they justify their behaviour.

1.3 Is international law really law?

One particular aspect of the discussion about international law has been the questioning by some writers of the very claim made to legal status. Much of the debate surrounding international law's status as law can be traced to the positivist legacy of John Austin. In his major theoretical work, *The Province of Jurisprudence Determined* (1955, London: Weidenfeld and Nicholson, pp 133, 140–41), he wrote:

> Laws properly so called are a species of commands ... And hence it inevitably follows that the law obtaining between nations is not positive law: for every positive law is set by a given sovereign to a person or persons in a State of subjection to its author ... the law obtaining between nations is law (improperly so called) set by general opinion. The duties

> which it imposes are enforced by moral sanctions: by fear on the part of nations, or by fear on the part of sovereigns, of provoking general hostility, and incurring its probable evils, in case they shall violate maxims generally received and respected.

HLA Hart also questioned the nature of international law, contrasting the 'clear standard cases' of law constituted by the legal systems of modern States with the 'doubtful cases' exemplified by primitive law and international law (see Hart, HLA, *The Concept of Law*, 1961, Oxford: Clarendon, p 3).

Other writers accept the nature of international law as law and cast doubt on the positivist use of municipal law as a model for law in general. Such writers argue that municipal law governs legal persons within a State and such law is derived from a legal superior. International law operates on a different plane. S Rosenne, in *Practice and Methods of International Law*, (1984, Dobbs Ferry, New York: Oceana, p 2), wrote:

> International law is a law of co-ordination, not, as is the case of most internal law, a law of sub-ordination. By law of co-ordination we mean to say that it is created and applied by its own subjects, primarily the independent States (directly or indirectly), for their own common purposes.

The implication here is that international law and municipal law are two different species of law. This issue will be further referred to in the context of the monist-dualist debate discussed in Chapter 17. It should be noted here, however, that not all municipal law can be considered to be a law of sub-ordination, derived from a legal superior. One only has to consider the development of public law in Britain to see an area of municipal law which is created and applied by its own subjects. Many of the rules of public law place restraints on government action, although it is the government, as majority party in the House of Commons, that arguably has the power to make the law as it chooses.

Other writers have countered arguments about the validity of international law by pointing to the behaviour of States. For example, JL Brierly, in *The Outlook for International Law* (1944, Oxford: OUP, p 5), has written:

> The best evidence for the existence of international law is that every actual State recognises that it does exist and that it is itself under obligation to observe it. States may often violate international law, just as individuals often violate municipal law, but no more than individuals do States defend their violations by claiming that they are above the law.

The fact is that States, the principal subjects of international law, do recognise a system of legal rules which they refer to as international law. Louis Henkin summed up the position in *How Nations Behave*, (2nd edn, 1979, New York: Columbia UP, p 47): '... almost all nations observe almost all principles of international law and almost all of their obligations almost all of the time'.

When Iraq invaded Kuwait in August 1990, Saddam Hussein did not argue that there was no system of law preventing Iraq acting in the way it did; rather, he sought to justify military action on the basis of compliance with the rules of international law. Of course, the fact that States refer to and justify their actions in the language of international law is not conclusive proof that it exists. It may be argued that States behave according to pure self-interest and only refer to international law for purposes of legitimation. Schwarzenberger has written that the primary function of law is to assist in maintaining the supremacy of force and the hierarchies established on the basis of power, and to give this overriding system the respectability and sanctity law confers. But this is not to deny international law's status of law. It can be, and has been, argued that municipal law exists to maintain the position of the ruling class. The actions of States cannot always be explained in terms of immediate self-interest. Even when extreme pragmatism governs State action and the result is the use of armed force, ultimately, it is the rules of international law that are used to make the peace. International law receives a bad press because it is the breakdowns that make the news – but just because a law is broken does not mean that it does not exist.

1.4 The enforcement of international law

International law is not imposed on States, in the sense that there is no international legislature. As has been seen, the traditional Western view is that international law is founded essentially on consensus. As will be seen in Chapter 12, it has generally been created in one of two ways: by the practice of States (custom) or through agreements entered into by States (treaties). Once international rules are established, they have an imperative character and cannot be unilaterally modified at will by States. Unlike municipal law, however, there is no uniform enforcement machinery. The full details of the various ways in which States are made to conform to their international obligations will be discussed throughout the book. The aim here is simply to introduce the range of mechanisms available.

1.4.1 The United Nations

Under Chapter VII of the Charter of the United Nations, the UN Security Council may take enforcement measures where it has determined the existence of a threat to the peace, breach of the peace, or act of aggression. This topic will be dealt with in more detail in Chapter 12. The Security Council's main role is in maintaining international peace and security rather than in enforcing international law, but the two functions will often overlap.

1.4.2 Judicial enforcement

Reference has already been made to judgments of the International Court of Justice, (ICJ) which is the judicial organ of the United Nations. Its main role is to resolve legal disputes between States and its judgments are binding on the parties to the dispute. In addition to the ICJ there are a number of specialised international tribunals dealing with particular areas of the law and it is not uncommon for States to establish ad hoc tribunals to resolve differences. The whole issue of the peaceful settlement of disputes will be dealt with in more detail in Chapter 11.

1.4.3 Loss of legal rights and privileges

A common enforcement method used by States is the withdrawal of legal rights and privileges. The best known example is the severing of diplomatic relations but sanctions falling short of this include trade embargoes, the freezing of assets and suspension of treaty rights. The adoption of such measures or, indeed, the mere threat of them can very often prove effective in enforcing international obligations.

1.4.4 Self-help

In very limited situations, international law does countenance self-help, in the sense of use of armed force. It is a fundamental rule of international law that the first use of armed force is prohibited, but a right of self-defence does exist and the actual use or threat of action in self-defence may be effective in enforcing international obligations. The law relating to the use of force, including the right of self-defence, is discussed in Chapter 12.

Two further points can be made about enforcement. First, an important aspect of law is its role in helping to predict future action. The action of individuals and States is generally predicated on a presumption that the law will be observed. Although the existing laws may be criticised and reforms demanded, it is in the general interest that law is upheld. An important factor influencing the observance of international law is therefore reciprocity – for example, it is in a State's own interests to respect the territorial sovereignty of other States as they will, in turn, respect its territorial sovereignty. Over 300 years ago, Grotius could state (*De Jure Belli ac Pacis, Libri Tres*, 1612, reproduced in *The Classics of International Law Series*, published by the Carnegie Endowment for International Peace):

> ... law is not founded on expediency alone. There is no State so powerful that it may not some time need the help of others outside itself, either for the purposes of trade or even to ward off the forces of many foreign nations united against it ... All things are uncertain the moment men depart from law.

The final point involves public opinion. Allusion has already been made to the role of law in the legitimation of action. States are ever keen to show that their actions are compatible with international law, and fear criticism based on the fact that they are failing to observe its rules. One only has to look at the role played by organisations such as Amnesty International in publicising abuses of international human rights law to recognise the effect that informed public opinion can have on State practice. Of course, no system of law can prevent atrocities being carried out. Just as municipal criminal law does not necessarily prevent the occurrence of murder and rape, international law cannot necessarily prevent genocide.

INTRODUCTION

Historical development

Throughout history, rules have existed to govern the conduct of international relations but the modern system of international law is usually traced back to the Peace of Westphalia 1648, which heralded the beginning of the nation State system. The rules which developed drew on doctrines of ecclesiastical law and of Roman law but also owed much to the work of legal theorists, the best known of whom is probably Hugo Grotius, whose main work, *De Jure Belli ac Pacis,* was completed in 1625. The main body of international law is to be found in agreement entered into by States (treaties) and in the practice of States (custom). Over-reliance on rules of custom has often been criticised by those States which have come into existence during the 20th century, who argue that they should not automatically be bound by rules based on the practice of Western States which they had no part in creating.

The nature of international law

International law should be distinguished from municipal, internal or domestic law and also from the rules of private international law (conflict of laws rules). Within international law, it is useful to note the distinctions between universal, particular, and general international law. The nature of international law has been an area of considerable controversy. The traditional view is that international law is exclusively concerned with governing the relations between, and the conduct of, States. This view has been increasingly doubted, especially since the establishment of the United Nations in 1945. A crude outline of the varying views is provided by the table at the end of the summary.

Is international law really law?

Some writers, particularly those adopting a positivist theory of law, have questioned whether international law can be regarded as law. The question has received less debate in recent times and most theorists now point to the fact that it is sufficient that States, as principal subjects of international law, themselves recognise a system of legal rules, which they refer to as international law.

The enforcement of international law

International law differs from most systems of municipal law in that there is no international legislature and no uniform enforcement machinery. This is not to say that international law cannot be, or is not, enforced. International law is enforced through the United Nations and the International Court of Justice. The role of self-help, either through diplomatic means or the use of armed force in self-defence, should not be underestimated.

View	**Subjects**	**Basis**	**Main proponents**
Traditional view	Exclusively States	Consensus of States to be bound	Oppenheim; PCIJ in the *Lotus* case (1927)
Modern view	Primarily States, but also international organisations and individuals	Consensus of States	Lauterpacht; ICJ in the *Reparation* case (1949)
American realists		Desire of justice in a political context	Louis Henkin
Sociological jurisprudence		International law is a process of decision making rather than a system of rules	Myres McDougal
Critical legal studies		Law is one of several political tools available for conflict resolution. The study of law involves an analysis of how subjects justify their behaviour and no universal definition of law is possible	Anthony Carty; Philip Allott; Martti Koskennieme

CHAPTER 2

THE SOURCES OF INTERNATIONAL LAW

2.1 Introduction

The term 'sources of law' has generated considerable debate among writers and is capable of conveying more than one meaning. The rules and norms of a legal system derive their authority from their source – the source is from where the authority of a legal system originates. The sources of law also articulate what the law is and where it can be found. Any legal system needs some criteria by which rules of behaviour are recognised and identified as 'laws'. When referring to municipal legal systems, some writers refer to formal and material sources. The formal sources are those legal procedures and methods for the creation of rules of general application which are legally binding on the addressees. The material sources provide evidence of the existence of rules which, when proved, have the status of legally binding rules of general application. The formal sources will usually refer to the constitutional mechanisms for law making. The material sources are the statutes and precedents where the specific rules of law are to be found.

The question of whether both formal and material sources exist in international law has been the subject of particular discussion. Some writers argue that formal sources do not exist in international law – as a substitute, there is a fundamental principle that the general consent of States creates rules of general application. I Brownlie states, in *Principles of Public International Law* (5th edn, 1998, Oxford: Clarendon, p 2):

> ... in international law the distinction between formal and material sources is difficult to maintain ... What matters then is the variety of material sources, the all important evidences of the existence of consensus among States concerning particular rules or practices.

Other writers have gone further than this, arguing that the whole idea of 'sources' of international law is flawed. For example, O'Connell has written, in his *International Law* (vol 1, 1970, London: Stevens, p 25):

> Sometimes the word 'source' is used to indicate the basis of international law; sometimes it is confused with the social origin and other 'causes' of the law; at others it is indicative of the formal law making agency and at others again it is used instead of the term evidence of the law ... As a figurative association the word 'source' is misleading and should be discarded.

For this reason, some writers will only refer to evidence of international law, and use the word, sources, only in quotation marks. This chapter discusses the sources of international law in the sense both of the mechanisms for law creation and of the methods by which rules of law may be identified as such. In other words, we are concerned here with finding out how new rules of international law may be created and with the process of identifying existing rules.

2.2 Article 38 of the Statute of the International Court of Justice

Article 38 of the Statute of the International Court of Justice states:

> 1. The court, whose function is to decide in accordance with international law such disputes as are submitted to it, shall apply:
>
> (a) international conventions, whether general or particular, establishing rules expressly recognised by the contesting States;
>
> (b) international custom, as evidence of a general practice accepted as law;
>
> (c) the general principles of law recognised by civilised nations;
>
> (d) subject to the provisions of Article 59, judicial decisions and the teachings of the most highly qualified publicists of the various nations, as subsidiary means for the determination of rules of law.
>
> 2. This provision shall not prejudice the power of the court to decide a case *ex aequo et bono*, if the parties agree thereto.

The traditional starting point for any discussion of the sources of international law has been Article 38 of the Statute of the International Court of Justice. Apart from a few formal changes, the statute is similar to the Statute of the Permanent Court of International Justice. The Permanent Court of International Justice (PCIJ) was created in 1920, under the auspices of the League of Nations, and the statute was drafted by an Advisory Committee of Jurists appointed by the Council of the League of Nations. The role and procedures of the International Court are discussed in Chapter 11. There follows here a more detailed analysis of Article 38 but it is worth inserting an initial word of caution: Article 38 does not actually use the term 'sources' but describes how the court is to decide disputes which come before it for settlement. Law is not necessarily simply defined in terms of how courts decide disputes. Article 38 does not refer to resolutions of the United Nations or other international organisations yet such resolutions may play an extremely important role in international society and may arguably constitute a source of law. A question that will be considered at the end of this chapter is the extent to which Article 38 is to be regarded as a comprehensive list of the sources of international law.

Another question that arises is whether Article 38, para 1 creates a hierarchy of sources. It is argued that there is no rigid hierarchy, but those drafting the article intended to give an order and, in practice, the court may be expected to observe the order in which they appear: (a) and (b) are obviously the important sources, and the priority of (a) is explicable by the fact that this refers to a source of mutual obligation of the parties – source (a) is, thus, not primarily a source of rules of general application although, as we shall see, treaties may provide evidence of the formation of custom. It may be useful here to note what E Lauterpacht has written, in *International Law, Collected Papers* (1970, Cambridge: CUP, vol 1, p 87), on the issue:

> The order in which the sources of international law are enumerated in the statute ... is, essentially, in accordance both with correct legal principle and with the character of international law as a body of rules based on consent to a degree higher than is law within the State. The rights and duties of States are determined, in the first instance, by their agreement as expressed in treaties – just as, in the case of individuals, their rights are specifically determined by any contract which is binding upon them. When a controversy arises between two or more States with regard to a matter regulated by treaty, it is natural that the parties should invoke and that the adjudicating party should apply, in the first instance, the provisions of the treaty in question.

2.2.1 Treaties

Treaties represent a source of law whose importance has grown since 1945. In this chapter, we are only concerned with treaties as a source of law. Chapter 3 deals with the mechanics of treaty making and enforcement in more detail. Treaties may be bipartite/bilateral or multipartite/multilateral and they may create particular or general rules of international law. A distinction is often drawn between law making treaties (*traité-lois*) and treaty contracts (*traité contracts*). The essence of the distinction lies in the fact that treaty contracts, being agreements between relatively few States, can only create a particular obligation between the signatories, an obligation which is capable of fulfilment, for example, an agreement between France, Germany and the UK to develop and build a new fighter jet. Law making treaties create obligations which can continue as law, for example, an agreement between 90 States to outlaw the use of torture. There has been a great increase in the number of law making treaties throughout this century. One reason for this growth is the increase in the number of States and the fact that many new States have a lack of faith in any rules of customary international law which they have not played a part in creating. The term, law making, can lead to confusion and it should be used with care – strictly speaking, no treaty can bind non-signatories. Even a multipartite treaty only binds those States which are party to it. The mere fact that a large number of States are party to a multilateral convention does not make it binding on non-parties, although its existence may be evidence of customary international law, as was discussed in the *North Sea Continental Shelf* cases (1969). For this reason, sometimes, the term, law making, is replaced by 'normative'. Normative treaties bind signatories as treaties, but may also provide evidence of rules of custom, which bind all States. Examples of normative treaties would include treaties operating a general standard setting instrument, for example, the International Covenant on Civil and Political Rights 1966; and treaties creating an internationally recognised regime, for example, the Antarctic Treaty 1959.

Customary law and treaty law have equal authority. However, if there is a conflict between the two, it is normally the treaty that prevails. This point is illustrated by the *Wimbledon* case (1923). In that case, the PCIJ, while recognising that customary international law prohibited the passage of armaments through the territory of a neutral State into the territory of a belligerent State, upheld Article 380 of the Treaty of Versailles, which provided that the Kiel canal was to be free and open to all commercial vessels and warships belonging to States at peace with Germany. In stopping a vessel of a State with which it was at peace, Germany was in breach of treaty obligations. It should, however, be noted that there is a presumption against the replacement of custom by treaty; treaties will be construed to avoid conflict with rules of custom, unless the treaty is clearly intended to overrule existing custom. Although it has been stated that treaty provisions will normally prevail over conflicting customary law rules, there is an important exception to this. Treaty provisions which conflict with peremptory norms of international law, *jus cogens*, will be void. Further discussion of the concept of *jus cogens* is to be found at 2.9.6.

2.3 Custom

In any society, rules of acceptable behaviour develop at an early stage and the international community is no exception. As contact between States increased, certain norms of behaviour crystallised into rules of customary international law. Until comparatively recently, the rules of general international law were nearly all customary rules.

2.3.1 Definitions of international custom

Custom in international law is a practice followed by those involved because they feel legally obliged to behave in such a way. Custom must be distinguished from mere usage, such as acts done out of courtesy, friendship, or convenience, rather than out of obligation or a feeling that non-compliance would produce legal consequences. Article 38 circumscribes customary law as 'international custom, as evidence of a general practice accepted as law'. The court cannot apply custom, only customary law, and sub-para 1(b) arguably reverses the logical order of events, since it is general practice, accepted as law, which constitutes evidence of a customary rule. Judge Hudson of the International Law Commission listed the following criteria for the establishment of a customary rule in a working paper for the ILC (UN Doc A/CN4/16, 3 March 1950, p 5):

(a) concordant practice by a number of States with reference to a type of situation falling within the domain of international relations;

(b) continuation or repetition of the practice over a considerable period of time;

(c) conception that the practice is required by, or consistent with, prevailing international law; and

(d) general acquiescence in the practice by other States.

How then is custom distinguished from behaviour which involves no legal obligation? The traditional view is that a rule of customary international law derives its validity from the possession of two elements: a material element and a psychological element. The material element refers to the behaviour and practice of States; whereas the psychological element, usually referred to as the *opinio juris sive necessitatis* or simply *opinio juris*, is the subjective conviction held by States that the behaviour in question is compulsory and not discretionary. Any alleged rule of customary law must therefore be checked as to its material and its psychological element.

It was stated, in the *Columbian-Peruvian Asylum* case (1950):

> The party which relies on a [regional] custom ... must prove that this custom is established in such a manner that it has become binding on the other party. The Colombian government must prove that the rule invoked by it is in accordance with a constant and uniform usage practised by the States in question, and that this usage is the expression of a right appertaining to the State granting asylum and a duty incumbent on the territorial State. This follows from Article 38 of the Statute of the Court ...

The ICJ, in the *North Sea Continental Shelf* cases (1969), concluded:

> Not only must the acts concerned amount to a settled practice, but they must also be such, or be carried out in such a way, as to be evidence of a belief that this practice is rendered obligatory by the existence of a rule of law requiring it. The need for such a belief, that is, the existence of a subjective element, is implicit in the very notion of the *opinio juris sive necessitatis*.

It should be noted that, in recent years, a number of writers have criticised this traditional view of customary law. The ICJ itself suggested a less rigorous test in the *Nicaragua* case (1986), stating:

> In order to deduce the existence of customary rules, the Court deems it sufficient that the conduct of States should, in general, be consistent with such rules, and that instances of State conduct inconsistent with a given rule should generally have been treated as breaches of that rule, not as indications of the recognition of a new rule.

In an article, 'The identification of International Law', in Cheng, B (ed), *International Law: Teaching and Practice*, (1982, London: Stevens, p 75), Sir Robert Jennings, former President of the ICJ, criticised the traditional view on the basis that it was outworn and inadequate, and commented:

> ... most of what we perversely persist in calling customary international law is not only not customary law, it does not even faintly resemble a customary law.

Critics of the traditional view argue that, although the ICJ speaks in terms of State practice and *opinio juris*, increasingly, its conclusions are determined by the application of legal rules that are largely treated as self-evident. The interpretation of State practice and *opinio juris* is never a straightforward automatic operation but involves a choice, usually justified on grounds of relevance, between conflicting facts and statements. Advocates of the non-traditional view, such as Martti Koskenniemi and Bruno Simma, argue that the study of international law must involve discussion of the way in which that choice is to be made. There is considerable merit to this view and an attempt will be made here to look critically at the way in which the ICJ deals with alleged rules of international custom.

2.4 The material element

In order to assert a binding rule of customary international law, it is necessary to demonstrate that the behaviour of States is, in general, in conformity with that rule. It is necessary, in other words, to provide evidence of State practice.

2.4.1 State practice

State practice includes any act, articulation, or other behaviour of a State which discloses the State's conscious attitude concerning a customary rule or its recognition of a customary rule. In 1950, the International Law Commission (ILC) listed the following classical forms of 'Evidence of Customary International Law':

(a) treaties;

(b) decisions of national and international courts;

(c) national legislation;

(d) diplomatic correspondence;

(e) opinions of national legal advisers; and

(f) practice of international organisations.

The list was not intended to be exhaustive but to provide a basis for discussion (see *YBILC*, 1950, New York: United Nations, pp 368–72).

There is some disagreement as to whether, for the purpose of the formation of customary law, State practice should consist merely of concrete actions, or whether it may also include abstract verbal, that is, written or oral, statements of State representatives, or their votes at diplomatic conferences or in UN bodies. Judge Read's dissenting opinion, in the *Anglo-Norwegian Fisheries* case (1951), explained the restricted view of State practice in more detail:

> ... customary law is the generalisation of the practice of States. This cannot be established by citing cases where coastal States have made extensive claims ... Such claims may be important as starting points, which, if not challenged, may ripen into historic title in the course of time ... The only convincing evidence of State practice is to be found in seizures, where the coastal State asserts its sovereignty over the water in question by arresting a foreign ship.

Dr Thirlway gives a similar view, in *International Customary Law and Codification* (1972, Leiden: AW Sijthoff, p 64):

> ... the fact that the practice is 'against interest' gives it more weight than the mere acceptance of a theoretical rule in the course of discussion by State representatives at a conference, and considerably more weight than the assertion of such a rule ... Claims may be made in the widest of general terms; but the occasion of an act of State practice contributing to the formation of custom must always be some specific dispute or potential dispute.
>
> The mere assertion *in abstracto* of the existence of a legal right or legal rule is not an act of State practice ... Such assertions can be relied on as supplementary evidence both of State practice and of the existence of the *opinio juris*.

Such views regard abstract statements as less, or not at all, relevant, apparently due to a reluctance to accept the notion that one body or conference could make law. However, States themselves do regard comments at conferences as constitutive of State practice and the courts do refer to abstract statements when identifying a customary rule. Also, the term 'practice' in Article 38 is general enough to cover any act or behaviour of a State and it is not clear in what respect verbal acts originating from a State could not be considered as behaviour of a State. It is also the case that the traditional evidence of State practice – diplomatic notes, instructions to State representatives – are often abstract and verbal. It could be argued that the restricted view of State practice is more compatible with a time when means of communication were much slower and there was less interaction between States. In the past, too, there has been a difficulty in obtaining evidence of State practice in situations not involving concrete actions. It is submitted that, today, such difficulties are no longer as great. Satellite communication and the development of techniques of information gathering and storage have made the collection of evidence of what States say far easier.

Of course, when using statements as evidence of State practice, it is necessary to look at the context and the manner in which they were made. Consideration must be given to whether they were made *de lege lata* (about the law that is in force) or *de lege ferenda* (about the law which it is desired to establish), against or not against national interest, or as trading ploys. Statements made *de lege lata* and against national interest are likely to provide more compelling evidence than those made *de lege ferenda* or supporting national interest. It is not always easy to discover a State's true motives behind its statements. It may be argued that it is unnecessary to look at motives since, whatever a State feels or believes when making a statement, other States may come to rely on the statement and the original State may become estopped from altering its position.

A further question concerns whether written texts such as conventions, ILC drafts, resolutions, etc, can be regarded as State practice. There seems no difficulty in regarding treaties as State practice, providing it is remembered that State practice must be accompanied by *opinio juris* for the creation of customary law. In the *North Sea Continental Shelf* cases, the ICJ stated that 'a very widespread and representative participation in the convention might suffice of itself' for a conventional rule to generate customary law – but it seems clear that *opinio juris* has to be demonstrated beyond mere contractual obligation in such cases. Mere participation in a conference and votes on single draft rules possess little value as practice, although votes on the draft text are of much more use, but usually only when accompanied by statements and explanations.

In the end, one of the main problems in evaluating the evidence for State practice is trying to ascertain what States actually do – their practice is not always consistent. For example, if one were looking at the law relating to military intervention in the internal affairs of other States, does one look at USSR practice in Afghanistan in 1980, which was denounced by the USA, or at USA practice in Grenada in 1983, which was denounced by the USSR? How does one reconcile a reluctance to intervene militarily in 'Yugoslavia' with military action taken against Iraq? It is exactly this sort of point that the critics of the traditional theories of international law wish to explore further. They are concerned to try and identify the basis on which the ICJ and others applying international law make decision about conflicting State practice. Attempts to distinguish between political and legal justifications of State action may often be fruitless. In many instances, assertion of the existence of customary rules of law may be little more than attempts to legitimise action taken for purely pragmatic, political reasons.

One final point should be made here. Although discussion has been of State practice, this should not be taken to mean that it is only the behaviour of States which is of interest. The practice of international organisations and even of individuals may well be taken into account in the attempt to establish the existence of a rule of customary international law.

2.4.2 The extent of the practice

The formation and existence of a customary rule requires general State practice. In the *North Sea Continental Shelf* cases, the ICJ postulated that 'State practice ... should ... have been extensive'. The term, general, indicates that common and widespread practice is required, although universal practice is not necessary. It seems, also, that practice must be representative in the sense that all the major political and socio-economic systems should be involved in the widespread practice. This marks a shift away from the position before the First World War, when Professor Westlake, in *International Law* (Part I, 1904, Cambridge: CUP, p 17) could argue that to prove the existence of a rule of custom:

> ... it is enough to show that the general consensus of opinion within the limits of European civilisation is in favour of the rule.

If practice is not widespread or general, it may still give rise to a local or regional customary rule/special rule, as was argued, unsuccessfully, in the *Asylum* case (1950). In that case, the ICJ held that, before State practice could be acknowledged as law, it had to be in accordance with a constant and uniform usage practised by the States in question. The case concerned political asylum; after an unsuccessful rebellion in Peru, one of the leaders was granted asylum in the Colombian embassy in Lima. Columbia sought a guarantee of safe conduct of the leader out of Peru, which was refused. Columbia took the matter to the ICJ and asked for a ruling that Columbia, as the State granting asylum, was competent to qualify the offence for the purposes of granting asylum – it argued for the ruling on the basis of treaty provisions and American law in general, that is, local/regional international custom. The court found that it was impossible to find any constant and uniform usage accepted as law. There was too much fluctuation and inconsistency.

In the *Rights of Passage over Indian Territory* Case (1960), the ICJ recognised the existence of a local custom overruling India's objection that no local custom could be established between only two States. The Court stated:

> It is difficult to see why the number of States between which a local custom may be established on the basis of long practice must necessarily be larger than two. The Court sees no reason why long continued practice between two States accepted by them as regulating their relations should not form the basis of mutual rights and obligations between the two States.

Inconsistency *per se* is not sufficient to negate the crystallisation of a rule into customary law – the inconsistency must be analysed and assessed in the light of such factors as subject matter, the identity of the States practising the inconsistency, the number of States involved and whether or not there are existing rules with which the alleged rule conflicts.

The practice of specially affected States is also often significant – for example, in the *North Sea Continental Shelf* cases, it was coastal States with a continental shelf who were specially affected; the practice of landlocked States was not significant. However, it is not true to say that, if all affected States follow a particular practice, then a rule of customary law comes into effect, since the practice of non-affected States may be sufficiently inconsistent to prevent the formation of a rule. It may be said that what is most significant is the adherence to a rule by all those States who had the opportunity to engage in such practice.

2.4.3 The practice of dissenting States and persistent objectors

If, and when, certain patterns of practice are emerging, or have emerged, States may wish to diverge or dissent from such practice. States may dissent from a customary rule from its inception onwards. The feasibility of such dissent was acknowledged by the ICJ, in the *Anglo-Norwegian Fisheries* case (1951). The case concerned the manner in which Norway calculated its territorial sea and the court found that Norway was not bound by the existing general rules of customary law relating to the matter. A persistent objector is not bound by the eventual customary rule if the State fulfils two conditions:

(a) the objections must have been maintained from the early stages of the rule onwards, up to its formation and beyond; and

(b) the objections must have been maintained consistently, since the position of other States, that may have come to rely on the position of the objector, has to be protected. The objector should not be able to rely on its own inconsistencies. Thus, if a State sometimes objects to, and at other times invokes, the rule, it will no longer be entitled to be regarded as a persistent objector. In all cases, the persistent objector bears the burden of proving its exceptional position.

It may be that States dissent from a customary rule after its formation. Their position is untenable because other States have come to rely on the subsequent objector originally conforming to the rule. Also, general customary law is binding on all States and cannot be the subject of any right of unilateral exclusion exercisable at will by any one State in its own favour. It should be noted, however, that a large number of subsequent objections may lead to desuetude or modification of the rule. It should also be noted that acquiescence over a period of time to an apparent breach of a general customary rule will lead to the result that the apparent breach cannot be challenged by those States acquiescing in it.

There has been some discussion regarding the situation of newly independent States. Such States have not participated in the creation of customary rules already in force when they come into existence, nor have they had any opportunity to oppose the rule's formation. It is open to the new State to contest the validity of customary rules or dispute their interpretation but it has no right to refuse to observe such rules, save in regard to those States which have expressly agreed to their waiver. When a new State begins to enter into relations with other States, it must be taken to accept the rules of international law which are then in force. When a State applies for membership of the UN, it must declare its acceptance of the principles of the Charter, the first purpose of which is the settlement of disputes 'in conformity with the principles of justice and international law' (Article 1(1)).

2.4.4 Duration of practice

In the *North Sea Continental Shelf* cases, the ICJ held that:

> Even without the passage of any considerable period of time, a very widespread and representative participation in the [practice] might suffice of itself ... Although the passage of only a short period of time is not necessarily, of itself, a bar to the formation of a new rule of customary law ... within the period in question, short though it might be, State practice ... should have been both extensive and virtually uniform.

There is no set time limit and no demand that the behaviour should have existed since time immemorial. The relative unimportance of time was highlighted by the ICJ in the *North Sea Continental Shelf* cases. The cases involved the Federal Republic of Germany, Denmark and Holland, and a dispute over the continental shelf. Denmark and Holland argued that the equidistance principle which was contained in the Convention on the Continental Shelf 1958 was customary law. The two States had argued that, even if no customary rule existed at the time of the Convention, a rule had since come into being, partly as a result of the impact of the Convention, and partly on the basis of subsequent State practice. The court was therefore required to look at the time requirement and it ruled, in rejecting their argument, that, although the passage of only a short period of time is not necessarily, or of itself, a bar to the formation of a new rule of customary international law, an indispensable requirement would be that the practice of States whose interests are specially affected should have been extensive and virtually uniform.

The length of time required to establish a rule of customary international law will therefore depend on other factors pertinent to the alleged rule. If, for example, the rule is dealing with subject matter about which there are no previously existing rules, then the duration of practice required is less than if there is an existing rule to be overturned. Time has also become less important as international communication has improved; it is much easier to assess a State's response to an alleged rule than it was in the past.

2.5 The psychological element

In addition to the material element, an alleged rule of customary international law also requires a psychological element, otherwise known as an *opinio juris sive necessitatis* (literally, belief/opinion of law or of necessity). State practice must occur because the State concerned believes it is legally bound to behave in a particular way – customary law must be distinguished from mere usage. The Statute of the International Court refers to 'a general practice accepted as law'. The essential problem then becomes one of burden and standard of proof. The position is probably as follows: the proponent of a custom has to establish a general practice and, having done this, must show that the general practice is due to a feeling of legal obligation. In many cases, the international court has been willing to assume the existence of an *opinio juris* on the basis of evidence of a general practice, or the previous determinations of the court or other international tribunals (for example, in the *Gulf of Maine* case (1984)). However, in a significant minority of cases, the court has adopted a more rigorous approach and has called for more positive evidence of the recognition of the validity of the rules in question. The first occasion where such an approach was taken was in the *Lotus* case (1927), where the court said:

> Even if the rarity of the judicial decisions to be found among the reported cases were sufficient to prove in point of fact the circumstances alleged by the agent for the French government, it would merely show that States had often, in practice, abstained from instituting criminal proceedings, and not that they recognised themselves as being obliged to do so; for only if such abstention were based on their being conscious of a duty to abstain would it be possible to speak of an international custom. The alleged fact does not allow one to infer that the States have been conscious of having such a duty; on the other hand ... there are other circumstances calculated to show that the contrary is true.

More recently, in the *Nicaragua v US (Merits)* case (1986), the ICJ stated:

> For a new customary rule to be formed, not only must the acts concerned amount to a settled practice, but they must be accompanied by the *opinio juris sive necessitatis.*

2.5.1 Treaties as evidence of customary law

A further issue is the extent to which a multilateral treaty can be used as evidence of customary international law. It is a general rule of international law, which is confirmed in Article 34 of the Vienna Convention on the Law of

Treaties 1969, that treaties cannot bind third parties without their consent. If a State wishes to enforce the provisions of a treaty against a non-party, it is necessary to argue that the provisions of the treaty are valid as rules of customary international law. Two possible situations arise:

(a) where the treaty is intended to be declaratory of existing customary international law; and

(b) where the treaty is constitutive of new law.

If the treaty on its face purports to be declaratory of customary international law, or if it can be established that it was intended to be declaratory of customary international law, then it may be accepted as valid evidence of the state of the customary rule. If the treaty, at the time of its adoption, was constitutive of new rules of law, then the party relying on the treaty as evidence of customary law will have the burden of establishing that the treaty has subsequently been accepted into custom.

The ICJ, in the *North Sea Continental Shelf* cases, recognised that it is possible for a treaty to contain norm-creating provisions which become accepted by the *opinio juris* and bind non-parties just as much as parties to the convention, but the court did lay down a series of conditions:

(a) the convention provision must be of a fundamentally norm-creating character such as could be regarded as forming the basis of a general rule of law;

(b) there must be widespread and representative participation in the convention particularly of those States whose interests are specifically affected; and

(c) there must be *opinio juris* reflected in extensive State practice virtually uniform in the sense of the provision invoked.

The following point should also be noted (Cassese, A, *International Law in a Divided World*, 1986, Oxford: Clarendon, p 180):

> Since treaties and custom are on the same footing, it follows that the relations between rules generated by the two sources are governed by those general principles which in all legal orders govern the relations between norms deriving from the same source: *lex posterior derogat priori* (a later law repeals an earlier law), *lex posterior generalis non derogat priori speciali* (a later law, general in character, does not derogate from an earlier law which is special in character), and *lex specialis derogat generali* (a special law prevails over a general law).

2.6 General principles of law

Article 38(1)(c) is one of the more problematic paragraphs in the Statute of the International Court of Justice and a knowledge of the history of the provision is an aid to its understanding. When the Advisory Committee of Jurists were discussing what law the Permanent Court should apply, there was consideration of whether the court should be restricted to applying custom and treaties or whether other sources of law might be allowed. The Belgian chairing the Committee, Descamps, proposed that the court should also apply 'the rules of law as recognised by the legal conscience of civilised nations'. The proposal was opposed by three members of the committee, who argued that the court should only apply rules and principles derived from the will of States and embodied in custom or treaties. To break the deadlock, Lord Phillimore, the British representative, proposed a compromise formula, *viz*, the court should be directed to apply 'the general principles of law recognised by civilised nations'. According to Lord Phillimore, the general principles were those 'which were accepted by all nations *in foro domestico* such as certain principles of procedure, the principle of good faith, and the principle of *res judicata*, etc'. The compromise was accepted and the phrase was included in the statute.

The original proposal has two main reasons behind it. Firstly, reflecting the spirit of the time, there was a view that the unshackled sovereignty of States was not necessarily a good thing and that peaceful settlement of disputes would be encouraged if international law was allowed to develop beyond the simple self-interests of States. It was also felt that the effectiveness of the court would be seriously undermined if it was unable to give a decision based on international law because of the absence of custom or treaty – such a situation being referred to as *non-liquet*. In municipal systems of law, the problem is tackled by deducing principles of law from already existing rules or from basic legal principles, such as justice and equity. A *non-liquet* situation was more likely to arise in international law and the formula 'general principles' would plug any gaps.

An important preliminary point to appreciate is that the ICJ has never itself made any express reference to Article 38(1)(c) of the statute. The formula 'general principles of law recognised by civilised nations' has only been used in individual or dissenting opinions (note that the ICJ delivers a single judgment of the court, to which individual assenting or dissenting judgments can be added). The prevailing view as to the meaning of Article 38(1)(c) is that it authorises the court to apply the general principles of municipal jurisprudence, in particular of private law, in as far as they are applicable to the relations of States. It is not thought to refer to principles of international law itself, which are to be derived from custom or treaty. International tribunals will often refer to 'well known' or 'generally recognised' principles such as the principle of the independence and equality of States. Such principles do not come within Article 38(1)(c). Lauterpacht, in *International Law*, (vol 1, 1970, Cambridge: CUP, p 69) states:

> [General principles] are, in the first instance, those principles of law, private and public, which contemplation of the legal experience of civilised

> nations leads one to regard as obvious maxims of jurisprudence of a general and fundamental character – such as the principle that no one may be judge in his own cause, that a breach of legal duty entails the obligation of restitution, that a person cannot invoke his own wrong as a reason for release from legal obligation, that the law will not countenance the abuse of a right, that legal obligations must be fulfilled and rights must be exercised in good faith, and the like.

A final point should be made about the term 'civilised nations'. The formulation is today outmoded and carries discriminatory connotations. It was criticised by Judge Ammoun of the ICJ in 1969 and there have been suggestions in the past that it should be changed.

2.6.1 Some examples

A number of decisions of the international court help illustrate the nature of general principles. In the *Chorzow Factory (Jurisdiction)* case (1927), the Permanent Court enunciated the principle that:

> ... one party cannot avail himself of the fact that the other has not fulfilled some obligation, or has not had recourse to some means of redress, if the former party has, by some illegal act, prevented the latter from fulfilling the obligation in question, or from having recourse to the tribunal which would be open to him.

Later on, in the *Chorzow Factory (Merits)* case (1928), the court observed:

> ... that it is a principle of international law, and even a general conception of law, that any breach of an engagement involves an obligation to make reparation.

In a number of cases, the international court has made use of the doctrine of estoppel as recognised by a number of municipal legal systems. Perhaps the clearest example came in the *Temple* case involving Thailand (formerly Siam) and Cambodia, formerly part of French Indo-China. The two States were in dispute over a section of the frontier. Cambodia successfully relied on a map of 1907, which the predecessor French authorities had produced at the request of the Siamese government. The map clearly showed the Temple area as part of French Indo-China. The Siamese authorities, far from protesting at the error, had thanked the French for preparing the map and requested a number of copies. Furthermore, in 1930, a Siamese prince paid a State visit to the disputed area and was officially received there by the French authorities. Together, these two events were seen by the international court as conclusive and it found that Thailand was precluded by its conduct from denying the frontier indicated on the map (the *Temple of Preah Vihear* case (1962)).

Other principles considered by the court have included the right to bring class actions (*actio popularis*), the *International Status of South West Africa* case

(1950), and the doctrine of corporate personality, in the *Barcelona Traction, Light and Power Company Limited* case (1970).

2.6.2 Good Faith

A general principle which has often been invoked by the ICJ is good faith. The principle of good faith is fundamental to international relations. Article 2(2) of the United Nations Charter obliges Member States to fulfil their Charter obligations in good faith and General Assembly Resolution 2625 (XXV) (Declaration on principles Concerning Friendly Relations and Co-operation among States, 1970) recognises the duty on States to undertake their international law obligations in good faith. In the *Nuclear tests* cases (1974), the ICJ stated:

> One of the basic principles governing the creation and performance of legal obligations, whatever their source, is the principle of good faith.

It should, however, be noted that, in the *Border and Transborder Armed Actions* Case (1988) between Nicaragua and Honduras, the ICJ emphasised the point that good faith, although one of the basic principles governing the creation and performance of legal obligations, is not, in itself, a source of legal obligation where none would otherwise exist.

2.6.3 Equity

Amongst these general principles, it could be argued that equity, in the sense of justice and fairness, is included and, in a number of cases, it has been used indirectly to affect the way in which substantive law is applied. The application of equity as a general principle should not be confused with Article 38, para 2, which states that, if both parties to a dispute agree, the court can decide a case *ex aequo et bono*, that is, the court can apply equity in precedence to all other legal rules.

The ICJ itself has, on a number of occasions, indicated that it considers the principles of equity to constitute an integral part of international law. In the *Diversion of Water from the Meuse* case (1937), Judge Hudson declared:

> What are widely known as principles of equity have long been considered to constitute a part of international law, and as such they have often been applied by international tribunals.

Over 40 years later, the ICJ confirmed this view, in the *Continental Shelf (Tunisia/Libyan Arab Jamahiriya)* case (1982):

> Equity as a legal concept is a direct emanation of the idea of justice. The court whose task is by definition to administer justice is bound to apply it ... [The Court] is bound to apply equitable principles as part of international law, and to balance up the various considerations which it regards as relevant in order to produce an equitable result.'

For a particularly full discussion of the place of equity within international law, readers are referred to the judgment of Judge Weeranmantry in the case concerning maritime delimitation in the area between Greenland and Jan Mayen (*Denmark v Norway* (1993)).

2.7 Judicial decisions

In the event of the court being unable to solve a dispute by reference to treaty law, custom or general principles, Article 38(1)(d) of the Statute of the ICJ provides that 'judicial decisions and the teachings of the most highly qualified publicists of the various nations' shall be applied 'as subsidiary means for the determination of rules of law'.

Judicial decisions may be applied, subject to the provisions of Article 59, which states:

> The decision of the court has no binding force except between the parties and in respect of that particular case.

In other words, there is no *stare decisis* in international law. Nevertheless, the ICJ does look at earlier decisions and take them into account. Value is seen in judicial consistency. However, caution should be exercised when looking at a particular decision. Decisions are by majority. In the event of even division, a decision may have been made by the president using a casting vote. Some dissenting judgments may be made more for political than for legal reasons. Arbitration decisions depend for their weight on the subject matter involved and the agreement between the States to submit the dispute to arbitration. The procedure of international tribunals is considered in more detail in Chapter 11.

Article 38 does not limit the judicial decisions that may be applied to international tribunals. If a municipal court's decision is relevant, it may be taken into account. The weight attached to it will depend on the standing of the court: for example, the US Supreme Court is held in high regard, particularly in disputes on State boundaries; similarly, the decisions of the English prize courts contributed to the growth of prize law (the law relating to vessels captured at sea during war). Municipal court decisions may also be evidence of State practice for the purpose of establishing the rules of customary international law.

2.8 The teachings of the most highly qualified publicists of the various nations

Historically, writers have performed a major role in the development of international law. The significance of jurists such as Grotius, Suarez and Gentilis has already been discussed in Chapter 1. Even today, States make plentiful reference to academic writings in their pleadings before the court. Writers have played an important part in the development of international law for two main reasons: (a) the comparative youth of a comprehensive system of international law; and (b) the absence of any legislative body. In the formative period, writers helped to determine the scope and content of international law. However, as the body of substantive law has increased, so the influence of writers has decreased (although writers still have an important role in developing new areas of law, for example, marine pollution). Who the most qualified writers are is a matter for subjective assessment; as is usual in these matters, death is often seen as an important qualification! It should be noted that the court itself does not usually make reference to specific writers.

2.9 Other possible sources

Over the last 30 years, there has been increasing support for the view that Article 38 should not be understood as a comprehensive and complete list of the sources of international law. On the one hand, examples can be found from the more recent decisions of the ICJ which seem to be based on rules of law not readily falling within the triad of sources created by the statute. On the other hand, it is argued that international law does not simply consist of the decisions of the ICJ. Indeed, between 1966 and 1980, the work load of the court decreased dramatically following the decision in the *South West Africa* case, second phase (1966). The decision was heavily criticised by the newly independent States, who were already distrustful of what they perceived as a European and American bias within the court. Rather than submit disputes to the ICJ, they preferred to seek remedies through the political organs of the UN. As the work of the UN has increased, it can be seen to have had a profound effect on the behaviour of States which cannot be ignored in any analysis of international law. For both these reasons, it is argued that the discussion of the sources of international law can no longer be confined to the provisions of Article 38. Support for this view can be found among the judges of the ICJ, for example, R Jennings, in 'The identification of International Law' in Cheng, B (ed), *International Law: Teaching and Practice* (1982, London: Stevens, p 9):

> We cannot reasonably expect to get very far if we try to rationalise the law of today solely in the language of Article 38 of the Statute of the International Court of Justice, framed as it was in 1920. It too needs urgent rethinking and elaboration ... To use Article 38 as it stands, as we constantly do still, for the purposes of analysing and explaining the elements and categories of the law today has a strong element of absurdity.

The editors of the ninth edition of Oppenheim (Jennings, R and Watts, A (Sir) (eds), *Oppenheim's International Law*, 9th edn, 1992, Harlow: Longman) take a slightly more cautious view, pointing out the fact that the ICJ itself has been able to deal with resolutions of international organisations in its judgments without 'remarking on the incompleteness of Article 38'. For example, in the *Legality of the Threat or Use of Nuclear Weapons* case (1996), the ICJ, in its advisory opinion, noted that

> General Assembly resolutions, even if they are not binding, may sometimes have normative value. They can, in certain circumstances, provide evidence important for establishing the existence of a rule or the emergence of an *opinio juris*.

Jennings and Watts suggested that the activities of international organisations 'are for the moment at least still properly regarded as coming within the scope of the traditional sources of international law'. The phrase 'for the moment' is significant, for the editors do consider that there may come a time 'when the collective actions of the international community within the framework provided by international organisations will acquire the character of a separate source of law'. The move in that direction clearly provides support for those who argue that theorising international law on the basis of the sovereign equality of nation States is increasingly losing its meaning.

2.9.1 Resolutions of international organisations

The exact status of resolutions of international organisations, in particular, resolutions of the United Nations General Assembly, has long been an area of controversy. Nonetheless, it is certainly true that the resolutions passed by the UN General Assembly have a far more significant role to play in the formation of international law than was envisaged in 1945, let alone in 1920 when Article 38 was drafted. When discussing the effect of resolutions, it may be useful to consider the categories suggested by B Sloan, in 'General Assembly resolutions revisited' (1987) 58 BYIL 93, who identifies three main categories of resolution:

(a) decisions:

by virtue of Article 17 of the UN Charter, the General Assembly may take decisions on budgetary and financial matters which are binding on the members. Failure to abide by budgetary decisions can ultimately lead to suspension and expulsion from membership. In addition, Article 2(5) of the Charter provides that:

> All members shall give the United Nations every assistance in any action it takes in accordance with the present Charter, and shall refrain from giving assistance to any State against which the United Nations is taking preventive or enforcement action.

Thus, arguably, resolutions that commit the UN to taking 'action' can be binding on Member States;

(b) recommendations:

Article 10 states:

> The General Assembly may discuss any questions or any matters within the scope of the present Charter ... and ... may make recommendations to the members of the United Nations or to the Security Council or to both on any such questions or matters.

The essence of 'recommendations' is that they are non-binding. They cannot, therefore, instantly create binding rules of international law in themselves. However, recommendations can be used as evidence of State practice and thus go towards the creation of customary rules of international law;

(c) declarations:

> Declarations are a species of General Assembly resolutions based on established practice outside the express provisions of Chapter IV of the Charter ... While the effect of declarations remains controversial, they are not recommendations and are not to be evaluated as such.

Since 1945, the General Assembly has adopted a number of resolutions which have been termed 'declarations' and have expressed principles of international law. Such declarations have often been adopted by unanimous vote or by consensus (that is, without voting). The most comprehensive was the Declaration on Principles of International Law concerning Friendly Relations and Co-operation among States (GA Resolution 2625 (XXV) (1970)). Other significant declarations have been the Declaration on the Granting of Independence to Colonial Territories and Peoples (GA Resolution 1514 (XV) (1960)); and the Declaration of Legal Principles Governing the Activities of States in the Exploration and Use of Outer Space (GA Resolution 1962 (XVIII) (1963)). Certain other resolutions, although not designated as 'declarations' have affirmed principles of international law. One example is the resolution entitled Affirmation of the Principles of International Law Recognised by the Charter of the Nuremberg Tribunal (GA Resolution 95 (I) (1946)). It should also be noted that some 'declarations' by the General Assembly are not intended to express legal rights and obligations; an important example is the Universal Declaration of Human Rights (GA Resolution 217 (III) (1948)), which is expressly stated to proclaim 'a common standard of achievement'.

It seems to be almost universally accepted today, therefore, that, in certain situations, UN resolutions can be used to establish binding rules of international law. Whether a particular resolution will be regarded as valid international law will depend on a number of criteria, including the context in which the resolution was passed, voting behaviour and analysis of the provisions concerned. In *Texaco Overseas Petroleum Co v Libya* (1978), an arbitration which arose after Libya had nationalised the property of two American oil companies, the arbitrator, Professor Dupuy, had cause to discuss the international law relating to nationalisation of foreign owned property. In particular, he referred to the General Assembly Resolution on Permanent Sovereignty over Natural Resources 1962 (GA Resolution 1803 (XVII) (1962)) and the Charter of Economic Rights and Duties of States 1974 (GA Resolution 3281 (XXIX) (1974)). Resolution 1803 had been adopted by 87 votes to two, with 12 abstentions. France and South Africa had voted against the resolution, and the Soviet bloc, Burma, Cuba and Ghana had abstained. The resolution recognised the right to expropriate foreign owned property where it was carried out for reasons of public utility, security or national interest and where compensation is paid. Arbitrator Dupuy, who had been appointed by the President of the ICJ commented:

> On the basis of the circumstances of adoption ... and by expressing an *opinio juris communis*, Resolution 1803 (XVII) seems to this tribunal to reflect the State of customary law existing in this field ... The consensus by a majority of States belonging to the various representative groups indicates without the slightest doubt universal recognition of the rules therein incorporated.

He then turned to consider the status of the Charter of Economic Rights and Duties of States 1974. This resolution was adopted by 120 votes to six with 10 abstentions. The States voting against were Belgium, Denmark, the Federal Republic of Germany, Luxembourg, the UK and the USA; those abstaining were Austria, Canada, France, Ireland, Israel, Italy, Japan, the Netherlands, Norway and Spain. The provisions of the Charter were much more favourable to the developing States. Arbitrator Dupuy found that there were several factors which mitigated against recognising the Charter as a source of international law:

> In the first place, Article 2 of this Charter must be analysed as a political rather than a legal declaration concerned with the ideological strategy of development and, as such, only supported by non-industrial States ... The absence of any connection between the procedures of compensation and international law and the subjection of this procedure solely to municipal law cannot be regarded by the tribunal except as a *de lege ferenda* formulation, which even appears *contra legem* in the eyes of many developed countries.

Since it now seems to be accepted that resolutions are capable of constituting rules of international law, debate now is focused on whether such resolutions constitute a source of law in their own right or whether they merely provide evidence of customary law or general principles of law. One resolution which has been the subject of much analysis is the Declaration on Outer Space which was passed in 1962. The main aim of the resolution was to establish a legal regime for outer space which incorporated the principles that space exploration was to be carried out for the benefit of all mankind, that 'outer space and celestial bodies' were not to be the subject of national appropriation, and that the use and exploration of outer space was to be carried out for peaceful purposes only. During the discussions leading to the adoption of the resolution, delegates to the General Assembly considered the legal effect of declarations in general and support was offered for the view that a declaration of legal principles, adopted unanimously could be, in effect, legally binding. A significant number of States expressed the view that the binding nature of such declarations was based on the fact that the declaration constituted State practice and also the necessary *opinio juris* to create a rule of custom. Such resolutions constituted, in the words of Bin Cheng, 'instant customary law' (Cheng, B, 'UN resolutions on outer space: instant international customary law?' (1965)). In the *Nicaragua* case (1986), the ICJ expressed the view that UN resolutions could constitute *opinio juris* which, together with evidence of State practice, could constitute a rule of custom. Until the provisions of Article 38 of the Statute of the ICJ are amended, it seems likely that international tribunals will continue to refer to resolutions in terms of evidence of international custom. Whether that is an accurate description of the procedure remains open to doubt.

2.9.2 Specialised agencies of the UN

The work of the specialised agencies of the United Nations, such as the International Labour Organisation and the International Maritime Organisation, should not be overlooked in any consideration of the development of international law. Such agencies have had a considerable role in promulgating international conventions in their areas of interest but the resolutions of such bodies have also had considerable effect.

2.9.3 Resolutions of regional organisations

Regional organisations, for example, the European Union, the Council of Europe, the Organisation of American States, and the Organisation for African Unity can, via their internal measures, demonstrate what they, as a regional group, consider to be the law. This is especially important in the area of human rights law, which is discussed in Chapter 14.

2.9.4 The International Law Commission and codification

The major difficulty with customary law is that it is diffuse and often lacks precision. In the light of this, attempts have been made to codify international law, an early example of which is provided by the Hague Conferences of 1899 and 1907 which did much to codify the laws relating to dispute settlement and the use of armed force. The codification and development of international law was a concern of the founders of the UN and that concern is reflected in Article 13(1) of the UN Charter, which provides:

> The General Assembly shall initiate studies and make recommendations for the purpose of:
>
> (a) promoting international co-operation in the political field and *encouraging the progressive development of international law and its codification* [emphasis added].

In 1947, under the auspices of the UN, the International Law Commission (ILC) was set up and charged with the task of progressively developing and codifying international law. The ILC is made up of 34 members from around the world who remain in office for 5 years each and who are appointed from lists supplied by national governments. The members of the ILC sit as individuals rather than as State representatives. Generally, the Commission works on its own initiative. Draft articles are prepared and sent for comment; a conference may then be convened, at which the draft articles are discussed, with the aim of producing a finished convention which can then be opened for signature. Conferences can last for some time – the Third Law of the Sea Conference had its opening session in New York in 1973 and the Law of the Sea Convention was finally opened for signature in December 1982. Ratified conventions are clearly a source of law, while the drafts are often highly persuasive statements of present State practice in a particular area of law.

Although the ILC is the most important international body engaged in the development and codification of international law, there do exist a number of other public organisations which are involved in the same mission. Such organisations generally specialise in particular areas of law, for example, the United Nations Commission on International Trade Law (UNCITRAL); the United Nations Educational, Scientific and Cultural Organisation (UNESCO). Additionally, there are also some private, independent bodies engaged in the development of the law: the International Law Association and the Institut de Droit International are two of the best known today, while the various Harvard Research drafts produced before the Second World War are still of value.

2.9.5 'Soft law'

A recent development in the study of the sources of international law has been the claim that international law consists of norms of behaviour of varying degrees of density or force. On the one hand, there are rules, usually contained in treaties, which constitute positive obligations, binding States objectively. On the other hand, there are international instruments, which, while not binding on States in the manner of treaty provisions, nonetheless constitute normative claims and provide standards or aspirations of behaviour. Such instruments can have an enormous impact on international relations and the behaviour of States but would not be considered law in the positivist sense. A growing body of writers has argued that both types of norms should be considered law and the distinction between the two is indicated by the terms 'hard law' and 'soft law'. The concept of soft law has been used significantly in the area of environmental protection which is discussed more fully in Chapter 16.

One particular benefit of soft law is that it allows States to participate in the formulation of standards of behaviour which they may not feel, at the time of formulation, ready to fully implement. For example, the Universal Declaration of Human Rights 1948 might be considered to be soft law, since it was expressed to be non-binding and, instead, set down aims for achievement. Since that time, it can be argued that most, if not all, of its provisions have been transformed into rules of hard law. Another example might be the Charter of Economic Rights and Duties of States 1974, which has already been mentioned. This has undoubtedly had an effect on the behaviour of States but is certainly a long way from hardening into a binding rule of law. It is clear that, within soft law, there will be varying degrees of hardness. Other examples of soft law would include the Final Act of the Conference on Security and Co-operation in Europe 1975 (the Helsinki Declaration), which was expressed to be non-binding; the OECD Guidelines for Multinational Enterprises; and the Gleneagles Agreement on the Sporting Boycott of South Africa. All undoubtedly have some legal effects, without creating legally binding obligations.

2.9.6 *Jus cogens* or peremptory norms

Having discussed the distinction between hard and soft law, it seems appropriate to turn to consideration of a duality of levels within hard law itself. Many municipal systems distinguish between *jus cogens* (rules or principles of public policy which cannot be derogated from by legal subjects, often referred to as *ordre public*) and *jus dispositivum* (norms which can be replaced by subjects in their private dealings). The idea that there are certain non-derogable fundamental norms in international law is not new. Even before the First World War, many writers had expressed the view that treaties which contravened certain fundamental norms would be void. The doctrine of international *jus cogens* was heavily influenced by natural law theories. Unlike the positivists, who argued that sovereign States enjoyed an almost complete freedom of contract, natural lawyers argued that States were not completely free in their treaty making powers. They argued that there were certain fundamental principles underpinning the international community which all States were obliged to respect.

In preparing the draft articles on the Law of Treaties, the ILC gave considerable thought to the doctrine of *jus cogens*. The ILC supported the idea that treaties conflicting with peremptory norms of international law would be void but it proposed no clear criteria by which such norms could be identified. An attempt at definition was made at the Vienna Conference and the result was seen in Article 53 of the Vienna Convention on the Law of Treaties 1969, which provides:

> A treaty is void if, at the time of its conclusion, it conflicts with a peremptory norm of general international law. For the purposes of the present convention, a peremptory norm of general international law is a norm accepted and recognised by the international community of States as a whole from which no derogation is permitted and which can be modified only by a subsequent norm of general international law having the same character.

The identical provision was included in the Vienna Convention on the Law of Treaties Between States and International Organisations or Between International Organisations 1986. The doctrine of *jus cogens* is further reflected in the Draft Articles on State Responsibility prepared by the ILC, which propose the notion of an international crime resulting from the breach by a State of an international obligation 'essential for the protection of fundamental interests of the international community' (*YBILC*, Vol II, 1976, New York: United Nations, p 73). Support for the existence of peremptory norms is also to be found in a number of judgments of the ICJ, notably in the *Nicaragua* case (1986), where the court identified the prohibition on the use of force as being 'a conspicuous example of a rule of international law having the character of *jus cogens*'. Other activities that have been identified as contravening *jus cogens* include slave trading, piracy and genocide.

Although it seems to be undisputed that international law recognises the concept of *jus cogens*, what is less clear is the way in which rules of *jus cogens* may be created. Since *jus cogens* has the status of a higher law, binding all States, it should not be possible for rules of *jus cogens* to be created by a simple majority of States and then imposed on a political or ideological minority. During discussions at the Vienna Conference on the Law of Treaties, a number of States stressed the need for universal acceptance of norms of *jus cogens* while the Austrian delegate argued that rules could only be regarded as having the status of *jus cogens* if there was 'the substantial concurrence of States belonging to all principal legal systems' (UNCLOT, Vol I, 1969, New York: United Nations, p 388), and the US representative argued that such a norm 'would require, as a minimum, the absence of dissent by any important element of the international community' (UNCLOT, Vol II, 1969, New York: United Nations, p 102). It therefore seems that the creation of a rule of *jus cogens* must, at the very least, meet the requirements of the establishment of a rule of customary law. As the Russian jurist, Gennady Danilenko, has written, in 'International *Jus Cogens*: issues of law making' (1991), p 65:

> As 'higher law' *jus cogens* clearly requires the application of higher standards for the ascertainment of the existence of community consensus as regards both the content and the peremptory character of the relevant rules. Only such an approach may ensure the required universality in the formation and subsequent implementation of rules designed to reflect and to protect the fundamental interests of the World Community.

THE SOURCES OF INTERNATIONAL LAW

Article 38 of the Statute of the International Court of Justice states:

1. The court, whose function is to decide in accordance with international law such disputes as are submitted to it, shall apply:

   (a) international conventions, whether general or particular, establishing rules ... expressly recognised by the contesting States;

   (b) international custom, as evidence of a general practice accepted as law;

   (c) the general principles of law recognised by civilised nations;

   (d) subject to the provisions of art 59, judicial decisions and the teachings of the ... most highly qualified publicists of the various nations, as subsidiary means for ... the ... determination of rules of law.'

Treaties

Treaties may be bilateral or multilateral and a further distinction is often drawn between law making or normative treaties and treaty contracts. Normative treaties are more akin to municipal legislation, although the general rule that treaties cannot bind third parties must always be remembered. Treaty contracts usually only involve a few States and create particular obligations which are capable of fulfilment.

Custom

Custom in international law is a practice followed by those concerned because they feel legally obliged to behave in such a way. A rule of customary international law needs to be distinguished from a general practice, which carries no legal obligation. To establish a rule of customary international law, it is necessary to demonstrate both a material element and a psychological element.

The material element refers to the practice of States. State practice includes treaties, legislation, diplomatic correspondence and the decisions of municipal courts. State practice should be extensive. This will usually mean widespread, although not necessarily universal, adherence to the rule. There is no specific time over which the practice must have occurred, although the shorter the time, the more extensive the practice would have to be.

The psychological element, often referred to as the *opinio juris*, refers to the distinction between custom and mere usage. The general practice must be one accepted as law and international tribunals will usually require some evidence of *opinio juris* together with the proof of State practice.

In general, rules of custom will be binding on all States although, exceptionally, it is possible for States, which have consistently objected to a rule since its inception, not to be bound by a particular rule. The burden of proving the exceptional position is on the persistent objector and the leading case on this point is the *Anglo-Norwegian Fisheries* case (1951).

Customary law and treaty law have equal authority although, if there is a conflict between the two, it is the treaty which prevails. Treaties should be interpreted to avoid such conflicts wherever possible.

General principles of law

The preferred view is that 'general principles of law' refers to principles of municipal law which may be applied by international tribunals where treaties or custom cannot resolve a particular problem. In a number of cases, the ICJ has made use of principles of equity and has stated them to be an integral part of international law.

Judicial decisions and the teachings of publicists

Judicial decisions, both of international and municipal tribunals, and the writings of publicists may be used by the ICJ as a subsidiary source of international law. Although there is no *stare decisis* in international law, the ICJ does make use of its own earlier decisions and has also referred to decisions of higher municipal courts. Less express use has been made of publicists, although States themselves will often make considerable use of them when arguing a particular position.

Other sources

Article 38 of the statute is the usual starting point for discussion of the sources of international law but many argue today that it should not be seen as a comprehensive list. In particular, there is considerable weight in the argument that certain UN resolutions do not constitute a source of international law. Much depends on the nature of the resolution and the manner in which it was adopted. Certainly, UN resolutions do not constitute a form of international legislation but clearly they have an important role to play in international law. The ICJ, in the *Nicaragua* case (1986), expressed the view that UN resolutions might constitute *opinio juris* which could, with evidence of State practice, constitute a rule of custom. Other writers have suggested that UN resolutions may be capable of constituting 'soft law' which can later harden into a legally binding rule.

CHAPTER 3

THE LAW OF TREATIES

Chapter 2 discussed the status of treaties as a source of international law. Chapter 3 is concerned with the mechanics of treaties: how they are concluded, interpreted, observed and terminated. In many respects, the law of treaties is to international law what the law of contract is to municipal law.

3.1 Introduction

Prior to 1969, the law of treaties consisted of customary rules of international law; many of the rules relating to treaties between States were codified in the Vienna Convention on the Law of Treaties (VCT) 1969, which was concluded on 23 May 1969 and entered into force on 27 January 1980, following receipt of the 35th ratification. The VCT 1969 is an early and important example of the codifying work of the International Law Commission. Also of interest is the Vienna Convention on Succession of States in Respect of Treaties (VCS) 1978, concluded on 23 August 1978, which entered into force on 6 November 1996, and the Vienna Convention on the Law of Treaties between States and International Organisations or between International Organisations (VCIO) 1986, concluded on 21 March 1986, which is not yet in force. The VCIO 1986 repeats most of the substantive rules contained in VCT 1969 and applies to those treaties which involve international organisations. In this chapter, reference will generally only be made to the relevant provisions of the VCT 1969. The VCT 1969 is not retroactive and only applies to treaties concluded after 27 January 1980. The rules of customary law still have an important role and it is important to decide the extent to which the Vienna Conventions codify existing customary law and the extent to which they introduce new rules of law. When studying the law of treaties, it is therefore important to be clear as to which rules are contained in the various Vienna Conventions and which rules are to be found in international custom.

3.2 Definitions

Article 2(1) of the VCT 1969 states:

> For the purposes of the present convention:
>
> (a) 'treaty' means an international agreement concluded between States in written form and governed by international law, whether embodied in a single instrument or in two or more related instruments and whatever its particular designation.

Article 2(1) of the VCIO 1986 states:

> For the purposes of the present convention:
>
> (a) 'treaty' means an international agreement governed by international law and concluded in written form:
>
> (i) between one or more States and one or more international organisations; or
>
> (ii) between international organisations,
>
> whether that agreement is embodied in a single instrument or in two or more related instruments and whatever its particular designation.

The VCT 1969 only applies to written agreements between States; VCIO 1986 deals with written agreements between States and international organisations or between international organisations. Although both conventions only apply to written agreements, this should not be taken to mean that agreements not in writing have no effect in international law; such unwritten agreements will still be regarded as treaties and will be governed by the customary law on treaties (subject to difficulties of proof of content). A useful definition has been provided by Paul Reuter, a French lawyer, who attended the Vienna Conferences on the Law of Treaties. He has written, in *Introduction to the Law of Treaties* (2nd edn, 1995, London: Kegan Paul, p 25):

> A treaty is an expression of concurring wills attributable to two or more subjects of international law and intended to have legal effects under the rules of international law.

Reuter identifies the following five essential components of a treaty.

3.2.1 An expression of concurring wills

The first requirement of a treaty is that there is an expression of will. This expression can be in a number of forms. The Vienna Conventions only apply where parties have expressed their will in writing and this will normally be the case. The ILC's commentary (*YBILC*, Vol II, 1966, New York: United Nations, p 189) on the draft articles reads:

> The restriction of the use of the term 'treaty' in the draft articles to international agreements expressed in writing is not intended to deny the legal force of oral agreements under international law or to imply that some of the principles contained in later parts of the commission's draft articles ... may not have relevance in regard to oral agreements.

Subjects of international law may express their will verbally by express oral declaration. It has been argued that conduct alone may also evidence an expression of a party's will to be bound. The more accepted view is that conduct alone cannot give rise to the creation of treaty obligations, although subjects of international law may find themselves bound to follow a particular path as a result of their conduct on the basis of estoppel or the creation of customary law obligations. The VCT 1969 itself clearly envisages the possibility of non-written obligations. For example, Article 11 provides:

> The consent of a State to be bound by a treaty may be expressed by signature, exchange of instruments constituting a treaty, ratification, acceptance, approval *or accession, or by any other means if so agreed* [emphasis added].

An example of an oral agreement is to be found in the case involving the *Legal Status of Eastern Greenland* (1933). The case arose from a dispute between Norway and Denmark over claims to sovereignty in Eastern Greenland. Denmark based its claim on the fact that during negotiations between government ministers, the Danish minister suggested to M Ihlen, the Norwegian foreign minister, that Denmark would raise no objection to Norwegian claims to Spitzbergen if Norway would not oppose Danish claims to Greenland at the Paris Peace Conference. A week after this conversation, in further negotiations, M Ihlen declared that Norway would 'not make any difficulty' concerning the Danish claim. The PCIJ found that the Spitzbergen question was interdependent on the Greenland issues and, as such, the court found that a binding agreement existed between the two States.

3.2.2 Concurring wills attributable to two or more parties

A basic point is that any treaty must have at least two parties. This is not to deny any legal effect to unilateral statements. While not constituting treaties, unilateral statements may be binding on States which make them. The matter was discussed in the *Nuclear Tests* cases (1974). The cases arose out of opposition by New Zealand and Australia to atmospheric nuclear testing carried out by France in the South Pacific. Australia and New Zealand brought proceedings before the ICJ but, before any decision was made, France indicated its intention not to hold any further tests in the region. The ICJ found that, in the light of the French declaration, it was no longer appropriate for it to give a decision on the merits of the case. In the course of its judgment, the ICJ declared:

> It is well recognised that declarations made by way of unilateral acts, concerning legal or factual situations, may have the effect of creating legal obligations. Declarations of this kind may be, and often are, very specific. When it is the intention of the State making the declaration that it should be bound according to its terms, that intention confers on the declaration the character of a legal undertaking, the State being thenceforth legally required to follow a course of conduct consistent with the declaration.

The intention is to be ascertained from all the circumstances surrounding the declaration and the ICJ did not lay down any specific form which the declaration had to take; it might be oral or in writing. The basis for the rule is the underlying obligation of good faith imposed on all subjects of international law and reference can also be made to application of the doctrine of estoppel which is discussed in Chapter 2.

3.2.3 Subjects of international law

Only those with international personality can be parties to treaties; effectively, this means States and international organisations. Whilst the majority of treaties are concluded between States, it should already be clear that it is possible for international organisations to undertake treaty obligations. It is not possible under international law for private individuals or companies to enter into treaties. The nature and requirements of the subjects of international law is dealt with in detail in Chapter 4.

Agreements between States themselves create no problem here but a number of marginal cases are becoming increasingly common. Instead of a State itself, the parties to an agreement may be other legal entities such as municipalities or public institutions. In such situations, the question arises as to whether such bodies have the power to commit their State and, if they do not, the degree to which it can it be said that they have concluded a treaty. On the whole, the problem is dealt with by application of the principles of agency and is resolved by looking at the extent to which the particular body can be implied to be acting as agent for the State concerned. Another problem arises in the case of agreements between States and entities which do not yet qualify as States (for example, national liberation organisations or provisional governments) but have been accorded some measure of international personality. In 1982, the Palestine Liberation Organisation issued a communication in which it purported to accede to the Geneva Conventions 1949 and additional Protocols dealing with the laws of war. Switzerland, as depository of the treaties, declined to accept the accession and sent a note (Embassy of Switzerland, 'Note of Information sent to State Parties to the Convention and Protocol', 13 September 1989) to State parties declaring:

> Due to the uncertainty within the international community as to the existence or the non-existence of a State of Palestine and as long as the issue has not been settled in an appropriate framework, the Swiss government, in its capacity as depository ... is not in a position to decide whether this communication can be considered as an instrument of accession ... The unilateral declaration of application of the four Geneva Conventions and of the additional Protocol I made on 7 June 1982 by the Palestine Liberation Organisation remains valid.

The exact status of the Israel-PLO accords agreed in 1992 thus remains a matter of debate.

3.2.4 An intention to produce legal effects

A further component of a treaty is the requirement of an intention to produce legal effects. An analogy may be drawn with the requirement in municipal contract law of an intention to be bound. Agreements will not be legally enforceable as treaties if it can be shown that one or more of the parties did not intend that the agreement should create binding legal obligations. So, for example, the Final Act of the Helsinki Conference on Security and Co-operation in Europe 1975 provided that it was to be 'not eligible for registration [as a treaty] under Article 102 of the Charter of the United Nations' and throughout the conference it was understood by the participants that the Final Act would not be legally binding. Such agreements may create 'soft law' as discussed in Chapter 2.

3.2.5 Legal effects under public international law

Perhaps the most important requirement of a treaty is that it is an agreement 'governed by international law'. In 1962, the ILC started a detailed study of the law of treaties and the Special Rapporteur, Sir Humphrey Waldock, stated in his first report to the ILC (*YBILC*, Vol II, 1962, New York: United Nations, p 32) that:

> The element of subjection to international law is so essential a part of an international agreement that it should be expressly mentioned in the definition. There may be agreements between States, such as agreements for the acquisition of premises for a diplomatic mission or for some purely commercial transaction, the incidents of which are regulated by the local law of one of the parties or by a private law system determined by reference to conflict of laws principles. Whether in such cases the two States are internationally accountable to each other at all may be a nice question; but even if that were held to be so, it would not follow that the basis of their international accountability was a treaty obligation.

An illustration of this point is provided by the *Anglo-Iranian Oil Co* case (1952). In that case, which arose after Iran had nationalised the oil industry, the UK sought to rely on an agreement made in 1933 between the Anglo-Iranian Oil Co and the government of Iran. The UK argued that the agreement was a treaty and, therefore, was binding on Iran. The argument was rejected by the ICJ, which found that the agreement was nothing more than a concessionary contract between a government and a foreign corporation.

3.2.6 Designation

It should be noted that the particular designation of the agreement does not govern its validity as a treaty – agreements may be entitled conventions, accords, final Acts, statutes, exchange of notes, protocols – they are all to be regarded as treaties for these purposes. The designation given may, however, be of relevance in indicating the nature of the transaction. For example, an 'agreement' is usually less formal than a 'treaty' and the term 'convention' will generally indicate a multilateral agreement.

3.3 Conclusion and entry into force of treaties

The making of a treaty will involve negotiation between the parties. Such negotiation will have to be carried out by representatives of the States concerned. An important consideration, therefore, is the extent of the power possessed by the representatives to bind their States.

3.3.1 Accrediting of negotiators

Once a State has decided to create a treaty, it is necessary to appoint representatives to conduct the negotiations. It is necessary that such representatives should be fully accredited and given sufficient authority to conduct negotiations, and conclude and sign the final treaty. As a general rule, such authority is contained in a formal document known as 'full powers' or often 'pleins pouvoirs'. Full powers can be dispensed with if practice between the negotiating States shows an intention to consider them as read and a gradual reduction in the use of full powers by States can be identified in the recent conduct of international relations.

In the case of multilateral agreements, which are generally concluded at international conferences, the practice is for a committee to be set up to investigate the validity of the accreditation of all delegates.

By virtue of Article 7 of the VCT 1969, three categories of person do not require full powers:

(a) heads of State, heads of government and ministers for foreign affairs have full powers for the purpose of performing all acts relating to the conclusion of a treaty;

(b) heads of diplomatic missions have powers for the purpose of adopting the text of a treaty between the accrediting State and the State to which they are accredited; and

(c) representatives accredited by States to an international conference or to an international organisation or one of its organs, have powers to act for the purposes of adopting the text in that conference, organisation or organ.

This provision reflects the rules in customary international law and, in the *Legal Status of East Greenland* case (1933), the special position of foreign ministers as representatives for the purpose of entering into international agreements was expressly recognised by the Permanent Court.

If an unauthorised person were to enter into an agreement, his/her actions would be without legal effect unless subsequently confirmed by the State. Article 8 of the VCT 1969 provides a further safeguard against abuse, by enabling a State to denounce an agreement entered into by an unauthorised person.

3.3.2 Negotiation and adoption

Negotiations concerning a treaty are conducted either through *pourparlers,* in the case of bilateral treaties, or at a diplomatic conference, in the case of multilateral treaties. The negotiators will maintain contact with their governments and usually, before actually signing a treaty, they will obtain a new set of instructions indicating the manner of signature. The procedure at diplomatic conferences runs to a standard pattern, with the appointment of committees and rapporteurs to manage the conference as efficiently as possible.

The aim of negotiation is the production of an agreed text of a treaty. The text is adopted by the consent of the parties. Article 9 of the VCT 1969 provides that the adoption of a treaty text at an international conference requires a two thirds majority of those present and voting, unless a two-thirds majority decides otherwise. A common practice over recent years has been for the final text of multilateral treaties to be adopted by a meeting of the relevant international organisation, for example, the UN General Assembly.

3.3.3 Authentication, signature and exchange

When the text of the treaty has been agreed upon and adopted, the treaty is ready for signing. Signing the treaty, which is usually a formal occasion, serves to authenticate the text. Signing is, therefore, essential to the validity of the treaty, unless other methods of authentication have been agreed.

Article 10 of the VCT 1969 provides that:

> The text of a treaty is established as authentic and definitive:
>
> (a) by such procedure as may be provided in the text or agreed upon by the States participating in its drawing up; or
>
> (b) failing such procedure, by the signature, signature *ad referendum* or initialling of the representatives of those States of the text of the treaty or of the final Act of a conference incorporating the text.

3.3.4 Effect of signature

The effect of signature depends upon whether the treaty is subject to ratification, acceptance or approval. If this is the case, then the signature means no more than that the delegates have agreed a text and have referred it to their governments for approval and ratification. Thus, in the *North Sea Continental Shelf* cases (1969), although the Federal Republic of Germany had signed the Continental Shelf Convention 1958, it was not bound by its provisions since it had not ratified it. For this reason, Denmark and Holland had to base their arguments on rules of customary international law. In keeping with the general requirement of good faith, Article 18 of the VCT 1969 provides that, where a State signs a treaty which is subject to ratification, there is an obligation to do nothing to defeat the object of the treaty until the State has made its intentions clear. Sometimes the treaty will provide that it is to operate on a provisional basis as from the date of signature.

If the treaty is not expressed to be subject to ratification, or is silent on the matter, the treaty is binding as from the date of signature (Article 12 of the VCT 1969). Where a treaty is constituted by an exchange of instruments between the parties, Article 13 of the VCT 1969 provides that such exchange may result in the parties becoming bound if:

(a) the instrument so provides; or

(b) it can otherwise be shown that the parties so intended.

3.3.5 Ratification

The next stage, if necessary, is for the delegates to refer the treaty back to their governments for approval. Ratification is the approval by the head of State or government of the signature to the treaty. Article 2 of the VCT 1969 defines ratification as the international act whereby a State establishes on the international plane its consent to be bound by a treaty. Ratification does not have retroactive effect, so States are only bound from the date of ratification, not the date of signature.

It used to be thought that ratification was always essential, but that is no longer the case. Nowadays, it is a question of the intention of the parties as to whether ratification is a mandatory requirement.

It should be noted that the method by which ratification is actually accomplished is a matter for individual States. In the UK, although treaties are signed and ratified under the royal prerogative without the need for reference to parliament, the practice is to lay the text of any treaty together with an explanatory memorandum detailing the main features of the treaty before both Houses of parliament for 21 days before ratification (this practice is known as the 'Ponsonby rule').

Generally, ratification has no effect until some notice of it is given to the other parties to the treaty. In the case of bilateral treaties, ratifications are simply exchanged between the parties. This is clearly impractical in the case of multilateral treaties, so multilateral treaties usually provide for the deposit of all ratifications with one central body; in nearly all cases, this function is performed by the secretariat of the United Nations.

3.3.6 Accessions and adhesions

When a State has not signed a treaty, it can only accede or adhere to it. Accession indicates that a State is to become a party to the whole treaty, whereas adhesion only involves acceptance of part of a treaty. Strictly speaking, States can only accede or adhere to a treaty with the consent of all the existing parties. In practice, the consent of existing parties to accession is often implied

3.3.7 Entry into force

When a treaty is to enter into force depends upon its provisions, or upon what the parties may otherwise have agreed. Treaties may be operative on signature, or on ratification. Multilateral treaties usually provide for entry into force only after the deposit of a specific number of ratifications, for example, Article 19 of the International Convention on the Elimination of all Forms of Racial Discrimination 1966 provides:

> This convention shall enter into force on the 30th day after the date of the deposit with the secretary general of the United Nations of the 27th instrument of ratification or instrument of accession.

VCT 1969 itself entered into force after the receipt by the secretary general of the 35th ratification. Sometimes a precise date for the entry into force of a treaty is given irrespective of the number of ratifications received.

3.3.8 Registration and publication

Article 102 of the United Nations Charter provides that all treaties entered into by members of the United Nations shall 'as soon as possible' be registered with the secretariat of the United Nations and be published by it. A similar provision was laid down in Article 18 of the League of Nations Covenant. Failure to so register and publish the treaty will mean that the treaty cannot be invoked in any UN organ. Most significantly, this would mean that a State would be unable to rely on an unregistered treaty in proceedings before the ICJ. This provision was included to try to combat the use of secret treaties which were considered to have a detrimental effect on international relations. Article 80 of the VCT 1969 provides that treaties shall, after their entry into force, be transmitted to the secretariat of the UN for registration or filing and recording, as the case may be, and for publication.

In fact, a considerable proportion of treaties are not registered. Paul Reuter suggests that statistical research based on the League of Nations and the United Nations Treaty Series shows that 25% of treaties have not been registered. Although the effect of non-registration of treaties has been discussed on a number of occasions before the ICJ, it is not possible to draw any definite conclusions.

3.4 Reservations

It can frequently happen that a State, while wishing to become a party to a treaty, considers that it can do so only if it can exclude or modify one or more particular provisions contained in the treaty. Ideally, such a State will be able to convince the other parties to amend the text of the treaty to incorporate its specific wishes. Often, however, this will not be possible and the regime of reservations allows a State, in certain circumstances, to alter the effect of the treaty in respect of its own obligations while preserving the original treaty intact as between the other parties.

3.4.1 Definitions

Article 2(1)(d) of the VCT 1969 defines a reservation as:

> ... a unilateral statement, however phrased or named, made by a State when signing, ratifying, accepting, approving or acceding to a treaty, whereby it purports to exclude or to modify the legal effect of certain provisions of the treaty in their application to that State.

The growth of reservations to treaties coincides with the growth in multilateral conventions. With regard to bilateral treaties, the two parties to the treaty may disagree over the precise terms of the treaty which is to bind them. If this is the case, they may re-negotiate the terms until they achieve full agreement. There will be no treaty in existence until both sides agree on the terms. From this, it follows that there can be no question of reservations to a bilateral treaty. In the case of multilateral treaties, it may not always be possible to get the full agreement of all the negotiating parties to every provision of the treaty. The general practice is for the text of such treaties to be adopted by two-thirds majorities. In the event of such a vote, those parties in the minority are in something of a dilemma; they can either refuse to become parties to the whole treaty, or they can accept the whole treaty even though they disagree with one or more of its provisions. The regime of reservations provides something of a compromise; those in the minority can become parties to the treaty without accepting all of the provisions therein.

Reservations should be distinguished from so-called 'interpretative declarations', whereby a State indicates the view which it holds about the substance of the treaty. Interpretative declarations are not intended as an attempt to derogate from the full legal effect of provisions of the treaty. In practice, the distinction between reservations and interpretative declarations may not always be clear cut. In *Belios v Switzerland* (1988), the European Court of Human Rights had to consider the nature of a declaration made by

Switzerland when it ratified the European Convention on Human Rights. Switzerland argued against a finding of the Commission that the declaration was a mere interpretative declaration which did not have the effect of a reservation. The court found that the declaration was a reservation and, in the course of its judgment, said:

> The question whether a declaration described as 'interpretative' must be regarded as a 'reservation' is a difficult one ... In order to establish the legal character of such a declaration, one must look behind the title given to it and seek to determine the substantive content.'

3.4.2 Validity of reservations

The formerly accepted rule for all kinds of multilateral treaty was that reservations were valid only if the treaty concerned permitted reservations and if all the other parties accepted the reservation. On this basis, a reservation constituted a counter-offer which required the acceptance of the other parties, failing which, the State making the counter-offer would not become a party to the treaty.

During the period of the League of Nations, the practice with regard to multilateral conventions was inconsistent. In 1927, the Committee of Experts for the Progressive Codification of International Law (the League of Nations equivalent of the International Law Commission) adopted a policy based on the absolute integrity of treaties and argued that reservations to treaties would not be effective without the full acceptance of all parties. At the same time, the members of the Pan-American Union (the forerunner of the Organisation of American States) adopted a more flexible policy, including the following key elements:

(a) as between States which ratify a treaty without reservations, the treaty applies in the terms in which it was originally drafted and signed;

(b) as between States which ratify a treaty with reservations and States which accept those reservations, the treaty applies in the form in which it may be modified by the reservations; and

(c) as between States which ratify a treaty with reservations and States which, having already ratified, do not accept those reservations, the treaty will not be in force.

A small number of States, principally from Eastern Europe, adhered to the view that every State had a sovereign right to make reservations unilaterally and at will, and to become a party to treaties subject to such reservations, even if they were objected to by other contracting States.

Matters came to a head following the unanimous adoption of the Convention on the Prevention and Punishment of the Crime of Genocide by the UN General Assembly in 1948. Article 9 of the Convention provided that disputes or cases arising under the Convention should be compulsorily within the jurisdiction of the ICJ. A number of States wished, for reasons of their own, to avoid being subject to the ICJ's compulsory jurisdiction, but the Convention contained no express provision allowing for reservations. The General Assembly therefore requested an advisory opinion from the ICJ on certain key questions:

(a) could a reserving State be regarded as being a party to the Convention while still maintaining its reservation if the reservation is objected to by one or more of the parties to the Convention but accepted by others? and

(b) if the answer to question (a) is in the affirmative, what is the effect of the reservation as between the reserving State and

- the parties which object to the reservation?
- those which accept it?

The court in the *Reservations to the Convention on Genocide* case (1951) ruled by seven votes to five, in response to question (a) that a State which has made and maintained a reservation which has been objected to by one or more of the parties to the Convention but not by others, can be regarded as being a party to the Convention if the reservation is compatible with the object and purpose of the Convention; otherwise, that State cannot be regarded as being a party to the Convention.

In response to question (b), again by a seven to five majority, the ICJ found that:

(a) if a party to the Convention objects to a reservation which it considers to be incompatible with the object and purpose of the Convention, it can consider that the reserving State is not a party to the Convention; and

(b) if, on the other hand, a party accepts the reservation as being compatible with the object and purpose of the Convention, it can in fact consider that the reserving State is a party to the Convention.

This judgment was not initially well received. It was felt that the compatibility test was too subjective and that the result of the decision would be further uncertainty. The International Law Commission reported in 1951, after the court had given its decision, and recommended a return to the traditional view that reservations required the unanimous consent of the parties to a treaty. However, views did gradually change. By 1959, the UN General Assembly had adopted the ICJ's position and, in 1962, the International Law Commission decided in favour of the compatibility test. That position was the one adopted by the VCT 1969 and represents customary international law. The relevant provisions are found in Articles 19–23. Article 19 provides that, in general, reservations are always permitted except in three instances:

(a) when the treaty explicitly forbids reservations;

(b) when the treaty does not permit the type of reservation being made; and

* A reservation is considered to have been accepted by a State if that State has made no objection within 1yr

(c) when the reservation is incompatible with the object and purpose of the treaty.

Some treaties provide mechanisms for deciding on compatibility of reservations; for example, Article 20 of the Convention on the Elimination of Racial Discrimination 1966 provides that a reservation shall be considered incompatible if at least two-thirds of the State parties to the Convention object to it.

Article 20 provides as follows:

1 A reservation expressly authorised by a treaty does not require any subsequent acceptance by the other contracting States unless the treaty so provides.

2 When it appears from the limited number of negotiating States and the object and purposes of a treaty that the application of the treaty in its entirety between all the parties is an essential condition of the consent of each one to be bound by the treaty, a reservation requires acceptance by all the parties.

3 When a treaty is a constituent instrument of an international organisation and unless it otherwise provides, a reservation requires the acceptance of the competent organ of that organisation.

4 In cases not falling under the preceding paragraphs and unless the treaty otherwise provides:

(a) acceptance by another contracting State of a reservation constitutes the reserving State a party to the treaty in relation to that other State if or when the treaty is in force for those States;

(b) an objection by another contracting State to a reservation does not preclude the entry into force of the treaty as between the objecting and reserving States unless a contrary intention is definitely expressed by the objecting State;

(c) an act expressing a State's consent to be bound by the treaty and containing a reservation is effective as soon as at least one other contracting State has accepted the reservation.

5 For the purposes of paras 2 and 4 and unless the treaty otherwise provides, a reservation is considered to have been accepted by a State if it shall have raised no objection to the reservation by the end of a period of 12 months after it was notified of the reservation or by the date on which it expressed its consent to be bound by the treaty, whichever is later.

Article 21 spells out the legal effects of reservations and sets down three main rules:

1 A reservation modifies the provisions of the treaty to which it relates as regards the reserving State in its relations with other parties and as regards the other parties in their relations with the reserving State.

2 A reservation does not modify the provisions of the treaty for the other parties to the treaty *inter se.*

3 When a State objecting to a reservation has not opposed the entry into force of the treaty between itself and the reserving State, the provisions to which the reservation relates do not apply as between the two States to the extent of the reservation.

Rule 3 was illustrated in the *English Channel* arbitration (1979) between France and the UK. During the course of the arbitration, it was necessary to consider the effect of reservations to Article 6 of the Continental Shelf Convention 1958, to which the UK had objected. The VCT 1969 does not apply to the Continental Shelf Convention, so the issue had to be decided in accordance with customary law. France argued that the combined effect of reservations and objections was to render Article 6 completely inapplicable as between Britain and France, whereas the UK sought to argue that the effect was to render the Article applicable *in toto.* The Court of Arbitration rejected both arguments and held that the combined effect of the reservation and the objection to it was to render Article 6 'inapplicable as between the two countries to the extent, but only to the extent, of the reservations'.

The VCT 1969 further provides that reservations and acceptances/objections to reservations must be in writing.

The topic of reservations is currently being considered by the International Law Commission. The ILC has indicated that, while it is fully satisfied with the reservations regime adopted in the Vienna Conventions, it may be useful to adopt a guide to practice in respect of reservations which, among other things, would contain model clauses on reservations to be inserted in multilateral conventions.

3.5 Application of treaties

The doctrine of *pacta sunt servanda,* the rule that treaties are binding on the parties and must be performed in good faith, is a fundamental principle of international law. The rule is included in the VCT 1969 by Article 26, which provides that: 'Every treaty in force is binding on the parties to it and must be performed in good faith'. As was mentioned in Chapter 1, the principle is derived from the *jus gentium* of the Roman legal system. There has been some discussion as to the question of whence the rule derives its authority and the precise status of the rule. The principle is certainly one of customary international law evidenced by widespread State practice and *opinio juris.* The fact that it is a recognised rule of customary international law enables the VCT

1969 itself to be binding. Arguably, *pacta sunt servanda* constitutes a higher rule of customary law, since it is difficult to envisage how a system of international law could operate without it. In this sense, it might be viewed as constituting one of the true sources of international law in the sense of a *grundnorm*, as identified by Kelsen. It could also be validly claimed to constitute a rule of *jus cogens*.

3.5.1 Non-retroactivity

Article 28 of the VCT 1969 reflects the customary rule of non-retroactivity of treaties. The provisions of a treaty do not bind a party in relation to any act or fact which took place or any situation which ceased to exist before the treaty entered into force for that State, unless a different intention appears from the treaty or is otherwise established. The rule applies to the VCT 1969 itself, which has no application to any treaty entered into before the VCT 1969 came into force. Where treaties are the subject of ratification, it is necessary to remember the rule expressed in Article 18 of the VCT 1969, which provides that States, having signed a treaty, should not act in any way to defeat the object and purpose of the treaty until it has made a clear final decision with regard to ratification. It should also be noted that treaties can apply to continuing situations. Although a situation may have arisen before a treaty came into force, it will be governed by the provisions of the treaty if it continues to exist after the treaty comes into force.

3.5.2 Territorial application

The general rule, reflected in Article 29 of the VCT 1969, is that, unless some other intention is made clear, a treaty applies to the entire territory of each party. The issue of territorial application arises where parties to a treaty have overseas territorial possessions, and the presumption is that a treaty applies to all the territory for which contracting States are internationally responsible. Thus, unless the contrary is explicitly indicated, treaties to which the UK is a party apply to the British colonies and all territory for which the UK is internationally responsible, for example, the Channel Islands and the Isle of Man.

3.5.3 Successive treaties

The problem of a later treaty being inconsistent with an earlier one is a complex issue, but Article 30 of the VCT 1969 sets out general rules that deal with the majority of cases. As far as UN members are concerned, the UN Charter prevails over any other international agreement which conflicts with it. Otherwise, the basic rules are:

(a) a prior treaty prevails over a later one in any instance of apparent disagreement when the later one specifies that it is subject to, or not incompatible with, the earlier one;

(b) where all the parties to the earlier treaty are also parties to the later treaty, the earlier (if still in effect) applies only to the extent that its provisions are compatible with those of the later treaty; and

(c) when the parties to the two treaties are not identical, the earlier applies between States that are parties to both only to the extent that the earlier is not incompatible with the later, while as between a State which is party to both treaties and a State which is a party to only one of the treaties, the treaty to which both are parties governs their mutual rights and obligations.

3.5.4 Treaties and third parties

The general rule expressed in the maxim, *pacta tertiis nec nocent nec prosunt*, is that treaties cannot bind third parties without their consent. The rule is affirmed in Article 34 of the VCT 1969. However, situations in which the rights and duties of third parties are involved have occasionally been created by treaties which are said to establish objective regimes, creating rights and obligations valid universally (*erga omnes*). *Erga omnes* is not a term used in the VCT 1969, but Article 36 does provide:

> 1 A right arises for a third State from a provision of a treaty if the parties to the treaty intend the provision to accord that right to a third State, or to a group of States ...

The International Law Commission considered that this provided the legal basis for establishing rights valid *erga omnes* and did not propose any special provision on treaties creating so-called objective regimes such as the Antarctic Treaty 1959. Certainly, there is less difficulty where a treaty creates rights for third parties than the situation where a treaty purports to impose obligations on non-parties. The subject of *erga omnes* obligations will be considered in more detail in connection with human rights law and environmental protection in Chapters 14 and 16. There are a number of examples of treaties establishing rights for third parties particularly with respect to rights over territory. The Constantinople Convention 1888 was, for a long time, considered to give a right of passage through the Suez Canal to States that were not parties to the agreement, as did the Treaty of Versailles 1919 with respect to the Kiel Canal.

It should not be forgotten that the provisions contained in treaties might bind non-parties as rules of customary international law either in situations where the treaty is itself a codification of existing international law or where the treaty leads to the gradual development of new rules of custom.

3.6 Amendment and modification

Prior to the VCT 1969, the customary law rule was that a treaty could not be revised without the consent of all the parties, although there was evidence that, by 1969, State practice had already begun to depart from the rule. The ILC, when considering the draft convention on treaties, noted the enormous increase in the number of multilateral treaties and the fact that obtaining the consent of all the parties would not always be possible (there are parallels here with the discussions about reservations). The VCT 1969 now draws a distinction between 'amendments' and 'modifications'. Amendment, covered by Article 40, denotes a formal change in a treaty intended to alter its provisions with respect to all the parties. Modification, dealt with in Article 41, indicates an agreement concluded between certain of the parties only, and intended to alter the provisions of the treaty between themselves alone. Modification is only allowed if:

(a) it is permitted by the treaty;

(b) it is not prohibited by the treaty;

(c) it does not affect the other parties to the treaty; and

(d) it is not incompatible with the treaty.

More usually, amendment or modification is achieved in the case of multilateral treaties by another multilateral treaty which comes into force only for those States which agree to the changes.

3.7 Treaty interpretation

Even when the text of a treaty has been agreed, there can remain considerable dispute about the precise meaning of specific clauses. The topic of treaty interpretation is one where there has been considerable dispute among academic writers. There are some writers, notably Stone, ('Fictional elements in treaty interpretation' (1955) 1 Sydney L Rev 344) who argue that there are no real rules or principles of treaty interpretation and any suggestion of rules or principles is merely an *ex post facto* rationalisation of a conclusion reached on other grounds. Such a view would lend support to the contemporary criticisms of a positive system of international law.

3.7.1 Aims and goals of interpretation

There is a measure of disagreement among jurists as to the aims of treaty interpretation. There are those who assert that the primary, and indeed only, aim of treaty interpretation is to ascertain the intention of the parties; this is generally referred to as the subjective approach. On the other hand, there are those who start from the proposition that there must be a presumption that the intention of the parties is reflected in the text of the treaty which they have drawn up, and that the primary aim of interpretation is to ascertain the meaning of this text; this is generally referred to as the objective or textual approach. Finally, there are those who maintain that the decision maker must first ascertain the object and purpose of a treaty and then interpret it so as to give effect to that object and purpose (the teleological or object and purpose approach).

It should be noted straight away that these three schools of thought are not mutually exclusive and a tribunal will probably draw on all three views to some extent when attempting to interpret a treaty.

3.7.2 Section 3 of the Vienna Convention on the Law of Treaties 1969

Section 3 of the VCT 1969 adopts a composite position. Article 31 states that treaties 'shall be interpreted in good faith in accordance with the ordinary meaning to be given to the terms of the treaty in their context and in the light of their object and purpose'.

3.7.2.1 Good faith

The principle of good faith underlies the most fundamental norm of treaty law – *pacta sunt servanda*. If the parties to a treaty are required to perform the obligations of a treaty in 'good faith', it is logical to interpret the treaty in 'good faith'.

3.7.2.2 Ordinary meaning

The ordinary meaning does not necessarily result from a strict grammatical analysis. In order to arrive at the ordinary meaning, account will need to be taken of all the consequences which reasonably flow from the text. It is also clear that the ordinary meaning of a phrase cannot be ascertained divorced from the context the phrase has in the treaty as a whole. In the *Employment of Women During the Night* case (1932), Judge Anzilotti said:

> I do not see how it is possible to say that an article of a convention is clear until the subject and aim of the convention have been ascertained, for the article only assumes its true import in this convention and in relation thereto. Only when it is known what the contracting parties intended to do and the aim that they had in view is it possible to say either that the natural meaning of terms used in a particular article corresponds with the real intention of the parties, or that the natural meaning of the terms used falls short of or goes further than such intention.

This view can be contrasted with the decision of the ICJ given in the advisory opinion in the *Competence of the General Assembly for the Admission of a State to the UN* case (1950), where the court said that:

> The first duty of a tribunal which is called upon to interpret and apply the provisions of a treaty is to endeavour to give effect to them in their natural and ordinary meaning in their context in which they occur. If the relevant

words in their natural and ordinary meaning make sense in their context, that is an end of the matter.

3.7.2.3 Special meaning

Paragraph 4 of Article 31 provides that a special meaning shall be given to a term if it is established that the parties so intended. In the *Eastern Greenland* case, the PCIJ stated:

> The geographical meaning of the word 'Greenland', that is, the name which is habitually used in maps to denote the whole island, must be regarded as the ordinary meaning of the word. If it is alleged by one of the parties that some unusual or exceptional meaning is to be attributed to it, it lies on that party to establish its contention.

3.7.2.4 The context, object and purpose

The context, for the purposes of interpretation, includes the text, its preamble and annexes and any agreement relating to the treaty made between all the parties, or made by some of the parties and accepted by the other, in connection with the conclusion of the treaty. The text of the treaty must be read as a whole. The preamble to the treaty will often provide assistance in ascertaining the object and purpose of a treaty.

3.7.2.5 Supplementary means of interpretation

Article 32 of the VCT 1969 provides:

> Recourse may be had to supplementary means of interpretation, including the preparatory work of the treaty and the circumstances of its conclusion, in order to confirm the meaning resulting from the application of Article 31, or to determine the meaning when the interpretation according to Article 31:
>
> (a) leaves the meaning ambiguous or obscure; or
>
> (b) leads to a result which is manifestly absurd or unreasonable.

Although Article 32 talks of 'supplementary means of interpretation', in practice, international tribunals tend to blur any differences between Articles 31 and 32, and the preparatory work often referred to by the French term *travaux preparatoires* are regarded as a considerable aid. In the *Employment of Women* Case, the PCIJ referred to the *travaux preparatoires* to confirm the clear meaning of the text. One possible restriction on the use of *travaux preparatoires* as an aid to interpretation arises where some of the parties to the dispute have not been involved in the preparatory work leading to the treaty. So, for example, in the *River Oder* case (1929), the PCIJ refused to allow reference to the preparatory work of the Treaty of Versailles 1919, on the grounds that several of the parties to the dispute had not taken part in the work of the conference which had prepared the treaty.

3.8 Multilingual treaties

Treaties are often drafted in two or more languages. In the case of bilateral treaties, the normal practice is that the treaty texts should be drawn up in the two languages of the parties, both texts being equally authentic. Multilateral conventions may be concluded in many languages: conventions concluded under the auspices of the UN will be drawn up in Arabic, Chinese, English, French, Russian and Spanish; the treaty by which Greece became a member of the European Union was concluded in eight languages. A more common practice is to conclude a treaty in two or three widely spoken languages and for these two or three texts to be equally authentic, and for a number of official translations to be deposited with the signed original. If a number of texts are equally authentic, they may be read in conjunction in order to ascertain the meaning of the convention.

3.9 Validity of treaties

The VCT 1969 represents both the codification of existing rules of customary international law and also the progressive development of international law. Part V of the Convention, which deals with invalidity, termination and suspension, represents more a 'progressive development' of the law than simple codification. In looking at the grounds of invalidity contained in the VCT 1969, it should be borne in mind that the customary law rules on validity may well not be as rigid or as settled.

3.9.1 Non-compliance with municipal law requirements

A State cannot plead a breach of its constitutional provisions as to the making of treaties as a reason for invalidating an agreement. Article 46 of the VCT 1969 provides that:

> 1 A State may not invoke the fact that its consent to be bound by a treaty has been expressed in violation of a provision of its internal law ... as invalidating its consent unless that violation was manifest and concerned a rule of its internal law of fundamental importance.
>
> 2 A violation is manifest if it would be objectively evident to any State conducting itself in the matter in accordance with normal practice and in good faith.

For example, where the representative of the State has had his/her authority to consent on behalf of the State made subject to a specific restriction which is ignored, the State will still be bound by that consent except where the other negotiating States were aware of the restriction on authority prior to the expression of consent.

3.9.2 Error

Unlike the role of mistake in municipal contract law, the scope of error in international law is very limited. In practice, given the number of people and the character of States involved in the negotiation and conclusion of treaties, errors are not very likely to occur.

Article 48 declares that a State may only invoke an error in a treaty as invalidating its consent to be bound if the error relates to a fact or situation which was assumed by that State to exist at the time when the treaty was concluded and formed an essential basis of its consent to be bound. The ground is not open to the State if it contributed to the error by its own conduct or the circumstances were such as to put it on notice of a possible error, or if the error related only to the wording of the text of the treaty.

3.9.3 Fraud and corruption

Where a State consents to be bound by a treaty as a result of the fraudulent conduct of another negotiating State, that State may, under Article 49 of the VCT 1969, invoke the fraud as invalidating its consent to be bound. Fraud itself is not defined in the VCT 1969. Since there are no examples of treaties being invalidated as a result of fraud, there is a lack of international precedents as to what constitutes fraudulent conduct.

If a State's consent to a treaty has been procured through the corruption of its representative, directly or indirectly by another negotiating State, the former State is entitled to claim that the treaty is invalid, under Article 50 of the VCT 1969.

3.9.4 Coercion

Use of coercion in the concluding of treaties will invalidate the treaty and may occur in one of two ways:

(a) coercion of State representatives:

Article 51 of the VCT 1969 provides that the expression of a State's consent to be bound by a treaty which has been procured by the coercion of its representative through acts or threats directed against him/her shall be without any legal effect. It has long been an accepted rule of customary international law that duress exercised against a representative concluding a treaty has been a ground for invalidating the treaty; and

(b) coercion of a State:

Article 52 VCT 1969 provides:

> A treaty is void if its conclusion has been procured by the threat or use of force in violation of the principles of international law embodied in the Charter of the United Nations.

There was considerable discussion about Article 52. In the 19th century, force had often been seen as a legitimate extension of diplomacy and treaties procured by force were not uncommon. The concept that a treaty may be void if its conclusion has been procured by threat or use of force is, therefore, of recent origin. At the Vienna Conference, discussion centred on the exact definition of force. A group of 19 African, Asian and Latin American States sought to define force as including any economic or political pressure. The vast majority of Western States opposed such a definition, arguing that it would seriously undermine the stability of treaty relations, given the width of possible interpretations of pressure. In the event, the 19 States did not push the issue to a vote, although the conference adopted a declaration which called upon States to refrain from economic and political coercion when negotiating and concluding treaties.

It should be noted that it is acceptance of the treaty that must be coerced. A peace treaty which is signed as a matter of choice between two independent States is valid even though its terms may have been influenced by a prior use of force.

There have been few recent examples of treaties brought about by the use of coercion. One of the best known cases involved the treaty between Germany and Czechoslovakia of March 1939, under which a German Protectorate was established in former Czechoslovakian territory. The treaty was signed by President Hacha of Czechoslovakia in Berlin at 2.00 am, after he had allegedly been subject to considerable personal threats and told that, if he did not sign, German bombers could destroy Prague within two hours.

In the *Fisheries Jurisdiction (Jurisdiction)* case (*UK v Iceland* [1973] ICJ Rep 1, p 14), the ICJ confirmed 'there can be little doubt, as is implied in the Charter of the United Nations and recognised in Art 52 of the Vienna Convention on the Law of Treaties, that, under contemporary international law, an agreement concluded under the threat of use of force is void'.

3.9.5 Unequal treaties

Many non-Western States take the view that treaties not concluded on the basis of the sovereign equality of all parties are invalid. Thus, treaties between economically powerful States and much weaker States under which the latter grants extensive privileges or facilities to the former should be set aside. For example, the 19th century treaties between the UK and China, under which China ceded Hong Kong Island and Kowloon and leased the New Territories to the UK was challenged by the Chinese government on the basis that they were not concluded between two equal States. On the whole, Western writers have regarded the concept of unequal treaties as too vague to be implemented.

3.9.6 *Jus cogens*

In the ILC's preparation of the Vienna Convention, considerable discussion took place about whether there were, in international law, certain rules so fundamental and of such universal importance that a State would not be entitled to derogate from them even by agreement with another State in a treaty. The ILC concluded that such rules did exist, for example, the prohibition on the unlawful use of force and the use of genocide.

Article 53 of the VCT 1969 provides:

> A treaty is void if, at the time of its conclusion, it conflicts with a peremptory norm of general international law. For the purposes of the present Convention, a peremptory norm of general international law is a norm accepted and recognised by the international community of States as a whole from which no derogation is permitted and which can be modified only by a subsequent norm of general international law having the same character.

Article 64 further provides that, if a new rule of *jus cogens* emerges, any existing treaty which conflicts with that rule becomes void and terminates.

3.9.7 The effect of invalidity

Article 69 of the VCT 1969 provides that, where the invalidity of a treaty is established, the treaty is void and its provisions have no legal effect. If acts have been performed in reliance on a void treaty, then States may require other parties to establish, as far as possible, the position with regard to their mutual relations that would have existed if the acts had not been performed. Acts performed in good faith in reliance on a treaty before its invalidity was invoked are not rendered unlawful by reason only of the invalidity of the treaty. Article 71 deals with the specific consequences arising where a treaty conflicts with *jus cogens*. In such a situation, the parties to the void treaty are under an obligation to bring their mutual relations into conformity with the peremptory norm. Where the treaty becomes void and terminates as a result of the development of a new rule of *jus cogens* under Article 64, the parties are released from any obligations further to perform the treaty, but rights and obligations created through the treaty prior to its termination are unaffected, provided that such rights or obligations do not themselves conflict with the new peremptory norm.

The answer to one question remains unclear: when a cause of invalidity arises, does it operate automatically, in the sense that anyone called upon to apply the treaty may judge whether or not it is valid, or is an international act of denunciation required on the part of the State that seeks to invoke the invalidity? The position at customary international law seems to be that, where the invalidity results from error or fraud, then an act of denunciation is required but on questions of coercion or violation of *jus cogens* there seems to be no real agreement. In practice, however, it will usually be the case that the question of invalidity will arise when a party to the treaty wishes to absolve itself from the obligations contained in it. It is therefore likely that some public act of denunciation will occur. Article 65 of the VCT 1969 provides that a party which seeks to impeach the validity of a treaty must notify the other parties and, providing no objection is received within three months of giving notice, that party may consider the treaty as void. If objections are made, there is a duty on the disputants to reach a peaceful settlement. The issue of peaceful settlement of disputes is dealt with in Chapter 11.

3.10 Termination of, suspension of and withdrawal from treaties

As important as the rules relating to the entry into force and application of treaties, are the rules by which treaty obligations may be suspended or brought to a permanent end.

3.10.1 By consent

Articles 54 to 59 of the VCT 1969 provide for various situations where a treaty may be terminated or suspended, or where a party may withdraw from a treaty by consent. The most straightforward situation will arise where the treaty either makes provision for termination, denunciation or withdrawal, or where all parties consent to a change. Where a treaty makes no provision for termination, denunciation or withdrawal, then the rule is that withdrawal and denunciation will not be allowed unless it is established that the parties intended to admit its possibility, or a right of termination and denunciation can be implied by the nature of the treaty. In such a case, a party wishing to denounce or withdraw from a treaty should give a minimum of 12 months' notice. The operation of a treaty may be suspended if provided for in the treaty or if all parties consent. In the case of multilateral conventions, two or more parties may conclude an agreement to suspend the treaty as between themselves, provided such suspension is not prohibited by the treaty and provided that it is not incompatible with the object and purpose of the treaty. If such an agreement to partially suspend a treaty is concluded, there is a duty on the two or more States to inform the other parties to the treaty.

3.10.2 Material breach

It has always been a rule of customary law that the breach of an important provision of a treaty by one party entitles the other parties to regard that agreement as at an end. The main question that arises is how important a breach needs to be before it will justify the termination of a treaty. The VCT 1969 refers to a 'material breach' as consisting in:

(a) a repudiation of the treaty not sanctioned by the present Convention; or
(b) the violation of a provision essential to the accomplishment of the object or purpose of the treaty.

A material breach will entitle the other parties to a treaty to terminate or suspend a treaty in whole or in part. In the case of multilateral treaties, those not in breach might decide to terminate or suspend the treaty only in respect of the party in breach. It is clear that a party responsible for a material breach cannot itself rely on that breach to terminate a treaty.

3.10.3 Supervening impossibility of performance

Article 61 of the VCT 1969 introduces a rule analogous to the doctrine of frustration in municipal contract law. If a treaty becomes impossible to perform as a result of the permanent disappearance or destruction of an object indispensable for the execution of the treaty, that impossibility may be invoked as a reason for terminating or suspending the treaty. Where the impossibility is only temporary, it may only be invoked as a ground for suspension of the treaty. An example of the operation of Article 61 would be the case of a treaty governing rights pertaining to a river. The treaty could be terminated if the river dried up permanently. The impossibility of performance cannot be invoked by a party where the impossibility results from the conduct of that party.

Linked to impossibility of performance is the doctrine of *force majeure*. (The doctrine will be discussed in more detail in Chapter 8, since it can provide a general defence to international responsibility.) The requirements of *force majeure* are that it must be irresistible, unforeseeable and external to the party relying on it. It may therefore exist under conditions which fall short of absolute material impossibility of performance. At the Vienna Conference on the Law of Treaties, Mexico proposed that *force majeure* should be included in Article 61 but the proposal was rejected. It therefore seems to be the case that, although *force majeure* may provide a defence for States accused of breaching treaty obligations, it will not result in the termination of the treaty. However, since a material breach of a treaty can result in the termination of that treaty, it may be argued that the ultimate effect of *force majeure* will be the same as a material impossibility of performance.

3.10.4 Fundamental change of circumstances

A fundamental change of the circumstances existing at the time the treaty was concluded has traditionally been a ground for withdrawal or termination. The rule is often referred to as the doctrine of *rebus sic stantibus*. Before the First World War, a number of treaties were brought to an end by States relying on fairly minor changes. Since that time, the law has been tightened up and it is clear that any change must be such as to radically alter the circumstances on the basis of which a treaty was concluded. In the *Fisheries Jurisdiction* case (1973), the ICJ declared that:

> International law admits that a fundamental change in the circumstances which determined the parties to accept a treaty, if it has resulted in a radical transformation of the extent of the obligations imposed by it, may, under certain conditions, afford the party affected a ground for invoking the termination or suspension of the treaty. This principle, and the conditions and exceptions to which it is subject, have been embodied in Article 62 of the Vienna Convention on the Law of Treaties, which may in many respects be considered as a codification of existing customary law on the subject ...

The conditions and exceptions which are indicated by Article 62 are that the change of circumstances must not have been foreseen at the time of the conclusion of the treaty; the existence of the circumstances must have constituted an essential basis of consent; and the effect of the change must be radically to transform the nature and extent of the obligations still to be performed under the treaty. A fundamental change of circumstances may not be invoked with regard to a treaty establishing a boundary, nor if the change is the result of a breach of any international obligation owed to any other party to the treaty by the party invoking it. The ICJ, in the *Gabcikovo-Nagymaros Project* case (1997), stressed the point that the plea of fundamental change of circumstances will only be accepted in exceptional cases.

3.10.5 Other possible grounds

Article 63 of the VCT 1969 provides that severance of diplomatic relations will not, in itself, affect treaty relationships, unless, of course, it amounts to a fundamental change of circumstances. There are a number of views as to the effect on a treaty of the outbreak of war. The VCT 1969 contains no provision relating to war, and it is certain that treaties governing war and peace, for example, the UN Charter and the Geneva Conventions 1949 are not terminated or suspended by war. The most sensible view seems to be that expressed by the New York State Court of Appeals in *Techt v Hughes* (1920): 'treaty provisions compatible with a state of hostilities, unless expressly terminated, will be enforced, and those incompatible rejected'.

3.10.6 The effect of termination or suspension

Article 70 of the VCT 1969 provides that termination of a treaty releases the parties from any further obligation to perform the treaty but does not affect rights and obligations or situations created prior to termination. The effect of suspension is to release the parties from their obligations for the period of suspension.

3.11 Dispute settlement

One of the main purposes of international law is to provide a framework for the peaceful settlement of disputes and Article 33 of the UN Charter places an obligation on States to settle their disputes by peaceful means. Clearly, this provision applies to disputes between parties to a treaty. Article 66 of the VCT 1969 deals with the specific question of disputes arising out of questions of validity, termination, withdrawal from or suspension of the operation of a treaty. If parties have not been able to settle the dispute themselves within a period of 12 months, then two procedures come into operation. In the case of disputes about the application or interpretation of a rule of *jus cogens,* the parties to the dispute may submit it to the ICJ for a decision. Disputes arising for other reasons are to be submitted to a conciliation procedure operated by the secretary general of the UN and detailed in an annex to the VCT 1969.

3.12 State succession

State succession involves the replacement of one State by another in the responsibility for the international relations of territory and has been a particularly controversial and unsettled area of law. In 1978, the Vienna Convention on the Succession of States in Respect of Treaties (VCS) was signed. The VCS only has 15 States as parties at present, although the basic rules are thought to reflect customary international law. As far as newly independent States are concerned, the VCS operates the 'clean slate' rule. In other words, by Article 16 of the VCS 1978, a newly de-colonised State:

> ... is not bound to maintain in force, or become a party to, any treaty by reason only of the fact that at the date of the succession of States the treaty was in force in respect of the territory to which the succession of States relates.

The only exception to this rule is in respect of treaties establishing boundaries or concerning other territorial matters, for example, treaties establishing objective regimes. Article 12 of the VCS 1978, which deals with obligations relating to territorial matters was considered by the ICJ, in the *Gabcikovo-Nagymaros Project* case (1997), and the court took the view that the Article reflected customary international law. This reflects general international practice with regard to the sanctity of boundaries and is in line with Article 62(2) of the VCT 1969, which provides that a fundamental change of circumstances cannot be invoked as a ground for terminating a treaty that establishes a boundary.

Of course, successor States may wish to become parties to treaties which had been in force with respect to the territory in question. In such a situation, a successor State may become a party by giving notice of succession. This rule will not apply where the application of the treaty to the successor State would be incompatible with the object and purpose of the treaty.

The VCS 1978 was adopted when questions of State succession arose, mainly as a result of de-colonisation. Recent events in Central and Eastern Europe have raised new questions and it is not yet possible to clearly identify a body of common State practice. Generally, the problem has been dealt with during negotiations leading to recognition of new States and in the drafting of new constitutions. In the case of German unification, many of the problems were dealt with in the Unification Treaty 1990 between the Federal Republic of Germany and the German Democratic Republic. Under the terms of unification, the GDR ceased to exist as a State and its territory was integrated into the FRG. As far as treaties to which the FRG is a party are concerned, the principle of moving treaty frontiers applies in that all treaties remain in force 'unless it appears that application of the treaty to the new territory would be incompatible with the object and purpose of the treaty or would radically change the conditions for its operation' (Article 15 of the VCS 1978). As far as treaties to which the GDR was a party are concerned, the position is more difficult. In the case of a union between two States which results in a new successor State, the VCS 1978 provides for the continuation of the treaties of both States to the extent that application of the treaties to the successor State is compatible with the object and purpose of the treaties, and does not radically change the conditions for its operation. Such treaties continuing in force shall, in general, only apply in respect of the part of the territory of the successor State in respect of which the treaty was in force at the date of succession. The situation envisaged here is exemplified by the short lived union of Egypt and Syria in the United Arab Republic, where the two States continued, in practice, to live a separate existence. The rules applicable to that situation do not seem to apply easily to the German situation. The preferred view seems to be that when States become dissolved, *prima facie*, no treaties pass to the successor State. and this rule applies where formerly sovereign territory is integrated into an existing State. Thus, treaties concluded by former sovereign parts of the Indian, American and Australian Federal States have been discontinued. Clearly, the option remains for the successor State to expressly choose to be bound by such treaties, but succession is not regarded as automatic.

With regard to those States which were formerly part of the Soviet Union, Russia has been regarded as a continuation of the Soviet Union and the other former Soviet republics have been regarded as successor States, except in the case of the Baltic republics of Latvia, Estonia and Lithuania, which are regarded as continuations of States which existed up until Soviet annexation in 1940. The Baltic States do not regard themselves as bound by treaties entered into by the former Soviet Union. The treaty obligations of the other former Soviet republics have been dealt with on a case by case basis. The same formula has been used in relation to the division of the former Czechoslovak Republic into the Czech Republic and the Republic of Slovakia, and in the case of the break up of the former Socialist Republic of Yugoslavia. The problem is complicated with regard to Yugoslavia since, while the Belgrade regime of Serbia and Montenegro considers itself to be the continuation of former Yugoslavia and refers to itself as the Republic of Yugoslavia, this claim is not recognised by the rest of the international community. The issue of succession to treaties has been considered by the ICJ in the case concerning the *Application of the Convention on the Prevention and Punishment of the Crime of Genocide* (1996), in which proceedings were brought by the government of Bosnia-Herzegovina against Serbia and Montenegro. Both parties regard themselves as parties to the Genocide Convention, although Serbia and Montenegro has not deposited an instrument of succession. Bosnia-Herzegovina argued that there was a customary law rule of 'automatic succession' which applies to human rights treaties. The ICJ, which was dealing with the jurisdictional issues of the case, found it unnecessary to make a ruling on the point. There have recently been discussions within the Council of Europe on the whole question of treaty succession and it has been suggested that matters could be clarified if there was an obligation on the depositories of treaties to contact successor States to ascertain their position with regard to the treaty obligations of those formerly responsible for the territory. It is likely that this area of law will be the subject of much further debate.

THE LAW OF TREATIES

The main source of the law of treaties is the Vienna Convention on the Law of Treaties (VCT) 1969. Although the provisions of the VCT 1969 broadly reflect customary international law, the treaty itself only applies to written agreements concluded between States after 27 January 1980 and all other treaties are governed by the rules of customary international law.

It is worth remembering Reuter's broad definition of a treaty as 'an expression of concurring wills attributable to two or more subjects of international law and intended to have legal effects under the rules of international law'. Treaties may, therefore, be unwritten and concluded by international law subjects other than States, for example, international organisations.

The various stages in treaty making and observance may be summarised as follows:

(a) accreditation of negotiators. Do representatives have the authority to conduct and conclude negotiations? Note the implied powers of heads of State, heads of government and foreign ministers – Article 7 of the VCT 1969;

(b) negotiation, through *pourparlers* (bilateral treaties) or at diplomatic conference (multilateral treaties);

(c) adoption and authentication of final text. Multilateral treaties require a two-thirds majority in favour of adoption. Authentication is usually achieved by signature;

(d) signature/exchange. Where a treaty is not subject to ratification, the treaty will become binding as from the date of signature or, in the case of treaties concluded by exchange of instruments, on the date of exchange;

(e) ratification. If ratification is required, the text of the treaty is referred back to the governments of the parties to the treaty. Where ratification is required, parties who have signed the treaty are under an obligation to do nothing to defeat the object of the treaty until such time as a firm decision has been made on ratification – Article 18 of the VCT 1969;

(f) reservations and entry into force (see Articles 19–23 of the VCT 1969). In the case of multilateral treaties, it is usual to make express provision for the entry into force of the treaty;

(g) registration, publication and application of treaty (see Article 102 of the UN Charter; *pacta sunt servanda*);

(h) adhesion and accession; State succession; interpretation (see Article 31 of the VCT 1969 and note the three approaches: subjective, objective and teleological);

(i) is the treaty valid? A treaty may be invalid on the following grounds:

- manifest non-compliance with municipal law;
- error, fraud and corruption;
- coercion; and
- violation of *jus cogens*.

CHAPTER 4

THE SUBJECTS OF INTERNATIONAL LAW AND THEIR RECOGNITION

4.1 Introduction

The principal question we are concerned with here is: to whom does international law apply? In order to be a subject of international law, an entity must have international personality; it must be capable of possessing international rights and duties and, as a consequence, must have the capacity to maintain such rights by bringing international claims. A subject of international law owes responsibilities to the international community and enjoys rights, the benefits of which must be claimed, and which, if denied, may be enforced to the extent recognised by the international legal system via legal procedures, that is, the entity will have procedural capacity. The question of who are the subjects of any legal system is clearly central to the nature of that legal system and, to some extent, the discussion about the subjects of international law has been dealt with in Chapter 1. In summary, the debate can be condensed into the question of whether States are the only subjects of international law. The position before the First World War seemed to be clear. Thus, in the first edition of Oppenheim's treatise on international law (1912, Harlow: Longman, p 5), it is stated that:

> Since the law of nations is based on the common consent of individual States, and not of individual human beings, States solely and exclusively are the subjects of international law.

By the end of the Second World War, the situation had changed and, in 1949, the ICJ declared, in the *Reparation for Injuries Suffered in the Service of the UN* case:

> The subjects of law in any legal system are not necessarily identical in their nature or in the extent of their rights, and their nature depends upon the needs of the community ... the court has come to the conclusion that the [United Nations] is an international person. That is not the same thing as saying that it is a State, which it certainly is not, or that its legal personality and rights and duties are the same as those of a State ... What it does mean is that it is a subject of international law and capable of possessing international rights and duties, and that it has capacity to maintain its rights by bringing international claims.

Today, it is no longer possible to consider States to be the sole and exclusive subjects of international law and this chapter, in addition to discussing the requirements of statehood, will also consider the international personality of international organisations and those entities which fall short of the full requirements of statehood, such as national liberation movements and provisional governments.

4.2 Independent States

While it is no longer accurate to talk in terms of States being the only subjects of international law, it is, without doubt, true that they continue to remain the most important subjects.

The traditional definition of a State for the purposes of international law is the one to be found in the Montevideo Convention on the Rights and Duties of States 1933, which was adopted by the seventh International Conference of American States and which provides (Article 1):

> The State as a person of international law should possess the following qualifications:
>
> (a) a permanent population;
>
> (b) a defined territory;
>
> (c) a government; and
>
> (d) a capacity to enter into relations with other States.

This definition has been subject to criticism, notably by James Crawford, whose major study on statehood, *The Creation of States in International Law,* was published in 1979 (Oxford: Clarendon). Nevertheless, the Montevideo definition continues to exert considerable influence. An alternative view of statehood is offered by Schwarzenberger and Brown (*Manual of International Law,* 6th edn, 1976, London: Stevens, p 43), who argue that an entity must satisfy a minimum of three conditions before it can be considered an independent State. Those conditions are:

(a) the entity must possess a stable government which does not recognise any outside superior authority;

(b) the government must rule supreme within a territory which has more or less settled frontiers; and

(c) the government must exercise control over a certain number of people.

It will be useful to examine the requirements of statehood in more detail.

4.2.1 Population and territory

States are aggregates of individuals and, accordingly, a permanent population living within a defined territory is regarded as a requirement of statehood. There are no limits as to size of population or territory. For example, the South

Pacific island of Nauru, which became independent in 1968, has less than 10,000 inhabitants and has a territory of less than 10 square miles. It is not a requirement that the population should hold the nationality of the State in question, merely that they should live there with some degree of permanence. As far as territorial boundaries are concerned, there is no requirement for absolutely settled borders. Israel was admitted to the United Nations in 1948, even though its borders were the subject of considerable dispute at the time. In the *Question of the Monastery at St Naoum* case (1924), the PCIJ recognised the State of Albania, even though its frontiers were not fixed. In *Deutsche Continental Gas-Gesellschaft v Polish State* (1929), the German-Polish mixed arbitral tribunal stated the position thus:

> In order to say a State exists ... it is enough that this territory has a sufficient consistency, even though its boundaries have not yet been accurately delimited, and that the State actually exercises independent public authority over that territory.

On the other hand, it is possible to cite a few situations where statehood was refused on the basis of unsettled frontiers, the classic example being that of Lithuania, which was refused membership of the League of Nations until border disputes with neighbouring States were settled. When considering the case of Israel in 1948, the US representative to the UN Security Council, Philip Jessup, attempted to provide the rationale behind the requirement of territory:

> ... both reason and history demonstrate that the concept of territory does not necessarily include precise delimitation of the boundaries of that territory. The reason for the rule that one of the necessary attributes of a State is that it shall possess territory is that one cannot contemplate a State as a kind of disembodied spirit. Historically, the concept is one of insistence that there must be some portion of the earth's surface which its people inhabit and over which its Government exercises authority.

4.2.2 Government

There is a strong case for regarding the possession of effective government as the single most importance criterion of statehood since, arguably, all the other requirements depend upon it. In 1920, a commission of jurists was appointed to investigate a dispute between Finland and the Soviet Union (the *League of Nations Commission of Jurists in the Aaland Islands dispute* (1920)), and it found that:

> Finland did not become a definitely constituted State until a stable political organisation had been created, and until the public authorities had become strong enough to assert themselves throughout the territories of the State without the assistance of foreign troops.

However, the application of the requirement of effective government has been far from straightforward. On 1 July 1960, the Republic of the Congo (now the

Democratic Republic of Congo, formerly Zaire) was granted independence by the former colonial power, Belgium, and admitted to membership of the UN. At the time, law and order had completely broken down and the government controlled very little of the territory, most of which was subject to the control of the Katangan secessionists. During the late 1970s and early 1980s it was doubtful as to the extent to which the State of Lebanon had any effective government. Most recently, the example of Bosnia-Herzegovina, shows that States may come into existence and be recognised by the international community, even though their governments have very limited control over their territory. Some authority for doubting the extent to which truly effective government is a requirement of statehood is provided by the Declaration on the Granting of Independence to Colonial Countries and Peoples (GA Resolution 1514 (XV) (1960)), which declares that inadequacy of political, economic, social or educational preparedness should never serve as a pretext for delaying independence. In view of State practice concerning the requirement of government, the position is correctly stated by J Crawford, who suggests the following conclusions in *The Creation of States in International Law* (1979, Oxford: Clarendon, p 45):

> First, to be a State, an entity must possess a government or a system of government in general control of its territory, to the exclusion of other entities not claiming through or under it.
>
> Secondly, international law lays down no specific requirements as to the nature and extent of this control, except, it seems, that it include some degree of maintenance of law and order.
>
> Thirdly, in applying the general principles to specific cases, the following must be considered: (i) whether the statehood of the entity is opposed under title of international law; if so, the requirement of effectiveness is likely to be more stringently applied; (ii) whether the government claiming authority in the putative State, if it does not effectively control it, has obtained authority by consent of the previous sovereign and exercises a certain degree of control; (iii) in the latter case at least, the requirement of statehood may be liberally construed; (iv) finally, there is a distinction between the creation of a new State on the one hand and the subsistence or extinction of an established State on the other. There is normally no presumption in favour of the status of the former, and the criterion of effective government therefore tends to be applied more strictly.

4.2.3 Independence

Most writers seem to be agreed that the capacity to enter international relations listed in Article 1 of the Montevideo Convention could be better expressed as 'independence' or 'sovereignty', in the sense of having full control over domestic and foreign affairs. The concept of 'capacity to enter into international relations' brings with it a degree of circularity: who has capacity to enter into legal relations? States; what are States? Those entities with capacity to enter into international relations. What is meant by the capacity to enter into relations with other States is independence in law from the authority of any other State. The point was summarised by Lauterpacht in *Recognition in International Law* (1978, New York: AMS, p 26 ff):

> The first condition of statehood is that there must exist a government actually independent of any other State ... If a community, after having detached itself form the parent State, were to become, legally or actually, a satellite of another State, it would not be fulfiling the primary condition of independence and would not accordingly be entitled to recognition as a State.

The classic example of this principle in operation is the case of Manchukuo. In 1931, Japan invaded the Chinese province of Manchuria. The following year it recognised the territory as constituting the independent State of Manchukuo. In fact, the government of Manchukuo was dominated by Japanese advisors and, in all important decisions, it appeared to follow the policy of Japan. The majority of States refused to recognise the independence of Manchukuo and continued to support Chinese claims to the territory. Some writers have considered the case of Manchukuo to be an example of the requirement of independence, although others have argued that Manchukuo did not become a legitimate State because it was established in circumstances contrary to principles of international law.

The principle of independence or sovereignty underlies international law. It is expressed to be a principle of the UN in Article 2 of the UN Charter and was confirmed in the Declaration on Principles of International Law Concerning Friendly Relations and Co-operation Between States 1970 adopted by the UN General, which provides:

> No State or group of States has the right to intervene, directly or indirectly, for any reason whatever, in the internal or external affairs of any other State.

4.2.4 Permitted derogations

There are a number of situations which are not regarded, in international practice, as derogating from formal independence, although, if extended far enough, they may derogate from actual independence:

4.2.4.1 Constitutional restrictions upon freedom of action

Provided no outside State has the power to alter the constitution, the fact that the State in question is constitutionally restricted is not seen as a derogation from formal independence. For example, the Constitution of the Republic of

Cyprus binds the Republic to permanently accept the stationing of foreign (Greek, Turkish and British) military forces on its territory.

4.2.4.2 Treaty obligations

One of the incidents of statehood is the ability to enter into treaty relations with other States and, thus, the conclusion of a treaty is usually a confirmation rather than a possible denial of statehood. However, questions may arise when a treaty purports to restrict a State's economic or political independence. In the *Austro-German Customs Union* case (1931), the PCIJ had cause to discuss the effect of treaty obligations on the independence of States. The case arose following an agreement between Austria and Germany to establish a customs union. Under the provisions of the peace treaties ending the First World War, Austria was obliged to abstain from any act which might directly or indirectly compromise its independence, unless it obtained the consent of the League of Nations. In the absence of such consent, the League of Nations asked for an advisory opinion as to whether the Austro-German Customs Union contravened the provisions of the peace treaties. On the facts, the PCIJ found that it did, but the case is of interest here for the general discussion of the issue of independence. Of particular interest is the dissenting judgment of Judge Anzilotti, who stated:

> It ... follows that the restrictions upon a State's liberty, whether arising out of ordinary international law or contractual agreements (treaties), do not as such in the least affect its independence. As long as these restrictions do not place the State under the legal authority of another State, the former remains an independent State however extensive and burdensome those obligations may be.

The PCIJ itself recognised that Austria remained a sovereign State in spite of the considerable restrictions that were placed on its authority by the provisions of the peace treaty.

4.2.4.3 The existence of foreign military bases

Clearly, the presence on its territory of the military forces of a hostile foreign State may well compromise the independence of a State. But the presence of foreign military bases pursuant to agreement will be no bar to statehood and there are a number of examples of this, such as the stationing of US troops in NATO countries and the British sovereign bases in Cyprus. The establishment of a 'security zone' by the Israel defence force in Lebanon during the second half of the 1980s and the stationing of Soviet troops in Czechoslovakia in 1968 and Afghanistan in 1980, and the use of US troops in Grenada and Panama raise more difficult questions, which will be dealt with in Chapter 12. In the context of the requirements of statehood, it should be noted that the international community continued to regard Lebanon, Czechoslovakia, Afghanistan, Grenada and Panama as sovereign States, despite the presence of foreign troops.

4.2.4.4 Membership of international organisations

Membership of international organisations is not seen as a bar to statehood, even if the organisation concerned has some degree of coercive authority. For example, membership of the UN is seen as a manifestation of statehood rather than a denial of it. The Treaty of Rome and associated treaties constituting the European Union clearly place restrictions on the freedom of Member States to act as they wish but it is accepted that, under international law, the Member States continue to be considered independent subjects of international law.

4.2.5 Permanence

There is no requirement that a State should endure for a specific minimum period – there are examples of States existing for a very short period but they have achieved full statehood. For example, the Mali Federation existed as a State from 20 June 1960 to 20 August 1960 and British Somaliland became an independent State on 26 June 1960 but united with Somalia to form the Somali Republic on 30 June 1960.

4.2.6 Legality

In recent years, the view has increasingly been put forward that, in addition to the criteria already mentioned, international law does not permit the creation of States in violation of fundamental principles of international law.

4.2.7 Self-determination

While discussion of the political principle of self-determination has a long history, the process of establishing it as a principle of international law is of more recent origin. It was discussed in the early days of the League of Nations, and the Mandate system was, to some degree, a compromise between outright colonialism and the principles of self-determination. In the period 1920–22, many of the treaties concluded by the Soviet Union enshrined self-determination as a legal right. However, the biggest impetus to recognition of self-determination as a legal principle came following the Second World War. The UN Charter (Article 1(2)) declared that one of its purposes was:

> To develop friendly relations among nations based on respect for the principle of equal rights and self-determination of peoples.

While it clearly enunciated the principle of self-determination, it left unclear the precise legal ramifications and this fact was seized upon by many Western jurists to deny that self-determination was in any way a legally enforceable right. In 1952, the General Assembly stated, in Resolution 637A (VII), that 'the right of peoples and nations to self-determination is a prerequisite to the full enjoyment of all fundamental human rights' and recommended that UN members 'shall uphold the principle of self-determination of all peoples and nations' while promoting 'realisation of the right of self-determination' for the peoples of colonial territories. Again, the resolution left unclear the precise legal implications of the principle.

In 1960, GA Resolution 1514 (XV), entitled the Declaration on the Granting of Independence to Colonial Countries and Peoples, was adopted 89 to 0, with 9 abstentions (Australia, Belgium, Dominican Republic, France, Portugal, South Africa, Spain, UK, US). Under the resolution, the General Assembly declared that:

> 2 All peoples have the right to self-determination; by virtue of that right they freely determine their political status and freely pursue their economic, social and cultural development.
>
> 3 Inadequacy of political, economic, social or educational preparedness should never serve as a pretext for delaying independence ...
>
> 6 Any attempt at the partial or total disruption of the national unity and the territorial integrity of a country is incompatible with the purposes and principles of the Charter of the United Nations.

In 1966, two conventions on human rights were signed – the International Covenant on Civil and Political Rights and the International Covenant on Economic, Social and Cultural Rights: both entered into force in 1976 and have been ratified by a large majority of States. The Covenants have a common Article 1, which States:

> 1 All peoples have the right of self-determination. By virtue of that right they freely determine their political status and freely pursue their economic, social and cultural development.

Subsequently, the Declaration of Principles of International Law Concerning Friendly Relations (GA Resolution 2625 (XXV) (1970)) confirmed the principle that self-determination is a right belonging to all peoples and that its implementation is required by the UN Charter in the case of alien subjugation or foreign domination. The Declaration went further in recognising that peoples resisting forcible suppression of their claim to self-determination are entitled to seek and receive support in accordance with the purposes and principles of the Charter.

Since the adoption of the Declaration in 1970, the ICJ has, on a number of occasions, confirmed that the principle of self-determination constitutes a binding norm of customary international law and, possibly, a rule of *jus cogens*. The extent of the right and the question of who may exercise the right will be considered in more detail in Chapter 14. Here, the concern is with the effect which the principle has upon claims to statehood and it must be admitted that the position remains unclear. In the case of the former Portuguese colony of Guinea-Bissau, the international community took the view that because of the *de facto* control of much of the territory by PAIGC, the national liberation movement, and in accordance with the principles of self-determination, Guinea-Bissau would be recognised as an independent State, despite the fact that the colonial power was still attempting to exercise effective control over the territory. That situation can be contrasted with the case of Namibia. There, in spite of the widely recognised claims of the people of Namibia to self-determination, and the fact that the liberation movement, SWAPO, had a high degree of allegiance from the population and exercised a fair degree of control in Namibia, there was no attempt to treat Namibia as an independent State. Instead, action was taken through the UN to bring about its independence and, in the interim period before independence, to provide for the protection of the rights of the Namibian people. Arrangements were worked out in conjunction with the South African authorities, who had maintained a claim to sovereignty over the territory, for the holding of elections and Namibia finally became independent in March 1990.

The most recent example of the question concerns Palestine. On 15 November 1988, the independent State of Palestine was proclaimed by the Palestine National Council meeting in Algiers. Although the right of the Palestinian people to self-determination has received widespread recognition, and although the PLO could demonstrate widespread allegiance throughout the West Bank and Gaza, together with some degree of control through the period of the *Intifadah*, there was little acceptance from the international community of Palestine's status as a State. The present view therefore seems to be that, although self-determination is certainly one of the criteria for statehood, it will not operate to the exclusion of other criteria.

One aspect of the application of the principle of self-determination does appear to be more settled. It now seems to be an accepted rule of international law that an entity created in defiance of the principle of self-determination cannot be considered a State. Arguably, this is one of the main reasons for considering that Manchukuo did not become a State. It also prevented the South African homelands such as Transkei and Bophutatswana becoming States.

4.2.8 States created by illegal use of force

It has already been stated that peoples resisting forcible suppression of their claim to self-determination are entitled to seek and receive support in accordance with the purposes and principles of the Charter. Use of force in such situations is not considered unlawful. However, if the peoples concerned do not have a valid claim to self-determination, intervention by third States will constitute an unlawful use of force and any subsequent 'State' established will have no validity in international law. An illustration of this point is provided by the Turkish Republic of Northern Cyprus. The Republic of Cyprus became an independent State in 1960. The population consisted of Greek and Turkish Cypriots and the president of the State was Archbishop Makarios. Initially, there was co-operation between the two communities in the running of government affairs but, in 1964, that co-operation came to an end and the Greek Cypriot wing of the Republic assumed the powers and functions of the government of Cyprus. The next 10 years saw considerable tension between the two communities and some sporadic fighting. However, on 15 July 1974, there was a military coup, inspired by the military regime operating in Greece at the time. On 20 July, Turkish troops landed in Cyprus and took control of an area of territory. The UN Security Council called for the withdrawal of all foreign troops from Cyprus. Although democracy was restored to Greece at the end of July, the Turkish troops did not leave and, instead, the area of Turkish control was extended. In 1975, a Turkish Federated State of Cyprus was proclaimed and its constitution was approved by a 99 per cent majority in a referendum. Talks between Greek and Turkish Cypriots aimed at reaching a federal solution of the Cyprus problem but met with little success. On 15 November 1983, the Turkish Republic of Northern Cyprus was proclaimed as an independent State and was immediately recognised as such by Turkey. However, the UN Security Council declared the declaration to be invalid and called for its withdrawal. (Security Council Resolution 541/1983) It further called on all States to recognise no Cypriot State other than the Republic of Cyprus. Since that time, there have been continued attempts to reach a solution based on a State of Cyprus with a single international personality and the Turkish Republic of Northern Cyprus has not been regarded as a State for the purposes of international law. Although there are some doubts as to its independence from Turkey, it seems clear that the main reason for denying statehood to the Turkish Republic of Northern Cyprus is the fact that it was established as a result of the unlawful use of force by Turkey in 1974. The question of what constitutes unlawful and lawful force will be considered in more detail in Chapter 12.

4.2.9 Extinction of statehood

Much of the previous discussion has been concerned with the creation of States and it is necessary make a short reference to the issue of extinction of States. The general rule seems to be that it is impossible to lose statehood involuntarily where such an event would lead to a complete absence of statehood within a particular territory. Even though existing States may, from time to time, lose many of the required attributes of statehood this will not mean that they cease to be States. Mention has already been made of Lebanon which, during much of the 1980s, had no real effective government yet continued to be a State. Invasion by hostile foreign forces, as in the cases of Kuwait in 1990 and Cambodia in 1979, did not prevent those two States from continuing to enjoy international personality. One of the starkest examples is provided by the case of the Baltic States of Lithuania, Latvia and Estonia, which became members of the UN following the collapse of the Soviet Union but which were widely regarded as continuations of States established before the Second World War. Of course, where States break up into constituent parts, new States may come into existence within a particular territory previously under the sovereignty of a single State. In such situations, it may be incorrect to speak in terms of the original State 'voluntarily' giving up its international personality but that will be the effect, provided the new States meet the requirements of statehood.

The most recent example of the problem of the extinction of States relates to former Yugoslavia. On 19 September 1992, the UN Security Council passed a resolution which, 'considering that the State formerly known as the Socialist Federal Republic of Yugoslavia [SFRY] has ceased to exist,' refused to recognise the Federal Republic of Yugoslavia (Serbia and Montenegro) as a continuation of the Socialist Republic and called upon the new State to apply for membership of the UN. On 22 September 1992, in the light of the Security Council resolution, the General Assembly resolved that the Federal Republic of Yugoslavia should apply for membership of the UN on the basis that the SFRY had ceased to exist. The new Federal Republic of Yugoslavia strongly protested against the resolution but, nonetheless, applied for membership of the UN as a new State on 23 September 1993.

It remains possible, of course, for States to agree to their own extinction. For example, the Republic of Czechoslovakia came to an end on 31 December 1992, with its division into the two States of the Czech Republic and Slovakia, and the GDR ceased to exist following the unification of East and West Germany on 3 October 1990.

4.3 Non-self-governing territories

There still exists, although the number is dwindling, a number of territories which have limited or restricted powers of control over their own affairs and can therefore not be considered as fully independent States. The question arises as to whether they possess any degree of international personality prior to full independence.

4.3.1 Colonies

Traditionally, international law has not regarded colonies as possessing any international personality, because the control of the colonies' foreign relations rested entirely in the hands of the colonial power. It has already been seen in Chapter 3 that there is a presumption that treaties will apply to a colonial power and its colonial possessions. However, with the development of the principle of self-determination, international law has come to recognise that, for certain purposes, 'pre-independent States' and national liberation movements may have some degree of international personality. For example, in 1974, the Palestine Liberation Organisation was accorded observer status at the United Nations, a position previously reserved solely for the representatives of sovereign States that were not at the time members of the UN. The head of the PLO was subsequently invited to address the UN General Assembly and PLO representatives have attended various UN conferences and meetings. Similarly, the UN General Assembly recognised the South West African People's Organisation (SWAPO) as the sole representative of the people of Namibia. However, the exact nature of the personality of liberation movements is far from clear and, in the case of *Tel-Oren v Libyan Arab Republic* (1984), a US Court of Appeal declined to accept a case against the PLO, in part, on the ground that the PLO's obligations under international law were unclear.

4.3.2 Protectorates

There are three situations where protection may be given by a foreign State:

(a) protection may be exercised over a territory which did not have international personality before the protectorate was created. This occurred in the late 19th century in respect of a number of territories in Africa and Asia for whom European States provided protection. In such situations, the entities in question only gained full international personality when it became clear that they were acting independently of the protecting State. For example, Kuwait became a British protectorate in 1899 and was gradually given increased control over its own affairs. Its independence was only formally acknowledged by the UK in 1961, although it seems clear that Kuwait had achieved statehood and international personality some time before then;

(b) protection may be exercised over an already existing State. The arrangement will usually be covered by agreement between the protecting and the protected State, and such protection does not usually affect the legal personality of the protected State. For example, Morocco was an independent State until the start of the 12th century, when it was divided into three parts: Tangiers became an international city, and the rest of Morocco was divided into a Spanish and a French zone. Foreign relations were completely within Spanish and French control, and France and Spain could conclude treaties on behalf of Morocco. Nevertheless, in the *Rights of US Nationals in Morocco* case (1952), the ICJ held that, during the period of the protectorate, Morocco had retained its international personality; and

(c) in a few specific cases, one State may exercise a protective power over a much smaller State without that smaller State losing its international personality, although the extent of that personality may be limited, for example, San Marino, Monaco and Liechtenstein.

4.3.3 Mandates and trust territories

The mandate system was introduced by the League of Nations to provide for the administration of those colonies and dependencies of the losing States in the First World War 'inhabited by peoples not yet able to stand by themselves under the strenuous conditions of the modern world' (Article 22 of the Covenant of the League of Nations 1919). The territories concerned were divided into three classes:

(a) class A territories were those parts of the Turkish Empire which were thought to be closest to independence and were put under the control of Britain or France. Only Iraq achieved independence under the Mandate system; Palestine (to the extent that Israel is an independent State), Transjordan (now the Hashemite Kingdom of Jordan), Syria and Lebanon only achieved independence as a result of the Second World War;

(b) class B territories comprised peoples (according to Article 22, para 5 of the League of Nations Covenant 1919):

> ... especially those of Central Africa, [who] are at such a stage that the mandatory must be responsible for the administration of the territory under conditions which will guarantee freedom of conscience and religion, subject only to the maintenance of public order and morals, the prohibition of abuses such as the slave trade, the arms traffic and the liquor traffic, and the prevention of the establishment of fortifications or military or naval bases and of military training of the natives for other than police purposes and the defence of the territory, and will also secure equal opportunities for the trade and commerce of other members of the League.

Included in the Class B territories were Tanganyika, British and French Togoland, the British and French Cameroons, and Rwanda. The territories concerned only gained independence after transfer to the UN trusteeship system; and

(c) class C territories included certain territories (Article 22, para 6 of the League of Nations Covenant):

> ... which, owing to the sparseness of their population, or their small size, or their remoteness from the centres of civilisation, or their geographical contiguity to the territory of the mandatory, and other circumstances, can be best administered under the laws of the mandatory as integral portions of its territory, subject to ... safeguards in the interests of the indigenous population.

Included in the Class C mandates were Namibia, Samoa, and New Guinea.

When the League of Nations was disbanded to be succeeded by the United Nations, a replacement was needed for the mandate system and an entirely new 'trusteeship system' was established under Chapter XI of the UN Charter. Those territories held under mandate were placed under the trusteeship system, which would involve the conclusion of a trusteeship agreement between the administering authority and the United Nations. According to Article 76 of the UN Charter, the main object of the system was:

> ... to promote the political, economic, social and educational advancement of the inhabitants of the trust territories, and their progressive development towards self-government or independence as may be appropriate to the particular circumstances of each territory and its peoples and the freely expressed wishes of the people concerned.

The traditional view of mandates and trusteeships was that, as long as they subsisted over a particular territory, that territory could not be regarded as having international personality. However, parallelling the situation with regard to colonies, increasingly, the view has been expressed that trust territories do possess some degree of separate status and international personality, similar to that accorded to organisations such as the PLO. In the *Namibia* case (1971), Judge Ammoun said:

> Namibia, even at the periods when it had been reduced to the status of a German colony or was subject to the South African mandate, possessed a legal personality which was denied it only by the law now obsolete ... It nevertheless constituted a subject of law ... possessing national sovereignty but lacking the exercise thereof.

All of the trust territories have now become independent States, or parts of such States. The last trust territory to obtain independence was the group of Western Pacific islands north of the equator which were administered by the USA as the UN Trust Territory of the Pacific Islands. In 1986, the US recognised the independence of the Federated State of Micronesia and the new state became a member of the UN in 1991. Palau, which had been administered as part of the Trust Territory of the Pacific Islands, did not wish to join the Federated States of Micronesia and, instead, became a fully independent state in 1994.

4.4 International Organisations

As was pointed out in Chapter 1, it is no longer possible to take the view that 'States solely and exclusively are the subjects of international law'. Developments during the twentieth century, notably the formation of the League of Nations in 1919 and the United Nations in 1945, have meant that international legal personality extends beyond individual sovereign States.

It is clear that international organisations are capable of possessing international personality and of being subjects of international law. The point was recognised by the ICJ in the *Reparations* case (1949). The functions, rights and duties of such organisations are governed by what Starke refers to as international constitutional law. Institutions will be defined by reference to their legal functions and responsibilities and the constitutions of such institutions will set out their powers, objects and purpose – analogies can perhaps be drawn with municipal company law and a company's memorandum and articles of association.

In deciding the existence and extent of an organisation's international personality, it will be useful to start with the instrument establishing the organisation. The instrument might itself bestow legal personality on the organisation. For example, Article 210 of the Treaty of Rome 1957 provides that 'the Community shall have legal personality'. Such express statements are useful since '[they] oblige the Members to accept the organisation as a separate international person, competent to perform acts which under traditional international law could only be performed by States ... [Such provisions] also clarify the status of the organisation for non-members. If a non-member were to doubt the organisation's competence to perform international acts, a clear constitutional provision may be of some assistance' (Schermers, HG, *International Institutional Law* (3rd edn, 1995, The Hague: Nijhoff).

In fact, as Bowett points out, '... specific acknowledgement of the possession of international personality is extremely rare' (Bowett, DW, *The Law of International Institutions*, 4th edn, 1982, London: Stevens, p 339). More often, international personality will be inferred from the powers or purpose of the organisation and from its practice. Professor Rama-Montaldo has taken the view that the ascription of international personality is automatic once an entity has fulfilled certain conditions. Professor Brownlie has identified those conditions as:

(a) a permanent association of States, with lawful objects equipped with organs to carry out those objects;

(b) a distinction between the organisation and its Member States; and

(c) the existence of legal powers exercisable on the international plane and not solely within the national system of one or more States.

4.4.1 The extent of personality

> ... it is permissible to assume that most organisations created by a multilateral inter-governmental agreement will, so far as they are endowed with functions on the international plane, possess some measure of

> international personality in addition to the personality within the system of municipal law of the members ... Possession of international personality will normally involve, as a consequence, the attribution of power to make treaties, of privileges and immunities, of power to undertake legal proceedings: it will also pose a general problem of dissolution, for in the nature of things, the personality of all such organisations can be brought to an end. [Bowett, DW, *The Law of International Institutions*, 4th edn, 1982, London: Stevens, p 339.]

There is some academic debate as to the legal consequences of legal personality for international organisations. Two principal schools of thought can be identified. The formal approach, associated with Professor Rama-Montaldo, argues that 'no specific rights or duties emerge from the fact that an organisation is endowed with international personality, but that it is necessary to have recourse to the provisions of the instrument setting up the organisation' (Rama-Montaldo, 'International legal personality and implied powers of international organisations' (1970) 44 BYIL 111). Such an approach dictates that no overall view can be taken of the rights and duties of international organisations: each individual organisation must be considered separately. Contrasting with the formal approach is the material approach, which takes the view that certain rights and duties automatically flow from the existence of personality. Professor Seyersted, advocating a material approach, argues that organisations have the same legal capacity as States, except in so far as such capacity is limited by provisions within the organisation's constitution, by the general purposes of the organisation and by practicalities: for example, an international organisation does not have a territory to defend or over which to assert jurisdiction.

The ICJ was called upon to consider the extent of the rights and duties of the UN in the *Certain Expenses of the United nations* case (1962):

> In the opinion of the court, the Organisation was intended to exercise and enjoy, and is in fact exercising and enjoying, functions and rights which can only be explained on the basis of a large measure of international personality and the capacity to operate upon an international plane ... It must be acknowledged that its Members, by entrusting certain functions to it, with the attendant duties and responsibilities, have clothed it with the competence required to enable those functions to be effectively discharged.

The court then went on to emphasise that this was to say that the UN was the same thing as a State. Professor White (*The Law of International Organisations*, 1996, Manchester: Manchester UP) has argued that this view is too traditionalist and that, while it may have been accurate in 1962, at the time of the Cold War and the superpower veto in the UN, international organisations have developed further since that time. In any event, Professor White argues, the opinion of the ICJ is not wholly without ambiguity and can be taken to support the concept of inherent, as opposed to implied, powers identified by

Professor Seyersted.

In the *Legality of the Use by a State of Nuclear Weapons* case (1996), the ICJ took the view that international organisations 'are invested by the States which create them with powers, the limits of which are a function of the common interests whose promotion those States entrust to them'. Again, this would seem to support a permissive view – international organisations have all the rights and duties of a State except in so far as those powers are limited by the States which create them and by practicalities. A restrictive view would limit the powers of an international organisation to those which are expressed in the constituent instrument or which can be implied as being essential to the performance of the organisation's constitutionally laid down duties. In the *Legality of the Use by a State of Nuclear Weapons* case, the ICJ had to consider whether the World Health Organisation (WHO) had the power to request an advisory opinion on the legality of the use of nuclear weapons. The ICJ considered Article 2 of the WHO constitution, which gave the WHO competence to deal with the effects on health of nuclear weapons. The Court took the view that such competence could not be extended to cover questions on the legality of the use of nuclear weapons. Such questions did not fall within the remit of the Organisation. It can be argued that the advisory opinion of the ICJ remains consistent with the more permissive view of the powers of international organisations.

4.4.2 The relationship between States and international organisations

One important aspect of the international legal personality of international organisations is the relationship it has with Member States and with third party States. As far as Member States are concerned, the existence of a separate legal personality for the organisation means that it can operate directly on the international plane rather than indirectly through the Member States.

As far as third party States are concerned, the question arises as to whether such third party States must recognise the international personality of international organisations. The general rule, as has been seen in Chapter 3, is that treaties are not binding on third parties. The question is one of private international law and the practice adopted by most States is that a domestic court determines legal status by reference to the applicable law. In the case of international organisations, the applicable law should be international law.

4.5 The United Nations

The best known international organisation possessing international personality is the United Nations and it may be useful here to give a brief summary of the powers and principal organs of the UN.

4.5.1 Purposes and principles

The purposes of the UN are stated in Article 1 of the UN Charter:

1 To maintain international peace and security, and to that end: to take effective collective measures for the prevention and removal of threats to the peace, and for the suppression of acts of aggression or other breaches of the peace, and to bring about by peaceful means, and in conformity with the principles of justice and international law, adjustment or settlement of international disputes or situations which might lead to a breach of the peace;

2 to develop friendly relations among nations based on respect for the principles of equal rights and self-determination of peoples, and to take other appropriate measures to strengthen universal peace;

3 to achieve international co-operation in solving problems of an economic, social, cultural or humanitarian character, and in promoting and encouraging respect for human rights and for fundamental freedoms for all without distinction as to race, sex, language, or religion; and

4 to be a centre for harmonising the actions of nations in the attainment of these common ends.

Article 2 lays down the operating principles for the organisation and members. The UN Charter is a multilateral treaty establishing the rights and duties of the signatory States – it is not subject to reservation or denunciation. Article 2(6) provides that members should ensure that States which are not members should act in accordance with the principles although, strictly speaking, as a treaty, the Charter cannot bind non-signatories. Article 2(7) states that nothing in the Charter shall authorise the UN to intervene in matters which are essentially within the domestic jurisdiction of any State. A matter will not be regarded as within the domestic jurisdiction if it amounts to a violation of international law, a violation of the rights of other States or a gross violation of human rights. Since the 1960s, the General Assembly has refused to regard any colonial situations as matters of domestic jurisdiction. Article 2(7) is a matter for political judgment rather than any legal interpretation.

4.5.2 Membership

Membership of the UN is dealt with in Chapter II of the Charter. The original members are those States which participated in the United Nations Conference on International Organisation held in San Francisco, or who previously signed the Declaration by the United Nations in 1942, and who subsequently signed and ratified the Charter. There were 51 original members. Since then, well over 100 other States have joined in accordance with Article 4 and, with the admission of Palau in December 1994, there are now 185 Member States. Membership of the UN is open to all peace loving States which accept the obligations contained in the Charter. Admission follows a decision of the General Assembly upon the recommendation of the Security Council. During the early days of the Cold War, membership was refused on 12 occasions for political reasons. In the *Admissions* case (1948), the ICJ was asked by the General Assembly for an advisory opinion on the question of admission. It declared that Article 4 was exhaustive on the matter and that, if a State fulfiled those requirements, then the Security Council was under a duty to make a recommendation of membership to the General Assembly. Since that time, membership has not been refused on overtly political grounds.

The General Assembly has certain powers to suspend membership of States and, in cases of persistent violation of the UN Charter, a State can be expelled. As a result of its pursuance of a policy of apartheid, South Africa's membership of the UN was suspended in 1974. The only incident of expulsion relates to the Federal Republic of Yugoslavia, whose exact membership status remains unclear. By a resolution passed on 22 September 1992, the General Assembly declared that the representatives of the Federal Republic of Yugoslavia would no longer be allowed to participate in the work of the General Assembly. Some commentators argued that this amounted to expulsion from the UN but, in a letter from the Legal Counsel of the UN to the representatives of Bosnia and Croatia, written on 29 September 1992, it was stated that Yugoslavia's membership in the UN was not at an end and its seat and nameplate remained in the General Assembly.

4.5.3 The organs of the UN

There are six principle organs: the General Assembly; the Security Council; the Economic and Social Council (ECOSOC); the Trusteeship Council; the Secretariat; and the International Court of Justice.

4.5.3.1 The General Assembly

The General Assembly is the plenary organ of the UN. Each member has one vote, although each member can send up to five representatives. The primary function of the General Assembly is to discuss matters within the scope of the Charter and to make recommendations to the members or to the Security Council. It meets in annual session, although emergency sessions can be called by a vote of any nine Security Council members or by a majority of the total membership. Voting can be by simple majority, although important measures, such as questions involving issues of peace and security, require a two-thirds majority of those present and voting (see Article 18 of the UN Charter). Actual voting can be by acclamation, show of hands or secret ballot. The effect of UN

General Assembly resolutions has already been discussed in Chapter 2. Although the General Assembly normally only meets in annual session, its work continues throughout the year in committees and subsidiary organs.

4.5.3.2 The Security Council

The Security Council consists of 15 members of the UN (until 1965, there were only 11 members). Five members are permanent: they are China, US, UK, Russia, and France. The other 10 members are elected by the General Assembly and serve for a period of two years. Each member has one representative. The primary function of the Security Council is to maintain peace and security. This is done either through encouragement of the peaceful settlement of disputes or through taking enforcement action.

The changes in the global political balance that have occurred since the break up of the Soviet Union have led to considerable debate about the role and membership of the Security Council. In particular, there have been calls for the number of permanent members to be increased. Germany has argued strongly that it should have a permanent seat on the Security Council. There have also been suggestions that there should be permanent Japanese representation, and resolutions from the Arab League have called for a permanent Arab seat.

4.5.3.3 The Economic and Social Council (ECOSOC)

ECOSOC comprises 54 members. Eighteen are elected every year by the General Assembly and they serve for a period of three years. Representatives from the five Permanent Security Council members are always elected. ECOSOC operates on a one member one vote system and decisions are by simple majority.

It operates under the authority of the General Assembly and has power to make recommendations. Article 62 deals with its functions:

> ECOSOC may make or initiate studies and reports with respect to international economic, social, cultural, educational, health, and related matters and may make recommendations with respect to any such matters to the General Assembly, to the members of the UN, and to the specialised agencies concerned.

It may also make recommendations for the purpose of promoting respect for, and observance of, human rights and fundamental freedoms.

4.5.3.4 The Trusteeship Council

This is concerned with the trust territories. With the independence of Palau in October 1994, the Trusteeship Council suspended its operations on 1

November 1994. It remains available for future use should new trust territories be created.

4.5.3.5 The Secretariat

The Secretariat consists of the Secretary General and his staff. The Secretary General is appointed by the General Assembly on the recommendation of the Security Council for a renewable period of five years.

4.5.3.6 The International Court of Justice

The ICJ is established by Art 92 of the UN Charter as the principal judicial organ of the UN. Its role will be discussed in detail in Chapter 11.

4.6 Individuals

Since the Second World War, it has gradually become more clear that individuals do enjoy a limited degree of personality in international law. Obligations are placed on individuals in connection with war crimes, crimes against humanity and piracy. Thus, following the Second World War, individual German nationals were tried by an international tribunal at Nuremberg for war crimes and international tribunals are trying individuals responsible for atrocities committed within the territory of former Yugoslavia and Rwanda. There is further discussion of this topic in Chapter 13. Individuals are also capable of bearing rights under international law and the last 45 years have seen a massive growth in international human rights law, which is discussed in detail in Chapter 14.

As Shaw points out, 'The essence of international law has always been its ultimate concern for the human being and this was clearly manifest in the natural law origins of classical international law' (Shaw, *International Law*, 4th edn, 1997, Cambridge: CUP). It was the growth of legal positivism that led to the centrality and exclusivity of the sovereign State in international law. Certainly, since 1945, 'individuals have become increasingly recognised as participants and subjects of international law' (Shaw, *International Law*).

4.7 Recognition

It will have been seen, during the course of the discussion of the subjects of international law, that international personality is a flexible concept and exists in varying degrees. Although a number of criteria can be put forward for deciding whether or not an entity is a subject of international law, in practice, much depends upon the reaction of existing States. A reaction favourable to the entity becoming an international person is known as recognition.

It has already seen that an important requirement of statehood is the capacity to enter into international legal relationships. This inevitably concerns the attitude of other States and, in particular, raises the question of recognition. Do other States recognise the new entity as a State? What are the implications if they do so recognise? What are the implications if they do not?

4.7.1 The theoretical issue

As is so often the case with international law, discussion of recognition has led to the development of two competing theories. The principal question which the two theories attempt to answer is whether recognition is a necessary requirement for, or merely a consequence of, international personality.

4.7.1.1 The constitutive theory

Underlying the constitutive theory is the view that every legal system requires some organ to determine with finality and certainty the subjects of the system. In the present international legal system, that organ can only be the States, acting severally or collectively, and their determination must have definitive legal effect.

The constitutive theory developed in the 19th century and was closely allied to a positivist view of international law. According to that view, the obligation to obey international law derives from the consent of individual States. The creation of a new State would create new legal obligations and existing States would need to consent to those new obligations. Therefore, the acceptance of the new State by existing States was essential. A further argument prevalent during the late 19th century was based on the view of international law as existing between 'civilised nations'. New States could not automatically become members of the international community; it was recognition which created their membership. This had the further consequence that entities not recognised as States were not bound by international law and nor were the 'civilised nations' so bound in their dealings with them. Oppenheim stated the position, in his *International Law,* (Vol I, 8th edn, 1955, Harlow: Longman, p 544), thus:

> The formation of a new State is ... a matter of fact and not law. It is through recognition, which is a matter of law, that such a new State become subject to international law.

Recognition is, therefore, seen as a requirement of international personality. A major criticism of this theory is that it leads to confusion where a new State is recognised by some States but not others. Lauterpacht attempted to get round this problem by alleging an international legal duty to recognise (Lauterpacht, *Recognition in International Law,* (1978, New York: AMS, p 6):

> To recognise a community as a State is to declare that it fulfils the conditions of statehood as required by international law. If those conditions are present, existing States are under a duty to grant recognition ... in granting or withholding recognition States do not claim and are not entitled to serve exclusively the interests of their national policy and convenience regardless of the principles of international law in the matter. Although recognition is thus declaratory of an existing fact, such declaration, made in the impartial fulfilment of a legal duty, is constitutive, as between the recognising State and the community so recognised, of international rights and duties associated with full statehood. Prior to recognition, such rights and obligations exist only to the extent to which they have been expressly conceded or legitimately asserted, by reference to compelling rules of humanity and justice, either by the existing members of the international society or by the people claiming recognition.

However, although States do make reference to the presence or absence of the factual characteristics of statehood when granting or refusing recognition, in the last resort, their decision will normally be based on political expediency; there is no real evidence that States themselves feel that there is a legal duty to recognise when the other requirements of statehood have been satisfied. The question arose with respect to the territory of former Yugoslavia. In June 1991, Slovenia and Croatia declared their independence. The European Union and its Member States did not recognise the two States immediately. In December 1991, Foreign Ministers of EU Member States adopted 'Guidelines on the recognition of new States in Eastern Europe and in the Soviet Union'. This provided that recognition would be accorded to those new States which agreed to respect five conditions. The five conditions included matters such as respect for human rights, guarantees for minorities, respect for the inviolability of frontiers, acceptance of commitments to regional security and stability and to settle by agreement all questions concerning State succession. Slovenia, Croatia and Bosnia-Herzegovina agreed to the conditions and were formally accorded recognition in early 1992. It is clear that the conditions set down by the European Union exceeded the normal requirements of statehood. The implication would, therefore, seem to be that the EU viewed recognition as a political measure, which was not required by any international obligation. It remains to be seen whether European practice will continue to use these conditions in all decisions on the recognition of new States or whether the application of the conditions will be restricted to the particular situation in the Balkans and Eastern Europe.

4.7.1.2 The declaratory theory

An early example of the declaratory theory is to be found in two provisions of the Montevideo Convention.

(a) Article 3:

> The political existence of the State is independent of recognition by other States. Even before recognition the State has the right to defend its integrity and independence ... and to organise itself as it sees fit. The exercise of these rights has no other limitation than the exercise of the rights of other States according to international law.

(b) Article 6:

> The recognition of a State merely signifies that the State which recognises it accepts the personality of the other, with all the rights and duties determined by international law.

For the adherents to the declaratory theory, the formation of a new State is a matter of fact not law. Recognition is a political act by which the recognising State indicates a willingness to initiate international relations with the recognised State and the question of international personality is independent of recognition. However, the act of recognition is not totally without legal significance, because it does indicate that the recognising State considers that the new entity fulfils all the required conditions for becoming an international subject.

The declaratory theory is more widely supported by writers on international law today and it accords more readily with State practice, as is illustrated by the fact that non-recognised 'States' are quite commonly the object of international claims by the very States which are refusing recognition; for example, Arab States have continued to maintain that Israel is bound by international law although few of them, until recently, have recognised Israel.

4.7.2 Non-recognition

The legal regime established by the Covenant of the League of Nations 1919 and the Kellogg-Briand Pact 1928 was the basis for the development of the principle that 'acquisition of territory or special advantages by illegal threat or use of force' would not create a title capable of recognition by other States. The principle achieved particular significance as a result of the Japanese invasion of Manchuria in 1931. The US Secretary of State, Stimson, declared that the illegal invasion would not be recognised, as it was contrary to the Kellogg-Briand Pact, which outlawed the use of war as an instrument of national policy. Thereafter, the doctrine of not recognising any situation, treaty or agreement brought about by non-legal means was often referred to as the Stimson doctrine.

However, State practice before the Second World War did not seem to support the view that the Stimson doctrine contained a binding rule of international law. The Italian conquest of Abyssinia (Ethiopia) was recognised, as was the German take-over of Czechoslovakia. After 1945, the principle was re-examined and the draft Declaration on the Rights and Duties of States, prepared by the ILC, emphasised that territorial acquisitions achieved in a manner inconsistent with international law should not be recognised by other States. Similarly, the Declaration on Principles of International Law 1970 adopted by the UN General Assembly included a provision to the effect that no territorial acquisition resulting from the threat or use of force shall be recognised as legal. There have been a number of occasions where the Security Council of the United Nations has called on States not to accord recognition to situations which have arisen as a result of unlawful acts, for example, Security Council Resolution, 20th November 1965:

> The Security Council, deeply concerned about the situation in Southern Rhodesia, ...
>
> 6 Calls upon all States not to recognise this illegal authority and not to entertain any diplomatic or other relations with it.

Recognition in such situations would itself be a breach of international law.

4.7.3 Recognition of governments

Although the practice of States is far from establishing the existence of a legal duty to recognise an entity which has established the factual characteristics of statehood, with regard to governments, the position is even more difficult. The problem of recognition of governments will arise when a new regime has taken power:

(a) unconstitutionally;

(b) by violent means; or

(c) with foreign help;

in a State whose previous and legitimate government was recognised by other States. Recognition in such circumstances may appear an endorsement of the new regime, and the recognising State may not wish to offer such endorsement or approval. Alternatively, it may be impractical not to acknowledge a factual situation, in which case, the recognising State may wish to indicate that recognition is inevitable once a given set of facts arise. Two approaches can therefore be identified: an objective approach, whereby recognition will occur if a given set of facts have occurred, or a subjective test, whereby recognition will depend on whether or not the new regime is going to act properly in the eyes of the recognising State.

One possible resolution of the problem of when to recognise is to avoid recognition altogether. In 1930, the Mexican Foreign Minister, Senor Estrada, rejected the whole doctrine of recognition on the ground that:

> ... it allows foreign governments to pass upon the legitimacy or illegitimacy of the regime existing in another country, with the result that situations arise in which the legal qualifications or national status of governments or authorities are apparently made subject to the opinion of foreigners. (Whiteman, 2 Digest of International Law, p 85.)

Henceforward, the Mexican government refused to make declarations granting recognition of governments. This Estrada doctrine, as it came to be known, denies the need for explicit and formal acts of recognition; all that needs to be determined is whether the new regime has in fact established itself as the effective government of the country.

Although slow at first to catch on, the Estrada doctrine has come to be followed by an increasing number of States. In 1977, the US announced that it would no longer issue formal declarations of recognition; the only question in future would be whether diplomatic relations continued with the new regime or not. Following the US practice, the UK has also de-emphasised recognition and there is now no formal recognition of new regimes, although the Foreign Office will still have to decide whether or not a new regime has effective control when considering matters such as trade and diplomatic relations.

4.7.4 *De facto* and *de jure* recognition

A distinction has sometimes been made in cases where governments have been accorded recognition between *de facto* and *de jure* recognition. Recognition of an entity as the *de facto* government can be seen as an interim step, taken where there is some doubt as to the legitimacy of the new government or as to its long term prospects of survival. For example, the UK recognised the Soviet government *de facto* in 1921 and *de jure* in 1924. In some situations, particularly where there is a civil war, both a *de facto* and a *de jure* government may be recognised: for example, during the Spanish Civil War, when the Republican government continued to be recognised as the *de jure* government but, as the Nationalist forces under General Franco took increasingly effective control of Spain, *de facto* recognition was accorded to the Nationalist government; eventually, the Nationalist government obtained full *de jure* recognition.

4.7.5 The legal effects of recognition in municipal law: UK practice

Since recognition is basically a political act, it is a decision for the executive branch of government and, in the UK, it is the Foreign Office which will answer questions about the status of entities which purport to have international personality. Such answers are usually given by means of an executive certificate. As has already been noted, in 1980, the British government announced that it was no longer intending to accord formal recognition to governments, although it would continue to recognise States. Of course, the substantive question of whether or not an entity is a government and thus entitled to the consequent immunities and privileges still remains but the courts will no longer have the benefit of an executive certificate to assist them. In *Republic of Somalia v Woodhouse Drake and Carey SA* (1993), Hobhouse J had to decide whether the interim government of Somalia, which was in a State of civil war at the time, was entitled to bring proceedings as the legitimate government of that State. In the course of his judgment, Hobhouse J identified four questions which the courts would consider when deciding whether a regime existed as the government of a State:

(a) had the regime come to power by constitutional means?

(b) what was the degree, nature and stability of administrative control exercised by the regime over the territory of the State?

(c) did the British government maintain any form of relationship with the regime?

(d) what was the extent of international recognition of the regime?

The status of international organisations raises a particular problem. Parliament passed the International Organisations Act 1968, which allows domestic legal personality to be conferred on international organisations by means of an Order in Council. As has already been seen, international organisations are established by agreement between States. The House of Lords confirmed, in *Maclaine Watson v Department of Trade and Industry* (1990), that the courts have no power to adjudicate on or enforce rights arising out of transactions entered into by sovereign States between themselves and that treaties do not automatically become part of English law.

There are a number of consequences of recognition and non-recognition and these will be illustrated here by reference to a number of important decisions made by the English courts.

4.7.6 *Locus standi*

Perhaps one of the most important consequences of recognition is that it gives the recognised entity *locus standi* in the courts. In *City of Berne v The Bank of England* (1804), the court refused to allow the revolutionary government of Berne to bring an action against the Bank of England, because the government was not recognised by the UK. A number of cases have arisen where recognition has been accorded to both a *de facto* and a *de jure* government. Since the British government declared that it would no longer accord formal recognition to governments, the problem may not arise in the same way in the future but, nonetheless, the cases are of historic interest and do shed some light on the way the courts deal with the whole problem of the status of foreign governments. In *Haile Selassie v Cable and Wireless Ltd (No 2)* (1939), the Emperor of Abyssinia (Ethiopia) was suing a British company for money owed under contract. At the time the action was brought, the British government recognised Haile Selassie as the *de jure* sovereign but recognised the Italian authorities as the *de facto* government. At first instance, it was held that, since the case concerned a debt recoverable in England and not the validity of acts done in Ethiopia, it was the *de jure* sovereign that was entitled to sue. The defendants appealed. Before the appeal was heard, the UK government extended *de jure* recognition to the Italian authorities. A basic principle of recognition is that it operates retroactively to the date when the authority of the government was first accepted as being established. The Court of Appeal therefore found that the *de jure* recognition of the Italian government of Ethiopia was deemed to operate from the date of *de facto* recognition. Since that occurred prior to the commencement of the action for the debt, Haile Selassie was deprived of any *locus standi* in the case.

In *Gur Corporation v Trust Bank of Africa* (1986), the Court of Appeal had to consider the status of the Republic of Ciskei, one of the homelands established by the government of South Africa. At first instance, Steyn J considered whether Ciskei had *locus standi* and asked the Foreign Office for its attitude to Ciskei. The Foreign Office replied that Ciskei was not recognised as an independent State and Steyn J therefore found that it had no *locus standi* to be joined as a party to the dispute. The issue was taken to the Court of Appeal, who investigated the establishment of Ciskei. The court found that the British government continued to regard South Africa as internationally responsible for the territory of Ciskei. Furthermore, it found that the government of the 'Republic of Ciskei' had been established under the South African Status of Ciskei Act 1981. The Court of Appeal therefore held that the government of the Republic of Ciskei was a subordinate body set up by the Republic of South Africa to act on its behalf and it therefore had *locus standi* in the present case.

The question of recognition was raised more recently in *Arab Monetary Fund v Hashim* (1990). The case was brought by the Arab Monetary Fund (AMF), which was an international organisation created by treaty. The UK was not a party to the treaty and no Order in Council had been made with respect to the AMF under the provisions of the International Organisations Act 1968. In those circumstances, the Court of Appeal found that the AMF could not bring the action. The decision was overturned by the House of Lords on the basis not that it was an international organisation and, therefore, entitled to sue irrespective of recognition but that it had been incorporated by Abu Dhabi law and, therefore, could be regarded as an Abu Dhabi corporation. The decision was based more on pragmatism than on strict legal principles and followed a line of reasoning which had been used in the earlier case of *Carl Zeiss Stiftung v Rayner and Keeler Ltd (No 2)* (1967).

4.7.7 Effectiveness of legislative and executive acts

A further consequence of recognition is that the courts will give effect to the legislative and executive acts of foreign governments. The classic example of this rule is the case of *Luther v Sagor* (1921). The plaintiffs in the case had owned a timber factory, which had been nationalised by the government of the Soviet Union in 1919. The defendants had bought a quantity of timber produced at the factory from the Soviet government in 1920. The plaintiffs claimed the timber on the basis that the nationalisation of the factory by the Soviet government should be ignored. When the case was heard at first instance, the Soviet government was not recognised by the UK, and the court therefore found in favour of the plaintiffs. By the time the case was heard by the Court of Appeal, the Soviet government had been accorded *de facto* recognition. The court found that recognition would operate from the date when the Soviet government had taken effective control, which was accepted as being December 1917. The nationalisation decree was therefore the act of a sovereign government and the UK courts would have to give effect to it. On that basis, the appeal was allowed.

In *Arantzazu Mendi* (1939), the House of Lords had to consider the rival claims of *de facto* and *de jure* government. The *Arantzazu Mendi* was a private ship registered in Bilbao, Spain. In the summer of 1937, following the capture of the region by Nationalist forces, the Republic government issued a decree requisitioning all ships registered in Bilbao. In early 1938, the Nationalist authorities issued a similar decree. While the *Arantzazu Mendi* was in London, the Republican government issued a writ to obtain possession of the ship in accordance with its requisition decree. This was opposed by the owners of the ship, who accepted the Nationalists' requisition. The Nationalists argued that since they had been recognised as the *de facto* government over the areas they actually controlled and since they controlled the region around Bilbao, the courts must give effect to their requisition decree and dismiss the Republican action. The House of Lords accepted this view, basing their finding on the fact that the Nationalist government was in effective control of the area and, therefore, was entitled to be regarded as the government of a sovereign State.

In the early 1950s, two cases raised again the distinctions between the *de facto* and *de jure* recognition and the question of retroactivity. *Gdynia Ameryka Linie v Boguslawski* (1953) concerned recognition of the Polish government in 1945. During the Second World War, the Polish government in exile was recognised as the *de jure* government of Poland. On 28 June 1945, the communist provisional government took effective control of the country and was recognised as the *de jure* government on 5 July. The case concerned the effect of executive action taken by the Polish government in exile on 3 July. The House of Lords emphasised the general principle of retroactivity, which would normally mean that all acts of the communist government would be given effect to as from 28 June. However, the acts of the government in exile with respect to issues under their control remained effective up until the withdrawal of recognition on 5 July. Therefore, the action taken by the government in exile on 3 July would be effective. A similar result obtained in *Civil Air Transport Inc v Central Air Transport Corporation* (1953).

4.7.8 Sovereign immunity

One of the underlying principles of international law has been the doctrine of sovereign equality and the consequence that one sovereign cannot exercise authority over another. The practical application of the doctrine means that the many activities carried out by a foreign State cannot be the subject of municipal court proceedings. For example, in *Kuwait Airways Corporation v Iraqi Airways Company* (1993), an English court dismissed a claim by Kuwait Airways arising out of the confiscation of civilian aircraft as a result of an Iraqi government directive, on the grounds that the directive was an exercise of sovereign authority and was, therefore, entitled to immunity. The law relating to sovereign immunity is discussed in detail in Chapter 7.

THE SUBJECTS OF INTERNATIONAL LAW AND THEIR RECOGNITION

To whom does international law apply

Historically, States were considered to be the only subjects of international law but, since the end of the First World War, this view has become increasingly untenable, although independent States continue to remain the most important subjects. An important point to grasp is that international personality is a flexible concept and may exist in varying degrees.

The requirements of statehood

Article 1 of the Montevideo Convention on the Rights and Duties of States 1933 provides:

> The State as a person of international law should possess the following qualifications:
>
> (a) a permanent population;
>
> (b) a defined territory;
>
> (c) a government;
>
> (d) a capacity to enter into relations with other States.

There are no limits as to the size of population or territory, nor is it necessary for the territory of a State to be undisputed. Together with territory and population, a State must possess some degree of effective, independent government, although the degree of effectiveness and independence necessary is not always clear. More recently, the view has emerged that an entity established in violation of fundamental principles of international law will not obtain statehood for the purposes of international law. Most importantly, statehood will be denied to those entities established in violation of principles of self-determination or created by the illegal use of force.

Non-self-governing territories

There are a number of territories which do not possess full independence but are, nevertheless, of significance to international law. The main examples are colonies, protectorates and, of historical interest, mandate or trust territories. The manner in which international law will apply to and affect such territories varies from case to case. A particular aspect of the law relating to self-determination has been according certain elements of international personality to liberation movements, most notably in the case of the PLO.

International organisations

International organisations have had an ever increasing importance in international law and it is clear that they are capable of possessing international personality. The consequences of such personality will usually depend on the details of the documents establishing the organisation and the purpose and context of the organisation.

The United Nations

The most important and best known international organisation is the United Nations, which was established under the UN Charter in 1945. Membership of the UN is open to all peace loving States. The work of the UN is carried out through the six principal organs; these are:

(a) the General Assembly – the plenary organ of the UN, in which each Member State has one vote;

(b) the Security Council – primarily responsible for peace and security and consisting of five permanent members (China, Russia, France, US and UK) and 10 other elected members;

(c) ECOSOC – the Economic and Social Council, comprising 54 elected members;

(d) the Trusteeship Council;

(e) the Secretariat; and

(f) the International Court of Justice (ICJ).

Individuals

Since the Second World War, individuals have come to enjoy a limited degree of personality in international law, particularly in the areas of human rights law and humanitarian law, which are dealt with in more detail in Chapters 13 and 14.

Recognition

In international law, much depends upon the extent to which a particular State of affairs is recognised by the international community. Much has therefore been written about the recognition of States and there have developed two competing theories.

The constitutive theory provides that every legal system requires that the subjects of the system are determined with certainty. In international law, it is argued that the determination is by States acting severally or collectively. On this basis, it is the act of recognition which constitutes a new State.

The declaratory theory suggests that the formation of a new subject of international law is a matter of fact not law. A new State can, therefore, come into existence irrespective of whether it has been recognised by existing States.

The majority of writers support the declaratory theory and it would seem to accord more with present State practice. However, although recognition may have limited consequences in the international sphere, it remains important at the municipal level, when questions of whether or not an entity is entitled to the rights and privileges of a State are to be decided. In this context, it is important to distinguish between the recognition of States and the recognition of governments. Many States, while continuing to accord official recognition to new States, have ceased to formally recognise governments.

CHAPTER 5

TERRITORIAL RIGHTS

5.1 Introduction

Territory is a tangible attribute of statehood and, within that particular geographical area which it occupies, a State enjoys and exercises sovereignty. Territorial sovereignty may be defined as the right to exercise therein, to the exclusion of any other State, the functions of a State. A State's territorial sovereignty extends over the designated land mass, sub-soil, the water enclosed therein, the land under that water, the territorial sea (the nature and extent of the territorial sea will be discussed in Chapter 9) and the airspace over the land mass and territorial sea (airspace will be considered in Chapter 10). It has already been seen, in Chapter 4, that territory is undoubtedly a basic requirement of statehood. As Jennings and Watts have written, in *Oppenheim's International Law* (Vol I, 9th edn, 1992, Harlow: Longman, p 563), '... a State without territory is not possible.'

The fundamental nature of territory and sovereignty over territory can be appreciated when an attempt is made to identify the causes of wars and international disputes throughout history: 99% of them could be classified ultimately as territorial disputes. As Philip Allott has written in *Eunomia New Order for a New World* (1990, Oxford: OUP, p 330):

> Endless international and internal conflicts, costing the lives of countless human beings, have centred on the desire of this or that State-society to control this or that area of the earth's surface to the exclusion of this or that State-society.

Rights and duties with respect to territory have, therefore, had a central place in the development of international law, and the principle of respect for the territorial integrity of States has been one of the most fundamental principles of international law. It should be pointed out, however, that there is a growing body of international law which operates outside concepts of exclusive territorial rights. As the need for interdependence has grown, and as technology has presented increasing problems as well as benefits, so international law has responded by developing concepts such as the 'common heritage of mankind' and rules for the regional and global protection of human rights and environmental rights. These matters are dealt with in more detail in Chapters 14 and 16. It is also important to note that title to territory in international law is, more often than not, relative rather than absolute. Thus, resolving a territorial dispute is a question of deciding who has the better claim rather than accepting one claim and dismissing another.

5.2 Basic concepts

Before discussing the rules relating to territorial rights, it is necessary to identify and define a number of basic concepts.

5.2.1 *Terra nullius* and *res communis*

Terra nullius consists of territory which is capable of being acquired by a single State but which is not yet under territorial sovereignty. In the age of European imperialism, there was a tendency for Western writers to consider as *terra nullius* those territories inhabited by non-Europeans which were not organised on the lines of European States. However, in the *Western Sahara* case (1975), the ICJ found that the State practice of the late 19th century was such as to indicate:

> ... that territories inhabited by tribes or peoples having a social and political organisation were not regarded as *terra nullius* – in such cases sovereignty was not acquired unilaterally through occupation but sovereignty could be acquired through agreements with local rulers – such agreements were regarded as derivative roots of title, and not original titles obtained by occupation of *terra nullius.*

Terra nullius may be contrasted with *res communis,* which denotes territory not capable of being claimed by any single State. The classic example of *res comunis* is the high seas and a more recent example is outer space. A further concept can be introduced here: the common heritage of mankind. The phrase was first used in the UN General Assembly Declaration of Principles Governing the Seabed and Ocean Floor (GA Resolution 2749 (XXV) (1970)), which recognised the seabed and ocean floor as the common heritage of mankind. The phrase was used in the Law of the Sea Convention 1982 and the Moon Treaty 1979. Like *res communis,* the common heritage of mankind is not susceptible to appropriation by States, but the concept goes further, in that it indicates that the exploitation and exploration of such areas should be for the benefit of mankind whereas, within *res communis,* States are free to explore and exploit as they see fit provided that, in doing so, they do not impinge the freedom of other States.

5.2.2 Intertemporal law

In many disputes, the rights of the parties may derive from legally significant acts concluded a long time ago, at a time when particular rules of international law may well have been different to what they are today. It has long been accepted as a principle of international law that, in such cases, the situation must be appraised or the treaty interpreted in the light of the rules of international law as they existed at the time. This principle was re-affirmed by Judge Huber, in the *Island of Palmas* case (1928), when he stated that:

> Both parties are also agreed that a juridical fact must be appreciated in the light of the law contemporary with it, and not of the law in force at the time when a dispute in regard to it arises or falls to be settled. The effect of discovery by Spain is therefore to be determined by the rules of international law in force in the first half of the 16th century.

Some confusion was caused by the fact that Judge Huber went on to note that, while the creation of particular rights was dependent upon the international law of the time, the continued existence of such rights depended upon their according with the evolution of the law. One possible implication of this would be that States would constantly have to re-establish title to territory on a basis approved by international law at the time. The potential problem is resolved by acknowledging the fact that title to territory in international law involves assessing the relative strength of competing claims. Creation of title is to be assessed according to contemporary law and creation coupled with effective occupation is likely to defeat most other rival claims apart, perhaps, from claims based on self-determination.

5.2.3 Critical date

The date on which a dispute over territory crystallises is known as the critical date. In many disputes, a certain date will assume particular significance in deciding between rival claims. The choice of the critical date or dates will lie with the tribunal deciding the dispute and will usually depend on the particular facts. Once a date is chosen, subsequent events relating to territorial claims will be ignored. Thus, in the *Island of Palmas* case, the US claimed the island as successor to Spain under a treaty of cession dated 10 December 1898. That date was chosen as the critical date and the case was decided on the basis of the nature of Spanish rights at that time. In the *Minquiers and Ecrehos* case (1953), France and Britain submitted two different critical dates but the ICJ did not specifically choose between the two. Since that case, tribunals have made little reference to the choice of critical date and have been more inclined to consider all the circumstances relating to a claim.

5.3 Title to territory

Traditionally, writers have referred to five means by which title to territory may be acquired:

(a) occupation of *terra nullius;*

(b) prescription;

(c) conquest;

(d) accretion; and

(e) cession.

These five modes will be discussed here, but it is important in this matter to note the words of Ian Brownlie, in *Principles of Public International Law*, (5th edn, 1998, Oxford: OUP, p 129):

> A tribunal will concern itself with proof of the exercise of sovereignty at the critical date or dates, and in doing so will not apply the orthodox analysis to describe its process of decision. The issue of territorial sovereignty, or title, is often complex, and involves the application of various principles of the law to the material facts. The result of this process cannot always be ascribed to any single dominant rule of 'mode of acquisition'. The orthodox analysis does not prepare the student for the interaction of principles of acquiescence and recognition with the other rules.

5.3.1 Occupation of *terra nullius*

Occupation is preceded by discovery. Discovery alone is insufficient to establish title. It can only serve to establish a claim which, in a reasonable period of time, must be completed by effective occupation. Published discovery can obviously establish a better claim in time, but is ineffective against proof of continuous and peaceful display of authority by another State.

The exact nature of effective occupation and title to territory was considered in the *Island of Palmas* case (1928). The case concerned the island of Palmas (or Miangos), which lies 50 miles south east of the Philippine island of Mindanao. Under the Treaty of Paris 1898, which brought to an end the Spanish-American War of 1898, Spain ceded the Philippines to the US. In 1906, a US official visited Palmas, believing it to be part of the territory of the Philippines, and found the Dutch exercising sovereignty. There followed a protracted dispute between the US and the Netherlands, which was finally submitted to arbitration in 1928. The US based its claim, as successor to Spain, principally on discovery. There was evidence that Spain had discovered the island in the 17th century but there was no evidence of any actual exercise of sovereignty over the island by Spain.

The arbitrator, Max Huber, took the view that the most that discovery alone could create was an inchoate title, which required completion within a reasonable time by effective occupation. On the other hand, Huber found that the Netherlands had shown a peaceful and continuous and public display of authority over the island from at least 1700. Such authority existed in 1898 and had never been the subject of challenge by any other State. On that basis, it was decided that the island of Palmas formed part of Netherlands territory.

An important and necessary condition of effective occupation is the actual taking of possession, and the nature of that possession will depend on the actual territory involved. Discovery must be reinforced by an intention or will (*animus occupandi*) to act as sovereign (this, again, depends on the facts);

normally, the exercise of exclusive sovereignty is evidenced when the State establishes an organisation capable of making its laws respected. In the *Island of Palmas* case, the arbitrator commented:

> Manifestations of territorial sovereignty assume ... different forms, according to conditions of time and place. Although continuous in principle, sovereignty cannot be exercised in fact at every moment on every point of a territory. The intermittence and discontinuity compatible with the maintenance of the right necessarily differ according to whether inhabited or uninhabited regions are involved, or regions enclosed within territories in which sovereignty is incontestably displayed or again regions accessible from, for instance, the high seas.

In the *Eastern Greenland* case (1933), the PCIJ held that occupation involved both the intention to act as sovereign and the adequate display or exercise of sovereignty. The intention is a matter of inference from all the facts – merely raising a flag is not enough. The second element is satisfied by some concrete evidence of possession or control or some symbolic act of sovereignty – it depends on the nature of the territory involved. In finding in favour of the Danish claim to Eastern Greenland, the court remarked that:

> 'It is impossible to read the records of the decisions in cases as to territorial sovereignty without observing that in many cases the tribunal has been satisfied with very little in the way of the actual exercise of sovereign rights, provided that the other State could not make out a superior claim. This is particularly true in the case of claims to sovereignty over areas in thinly populated or isolated countries.

This point is further illustrated by the *Clipperton Island* case (1932), which concerned a dispute between France and Mexico. In November 1858, a French naval officer, on board a ship sailing about half a mile off Clipperton, proclaimed French sovereignty over the island. The French crew had had difficulties landing on the island – they eventually did land but left without leaving any visible signs of sovereignty. Declarations of sovereignty were subsequently published in Hawaii both in French and English. Until 1897, no positive or apparent act of sovereignty could be recalled by France or any other power. The island had no population, no administration (although a concession for the exploitation of guano had been given by the French government but had not been used). In 1897, a French boat discovered three Americans on the island and explanations were demanded from the US government, which said it made no claim to sovereignty. A month later Mexico sent a gun boat to the island in response to what was thought to be an English invasion. Mexico had ignored the French claim and always believed that the island belonged to Mexico, as successors to Spain. The Mexican flag was hoisted over the island. In January 1898, the French returned and the dispute commenced. The arbitrator found that, even if the Spaniards had discovered the island at the beginning of the 18th century, they had never shown any intention to exercise sovereignty and so, in 1858, the island was *terra nullius*. The question was therefore whether France had established title. It was found that France had made clear its intention to occupy the island, had asserted sovereignty and that nothing that had happened since 1858 could defeat France's claim.

5.3.2 Prescription

There are many similarities between claims based on prescription and those based on occupation. Both require peaceful and continuous effective control of territory. However, the two modes of acquisition are distinguished by the fact that occupation will only arise in respect of *terra nullius*. Prescription can validate an otherwise doubtful title. It depends on public control and the implication that other States see the effective control and acquiesce in the assumption of sovereignty. Protests by other States can defeat a claim based on prescription. Traditionally, it was thought that, in order to be effective, protests had to involve the threat or use of armed force. As the use of armed force gradually became restricted by international law, so diplomatic protest came to suffice. There remains some discussion as to the precise requirements of effective protest. Some writers have argued that diplomatic protest must, within a reasonable time, be followed by reference of the matter to the UN or the ICJ.

The issue of protest was raised in relation to the dispute between Argentina and the UK over sovereignty over the Falkland Islands (Malvinas). In 1982, the British Foreign Secretary stated that Britain's claim to the Falkland Islands rested partly on principles of prescription. According to Argentinian accounts, the Falkland Islands were first discovered by Spain, in 1520. Britain claims that the islands were first discovered by Britain in 1592. The islands remained unoccupied until 1764, when a French settlement was established on East Falkland. This settlement was sold to Spain two years later and was maintained by Spain until 1811. Meanwhile, a British settlement had been established in West Falkland in 1766. The British settlers were expelled by Spain in 1770 but returned in 1771 only to withdraw completely in 1774, leaving behind the Union flag and a plaque affirming British ownership of the island. Argentina became independent in 1816 and the Falkland Islands remained unoccupied until 1820, when the Argentinian government took possession of them, claiming sovereignty as successor to Spain. The occupation of the islands was advertised in the *London Times*. Between 1820 and 1829, Argentina performed a number of sovereign acts in relation to the Falklands and it was only in 1829, when a political and military commander was appointed, that Britain protested to the Argentinian government. In 1831, the Argentinian commander of the Falklands seized three American ships for unlawful sealing in Argentinian waters. In retaliation, the US destroyed the settlement on East Falkland and declared the islands to be free of all government. In 1833, the British purported to exercise rights of sovereignty over the islands by expelling the remainder of the Argentinian garrison and the islands remained in continuous British possession until 2 April 1982, when an Argentinian force invaded the islands. The Argentinian government had formally protested against Britain's occupation of the islands in 1833, 1834, 1841 and 1842. In 1849, Argentina sent a note to the British government indicating that it intended to make no further protest in respect of Britain's occupation since to do so seemed to be pointless. Nevertheless, Argentina pointed out that in no way should their lack of protest be taken to indicate acquiescence. Argentina resumed its protest in 1884 and has continued on a regular basis ever since. The Foreign Affairs Committee of the House of Commons was unable to reach a categorical conclusion on the legal validity of either Britain's or Argentina's claim to the Falklands. Clearly, it was the view of the British Foreign Secretary, in 1982, that Argentine's failure to protest between 1849 and 1884 amounted to acquiescence to Britain's claims to the Falklands.

The main issue regarding prescription therefore seems to be the question of whether a claim based on it will only succeed with evidence of positive acquiescence, or whether such a claim can only be defeated by evidence of positive protest. Traditionally, claims based on prescription were substantiated by evidence of open, continuous, effective and peaceful occupation which would seem to suggest that only active and effective protest will defeat such a claim. However, this view would seem to legitimise the claims of powerful States against the weak and may be incompatible with modern views of international law. The preferred view seems to be that of Brownlie, who points out that claims based on prescription rely on the acquiescence of other States:

> If acquiescence is the crux of the matter (and it is believed that it is) one cannot dictate what its content is to be, with the consequences that the rule that jurisdiction rests on consent may be ignored, and failure to resort to certain organs is penalised by loss of territorial rights. [Brownlie, I, *Principles of Public International Law*, 3rd edn, 1998, Oxford: OUP, p 154.]

Such a view would cast doubts on Britain's claims to the Falklands if they are based solely on prescription. However, the UK government has relied heavily on principles of self-determination to strengthen its case. The extent and implementation of a right to self-determination is discussed in Chapter 14. It has also been suggested that Britain would have been better to base its claim on conquest and subsequent annexation in 1833. As will be discussed at 5.3.3, below, such a claim would have been valid under principles of intertemporal law. However, for largely political reasons, Britain has not seen fit to found its claim on such a basis.

There is no prescribed time period necessary for a claim based on prescription to succeed; much will depend on the circumstances of the case, although, in *British Guiana v Venezuela Boundary* arbitration (1899), the arbitrators were instructed by treaty that adverse holding or prescription during a period of 50 years would establish a good title.

As has already been pointed out, claims to territory are rarely based on just one of the traditional grounds and some writers have doubted the utility of the doctrine of prescription. Nevertheless, the possibility of obtaining title by prescription has been recognised by a number of international tribunals, notably in the *Chamizal* arbitration (1911) and the *Frontier Land case* (1959).

5.3.3 Conquest and annexation

The third traditional mode of acquisition is of historic interest only. Under the Kellogg-Briand Pact 1928, war was outlawed as an instrument of national policy and the Stimson doctrine of Non-Recognition 1932 called upon States not to recognise changes brought about by use of force. Thus, the State of Manchukuo was not recognised, as it resulted from the conquest of Manchuria by the Japanese. Article 2(4) of the UN Charter prohibits States from using or threatening to use force against the territorial integrity or political independence of any State. Prior to the First World War, however, the use of armed force was not illegal and it was possible for territory to change hands following its use. Conquest itself was not sufficient to give title to territory and gave rise only to rights of belligerent occupation. In order to give effective title, physical occupation had to be combined with an intention to occupy as sovereign. This intention was usually evidenced by a formal declaration of annexation by the conquering State. Such a declaration of annexation would only be effective when hostilities had ceased. In practice, examples of title created by conquest are rare, because the annexation of territory after a war was usually confirmed by an express ceding of the territory from conquered to conqueror in the subsequent peace treaty.

Since 1945, there have been a number of cases in which territory has been occupied as a result of the use of force. The most notable recent example is, of course, Iraq's invasion and annexation of Kuwait, in August 1990. Although Iraq sought to justify its action on the basis of historic claims to the territory, such claims were rejected by the international community and, in resolution 662, the UN Security Council declared that:

> Annexation of Kuwait by Iraq under any form and whatever pretext has no legal validity, and is considered null and void.

The situation with regard to the territory taken by Israel during the course of the 1967 Six Day War remains more complicated. Until 1947, Palestine had been the subject of a League of Nations mandate which was administered by Britain. In 1947, the UN recommended partition of Palestine into a Jewish and an Arab State. The partition plan proved to be unworkable and, in May 1948, Israel declared itself an independent State. There followed a period of war which was ended by a number of armistice agreements concluded between Israel and each of its neighbours. Under these agreements, Israel retained more territory than would have been allocated to the Jewish State under the partition plan. There were a number of violations of the armistice agreements, the most major one being in 1956, when Israel invaded the Egyptian Sinai peninsula but later withdrew to the 1949 borders. In 1967, Israel again invaded the Sinai peninsula, together with East Jerusalem, the West Bank and the Gaza Strip, and the Golan Heights. This time the territory was not returned, despite UN Security Council resolution 242, which called for the withdrawal of Israeli armed forces from territories occupied in the conflict. The territory taken from Egypt in the Sinai Peninsula was returned following the peace treaty between the two States in 1979. Israeli civilian law was extended to East Jerusalem in 1967 and to the Golan Heights (which had previously been part of Syria) in 1981. The extension of Israeli law has been declared invalid by the UN and the prevailing opinion is that Israel continues to be in belligerent occupation of the territory taken in 1967. Apart from its claims on East Jerusalem, Israel has not made any express claim to title to the territory occupied in 1967 but argues that the traditional rules relating to belligerent occupation do not apply. Those rules are discussed in Chapter 14. Final clarification of the territorial status of much of the area awaits implementation of the PLO-Israel Accords of 1991 and conclusion of peace treaties between Israel and its neighbours.

Some doubts about the clarity of the law relating to conquest are created by the Indian invasion of Goa in 1961. Goa was a Portuguese colony at the time, although India maintained that it was an integral part of India and, as such, the invasion amounted to an act of self-determination. The invasion was criticised by a number of States but the Security Council was unable to agree on a clear policy. Following the Portuguese revolution in 1974, the new government recognised the Indian title to Goa. It is clear that, today, Goa forms part of the territory of India. There remains some doubt, however, as to who had title to the territory between 1961 and 1974, and the precise effect of Portuguese recognition of Indian claims. The suggestion is that it is recognition by the international community of India's claims that validated an otherwise illegal act. What is prohibited under international law is the unlawful use of force, and force used to obtain self-determination may be regarded as lawful. The whole question of the use of force is discussed in Chapter 12.

5.3.4 Cession

The possibility of cession of territory under the provision of a peace treaty has already been mentioned at 5.3.3, above. Cession involves a complete transfer of sovereignty by the owner State to some other State, and may involve a part or all of the owner State's territory. Traditionally, there was no bar on the extent to which one State could cede territory to another, although, today, a treaty which purported to provide for the cession of territory in conflict with principles of self-determination would violate *jus cogens* and, therefore, be invalid. It should be noted that the principle *nemo dat quod non habet* applies in international law just as in municipal law – it is not possible for a State to cede what it does not possess.

Cession need not only arise in cases of transfer of territory from losing to victorious State following a war. In the past, land has been ceded in an exchange agreement, for example, Britain and Germany exchanged Heligoland and Zanzibar by a treaty made in 1890 and, in 1867, Russia ceded Alaska to the US in exchange for payment.

5.3.5 Accretion

It is possible for States to gain or lose territory as a result of physical change. Such changes are referred to as accretion and avulsion. Accretion involves the gradual increase in territory through the operation of nature, for example, the creation of islands in a river delta. Avulsion refers to sudden or violent changes, such as those caused by the eruption of a volcano. The distinction between avulsion and accretion can be significant in boundary disputes, which will be discussed at 5.4.

5.3.6 Other possible modes of acquisition

As has already been stated, issues of title to territory are complex and will usually involve the application of a number of principles. In practice, cases rarely fall neatly into one of the five categories mentioned and claims to territory will be based on a combination of factors. In addition to the five modes of acquisition that have been discussed, a number of others have been suggested from time to time. Among those that can be clearly identified are: adjudication; disposition by joint decision; and continuity and contiguity.

5.3.6.1 Adjudication

In certain situations, territory may accrue to one State by virtue of a decision of an international tribunal. This is most likely to occur in the context of boundary disputes. Thus, in the *Frontier Dispute* case (1985), Burkina Faso and Mali agreed to submit their boundary dispute to a chamber of the ICJ and agreed to accept that tribunal's finding.

5.3.6.2 Disposition by joint decision

Following both World Wars, the victorious States assumed powers of disposition with regard to the territory of the defeated States. More often than not, such dispositions were subsequently confirmed by the provisions of a peace treaty and thus may be thought to come within the concept of cession. However, it is believed that such dispositions remain valid irrespective of any subsequent treaty and are today justified on the basis of the entitlement of the international community to impose collective sanctions on aggressor States.

5.3.6.3 Continuity and contiguity

The two principles of continuity and contiguity relate to occupation. Under the principle of continuity, an act of occupation in a particular area extends sovereignty so far as it is necessary for the security and natural development of the area of claim. Thus, for a long period, France claimed that its eastern border should follow the west bank of the River Rhine. A more modern example, although not expressed as such, would be Israel's wish to claim the strategically significant Golan Heights from Syria. Connected to the principle of continuity is the hinterland doctrine, under which coastal settlements were deemed to extend over the area of immediate hinterland.

The principle of contiguity involves the extension of sovereignty to all areas that are geographically pertinent to the area of claim. The possibility of such a principle was rejected by Max Huber in the *Island of Palmas* case. It is in respect of the polar regions that the principle has been most used. Both Russia and Canada have made claims in respect of the Arctic based on the sector principle, which is itself an adaptation of the contiguity principle. Other Arctic States have not followed this example and a major argument against any territorial claims to the Arctic is that, since the area consists almost entirely of frozen sea, it constitutes a part of the high seas and is therefore not capable of national appropriation. As regards Antarctica, both Chile and Argentina have made claims based on the contiguity principle, although such claims have not gone unopposed. Under the Antarctic Treaty 1959, all claims to national sovereignty were suspended and it is argued that Antarctica now constitutes part of the common heritage of mankind, incapable of national appropriation. There is further discussion of the regime pertaining in Antarctica in Chapter 16.

5.4 Boundaries

Disputes over territory may often arise in the context of boundary disputes and a number of principles exist which may be of assistance in the determination of borders between States. Sometimes, a boundary will be evidenced by some physical barrier but, more often than not, the border is an invisible line and, where relations between neighbouring States are friendly, agreement will be reached to enable free movement of officials across the border and joint exploitation of resources which straddle the borderland. For example, as a result of modern surveying techniques the border between France and the UK in the Channel Tunnel has been pinpointed with immense accuracy, yet agreement between the two States has been reached to provide for customs officials from one State to operate in the other and for the police of one State to carry out arrests in the Tunnel environs of the other State.

Two particular aspects of boundaries will be considered here. The first relates to boundary disputes which arise following de-colonisation. The principle which is commonly applied is known as *uti possidetis juris*. The principle was first applied during the break up of the Spanish Empire in South America, when the newly independent States agreed that their boundaries would conform to those set down by the former colonial power. The principle was adopted by the Organisation of African Unity in 1964, when it declared that colonial boundaries existing at independence constituted a tangible reality which all Member States pledged themselves to respect. The principle was recognised by the ICJ, in the *Frontier Dispute* case (1986), and is reflected in the Vienna Convention on the Succession of States in Respect of Treaties 1978, which provides that treaties establishing boundaries are an exception to the general rule that successor States start with a clean slate in respect of treaties entered into by their predecessors. Further confirmation of the universal nature of the principle came when the EC Arbitration Commission on Yugoslavia 1993 declared that it applied to newly independent States formerly part of a federation.

The other aspect of boundaries to be considered relates to those boundaries formed by rivers. There are a number of well-recognised principles which operate with regard to river boundaries in the absence of any express agreement. As far as non-navigable rivers are concerned, the boundary will follow the median line between the two banks. If the river is navigable, the boundary follows the median line of the principal navigation channel, known as the 'thalweg'. Of course, rivers can be subject to physical changes and the effect of such changes depends on whether they are a result of accretion or avulsion. Where physical change is gradual (accretion), the boundary will reflect the changes. However, where avulsion occurs, the boundary will follow its original course.

5.5 Rights of foreign States over territory

It is a general rule of international law that States have exclusive sovereignty over their territory. However, there are a number of exceptions whereby a foreign State(s) may be granted certain rights over the territory of another independent sovereign State. Such situations include leases, for example, the 99 year lease granted by China to the UK in respect of the New Territories and Kowloon, and servitudes.

Servitudes occur where territory belonging to one State is made to serve the interests of territory belonging to another State. The State enjoying the benefit may be entitled to do something on the territory concerned, for example, exercise a right of way, or take water for irrigation; alternatively, the

State on whom the burden falls may be obliged to refrain from doing something, for example, an obligation not to fortify.

Servitudes are normally created by treaty, although very occasionally they have been created as a result of long usage. For example, in the *Rights of Passage* case (1960), the ICJ recognised that Portugal had a right of passage across Indian territory between its colonial possessions of Daman and Goa and that such a right for peaceful purposes existed on the basis of a local customary law between India and Portugal. Such problems as arise will generally involve issues of State succession. The term is adapted from Roman law, where servitudes ran with the land and bound successors in title. The question then arises as to whether this is also true of international law? There have been a number of instances where international tribunals have held the successor States bound. In the *Free Zones of Upper Savoy and District of Gex* case (1932), the PCIJ held that France was obliged to perform a promise made by Sardinia to maintain a customs-free zone in territory which France had subsequently acquired from Sardinia.

It remains unclear exactly what type of obligation survives changes of sovereignty. For example, under the Lease-Lend Agreement 1940, the UK granted the USA military bases on certain British islands in the West Indies: the USA considered that its rights would lapse when the islands became independent. Also of relevance is the *North Atlantic Fisheries* arbitration (1910), in which a panel of arbitrators had to consider the effect of an 1818 treaty between the UK and the USA, which stated that 'the inhabitants of the US shall have, for ever, in common with the inhabitants of the UK, the liberty to take fish of every kind from the seas off the Newfoundland coast': the arbitrators held that this provision did not create a servitude which prevented UK making regulations limiting the fishing rights of all persons, including US nationals, in the area concerned. Arguments have followed as to the precise nature of the decision and it is pointed out that the arbitrators drew a distinction between express grant of sovereign rights and purely economic rights; by this, the tribunal implicitly accepted a class of limited servitudes. Clearly, with regard to some benefits, such as the right to take water from neighbouring States, it seems more appropriate that they should run with the land rather than be personal to the present title holder.

Servitudes can exist for the benefits of more than just one State. For example, the *Aaland Islands* case (1920) concerned an agreement made in 1856 between Russia, France and Britain, under which Russia agreed not to fortify islands lying near Stockholm in the Baltic. Sweden was not part of the treaty. In 1918, the islands became part of Finland, which began fortifying the islands. Sweden complained to the League of Nations and a Committee of Jurists decided that Sweden could claim the benefit of the 1856 treaty on the basis that Finland had succeeded to Russia's obligations and the treaty was designed to preserve the balance of power; therefore, all States directly interested could invoke it.

It has been suggested that a similar interpretation should be placed on treaties governing the Panama and Suez Canals. Servitudes are particularly important with regard to rivers and canals. There is a customary rule that foreign ships can be excluded from internal waters and this is especially hard on land-locked States. Since 1815, most major rivers have been open to navigation (either to all States, riparian States, ships of all States, or parties to a particular treaty). In 1888, the Convention of Constantinople opened the Suez Canal to all nations; in 1901 and 1903, similar agreements dealt with the Panama Canal. Egypt succeeded to Turkey's obligations and, although the Suez Canal Company was nationalised in 1956, in 1957, Egypt publicly declared that it would keep the canal open to all nations. It was widely understood that Egypt breached its international obligations when it attempted to close the canal to Israeli shipping. It is believed that the 1888 treaty internationalises and institutionalises the use of the canal; the canal is, effectively, an easement across Egyptian territory. The present status of the Panama Canal is governed by the Panama Canal Treaty 1977 between Panama and the US. Under the provisions of the treaty, the canal is to remain open to peaceful transit by the vessels of all nations. Discussion of the rights of passage of foreign States through the territorial sea takes place in Chapter 9.

TERRITORIAL RIGHTS

Territory is a basic requirement of statehood and, within its territory, a State enjoys and exercises sovereignty. Territorial sovereignty extends over the designated land mass, sub-soil, inland waters, territorial sea and the airspace above the land, internal waters and territorial sea. Although, historically, States were considered to have absolute and exclusive sovereignty over their territory, more recently, there has developed a body of rules, particularly in the fields of human rights and environmental protection, which have placed limits on such sovereignty.

Title to territory

Traditionally, there have been five means of acquiring title to territory:

(a) occupation of *terra nullius* – discovery alone is insufficient to establish title and it must be accompanied by effective occupation. What constitutes effective occupation will depend on the nature of the territory concerned (*Eastern Greenland* case (1933));

(b) prescription;

(c) conquest – this method, although of historical interest, is no longer a permitted way of obtaining title to territory;

(d) accretion and avulsion; and

(e) cession.

The creation of title is to be judged according to the contemporary rules of law and not according to the law in force at the time of the dispute. The traditional means of acquisition should not be thought of as mutually exclusive nor as a comprehensive list. Other factors, such as tribunal decisions and continuity or contiguity, may be significant.

Boundaries

A potential cause of dispute between neighbouring States is determination of territorial boundaries. Ultimately, this will have to be achieved by agreement and such agreement may often provide for free movement of officials across the border and joint exploitation of borderland resources. As far as the boundaries of former colonial territories are concerned, the presumption is that the colonial borders will continue to be respected and this principle has more recently been applied in the case of the break up of federal States, as in the case of former Yugoslavia. There are a number of accepted principles which apply in situations where a boundary follows the course of a river. The normal rule is that the boundary will follow the median line.

Rights of foreign States

International law recognises the possibility of foreign States acquiring certain limited rights over territory. Such rights are often referred to as servitudes and they may involve positive or negative obligations. They are normally created by treaty, although it is possible for them to develop through usage over a long period of time.

CHAPTER 6

JURISDICTION

6.1 Introduction

A fundamental principle of international law is the sovereign equality of States. This principle is reflected in the rule which prohibits the interference by one State in the domestic affairs of another. It is the international norms relating to jurisdiction which provide guidance on what is and what is not within the internal competence of a State. Jurisdiction refers to the power of a State to govern persons and property and situations. As Lord Macmillan declared in *The Christina* (1938):

> It is an essential attribute of the sovereignty of this realm, as of all sovereign independent States, that it should possess jurisdiction over all persons and things within its territorial limits and in all cases, civil and criminal, arising within these limits.

A number of different categories and types of jurisdiction should be identified from the outset. First, it is necessary to distinguish between prescriptive jurisdiction, which indicates the power to prescribe rules, and enforcement jurisdiction, which refers to the power to enforce rules. It is also useful to distinguish between legislative, executive and judicial jurisdictions. Legislative jurisdiction refers to the power of the State to make binding laws within its territory. Clearly, there are limits on the 'legislative supremacy' of a State. A State which adopts laws that are contrary to international law will render itself liable for the breach of international law on the international plane, although the internal constitutional position may be such that the municipal courts have to give effect to the municipal law. Executive jurisdiction refers to the capacity of the State to act within the borders of another State. Since States possess territorial sovereignty, it follows that, generally, State officials may not exercise their functions on foreign soil without the express consent of the host State. Judicial jurisdiction refers to the power of the municipal courts to try cases in which a foreign factor is present. It is the exercise of judicial jurisdiction which has received most discussion.

International law concerns itself with the propriety of the exercise of jurisdiction; exercise itself is a matter for the discretion of the State concerned. Jurisdiction has primarily and historically been exercised on a territorial basis, but there are occasions when States exercise jurisdiction outside their own territory. The PCIJ, in the *Lotus* case (1927), confirmed that:

> A State may not exercise its power in any form in the territory of another State. In this sense jurisdiction is certainly territorial; it cannot be exercised by a State outside its territory except by virtue of a permissive rule derived from international custom or from a convention.

However, the court went on to suggest that this rule really only applied to enforcement jurisdiction; a State could exercise prescriptive jurisdiction in its own territory in respect of acts which occurred abroad, provided that there was no positive rule of international law prohibiting such an exercise of power.

It should be recognised that much of the discussion of jurisdiction involves the identification of principles rather than the assertion of rigid rules of law. In this context, the words of Sir Gerald Fitzmaurice, in the *Barcelona Traction* case (1970), are of relevance:

> It is true that under present conditions international law does not impose hard and fast rules on States delimiting spheres of national jurisdiction in such matters ... but leaves to States a wide discretion in the matter. It does, however, (a) postulate the existence of limits – though in any given case it may be for the tribunal to indicate what these are for the purposes of that case; and (b) involve for every State an obligation to exercise moderation and restraint as to the extent of the jurisdiction assumed by the courts in cases having a foreign element, and to avoid undue encroachment on a jurisdiction more properly appertaining to, or more appropriately exercisable by, another State.

In addition to jurisdiction exercised on a territorial basis, there are a number of other relevant principles which can be identified and which have received varying degrees of international acceptance. The commentary to the Harvard Research Draft Convention on Jurisdiction with Respect to Crime 1935 identified five general principles, namely:

(a) the territorial principle;

(b) the protective principle;

(c) the nationality principle;

(d) the passive personality principle; and

(e) the universality principle.

Discussion of the application of these principles will form the main part of this chapter. Before looking at them in detail, it is necessary to consider some issues raised by the assertion of civil jurisdiction. One final introductory point needs to be made. This chapter is concerned with the exercise of jurisdiction by States on the municipal plane. Questions of jurisdiction also arise on the international plane and the subject of international criminal jurisdiction is discussed in Chapter 8.

6.2 Civil jurisdiction

The rules relating to the exercise of civil jurisdiction have tended to be more flexible than those relating to criminal jurisdiction. Some writers have argued that there, in fact, exist no clear rules of customary international law governing the exercise of civil jurisdiction, although there are an increasing number of treaties dealing with the matter. The traditional rule in the common law countries was that courts would have jurisdiction over civil disputes if the defendant was present in the territory, no matter for how short a period. Civil law countries have tended to operate on the basis that the defendant is habitually resident within the territory where jurisdiction is to be assumed. The position within the European Union is governed by the Brussels Convention on Jurisdiction and Enforcement of Judgments in Civil and Commercial Matters 1968. This provides the general rule that persons domiciled in a contracting State must be sued in the courts of that State alone, although there are two main exceptions to this rule. The Brussels Convention is incorporated into English law by the Civil Jurisdiction and Judgments Act 1982. The 1982 Act has since been amended to incorporate the Lugano Convention 1989, which extends the Brussels Convention regime to those States which are members of the European Free Trade Association.

As far as matrimonial cases are concerned, the generally accepted ground for exercising jurisdiction is the domicile or habitual residence of the party bringing the action and this rule is reflected in the Hague Convention on the Recognition of Divorces and Legal Separations 1970.

For a full discussion of the rules relating to the exercise of civil jurisdiction, reference should be made to a textbook on private international law. As far as public international law is concerned, questions of jurisdiction have usually arisen when a State has attempted to exercise criminal jurisdiction over non-nationals or in respect of actions that have occurred outside the State's own territory.

6.3 Territorial principle

The ability of a State to exercise jurisdiction over crimes committed within its territory is an essential attribute of sovereignty and the territorial principle has received universal recognition.

According to the territorial principle, events occurring within a State's territorial boundaries, and persons within that territory, albeit temporarily, are subject to local law and the jurisdiction of the local courts. The principle has practical advantages in terms of availability of witnesses.

Application of the territorial principle will usually be straightforward where the crime has been committed wholly within the territory. However, it is not always possible to decide on the exact location of the crime. The activities constituting the offence may have taken place in more than one State: for example, suppose X fires a gun in State A, killing someone in State B; which State can claim territorial jurisdiction? Under what is known the subjective territoriality principle, State A has jurisdiction, since that is where the offence was commenced. Under the objective territoriality principle, State B has jurisdiction, since that is where the offence was completed and had its effect. Both principles are recognised by international law and thus, in the example, both State A and State B would have concurrent jurisdiction.

An example of the subjective territorial principle is found in *Treacey v DPP* (1971). The appellant had written and posted in the Isle of Wight a letter addressed to Mrs X in Germany, which demanded money with menaces. Mrs X received the letter in Germany but informed the British police. Treacey was convicted of blackmail and his conviction was upheld by a majority in the House of Lords. Lord Diplock stated that:

> There was no principle of international comity to prevent parliament from prohibiting under pain of punishment persons who are present in the United Kingdom, and so owe local obedience to our law, from doing physical acts in England, notwithstanding that the consequences of those acts take effect outside the United Kingdom.

In *DPP v Doot* (1973) the respondents were convicted of conspiracy to import cannabis into the UK. The House of Lords held that the English courts had jurisdiction over the case, even though the actual conspiracy took place abroad, since the offence continued to occur in England when the conspiracy was carried out. Lord Wilberforce stated:

> The present case involves 'international elements' – the accused are aliens and the conspiracy was initiated abroad – but there can be no question here of any breach of any rules of international law if they are prosecuted in this country. Under the objective territorial principle ... or the principle of universality (for the prevention of narcotics falls within this description) or both, the courts of this country have a clear right, if not a duty, to prosecute in accordance with our municipal law.

It should be noted that, more recently, the English courts have moved away from a strict application of the subjective or objective territorial principle. Thus, in *Somchai Liangsiriprasert v Government of the USA* (1991), Lord Griffiths commented:

> The English courts have decisively begun to move away from definitional obsessions and technical formulations aimed at finding a single *situs* of a crime by locating where the gist of the crime occurred or where it was completed. Rather, they now seem by an examination of relevant policies to apply the English criminal law where a substantial measure of the activities constituting a crime takes place in England, and restrict its application in such circumstances solely in cases where it can seriously be

> argued on a reasonable view that these activities should, on the basis of international comity, be dealt with by another country.'

A controversial example of the application of the objective territorial principle is provided by the *Lotus* case (1927). The case arose following a collision on the high seas between a Turkish and a French ship. As a result of the collision, the Turkish vessel sank and a number of crew members and passengers drowned. The French ship put into port in Turkey and a number of French crew members were arrested and subsequently tried and convicted of manslaughter. France raised objections to the exercise of jurisdiction by Turkey and the dispute was submitted to the PCIJ. Turkey argued that ships on the high seas formed part of the territory of the State whose flag they fly. They therefore argued that jurisdiction could be exercised on the basis of the objective territorial principle, since the consequences of the French act had occurred on Turkish territory. The PCIJ found in favour of Turkey by the casting vote of the president of the court. The decision has been criticised for the suggestion it makes that States have a wide measure of discretion to exercise jurisdiction which is only limited to the extent that there are specific prohibitive rules. In other words, the onus is on the one disputing jurisdiction to provide evidence of a rule restricting jurisdiction. The better view today seems to be that it is the one asserting jurisdiction that must show a relevant permissive rule of international law. It is also important to note that the view that a ship forms part of the territory of the flag State is no longer correct. Questions of jurisdiction on board ships are discussed in Chapter 9 and jurisdiction on board aircraft will be dealt with in Chapter 10.

6.4 Protective or security principle

Under the protective or security principle, a State can claim jurisdiction over offences committed outside its territory which are considered injurious to its security, integrity or vital economic interests. The principle remains ill-defined and there are uncertainties about how far it can extend. There remains a considerable danger of abuse. Nevertheless, a large number of States have used the principle to a greater or lesser extent. The commentary to the Harvard Research Draft Convention stated:

> In view of the fact that an overwhelming majority of States have enacted such legislation [relying on the protective principle], it is hardly possible to conclude that such legislation is necessarily in excess of competence as recognised by contemporary international law.

It has been suggested that the principle was applied in the case of *Joyce v DPP* (1946), which involved the trial for treason of the Nazi propagandist William Joyce, also known as Lord Haw-Haw. Joyce was born in the US but, in 1933, he fraudulently acquired a British passport by declaring that he had been born in Ireland. In 1939, he left Britain and began work for German radio, broadcasting propaganda to Britain. The House of Lords had to decide whether the British courts had jurisdiction to try him for treason. They decided that jurisdiction did exist. Lord Jowitt LC answered the question as to whether the English courts could have jurisdiction to try an alien for a crime committed abroad by stating:

> There is, I think, a short answer to this point. The statute in question deals with the crime of treason committed within or ... without the realm ... No principle of comity demands that a State should ignore the crime of treason committed against it outside its territory. On the contrary a proper regard for its own security requires that all those who commit that crime, whether they commit it within or without the realm, should be amenable to its laws.

The House of Lords also found that jurisdiction could be based on the fact that Joyce owed allegiance to the British Crown. Although he was not a British national and the act of treason had occurred outside the UK, Joyce had availed himself of a British passport and could thereby be deemed to owe allegiance to the Crown and be liable for breach of that allegiance.

The protective personality principle is most often used in cases involving currency, immigration and economic offences. For example, s 170 of the UK Customs and Excise Management Act 1979 creates jurisdiction over acts done abroad, whether committed by UK nationals or not, to further the fraudulent evasion of import restrictions and duties

6.4.1 The effects doctrine

A development which is linked to the protective principle and to the objective territorial principle is the emergence of a particular type of extra-territorial jurisdiction known as the effects doctrine. According to this doctrine, States claim jurisdiction over acts committed abroad which produce harmful effects within the territory. The rationale behind the effects doctrine is the need to protect national economic interests. The effects doctrine has been particularly significant in the area of US anti-trust or anti-cartel law. In the *Alcoa* decision (*US v Aluminium Co of America* (1945)), the US Second Circuit Court of Appeals stated that:

> Any State may impose liabilities, even upon persons not within its allegiance, for conduct outside its borders that has consequences within its borders which the State reprehends.

The court suggested that jurisdiction would be founded if two conditions were met: the performance of a foreign agreement must be shown to have had some effect in the US and, secondly, this effect must have been intended. The decision provoked widespread opposition outside the US. In *British Nylon Spinners Ltd v Imperial Chemical Industries Ltd* (1953), the UK Court of Appeal was willing to issue an injunction preventing compliance with an order of the US courts made as a result of the application of the effects doctrine.

In the face of widespread opinion that the *Alcoa* decision contravened international law, application of the effects doctrine was modified in *Timberlane Lumber Co v Bank of America* (1976), in which it was stated that the courts had to take into account the economic interests of other nations and the nature of the relationship between the defendants and the US. US courts would only exercise extra-territorial jurisdiction if the interests of the US and the effects on US foreign trade were sufficiently strong vis à vis the interests of other States. In spite of this modification, application of the doctrine continues to be criticised and a number of States have taken action themselves to protect their national companies. For example, under the UK Protection of Trading Interests Act 1980, the Secretary of State can prohibit the production of documents or information to a foreign State's courts if that foreign State is indulging in extra-territorial action relating to the control and regulation of international trade. Furthermore, a UK national or resident can sue in an English court for recovery of damages paid under the judgment of a foreign court in such a situation.

The situation with regard to the effects doctrine was exacerbated in the US by an amendment to the Cuban Democracy Act 1992. The Helms-Burton legislation, in March 1996, provided for the institution of legal proceedings in the US against foreign persons deemed to be trafficking in property expropriated by Cuba from US nationals. The enactment led to international protests and the Inter-American Juridical Committee of the OAS concluded that such a purported exercise of jurisdiction would be contrary to international law.

In practice, little use has been made of such counter-legislation and, further, the US seems to have moderated its position, such that jurisdiction will only be asserted if the main purpose of an anti-trust agreement is to interfere with US trade and such interference actually occurs. It is submitted that, implemented in this way, the effects doctrine would be little different in practice from the objective territorial principle and the traditional passive personality principle.

There has been discussion as to the extent to which the effects doctrine has been applied by the European Court. In the *Dyestuffs* case (*ICI v Commission* (1972)), the court exercised jurisdiction over ICI (for the purposes of the case, a national of a non-EEC country) to control the activities of a price-fixing cartel which had been established outside the EEC but which was having effects within the EEC. The European Commission and the Advocate General had supported jurisdiction on implementation of the effects doctrine, although this position had been criticised by a number of Member States. The Court, however, sought to justify the exercise of jurisdiction on the fact that ICI was operating through subsidiaries within the EEC. In the *Woodpulp* case (*Ahlstrom*

Osakeyhtio v Commission (1988)), the court went further, in exercising jurisdiction over 41 woodpulp producers and two trade associations all of which were non-EEC nationals. The court stated:

> An infringement of Article 85, such as the conclusion of an agreement which has the effect of restricting competition within the Common Market, consists of conduct made up of two elements, the formation of the agreement, decision or concerted practice and the implementation thereof. If the applicability of prohibitions laid down under competition law were made to depend on the place where the agreement, decision or concerted practice was formed, the result would obviously be to give undertakings an easy means of evading those prohibitions. The decisive factor is therefore the place where it is implemented.

The court went on to state that it was immaterial to the exercise of jurisdiction whether the producers in the case operated through intermediaries or subsidiaries within the Community and further claimed that the exercise of jurisdiction in the case was covered by the territoriality principle. Critics of the decision, such as Dr Francis Mann, have argued that the decision goes further than the *Alcoa* case and is incompatible with the rules of international law. Others have sought to suggest that the decision is only an extension of the objective territorial principle. It seems accurate to state that the effects doctrine *per se* cannot be supported by any of the sources of international law, although supporters of the effects doctrine point to the *dictum* of the PCIJ in the *Lotus* case as authority for the view that any assertion of jurisdiction is lawful unless it is specifically prohibited.

6.5 Nationality principle

Most civil law systems claim a wide jurisdiction to punish crimes committed by their nationals, even on the territory of a foreign State. Those States which make little use of the nationality principle do not appear to protest about its use elsewhere. Although a State may not enforce its laws within the territory of another State, it can punish crimes committed by nationals extra-territorially when the offender returns within the jurisdiction. Jurisdiction based on nationality is less usual in common law countries, although there may be exceptions with regard to serious offences. For example, under English law, the courts have jurisdiction over British nationals who have committed murder or manslaughter, bigamy or treason outside the territory of the UK. It should also be noted that s 70 of the Army Act 1955 provides for the jurisdiction of the UK military legal system over UK military personnel, wherever they are stationed.

As a general rule, international law sets no limits on the right of a State to extend its nationality to whomsoever it pleases. In the *Nationality Decrees in Tunis and Morocco* case (1923), the PCIJ stated that:

> In the present state of international law, questions of nationality are, in the opinion of the court, in principle, within the [jurisdiction of the State].

This position was confirmed in Article 1 of the Hague Convention on the Conflict of Nationality Laws 1930, which provides that:

> It is for each State to determine under its own law who are its nationals. This law shall be recognised by other States in so far as it is consistent with international conventions, international custom and the principles of law generally recognised with regard to nationality.

In the *Nottebohm* case (1955), the ICJ stated:

> According to the practice of States, to arbitral and judicial decisions and to the opinions of writers, nationality is a legal bond having as its basis a social fact of attachment, a genuine connection of reciprocal rights and duties. It may be said to constitute the juridical expression of the fact that the individual upon whom it is conferred ... is in fact more closely connected with the population of the State conferring nationality than with that of any other State.

Thus, the general rule is that there should be some genuine link between a State and the person to whom it grants nationality. The two most important bases upon which nationality is founded are descent from parents who are nationals (*jus sanguinis*) and birth within the territory of the State (*jus soli*). It is also possible for individuals to change nationality, for example, by marriage or by naturalisation based on residence. The issue of nationality is considered in more detail in the context of nationality of claims in Chapter 8.

6.6 Passive personality principle

Under the passive personality principle, jurisdiction is claimed on the basis of the nationality of the actual or potential victim. In other words, a State may assert jurisdiction over activities which, although committed abroad by foreign nationals, have affected or will affect nationals of the State. The Harvard Research Draft Convention on Jurisdiction with Respect to Crime 1935 did not list the passive personality principle as a basis of jurisdiction and the commentary to the Draft Convention indicated that State practice with regard to the principle was inconclusive. The principle was rejected by all six dissenting judges in the *Lotus* case. It is argued that, in most cases, jurisdiction based on the passive personality principle could also be justified on the protective and the universality principles.

The commonly cited example of the principle is the *Cutting* case (1886). Cutting, a US national, had published defamatory statements amounting to a criminal offence under Mexican law against a Mexican national, though the publication had taken place in Texas. Cutting was convicted of the offence, *inter alia*, on the ground that Mexico was entitled to exercise jurisdiction on the basis of the passive personality theory. This view was strongly contested by the US and eventually Cutting was released, although Mexico claimed that the release was due only to the fact that the victim of the defamation withdrew from the action.

The prevailing view has, until recently, been that the passive personality principle should not be regarded as a proper basis for exercising jurisdiction. The main ground of objection to the principle is the fact that it seems to base jurisdiction solely on the fortuitous fact of the victim's nationality, which may very often be irrelevant to the commission of the offence itself. However, within the last 10 years, the US has begun to alter its practice, and it remains to be seen what effect this will have on State practice around the world. The first major indication of the change concerned the *Achille Lauro* affair, in which the US sought extradition from Italy of the leader of the group which had hijacked the *Achille Lauro* in 1985. The sole link between the US and the hijacking was that the hijackers had killed Leon Klinghoffer, a US national. Further confirmation of the US change in attitude was provided by the decision of the Court of Appeal, District of Columbia, in *United States v Yunis* (1991). Yunis, a Lebanese national, was charged with hostage taking and piracy in connection with the hijacking, in 1985, of a Royal Jordanian Airline aircraft on which US citizens were travelling. The Court of Appeal upheld the decision of the lower court, which found that the passive personality principle did authorise States to assert jurisdiction over offences committed against their citizens abroad. Chief Judge Mikva stated:

> Under the passive personality principle, a State may punish non-nationals for crimes committed against its nationals outside its territory, at least where the State has a particularly strong interest in the case.

Yunis unsuccessfully argued that the passive personality principle could only apply where the victims were chosen precisely because they were nationals of a particular State, which was not the case here. The court also based jurisdiction on the universality principle and it is suggested that, in both this case and in the *Achille Lauro* incident, jurisdiction could, and probably should, have been based on the universality principle alone, given the nature of the offences involved. The universality principle is discussed at 6.7. In *United States v Alvarez-Martin* (1992), Dr Alvarez-Martin was a Mexican national who was accused of participating in the torture and murder of a US special agent in the Drug Enforcement Agency. The torture and murder had taken place in Mexico. Although there was an extradition treaty between Mexico and the US, Alvarez-Martin was abducted by US agents and flown to the US. At first instance, the district court upheld Mexican complaints that it lacked jurisdiction to hear the case. The decision was upheld in the Court of Appeal and the US government appealed to the Supreme Court. It held that the US courts had jurisdiction to try the accused as long as the manner in which he was brought to the court did not breach any treaty obligations between the two States. The court examined the extradition treaty and found that the abduction of Alvarez-Martin did not contravene any express or implied provisions of the treaty. It therefore held that the US courts had jurisdiction. The court ignored the possibility of the abduction being prohibited by customary international law and the decision seems to provide further evidence of the use of the passive personality principle, since the only connection the US had with the case was the fact that the victim of the crime was a US national. It remains possible to argue that jurisdiction in this case could have been based on the universality principle, since the offence involved allegations of torture.

6.7 Universality principle

It has been seen that, so far, all the bases of jurisdiction have in some way involved a connection with the State asserting jurisdiction; events have taken place within the territory of the jurisdictional State or they have been committed by or against nationals or in some other way impinge on the interests of the State claiming jurisdiction. International law further recognises that, where an offence is contrary to the interests of the international community, all States have jurisdiction, irrespective of the nationality of the victim and perpetrator and the location of the offence. The rationale behind the universality principle is that repression of certain types of crime is a matter of international public policy.

The origins of universal jurisdiction can be traced to the fight against piracy. Customary international law provides that any State can exercise jurisdiction over pirates, provided the alleged pirate is apprehended on the high seas or within the territory of the State exercising jurisdiction. Clearly the nature of piracy makes it difficult, if not impossible, for jurisdiction to be based on any of the other principles: the offence is, by definition, committed outside the territory of any particular State; the nationality of the pirates would not always be possible to ascertain; and those apprehending the pirates would very often not have been the victims of the act of piracy. The rule of customary international law was affirmed in Article 19 of the Convention on the High Seas 1958 and is included in Article 105 of the Law of the Sea Convention 1982.

Piracy under international law (or piracy *jure gentium*) must be distinguished from piracy under municipal law. Offenders that may be characterised as piratical under municipal law may not fall within the definition under international law and, thus, are not susceptible to universal jurisdiction. Piracy *jure gentium* was defined in Article 15 of the High Seas Convention 1958:

Piracy consists of any of the following acts:

(1) any illegal acts of violence, detention or any act of depredation, committed for private ends by the crew or the passengers of a private ship or private aircraft, and directed:

(a) on the high seas, against another ship or aircraft, or against persons or property on board such a ship or aircraft;

(b) against a ship, aircraft, persons, or property in a place outside the jurisdiction of any State;

(2) any acts of voluntary participation in the operation of a ship or of an aircraft with knowledge of facts making it a pirate ship or aircraft;

(3) any act of inciting or of intentionally facilitating an act described in sub-para 1 or sub-para 2 of this article.

The law relating to piracy and the more general issue of jurisdiction on board ships is considered in more detail in Chapter 9.

A number of other offences have since joined piracy in being regarded as capable of being subject to universal jurisdiction. One of the earliest offences to be so recognised was slave trading. By the second half of the 19th century, it was widely accepted that customary international law prohibited the slave trade and a number of States began to assert jurisdiction over offences connected with slavery on the basis of the universality principle. For example, s 26 of the UK's Slave Trade Act 1873 provides that the English courts have jurisdiction over certain slavery offences irrespective of where or by whom they are committed. The Slavery Convention 1926 further provides for universal jurisdiction over such offences. Since 1945, universal jurisdiction has been provided for in a number of treaties on matters of international concern, for example, torture, drug trafficking, attacks on diplomats, hostage taking and the hijacking and sabotage of aircraft. Jurisdiction over offences relating to aircraft is discussed in more detail in Chapter 10.

There has been some discussion of the basis of jurisdiction over war crimes and other breaches of the laws of war. Many writers consider that the exercise of jurisdiction over war crimes is a further example of the universality principle and the classic example given is the *Eichmann* case (1961). Adolph Eichmann was head of the Jewish Office of the German Gestapo and, as such, had been responsible for the carrying out of Hitler's 'Final Solution'. In 1960, he was abducted by Israeli agents in Argentina and brought to Israel, where he was charged with war crimes, crimes against humanity and crimes against the Jewish people. During the course of his trial in Jerusalem, his lawyers made objections to Israeli jurisdiction. It was argued that Eichmann had been a German national at the time of the offences, which had been carried out elsewhere than on the territory of Israel against persons who were not Israeli nationals. At the time of the offences, of course, Israel did not exist as a State. The Jerusalem District Court found that it did have jurisdiction, stating that:

> The abhorrent crimes defined in the [Israeli Nazi and Nazi Collaborators (Punishment) Law 1951] are not crimes under Israeli law alone. These crimes, which struck at the whole of mankind and shocked the conscience of nations, are grave offences against the law of nations itself (*delicta juris gentium*). Therefore, so far from international law negating or limiting the jurisdiction of countries with respect to such crimes, international law is, in the absence of an international criminal court, in need of the judicial and legislative organs of every country to give effect to its criminal interdictions and to bring the criminals to trial. The jurisdiction to try crimes under international law is universal.

Brownlie argues, correctly, it is submitted, that a distinction needs to be drawn between such cases where what is being punished is the breach of international law (*delicta juris gentium*) and the true application of the universality principle, where international law merely provides that States have a liberty to assert jurisdiction over certain specific acts which are not themselves necessarily breaches of international law. The distinction may be important, since the strict application of the universal principle would seem to depend upon the municipal law of the State asserting jurisdiction, whereas jurisdiction over international crimes involves interpretation of the provisions of international law. Thus, in the *Barbie* case (1983), the French court found that it had jurisdiction over crimes against humanity committed by Klaus Barbie on the basis of the provisions of the relevant international agreements which were not subject to the usual statutory limitations of French law. The subject of war crimes and crimes against humanity is discussed in more detail in Chapter 13.

6.7.1 International criminal jurisdiction

It has been seen, in the *Eichmann* case, that one of the reasons for allowing States to assert jurisdiction over crimes against international law is the absence of an international criminal tribunal. Over the last century, there has been considerable discussion about the possibility of setting up such a tribunal. The discussion intensified as the Second World War came to an end and the two tribunals established in Nuremberg and Tokyo to try German and Japanese war criminals were seen as possible prototypes for a permanent international criminal court. Article VI of the Genocide Convention 1948 recognised the jurisdiction of an international criminal court should one be established, but there was no requirement that such a court should be established. The United Nations in fact prepared two drafts for an international criminal court, in 1951 and 1953, but the developing Cold War meant that neither draft achieved reality. The end of the Cold War and events in Iraq, Yugoslavia and Rwanda have resulted in renewed interest in a permanent court. The work of the International Criminal Tribunals for Yugoslavia and Rwanda, together with that of the Nuremberg and Tokyo tribunals, is discussed in Chapter 13. The ILC has now prepared a new draft statute for a permanent international tribunal, which has been submitted to a diplomatic conference in Rome, in June/July 1998. The tribunal would have jurisdiction over a number of specified international crimes. At the same time, the ILC is also preparing a draft Code of Crimes against the Peace and Security of Mankind, which could, ultimately, provide the law over which an international criminal court would have jurisdiction.

6.8 Double jeopardy

It has already been seen that very often it will be the case that more than one State has jurisdiction over a particular act. In such situations, the question of double jeopardy arises: if a person is acquitted or convicted in one State, can they subsequently be prosecuted for the same offence in another State? There is no completely unequivocal answer: the Harvard Draft Convention does provide that no State should prosecute or punish an alien who has been prosecuted in another State for much the same crime; but no reference is made to nationals who have been prosecuted in another State. The English courts have generally held that an acquittal or conviction by a court of competent jurisdiction outside England is a bar to indictment for the same offence before any court in England. However, before a plea of *autrefois* convict or acquit can be sustained, it must be shown that the defendant stands in jeopardy of punishment for a second time. Thus, in *R v Thomas* (1984), the defendant could be tried in England for an offence for which he had already been tried and convicted of in Italy, since he had been tried and convicted in his absence and there appeared little likelihood of his actually serving sentence in Italy.

6.9 Extradition

The term, extradition, denotes the process whereby, under treaty or upon a basis of reciprocity, one State surrenders to another State at its request a person accused or convicted of a criminal offence committed against the laws of the requesting State, such requesting State having jurisdiction. The rationale behind the law and practice of extradition is as follows:

(a) a desire not to allow serious crimes to go unpunished. Frequently a State in whose territory a criminal has taken refuge cannot prosecute for the offence because of a lack of jurisdiction. It will therefore surrender the criminal to a State that can try and punish the offence; and

(b) the State on whose territory the offence has been committed is the best able to try the offence because of the availability of evidence, etc.

Extradition developed in the 19th century through the use of bilateral treaties and the principle was accepted that there was no right to extradite, although there is also no rule forbidding the surrender of offenders. In England, extradition is governed by the Extradition Act 1989. Extradition is more principally a matter for municipal law, although a number of general principles can be discerned.

Before extradition can be ordered, two conditions must be satisfied:

(a) there must be an extraditable person; and

(b) there must be an extraditable crime. Such crimes are usually listed in the extradition agreement and, very often, political crimes, military offences and religious offences are not extraditable. Obviously, the definition of such crimes is an area for much argument and there have been a number of cases involving arguments about the extent to which acts of terrorism constitute political crimes.

A usual requirement is that of double criminality, that is, the act should be a crime in both States. Furthermore, it is a general principle that a State should not try an offender for any offence other than the one for which he was extradited.

A particular question that has been raised in the *Lockerbie* case (1992) is whether, in situations where more than one State has jurisdiction over an offence, a State can insist on the extradition of a defendant from a State which is willing to prosecute the offence itself. The matter was not considered by the ICJ when Libya made its request for provisional measures of protection nor when the ICJ decided it had jurisdiction to hear the merits of the case. If, as seems likely, those suspected of the Lockerbie bombing are tried in a neutral country, the ICJ will be unlikely to consider the merits.

6.10 Asylum

Linked to the question of extradition is asylum. It involves two elements: shelter and a degree of active protection. It may be either territorial asylum, granted by a State on its territory, or extra-territorial asylum, granted in consular premises, diplomatic missions, etc. The general view is that every State has a right to grant territorial asylum subject to the provisions of any extradition treaty in force. The granting of territorial asylum is regarded as an aspect of State territorial sovereignty. A more important question is whether there ever exists any duty to grant asylum. The right to grant extra-territorial asylum is more controversial and needs to be established in each case, since it involves a derogation from territorial sovereignty.

Article 14 of the Universal Declaration of Human Rights 1948 provides that:

> (1) Everyone has the right to seek and enjoy in other countries asylum from persecution.
>
> (2) This right may not be invoked in the case of prosecutions genuinely arising from non-political crimes or from acts contrary to the purposes and principles of the United Nations.

A resolution of the UN General Assembly, the Declaration on Territorial Asylum, which was adopted on 14 December 1967 (GA Resolution 2312 (XXII) (1967)), recommended a number of practices and standards:

(a) a person seeking asylum from persecution should not be rejected at the frontier: the individual case should be considered properly (this is generally known as the principle of non-refoulement);

(b) if a State finds difficulty in granting asylum, international measures should be taken to try and alleviate the burden; and

(c) asylum should be respected by all other States.

The preamble to the declaration made clear that the grant of asylum to persons fleeing persecution is a peaceful and humanitarian act that cannot be regarded as unfriendly by any other State. It now seems to be accepted that the principle of non-refoulement is part of customary international law and is a fundamental rule of refugee law. Refugees are defined as those having a well founded fear of persecution. What has yet to be settled is how the phrase 'well founded fear of persecution' is to be construed. In particular, it is not clear whether the test is an objective or a subjective fear; whether it depends solely on the refugees' own perceptions or whether the views of the receiving or the alleged persecuting State are significant. There are a number of treaties dealing with the rights of refugees, in particular, the Refugee Convention 1951 as amended by the Protocol 1967.

As far as extra-territorial asylum is concerned, there exists no general right to grant diplomatic asylum. This point was confirmed by the ICJ, in the *Asylum* case (1950). Exceptionally, extra-territorial asylum may be granted:

(a) as a temporary measure to individuals in physical danger;

(b) where there is a binding local customary rule that diplomatic asylum is permissible; and

(c) under special treaty.

6.11 Illegal seizure of offenders

Article 16 of the Harvard Draft Convention provided that no State should have jurisdiction over an offender who had been brought within its territory as a result of measures which themselves breached international law. However, the article appears to be more in the nature of *lege ferenda* than of *lex lata*. State practice seems to establish that the illegal seizure of offenders in the territory of another State is not, of itself, a bar to the exercise of jurisdiction. In the *Eichmann* case (1961), the defendant was unlawfully seized by Israeli agents in Argentina, and transported to face trial in Israel. In *United States v Yunis* (1991), the US courts found that they had jurisdiction, although Yunis, a Lebanese national, had been lured onto a yacht in the Mediterranean by FBI agents and then arrested once the yacht entered the high seas. In both cases, there was in existence no formal extradition arrangements between the countries involved and, thus, some writers have argued that seizure of offenders would negate any claim to jurisdiction if extradition would have been possible. However, in *United States v Alvarez-Martin* (1992), the Supreme Court held that the US courts had jurisdiction, in spite of the fact that Dr Alvarez-Martin had been seized by US Drug Enforcement agents in Mexico, although an extradition treaty was in force between the US and Mexico. In *R v Plymouth Justices ex p Driver* (1986), the British police wished to interview Driver, who was in Turkey. No extradition arrangements existed between the UK and Turkey and the police therefore asked the Turkish authorities for assistance. As a result, Driver was detained and transported to Britain where he was charged with murder. He argued that the English courts had no jurisdiction but the Divisional Court held that, once a person was lawfully in custody within the jurisdiction, the courts had no power to inquire into the circumstances by which that person came into the jurisdiction.

Of course, while the manner in which a defendant is brought before the court may not be a ground for denying jurisdiction, it is possible that the manner in which a defendant is seized may involve other breaches of international obligations. In general, the seizure of defendants by government agents acting outside the territory will amount to a breach of the principle of non-intervention in the domestic affairs of another State and will give rise to international liability. In the *Eichmann* case, the Argentinian authorities made strong protests to Israel about the capture of Adolph Eichmann, although the dispute between the two States was resolved before the case came to trial.

6.12 The wrongful exercise of jurisdiction

As was stated at the beginning of this chapter, international law is concerned with the propriety of the exercise of jurisdiction. The exercise of jurisdiction over aliens and with respect to events occurring outside the territory may well constitute interference in the domestic affairs of another State. In general, international law prohibits such intervention and it therefore follows that a wrongful exercise of jurisdiction may give rise to liability to another State, even in the absence of any intention to harm that other State.

JURISDICTION

Jurisdiction refers to the power of a State to govern persons and property and situations – it is an essential attribute of sovereignty. It is necessary to distinguish between prescriptive jurisdiction and enforcement jurisdiction, and also between legislative, executive and judicial jurisdiction. Most discussion has centred on the exercise of judicial jurisdiction, that is, the power of municipal courts to try cases in which a foreign element is present. Although rules exist governing the exercise of civil jurisdiction, the main concentration is on the exercise of criminal jurisdiction.

Bases of criminal jurisdiction

From State practice, it is possible to identify a number of principles which have been adopted.

- Territorial principle

  This is the most accepted and most used basis of jurisdiction. A State has jurisdiction over property and persons and events occurring within its territory (see the *Lotus* case (1927)). Where crimes are committed in more than one State, there is the possibility of adopting the objective territorial principle (where was the offence completed?) or the subjective territorial principle (where was the offence commenced?). The decision in *Somchai Liangsiriprasert v Government of USA* (1991) suggests the English courts are moving away from a strict choice between subjective and objective principle and, instead, will look for a genuine link between the crime and the UK.

- Protective or security principle

  Jurisdiction is claimed over offences which are considered injurious to State security or integrity, or vital economic interests. The principle is controversial and there are many who dispute its validity. One manifestation of the principle is to be found in the Effects Doctrine. This was first identified in the *Alcoa* case (1945), where jurisdiction was claimed on the basis of conduct committed outside the territory which had deleterious effects within the territory of the State claiming jurisdiction. The doctrine has been much criticised, although a modified version has continued to be used both in the US and by the European Court.

- Nationality principle

  It is generally accepted that States may exercise jurisdiction over their nationals even in respect of offences committed abroad.

- Passive personality principle

  Here, jurisdiction is claimed on the basis of the nationality of the victim. The classic example is the *Cutting* case (1886), although, more recently, the principle has been revived in the case of the *Achille Lauro* incident and in *US v Alvarez-Martin* (1992).

- Universality principle

  International law recognises that, where an offence is contrary to the interests of the international community, all States may claim jurisdiction, irrespective of the nationality of the victim and perpetrator or the location of the offence. Traditionally, universal jurisdiction has been claimed in respect of piracy on the high seas. It may also arise in connection with war crimes and certain terrorist offences.

Wrongful exercise of jurisdiction may give rise to international responsibility.

It may often be the case that more than one State can exercise jurisdiction over a particular offence. In practice, the deciding factor will be the location of the offender. Once the offender has been tried in one State, there is an argument to suggest that the rule of double jeopardy will apply and he or she cannot be tried again for the same offence in another jurisdiction. However, there is no clear rule of international law to this effect.

Two issues relating to the question of jurisdiction are extradition and asylum. As far as extradition is concerned, there is no right to extradite nor is there a rule forbidding extradition. The rules relating to extradition between particular States therefore depend upon the existence of a bilateral extradition treaty between the two States. It should be noted, however, that the manner in which an offender is brought before the courts will not generally affect jurisdiction, although it may involve other breaches of international obligations. Linked to extradition is asylum. All States have the right to offer territorial asylum to foreign nationals, subject to the provisions of any extradition treaty in force. More controversial is the question of whether there is any duty to grant asylum. It is a general principle that a person seeking asylum from persecution should not be rejected at the frontier (non-refoulement) and their case should be considered properly. The position of refugees is largely governed by the Refugee Convention 1951, as amended.

CHAPTER 7

IMMUNITIES FROM NATIONAL JURISDICTION

7.1 Introduction

As was seen in Chapter 6, the principal basis for jurisdiction is territorial. States are recognised as having authority over people, things and events within their own territory and, therefore, may exercise jurisdiction over them. However, international law does recognise that certain people, things and events are entitled to immunity from the enforcement of local law. It should be noted that immunity is from enforcement rather than from the law itself. It is these exceptions to territorial enforcement which are the subject of this chapter. Traditionally, there have been two beneficiaries of the exception: foreign States and foreign diplomats. More recently, international organisations have also been accorded certain immunities.

Today, immunity from jurisdiction may be enjoyed by:

(a) foreign States and heads of foreign States (including public ships of foreign States);

(b) armed forces of foreign States;

(c) diplomatic representatives and consuls of foreign States; and

(d) international organisations.

An initial point that should be noted is the distinction to be drawn between the related concepts of immunity and non-justiciability. Where an issue is non-justiciable, the municipal court has no competence to assert jurisdiction at all. A non-justiciable matter is one that cannot be the subject of judicial proceedings before a municipal court. Immunity arises where the municipal court would ordinarily have jurisdiction but, because of the identity of one of the parties involved, the court will refrain from exercising that jurisdiction. One of the consequences of the distinction is that it is possible for immunities to be waived but the courts will never be able to consider matters which are non-justiciable. This chapter is principally concerned with immunities.

7.2 State immunity

From the earliest days of international law, it has been recognised that the heads of foreign States enjoy certain privileges and immunities.

7.2.1 The basis of State immunity

The traditional view of immunity was set out by Chief Justice Marshall of the US Supreme Court in *Schooner Exchange v McFaddon* (1812). The case concerned a ship, the *Schooner Exchange*, whose ownership was claimed by the French government and by a number of US nationals. The US Attorney General argued that the court should refuse jurisdiction on the ground of sovereign immunity. Chief Justice Marshall stated:

> The full and absolute territorial jurisdiction being alike the attribute of every sovereign, and being incapable of conferring extraterritorial power, would not seem to contemplate foreign sovereigns nor their sovereign rights as its objects. One sovereign being in no respect amenable to another; and being bound by obligations of the highest character not to degrade the dignity of his nation, by placing himself or its sovereign rights within the jurisdiction of another, can be supposed to enter a foreign territory only under an express licence, or in the confidence that the immunities belonging to his independent sovereign station, though not expressly stipulated, are reserved by implication, and will be extended to him.

State immunity developed from the personal immunity of sovereign heads of State. At an international level, all sovereigns were considered equal and independent. It would be inconsistent with this principle if one sovereign could exercise authority over another sovereign. The immunity of sovereigns is expressed in the maxim *par in parem non habet imperium*. In medieval times, ruler and State were regarded as synonymous and sovereignty was regarded as a personalised concept. By the time of *Schooner Exchange v McFaddon*, it was clear that a sovereign had a representative character and that actions taken on behalf of the sovereign or in the name of the sovereign were capable of attracting the same immunities.

State immunity can also be linked to the prohibition in international law on one State interfering in the internal affairs of another. In *Buck v Attorney General* (1965), the Court of Appeal was called upon to discuss the validity of certain provisions of the Constitution of Sierra Leone and refused on the basis that it lacked jurisdiction. In the course of his judgment, Diplock LJ stated:

> The only subject matter of this appeal is an issue as to the validity of a law of a foreign independent sovereign State ... As a member of the family of nations, the government of the United Kingdom observes the rules of comity, videlicet the accepted rules of mutual conduct as between State and State which each State adopts in relation to other States and expects other States to adopt in relation to itself. One of those rules is that it does not purport to exercise jurisdiction over the internal affairs of any other independent State, or to apply measures of coercion to it or its property, except in accordance with the rules of public international law. One of the commonest applications of this rule ... is the well known doctrine of

> sovereign immunity ... the application of the doctrine of sovereign immunity does not depend upon the persons between whom the issue is joined, but upon the subject matter of the issue.

The question arises as to whether immunity arises *ratione personae* or *ratione materiae*; this quotation would seem to support the view that immunity applies only *ratione materiae* but other writers, such as I Sinclair ('The law of sovereign immunity; recent developments' (1980) 167 Hague Recueil 113), are not so sure:

> ... does [immunity] apply *ratione personae* or *ratione materiae*? The answer is probably both. Immunity applies *ratione personae* to identify the categories of persons, whether individuals, corporate bodies or unincorporated entities, by whom it may *prima facie* be claimable; and *ratione materiae* to identify whether substantively it may properly be claimed ...

It seems better to suggest a two fold test: first, is the entity concerned entitled to immunity (*ratione personae*)? and, then, if the answer is yes, is the act itself one which carries immunity (*ratione materiae*)?

7.2.2 Absolute and restrictive immunity

The traditional doctrine of State immunity was absolute, in that immunity attached to all actions of foreign States. With the rise of industrialisation during the 19th century, States became more involved in commercial activities, particularly in the area of railways, shipping and postal services. The emergence of the Communist States in the first half of the 20th century and the increasing use of nationalisation as a tool of economic development resulted in a massive growth in the commercial activity of States. It became increasingly common for private individuals and corporations to enter into contracts with foreign State trading organisations. Should a dispute subsequently arise, the foreign State trading organisation would be able to rely on the doctrine of sovereign immunity and deny the other party the protection of municipal law. This situation led to calls for the modification of the absolute immunity of States and for a distinction to be drawn between the public acts of States (acts *jure imperii*) and private acts (trading and commercial acts – acts *jure gestionis*). Under a restrictive view of immunity, it would only be acts *jure imperii* that would attract immunity. In *Dralle v Republic of Czechoslovakia* (1950), the Supreme Court of Austria carried out a comprehensive survey of State practice and concluded that, in the light of the increased commercial activity of States, the classic doctrine of absolute immunity had lost its meaning and was no longer a rule of international law. In 1952, the US State department issued the Tate letter, which stated that immunity would only be given to public acts and no longer to private acts. This restrictive approach was supported by four justices of the Supreme Court in *Alfred Dunhill of London Inc v Republic of Cuba* (1976) and the doctrine of restrictive immunity was confirmed in the US Foreign Sovereign Immunities Act 1976.

It should be noted that the doctrine of absolute immunity still applies to heads of State and is usually extended to such members of their family that form part of their household.

7.2.3 The British position

British practice with regard to State immunity has undergone a series of changes. In the mid 19th century, the authorities seemed to conflict and there was certainly some evidence of a restrictive view being taken. For example, in *De Haber v Queen of Portugal* (1851), the Lord Chief Justice seemed to favour a restrictive view of immunity, when he said at p 207:

> ... an action cannot be maintained in an English court against a foreign potentate for anything done or omitted to be done by him *in his public capacity* as representative of the nation of which he is head ... no English court has jurisdiction to entertain any complaints against him in that capacity [emphasis added].

The case seen for a long time as the main authority on State immunity was *The Parlement Belge* (1880). In that case, which concerned a mail ship owned and controlled by the King of Belgium and crewed by the Royal Belgian Navy, the Court of Appeal held that it lacked jurisdiction 'over the person of any sovereign ... of any other State, or over the public property of any State which is destined to its public use'. 40 years later, the Court of Appeal, in *The Porto Alexandre* (1920), relied on *The Parlement Belge* to find that immunity attached to a ship which had been requisitioned by the government of Portugal and used to carry cargo belonging to a private company. It was argued that the ship was engaged on an ordinary commercial undertaking but the court held that that was not capable of displacing the rule of absolute immunity laid down in *The Parlement Belge*.

The doctrine of absolute immunity was seen at its most extreme in *Krajina v The Tass Agency* (1949). In that case, Krajina claimed damages for a libel contained in the *Soviet Monitor* which was published by the London office of the Tass news agency. The Soviet Ambassador to the UK certified that Tass was a department of State of the Soviet Union and the Court of Appeal accordingly decided that it was entitled to immunity. The decision provoked widespread criticism and led to the setting up of a government committee to consider the whole question of State immunity. The committee found that the UK did accord a greater immunity than that granted by many other States but was unable to agree on the question of the degree of immunity required by international law. The courts continued to apply the absolute doctrine, although, in *Rahimtoola v Nizam of Hyderabad* (1958), Lord Denning, in a dissenting judgment, put the case strongly for adopting a restrictive approach.

By the 1970s, a significant number of States had adopted the restrictive approach and, following lengthy discussions, the Council of Europe promulgated the European Convention on State Immunity 1972 which the UK signed. Its provisions were incorporated into English law by the State Immunity Act 1978, which entered into force on 22 November 1978. Before the Act came into force, the British courts had already shown a change in approach in two notable cases: *The Philippine Admiral* (1977) and *Trendtex Trading Corporation Ltd v Central Bank of Nigeria* (1977). The latter case was notable for the judgment of Lord Denning to which reference has already been made in Chapter 2. In that case, the Court of Appeal held that restrictive immunity was now firmly established as a rule of customary international law and it could therefore be incorporated into the common law without need for an Act of Parliament. This point was confirmed by the House of Lords in *I Congreso del Partido* (1981), a case which concerned matters occurring before the State Immunity Act came into force.

The State Immunity Act 1978 provides, in s 1, that States are immune from the jurisdiction of the courts of the UK, except as provided in the Act. The Act contains 10 provisions which create exceptions to the main rule. Probably the most important exception is provided in s 3:

> (1) A State is not immune as respects proceedings relating to:
>
> (a) a commercial transaction entered into by the State; or
>
> (b) an obligation of the State which by virtue of a contract (whether a commercial transaction or not) falls to be performed wholly or partly in the United Kingdom.

Sub-section 3(3) lists those transactions which will be considered commercial:

> (a) any contract for the supply of goods or services;
>
> (b) any loan or other transaction for the provision of finance and any guarantee or indemnity in respect of any such transaction or of any other financial obligation; and
>
> (c) any other transaction or activity (whether of a commercial, industrial, financial, professional or other similar character) into which a State enters or in which it engages otherwise than in the exercise of sovereign authority;
>
> but neither paragraph of sub-s (1) above applies to a contract of employment between a State and an individual.

It is clear that the pre-Act cases will still be of relevance in deciding when an act is done in the exercise of sovereign authority.

In *Kuwait Airways Corporation v Iraqi Airways Co* (1995), the House of Lords considered the State Immunity Act 1978. The case arose following the Iraqi invasion of Kuwait in August 1990. Aircraft belonging to Kuwait Airways were transported from Kuwait to Iraq by the defendants, acting under Iraqi Government orders. Subsequently, the Iraqi government purported to dissolve Kuwait Airways and transfer its assets to the defendants. Kuwait Airways brought the action for damages arising out of the wrongful interference by Iraqi Airways with a number of aircraft. The defendants claimed State immunity. The House of Lords took the view that the central question was whether the acts taken by Iraqi Airways were performed in the exercise of sovereign authority and the answer to this question depended on whether the acts are of their own character a governmental act, as opposed to an act which any private citizen can perform. Lord Goff made clear that it was insufficient that the act was carried out on the directions of the State, because such an act need not possess the character of a governmental act. Accordingly, the House of Lords decided, by a majority of three to two, that the actions taken prior to the purported dissolution of Kuwait Airways were performed in the exercise of sovereign authority but that, once the aircraft were vested in Iraqi Airways by the Iraqi government, the action by the company ceased to be action in exercise of government authority.

7.2.4 The current legal position

It is difficult to State the current position with regard to State immunity with any clear certainty. Most writers stress the trend towards the restrictive approach in the practice of States without going as far as to claim it as an unopposed rule of customary international law. Even if the restrictive view is accepted as reflecting customary law, there remains the problem of clearly distinguishing between acts *jure imperii* and acts *jure gestionis*. One aspect of the distinction is whether the deciding factor should be the nature of the activity in issue or whether it is the purpose of the transaction which is more significant. Certainly, the US and the UK cases seem to favour a distinction based on the nature of the transaction involved and, in the *Empire of Iran* case (1963), the German Constitutional Court stated:

> As a means of determining the distinction between *actus jure imperii* and *jure gestionis* one should refer rather to the nature of the State transaction or the resulting legal relationships, and not to the motive or purpose of the State activity.

In 1986, the ILC published its Draft Articles on Jurisdictional Immunities of States and Their Property, and these have since been revised in the light of the comments of States. The draft articles provide for the immunity of States, subject to a number of exceptions. 'State' is defined in Article 3 and includes the organs of government, political subdivisions of the State, State agencies and representatives of the State acting in an official capacity. Of particular interest in the context of the discussion about acts *jure imperii* and acts *jure gestionis,* is Article 3(2), which provides:

> In determining whether a contract for the sale or purchase of goods or the supply of services is commercial, reference should be made primarily to the nature of the contract, but the purpose of the contract should also be taken into account if, in the practice of that State, that purpose is relevant to determining the non-commercial character of the contract.

The latest draft was published in 1991 and the Sixth Committee of the UN General Assembly is currently debating whether to recommend that the General Assembly convenes an international conference to produce a convention on the matter.

7.3 Foreign armed forces

Members of the armed forces usually enjoy limited immunities from local jurisdiction while in the territory of a foreign State. Obviously, such immunities only apply where the forces are present with the consent of the host State. The nature and extent of the immunities generally depends on the circumstances under which they were admitted, although simple admission itself can produce legal consequences. The receiving State impliedly agrees not to exercise jurisdiction in such a way as to impair the integrity and the efficiency of the force. The general rule is that the commander of visiting forces has exclusive jurisdiction over offences committed within the area where the force is stationed or while members of the force are on duty. Usually, the status and immunities of foreign troops will be the subject of specific agreement. Thus, under the North Atlantic Treaty Agreement 1951, the sending State has the primary right to exercise jurisdiction over NATO troops stationed abroad in other Member States.

7.4 Diplomatic immunity

The rules concerning diplomatic relations have always been an important aspect of international law and, arguably, form one of the most accepted areas of the law. In the *US Diplomatic and Consular Staff in Tehran* case (1980), the ICJ confirmed the fundamental nature of the law on diplomatic immunity:

> ... the maintenance of which is vital for the security and well being of the complex international community of the present day.

7.4.1 The basis of diplomatic immunity

There have been three principal theories justifying diplomatic immunity: personal representation; extra-territoriality; and functional necessity.

7.4.1.1 Personal representation

This theory dates back to the time when diplomatic relations involved the sending of personal representatives of the sovereign. Immunity attaching to diplomatic representatives was seen as an extension of sovereign immunity.

7.4.1.2 Extra-territoriality

This theory was founded on the belief that the offices and homes of the diplomat were to be treated as though they were the territory of the sending State. In 1758, Emmercich de Vattel wrote: '... an ambassador's house is, at least in all common cases of life, like his person, considered as out of the country.' The theory always rested on a fiction and is now no longer respected.

7.4.1.3 Functional necessity

The preferred rationale for the privileges and immunities attaching to diplomats is that they are necessary to enable them to perform diplomatic functions. Modern diplomats need to be able to move freely and be unhampered as they report to their governments. They need to be able to report in confidence and to negotiate on behalf of their governments without fear of let or hindrance. Diplomatic immunity is not for the benefit of individuals, but to ensure the efficient performance of the functions of diplomatic missions as representing States.

7.4.2 The international law on diplomatic relations

Until the end of the 1950s, the source of diplomatic law was customary international law. In 1957, the ILC undertook to produce a draft convention on diplomatic relations. This draft formed the basis for the Vienna Convention on Diplomatic Relations 1961 (referred to in this chapter as the Vienna Convention), which was signed on 18 April 1961 and entered into force on 24 April 1964. The Convention was widely regarded as codifying existing rules of customary law and the vast majority of States are party to it. The Convention emphasises the functional necessity of diplomatic immunity and the main functions of a diplomatic mission are set down in Article 3. These functions include representing the sending State in the receiving State; protecting the interests of the sending State; negotiating with the receiving State; reporting on conditions and developments within the receiving State; and generally promoting and developing friendly relations between sending and receiving States. The Vienna Convention became part of UK law by virtue of the Diplomatic Privileges Act 1964.

The first point to be noted is that there is no right to diplomatic relations. Such relations exist only by consent and a receiving State may declare any member of a diplomatic mission *persona non grata*, in which case the sending State must withdraw the diplomatic agent or face the withdrawal of immunity. This rule is now to be found in Article 9 of the Vienna Convention 1961. Declaring members of a mission *persona non grata* amounts to a unilateral act on the part of the receiving State. More usually, disputes about diplomatic staff are resolved by agreement between the sending and the receiving State (the latter will ask that the sending State withdraws particular members of its mission). The sending State will normally comply with such a request rather than declaring individuals to be *persona non grata*.

7.4.3 The diplomatic mission

The premises of the diplomatic mission, which includes the embassy buildings and compound, together with the residence of the head of the mission are inviolable, by virtue of Article 22 of the Vienna Convention. This is not to say that the premises of the diplomatic mission constitute part of the territory of the sending State but does mean that they are inaccessible to agents of the receiving State without the consent of the head of the mission. In observing this rule, the English courts refused to issue a writ of *habeas corpus* with regard to a Chinese dissident who was being held against his will in the Chinese embassy in London, in what was known as the *Sun Yat Sen* incident.

An incident in London in 1984 illustrates some aspects of diplomatic immunity. A demonstration was held outside the Libyan diplomatic mission in London to protest against the government of Colonel Ghaddafi. The mission had asked unsuccessfully for the demonstration to be banned and a counter demonstration of Ghaddafi supporters was separated from the main demonstration by a large number of police. During the demonstration, shots were fired from a window of the mission. One of the shots killed WPC Fletcher and a number of demonstrators were injured. No attempt was made by the British authorities to enter the mission at the time but diplomatic relations were severed and the Libyan mission was evacuated. After the diplomats had left, the building was searched. The British authorities argued that they had done sufficient to protect the mission consistent with Article 22 of the Vienna Convention – it was argued that maintaining the peace of the mission did not require complete isolation from hostile public opinion. The inviolability of the mission premises was observed until diplomatic relations were severed, after which time the only obligation on the host State is merely to protect the premises of the mission.

The inviolability of the diplomatic mission also means that the receiving State is under a duty to afford all reasonable protection to it. It was a failure to adequately protect the US embassy in Tehran which led to the *US Diplomatic and Consular Staff in Tehran* case (1980). On 4 November 1979, following the revolution in Iran, a number of Iranian nationals seized the US embassy and took the personnel inside hostage. Although the ICJ found that the initial hostage taking could not be attributed to the Iranian government, it had been aware of the threat posed to the embassy and had the means available to provide adequate protection. The court therefore found that Iran's failure to prevent the seizure of the embassy amounted to a breach of its international obligations.

7.4.4 Diplomatic personnel

The Vienna Convention provides for varying degrees of immunity which are dependant on the status of the person concerned. There are five main categories of person, each attracting differing degrees of immunity:

(a) the head of the mission (the ambassador or *chargé d'affaires*);

(b) the members of the diplomatic staff;

(c) the members of the administrative and technical staff;

(d) the members of the service staff; and

(e) private servants.

The appointment of the head of the mission requires the consent of the receiving State and details of all other members of the mission must be given to the receiving State if immunity is to be invoked. The receiving State can set limits on the size of a particular mission or refuse, on a non-discriminatory basis, to accept officials of a particular category.

The head of the mission and the members of the diplomatic staff are also referred to as diplomatic agents and they receive the highest degree of immunity. Article 29 of the Vienna Convention provides that the person of a diplomatic agent shall be inviolable. He or she shall not be subject to any form of arrest or detention and the receiving State has a duty to ensure their protection. Article 31 further provides that diplomatic agents enjoy complete immunity from the criminal jurisdiction of the receiving State and extensive immunity from civil and administrative jurisdiction. These immunities extend to the families of diplomatic agents if they are not nationals of the receiving State.

Members of the administrative and technical staff and their families, provided they are not nationals of the receiving State, enjoy similar immunities to diplomatic agents, apart from the fact that their immunity from civil and administrative jurisdiction does not extend to acts performed outside the course of their duties.

Members of the service staff who are not nationals of the receiving State enjoy immunity in respect of acts performed in the course of their duties. Private servants, who are not nationals of the receiving State, only enjoy exemption from local taxation, unless there is specific agreement which extends their immunities.

The immunities granted to diplomatic personnel can be seen to be quite extensive, although Article 41 provides that all persons enjoying such immunities are under a duty to respect the laws and regulations of the receiving State. From time to time, a particular instance of law breaking by a diplomatic agent receives widespread publicity and there are calls for the immunities to be restricted. It is always possible for immunity to be waived by the sending State under Article 32 of the Vienna Convention. Furthermore, in cases of serious abuse of immunity, it is possible for the receiving State to declare the diplomatic agent *persona non grata*.

7.4.5 Diplomatic communications

As has already been indicated, one of the functions of a diplomatic mission is to report on conditions and developments within the receiving State. This function can only be achieved if diplomatic staff enjoy a reasonable freedom of movement and communication. Article 26 of the Vienna Convention provides that all members of the diplomatic mission shall enjoy freedom of movement, subject to restrictions imposed on grounds of national security.

Article 24 provides that the archives and documents of the mission shall be inviolable. Perhaps the area of diplomatic law which has led to the greatest amount of debate concerns the diplomatic bag. Article 27 requires the receiving State to allow and protect freedom of communication for the mission and states that the official correspondence of the mission shall be inviolable. Paragraph 3 provides that 'the diplomatic bag shall not be opened or detained'. Apart from the requirement that the bag shall be externally marked and only used for diplomatic documents or articles intended for official use, there is no indication as to what constitutes the diplomatic bag. In practice, the 'bag' has a range from a small package to a collection of large crates. There have been allegations of the use of diplomatic bags to smuggle drugs and weapons. In 1964, a crate purporting to be an Egyptian diplomatic bag was opened at Rome airport and inside was found a bound and drugged Israeli. In 1984, a former Nigerian minister, Mr Dikko, was kidnapped in London and placed in a crate. The crate was taken to Stansted Airport by a Nigerian diplomat but, since the crate did not itself contain any external diplomatic markings, it was opened and Mr Dikko was released. A number of States have since argued that it is permissible to subject the diplomatic bag to electronic or other similar screening, although this has not been universally accepted. Certainly, the Draft Articles on the Diplomatic Courier and Diplomatic Bag 1989 adopted by the ILC provide for the absolute inviolability of the diplomatic bag. In practice, it seems that a State has limited scope for protest when its diplomatic bags are opened to reveal weapons, drugs or other non-official articles. The lesson for customs and other officials of the receiving State seems, therefore, to be that a diplomatic bag should only be opened when there is a 100% certainty of finding prohibited items.

7.5 Consular immunity

The primary function of consulates, vice consulates, and consular posts is to represent and deal with nationals of the sending State. They enjoy certain immunities but these immunities are not as extensive as those enjoyed by diplomatic agents. The law relating to consular relations is contained in the Vienna Convention on Consular Relations 1963, which entered into force in 1967.

As in the case of diplomatic relations, consular relations can only exist by agreement between the two States and, by virtue of Article 23 of the Convention, it is possible for the receiving State to declare a consular official *persona non grata*. The Convention provides for the inviolability of the consular premises and the consular archives and documents. Consular staff are entitled to freedom of movement, subject to the requirements of national security, and to freedom of communication. Consular officials do not, however, enjoy compete immunity from the local criminal jurisdiction. Although they are not liable to arrest or detention, save in the case of a grave crime, they can be subjected to criminal proceedings. Their immunity from civil and administrative jurisdiction only extends to acts performed in the exercise of consular functions. Members of the consular staff's family do not enjoy significant immunities.

7.6 International organisations

International organisations operate in particular States and will often require the same immunities and privileges as diplomatic missions if they are to carry out their functions effectively. Unfortunately, there is no general law applicable to the relations between international organisations and host States. Such immunities and privileges as particular international organisations enjoy must, therefore, be the subject of specific agreement between the organisation and the host State. Very often the privileges and immunities are provided for in the constituent charter of the organisation or in subsequent supplementary agreements. The position of the UN is dealt with in the Convention on the Privileges and Immunities of the UN 1946.

With the growth in the number of international organisations and the consequent increase in the number of agreements dealing with their immunities and privileges, there has been some debate as to whether there exist any rules of customary international law governing the matter. The Third Restatement of the Foreign Relations Law of the US seems to suggest that there is, stating that international organisations are entitled to:

> ... such privileges and immunities as are necessary for the fulfilment of the

> purposes of the organisation, including immunity from legal process and from financial controls, taxes and duties.

However, the English courts in the *International Tin Council* cases (1987–89) took the view that customary international law gave no such entitlement to international organisations. The position does not seem to be clear and the subject is currently being examined by the ILC.

IMMUNITIES FROM NATIONAL JURISDICTION

It has already been seen that the principal basis for the exercise of jurisdiction is territorial. However, international law recognises that certain people, things and events are immune from the enforcement of the local law. It should be understood that the immunity is from enforcement of the law and not from the law itself. It follows from this that it is always possible for immunities to be waived.

There are fours main categories of immunity.

- State immunity

  This is the immunity enjoyed by foreign States and the heads of foreign States. Traditionally, immunity was absolute and attached to all activities carried out by a foreign State. However, by the 20th century, the increasing involvement of States in commercial activity gradually led to demands for a more restrictive approach to immunity. A distinction was drawn between public acts (acts *jure imperii*) and private acts (acts *jure gestionis*) and many States would only grant immunity to acts *jure imperii*.

  Dunhill of London Inc v Republic of Cuba (1976).

  The Parlement Belge (1880).

  Krajina v The Tass Agency (1949).

  Trendtex Trading Corporation Ltd v Central Bank of Nigeria (1977).

  State Immunity Act 1978.

  ILC Draft Articles on Jurisdictional Immunities of States and Their Property 1986.

- Foreign armed forces

  It is usual for foreign armed forces to enjoy limited immunities from local jurisdiction. Such immunities are usually dealt with in the agreement under which the forces enter the foreign territory.

- Diplomatic and consular immunities

  There is no right to diplomatic or consular relations and abuses of the system of privileges and immunities may result in diplomatic or consular agents being expelled or in the breaking of diplomatic relations.

  Vienna Convention on Diplomatic Relations 1961.

  Vienna Convention on Consular Relations 1963.

  US Diplomatic and Consular Staff in Tehran case (1980).

- International organisations

  There is no general law applicable to international organisations and the immunities enjoyed by them will depend upon specific agreements. The position of the UN is dealt with in the Convention on the Privileges and Immunities of the UN 1946.

CHAPTER 8

STATE RESPONSIBILITY

8.1 Introduction

A corollary of binding legal obligations is legal responsibility for a breach of those obligations. This chapter is concerned with the general rules of international law which determine whether an international subject is in breach of its international obligations. The term 'State responsibility' reflects the fact that, historically, States were the sole subjects of international law. The term now covers the responsibility of all those with international personality. These rules are often referred to as second level rules, in that, while they seek to determine the consequences of a breach of a legal obligation, they do not concern themselves with the nature and content of that obligation. The obligation will be found in the law of the sea, the law of treaties, etc. However, in common with the majority of textbooks, reference will be made in this chapter to the particular content of the rules relating to the treatment of foreign nationals. The rules relating to the settlement of disputes arising from breaches of international obligations are dealt with in Chapter 11. It should be noted that responsibility will only arise where there has been a breach of international legal obligations; liability may arise even where there has been no breach of international law. Such liability is currently under consideration by the ILC.

In recent years, the area of State responsibility has been the subject of much work by the ILC, who have produced a set of Draft Articles on State Responsibility. Although these articles have yet to be adopted into a binding international convention, they do form the starting point for most discussions about the topic. Article 1 of Part I of the Draft Articles provides:

> Every internationally wrongful act of a State entails the international responsibility of that State.

According to Article 3, an 'internationally wrongful act' occurs when:

> (a) conduct consisting of an action or omission is attributable to the State under international law; and
>
> (b) that conduct constitutes a breach of an international obligation of the State.

It should be noted that international law is only concerned with the wrongful acts of one international person against another on the international plane. Such wrongful acts can be divided into two main categories: direct and indirect. Direct wrongs occur when the victim is the State itself, for example, when its territory is invaded by another State, or where the obligations of a treaty to which it is a party are broken by another State. Indirect wrongs arise when the victim is a national of the State and the wrong done to him or her goes unremedied. The issue remains one between two States and any reparation is a matter for the States to deal with. An indirect wrong would occur if a national was tortured by the officials of a foreign State.

8.2 Fault

There has been some debate as to whether the responsibility of States for unlawful acts or omissions requires an element of fault or whether liability is strict. The ILC Draft Articles provide no assistance in the matter and there are a number of conflicting authorities. Brownlie has argued that the nature of liability will depend on the precise nature of the particular obligation in issue and suggests that the discussions of the ILC tend to support this view.

8.2.1 Objective or risk responsibility

The view that seems to attract majority support is that an objective test should be applied to the actions of States. Provided that the acts complained of can be attributed to the State, then it will be liable if those acts constitute a breach of international law, regardless of any question of fault or intention. There are certain defences available, but the burden of establishing them will be placed upon the defence once the fact of the breach of an obligation is established. The most cited example of the objective test is to be found in the judgment of Verzijl in the *Caire* claim (1929). Caire was a French national who was asked to obtain a large sum of money by a major in the Mexican army. He was unable to obtain the money and was subsequently arrested, tortured and killed by the major and a number of soldiers. France successfully pursued a claim against the Mexican government, which was heard by the French-Mexican Claims Commission. The principal question for the Commission was whether Mexico could be responsible for the actions of individual military personnel who were acting without orders and against the wishes of their commanding officer and independently of the needs and aims of the revolution. Verzijl gave support to the objective responsibility of the State, according to which a State is responsible for the acts of its officials and organs even in the absence of any fault of its own. He continued by finding a State to be responsible:

> ... for all the acts committed by its officials or organs which constitute offences from the point of view of the law of nations, whether the official or organ in question has acted within or exceeded the limits of his competence ... [provided that] they must have acted at least to all appearances as competent officials or organs, or they must have used powers of methods appropriate to their official capacity.

Similarly, in the *Jessie* case (1921), the British-American Claims Arbitral Tribunal held the US responsible for the action of its revenue officers, who had boarded and searched a British ship on the high seas. The officers had acted in good faith, mistakenly believing that they were empowered to carry out the search by virtue of municipal law and an agreement between the UK and the USA. The tribunal laid down the principle that:

> Any government is responsible to other governments for errors in judgment of its officials purporting to act within the scope of their duties and vested with powers to enforce their demands.

8.2.2 Subjective responsibility

A number of writers, most notably Hersch Lauterpacht, have argued that the responsibility of States depended on some element of fault. Such fault is often expressed in terms of intention to harm (*dolus*) or negligence (*culpa*). A number of cases are commonly cited to support the subjective view. The *Home Missionary Society* claim (1920) arose following a rebellion in the British protectorate of Sierra Leone. During the course of the rebellion, property belonging to the Home Missionary Society was destroyed or damaged and a number of missionaries were killed. The US brought a claim on behalf of the Missionary Society against the UK. The tribunal dismissed the claim and noted that:

> It is a well established principle of international law that no government can be held responsible for the act of rebellious bodies of men committed in violation of its authority, where it is itself guilty of no breach of good faith, or of no negligence in suppressing insurrection.

Those advocating the objective doctrine have argued that the *Home Missionary Society* claim was concerned with a specific question of State responsibility for the acts of rebels (which is discussed at 8.3.4) and that the case cannot be used to establish a general rule.

Another case which has been cited in support of subjective responsibility is the *Corfu Channel (Merits)* case (1949). The case arose following the sinking by a mine of a British warship in Albanian territorial waters. The UK brought a claim against Albania arguing first, that Albania itself had laid the mines. However, it adduced little evidence on this point and its main argument was that the mines could not have been laid without the knowledge or connivance of the Albanian authorities. The ICJ found that the laying of mines could not have been achieved without the knowledge of the Albanian government. This being so, Albania's failure to warn British naval vessels of the risk of mines gave rise to international responsibility. In the course of its judgment, the court stated that:

> It cannot be concluded from the mere fact of the control exercised by a State over its territory and waters that that State knew, or ought to have known, of any unlawful act perpetrated therein, nor yet that it necessarily knew, or should have known, the authors. This fact, by itself and apart from other circumstances, neither involves *prima facie* responsibility nor shifts the burden of proof.

Lauterpacht subsequently remarked that 'the *Corfu Channel* case ... provided an instructive example of the affirmation of the principle that there is no liability without fault' (in Lauterpacht, INIT (ed),*Oppenheim's International Law*, Vol 1, 8th edn, 1955, Harlow: Longman, p 343). However, it is worth noting that the Soviet judge in the case understood the decision to be an application of the objective responsibility doctrine and dissented from it on that ground. He argued that responsibility could only arise on the basis of *culpa*, a more exacting test than mere fault, since it requires a wilful and malicious act or a culpably negligent act, that is, guilt rather than mere inadvertence or carelessness. Brownlie has stated (*Principles of Public International Law*, 5th edn, 1998, Oxford: OUP, p 442) that liability in the case arose out of the particular legal obligation of Albania identified by the court 'not to allow *knowingly* its territory to be used for acts contrary to the rights of other States' (emphasis added).

It is submitted that much of the confusion arising from questions of the nature of responsibility stems from the tendency to equate objective responsibility with the municipal law doctrine of strict liability and to regard strict liability as an absolute liability from which no exculpation is possible. It has already been indicated that objective responsibility does admit the possibility of defences. Discussion about the nature of responsibility highlights the dangers of discussing the topic in isolation from the substantive 'first level' rules of international law. It is for this reason that writers, such as Philip Allott, have criticised the whole concept of a separate category of 'State responsibility'. In an article written in 1988 ('State responsibility and the unmaking of international law' (1988) 29 Harvard International LJ 1), he wrote:

> In the terms of legal analysis, wrongdoing gives rise to a liability in the offender owed to others who have rights which may be enforced by legal processes. Liability is not a consequence of some intervening concept of responsibility. It is a direct consequence flowing from the nature of the wrong ... and the nature of the actual wrongful act in the given case.

In individual cases, what is important is the particular obligation which has been breached. As Brownlie has stated (*The System of the Law of Nations: State Responsibility*, 1983, Oxford: OUP, Pt I, p 40):

> It must always be borne in mind that the rules relating to State responsibility are to be applied in conjunction with other, more particular rules of international law, which prescribe duties in various precise forms. Indeed, the basic concept of responsibility is a necessary but not a

> sufficient condition for breaches of particular legal duties ... The relevance of fault, the relative 'strictness' of the obligation, will be determined by the content of each rule ... it would be pointless to embark on an examination of a question, framed in global terms, whether State responsibility is founded upon fault (that is, *culpa* or *dolus*) or strict liability: the question is unreal.

8.3 Imputability

As has already been stated, international law is concerned with the responsibility of international persons and, in the main, that will mean States. Because, ultimately, a State can act only through individuals, and individuals may act for reasons of their own, distinct from the intentions of their State, it becomes necessary to know which actions of which persons may be attributed, or imputed, to the State. A State will only be liable for acts which can be attributed or imputed to it; it is not liable for all the private actions of its nationals.

8.3.1 Organs of the State

Article 5 of part I of the ILC Draft Articles provides that:

> ... conduct of any State organ having that status under the internal law of that State shall be considered as an act of the State concerned under international law, provided that organ was acting in that capacity in the case in question.

Article 6 states that:

> The conduct of an organ of the State shall be considered as an act of that State under international law, whether that organ belongs to the constituent, executive, judicial or other power, whether its functions are of an international or an internal character and whether it holds a superior or a subordinate position in the organisation of the State.

This reflects the customary law position that a State is liable for the actions of its agents and servants whatever their particular status. Thus, when, in July 1985, French secret agents sank the Greenpeace ship *Rainbow Warrior*, France became internationally liable and the tribunal was not concerned with the issue of whether this act of State terrorism was ordered at a high or low level within the French government (*Rainbow Warrior* arbitration (1987)).

Article 7 extends responsibility to quasi-governmental organisations, that is, those organs which, although not part of the formal structure of government, exercise elements of governmental authority, when they act in a governmental capacity. The Commentary to the Draft Articles gives as an example the case of a railway company to which certain police powers have been granted.

Where one State, or an international organisation, has made available its representatives to another State, as, for example, where it sends members of its medical agencies to assist in an epidemic or natural disaster, responsibility for their actions lies with the receiving State. This is often provided for in the agreement under which such assistance is given and it is also reflected in Article 9 of the Draft Articles. The Commentary to Article 9 gives the specific example of the UK Privy Council acting as the highest court of appeals for New Zealand.

8.3.2 Individuals

Article 8 of the Draft Articles provides that:

> The conduct of a person or a group of persons shall also be considered as an act of the State under international law if:
>
> (a) it is established that such person or group of persons was in fact acting on behalf of that State; or
>
> (b) such person or group of persons was in fact exercising elements of the governmental authority in the absence of official authorities and in circumstances which justified the exercise of those elements of authority.

In the *US Diplomatic and Consular Staff in Tehran* case (1980), the ICJ considered the status of the students who initially took possession of the US Embassy in Tehran:

> No suggestion has been made that the militants, when they executed their attack on the embassy, had any form of official status as recognised 'agents' or organs of the Iranian State. Their conduct in mounting the attack, overrunning the embassy and seizing its inmates as hostages cannot, therefore, be regarded as imputable to that State on that basis ... Their conduct might be considered as itself directly imputable to the Iranian State only if it were established that, in fact, on the occasion in question the militants acted on behalf of the State, having been charged by some competent organ of the Iranian State to carry out a specific operation.

However, the court went on to find that the status of the students changed during the occupation of the embassy. On 17 November 1979, the Ayatollah Khomeini issued a decree which declared that the premises of the embassy and the hostages would remain as they were until the US handed over the Shah for trial.

The ICJ commented:

> The approval given to these facts by the Ayatollah Khomeini and other organs of the Iranian State, and the decision to perpetuate them, translated continuing occupation of the embassy and detention of the hostages into acts of that State. The militants, authors of the invasions and jailers of the

> hostages, had now become agents of the Iranian State for whose acts the State itself was internationally responsible.

In *Yeager v Iran* (1987), the Iran-US Claims Tribunal had to consider the status of 'revolutionary guards' who had detained Mr Yeager for a number of days. Iran argued that the conduct of the guards was not attributable to it. The tribunal stated:

> ... attributability of acts to the State is not limited to acts of organs formally recognised under internal law. Otherwise a State could avoid responsibility under international law merely by invoking its internal law. It is generally accepted under international law that a State is also responsible for acts of persons, if it established that those persons were in fact acting on behalf of the State. An act is attributable even if a person or group of persons was in fact merely exercising elements of governmental authority in the absence of official authorities and in circumstances which justified the exercise of those elements of authority.

On the facts, the tribunal found that the actions of the guards were attributable to the Iranian State.

The rule enunciated in Article 8 will generally apply to activities taking place within the territory of the responsible State. Where the actions complained of take place outside the territory of the responsible State, it appears that a slightly stricter test will be applied. This can be seen in the decision of the ICJ in the *Military and Paramilitary Activities in and against Nicaragua (Merits)* case (1986). One aspect of the case was the question of whether the activities of the contras (who, Nicaragua argued, were recruited, organised, financed and commanded by the US government) could be attributed to the US. The contras were acting outside US territory and the court took the view that:

> US participation, even if preponderant or decisive, in the financing, organising, training, supplying and equipping of the contras, the selection of military or paramilitary targets, and the planning of the whole of its operation, is still insufficient of itself ... for the purpose of attributing to the US the acts committed by the contras ... For this conduct to give rise to the legal responsibility of the US, it would have to be proved that the State had effective control of the military or paramilitary operations in the course of which the alleged violations were committed.

In general, a State will not be liable for the acts of private individuals which cannot be attributed to it and this is confirmed in Article 11 of the Draft Articles. However, responsibility may still arise if it is shown that there existed a duty to exercise due diligence and that diligence was not exercised. It was seen in Chapter 7 that States are under a duty to protect the premises of diplomatic missions within their territory. Therefore, a failure to provide adequate protection will give rise to responsibility should a diplomatic mission be attacked by a group of private individuals. It was for this reason that the Irish government admitted responsibility for the sacking by private individuals of the British embassy in Dublin in 1972.

8.3.3 *Ultra vires* acts

The mere fact that a State organ or official acts outside municipal law or express authority does not automatically mean that a State will not be responsible for their actions. Article 10 of part I of the Draft Articles provides that:

> The conduct of an organ of a State, of a territorial government entity empowered to exercise elements of the governmental authority, such organ having acted in that capacity, shall be considered as an act of the State under international law even if, in the particular case, the organ exceeded its competence according to international law or contravened instructions concerning its activity.

An act may be attributed to a State even where it is beyond the legal capacity of the official involved, providing, as Verzijl noted in the *Caire* claim, that the officials 'have acted at least to all appearances as competent officials or organs or ... have used powers or methods appropriate to their official capacity'. In the words of the Commentary to the ILC Draft Articles: 'The State cannot take refuge behind the notion that, according to the provisions of its legal system, those actions or omissions ought not to have occurred or ought to have taken a different form.'

In the *Union Bridge Company* claim (1924), a British government official wrongly appropriated neutral property during the Boer War. The arbitration tribunal held Britain liable and commented:

> That liability is not affected either by the fact that [the official appropriated the property] under a mistake as to the character and ownership of the material or that it was a time of pressure and confusion caused by war, or by the fact, which, on the evidence, must be admitted, that there was no intention on the part of the British authorities to appropriate the material in question.

The *Youman's* claim (1926) arose from a situation in which Mexican troops, who were sent to protect US nationals besieged by rioters, joined in the attack, in which the US nationals were killed. The Mexican authorities argued that, since the soldiers had acted in complete disregard of their instructions, Mexico could not be responsible for the deaths. The tribunal recognised that a State might not be responsible for the malicious acts of officials acting in a personal capacity but held that a State would almost invariably be responsible for wrongful acts committed by soldiers under the command of an officer. The soldiers in this case had been under the immediate supervision and in the presence of their commanding officer.

The ILC recognised that there was a distinction between action by officials in a private capacity and action done in an official capacity, but provided little assistance on how the distinction was to be made. It will, therefore, depend on the facts of the particular event. It would appear that, in the case of high level officials, there is a greater presumption that their acts are within the scope of their authority and Brownlie suggests that, in the case of military leaders and cabinet ministers, it is inappropriate to use the dichotomy of official and personal acts. An analogy may be drawn with the rules relating to diplomatic immunity: diplomatic agents enjoy the highest level of immunity from jurisdiction, whereas lower level diplomatic staff will only attract immunities in respect of activities carried out in the exercise of their official functions. An example of the distinction is seen in the *Mallen* claim (1927). Mallen, the Mexican consul in Texas was twice assaulted by the Deputy Constable of Texas. On the first occasion, the constable had met Mallen in the street, had threatened to kill him and had slapped his face. On the second occasion, the constable had boarded a train on which Mallen was travelling, attacked him and then demanded the train stop so that he could take Mallen to jail. The tribunal found that the first assault had been a private act and no responsibility on the part of the US could arise. However, on the second occasion, it was clear that the constable had taken advantage of his official position. It was established that the constable had shown his official badge to assert his authority and the tribunal pointed out that a private individual would not have been able to take Mallen to jail. It therefore held the US responsible for the second assault, since the constable had been acting with apparent authority, even though his behaviour was wholly unreasonable and had been motivated by a private vendetta.

8.3.4 Insurrectionaries

Article 11 of the Draft Articles makes it clear that the conduct of a person or persons not acting on behalf of the State will not be considered as an act of the State under international law. It therefore follows that the actions of rebels and insurrectionaries will not normally be considered as acts of the State and this is provided for in Article 14. However, the State is required to show due diligence, and may be liable if it has provided insufficient protection for aliens (the special protections for diplomatic and consular staff should be noted in this context).

Where an insurrectionary movement is successful and the revolutionaries take over the government, the new government will be liable for the actions of the insurrectionaries before they took power. In the *Bolivar Railway Company* claim (1903), the tribunal held Venezuela liable for the acts of successful revolutionaries committed before they had taken power. The conclusion was justified on the grounds that:

> Nations do not die when there is a change of their rulers or in their forms of government ... The nation is responsible for the obligations of a successful revolution from its beginning, because, in theory, it represented *ab initio* a changing national will, crystallising in the finally successful result ... success demonstrates that from the beginning it was registering the national will.

In *Short v Iran* (1987), the Iran-US Claims Tribunal considered the claim of an American national who had been evacuated from Iran three days before the Islamic revolutionary government took office. He was evacuated on the orders of his American employers because of the worsening situation in Iran at the time and he sought compensation from the new government of Iran for loss of salary arising out of what he alleged to be his expulsion from Iran. The tribunal stated:

> Where a revolution leads to the establishment of a new government, the State is held responsible for the acts of the overthrown government insofar as the latter maintained control of the situation. The successor government is also held responsible for the acts imputable to the revolutionary movement which established it, even if those acts occurred prior to its establishment, as a consequence of the continuity existing between the new organisation of the State and the organisation of the revolutionary movement.

The tribunal, however, went on to point out that the same rules of attributability apply to revolutionary movements as apply to States. In other words, it must be established that the acts complained of are the acts of agents of the revolutionaries and not the acts of mere supporters.

8.4 International crimes

A distinction is sometimes drawn between international crimes and international delicts. Article 19 of part I of the ILC Draft Articles provides that all breaches of international obligations are internationally wrongful acts. But an internationally wrongful act which results from the breach by a State of 'an international obligation so essential for the protection of fundamental interests of the international community that its breach is recognised as a crime by that community as a whole' constitutes an international crime. All other wrongful acts are international delicts. Article 19(3) lists some examples of specific international crimes:

(a) serious breaches of the law on peace and security;

(b) serious breaches of the right to self-determination;

(c) serious breaches of international duties on safeguarding the human being (for example, slavery, genocide, apartheid); and

(d) serious breaches of obligations to protect the environment.

The commentary to the Draft Articles makes it clear that an international crime is not the same as a crime at international law. It is States who are responsible for international crimes, whilst individuals bear responsibility for crimes at international law.

Many Western writers have argued that the concept of international crime is of no legal value and that, in principle, it cannot be justified. They argue that domestic criminal law involves a connection between criminal intention and a criminal act and that States, as institutions, are not capable of criminal intention. This view is countered by those who argue that the word 'crime' in Article 19 carries a different meaning from that it usually has. The purpose of classifying certain acts as 'international crimes' is to highlight their objectionable nature and to indicate that such acts constitute a threat to mankind as a whole. In consequence, all States have a legitimate interest and a right to invoke the criminal responsibility of a State and demand the cessation of the crime and the making of reparation. The concept of 'international crime' is very much tied up with the concept of *erga omnes* obligations, that is, obligations which are owed to the international community as a whole. The existence of such obligations was recognised by the ICJ in the *Barcelona Traction* case (1970).

8.5 State responsibility for the treatment of aliens

As was indicated at 8.1, a State may suffer injury indirectly when the victim of wrongful behaviour is one of its nationals. Not every injury suffered by an foreign national abroad will constitute an international wrong. The injury will only give rise to issues of State responsibility if it can in some way be linked to the foreign State. As was indicated at 8.3.2, a State will not generally be liable for the acts of private individuals but responsibility will arise if the State can be shown to have connived at or failed to take adequate measures to prevent injuries to foreigners, or if, after the event, the foreign authorities fail to make an adequate attempt to provide justice.

Where the respondent State is involved in the wrongful act itself, either through its organs or officials, it is appropriate to talk of *prima facie* breaches of international law. The State of the injured national has the right to intervene on the diplomatic level to insist that the respondent State remedy the wrong it has committed. The matter is on the international plane from the start, even if it only gives rise to State responsibility if the respondent State fails to provide adequate redress through local remedies.

8.5.1 Standard of treatment

One area of considerable controversy is the standard of treatment to be accorded to foreign nationals. A State will only be responsible for treatment of aliens which falls below this standard. There are two conflicting views. Most

Western States adhere to the concept of an international minimum standard of treatment. Every State is under a duty to treat aliens within its territory in accordance with this standard. This is so even if municipal law imposes a lower standard of treatment with respect to home nationals. This view was applied, in the *Neer* claim (1926), by the US-Mexican Claims Tribunal and, in the *Chevreu* case (1931), by an Anglo-French arbitral tribunal. Proponents of the international minimum standard have sought to argue that the concept is inextricably linked to the international law of human rights, which is discussed in Chapter 14.

The opposing view is that foreign nationals are only entitled to be treated in the same manner as home nationals. This national standard would imply that the only thing to guard against is discrimination against foreign nationals. Article 9 of the Montevideo Convention on the Rights and Duties of States 1933 reflected this view by providing that 'foreigners may not claim rights other or more extensive than those of the nationals'. The national standard has been most strongly advocated by the developing States in the context of nationalisation of foreign owned property. This topic is discussed in Chapter 15.

It seems clear that it is not possible to discern a general rule of international law relating to treatment of aliens. Much depends upon the particular rights being asserted. What is more certain is that it is for international law to decide which standard operates in a particular case and this is related to the general principle that provisions of municipal law cannot be used as a defence to breaches of international obligations.

8.6 *Locus standi* and the right to bring claims

The general rule is that it is only injured States which are able to bring international claims against other States for a breach of some international obligation. The principle was strictly applied in the second phase of the *South West Africa* case (1966), when the ICJ held that Liberia and Ethiopia had no legal interest in South Africa's treatment of the inhabitants of Namibia. Although both States had been original members of the League of Nations and, therefore, had certain rights under the mandate agreement between the League and South Africa, the court held that enforcement of the mandate was a matter for the League alone and individual members suffered no injury and therefore had no independent right to bring claims arising out of breaches of its provisions. Article 5(1) of the ILC Draft Articles on State Responsibility, Part II (1985) provides that an injured State is any State, a right of which is infringed by the act of another State, if such an act constitutes an internationally wrongful act. Article 5(2) lists a number of situations in which injury will have occurred and this includes breaches of treaty obligations, both bilateral and multilateral, together with breaches of customary international law. Thus, for example, breaches of the European Convention on Human Rights by a State party may be pursued by any other State party to the convention and there is no requirement that the victim of the human rights abuse should be a national of the claiming State.

Article 5(3) of the Draft Articles goes further by providing that, if the internationally wrongful act constitutes an international crime (see 9.4), then 'injured State' means all other States. This idea of collective responsibility is one of the most controversial areas of State responsibility and Article 5(3) cannot in any way be said to express an existing rule of international law. The concept of international crimes and *erga omnes* obligations is of particular relevance to claims arising out of human rights abuses, breaches of humanitarian law and environmental damage, and is further discussed in Chapters 13, 14 and 16.

8.7 Nationality of claims

Where a State has suffered directly from an internationally wrongful act, such as the breach of a treaty obligation owed to it, there will be little difficulty in establishing its right to bring an international claim. However, States may also suffer indirectly. Internationally wrongful acts can occur in respect of the treatment of individuals or corporations. In such situations, the claiming State needs to establish its right to make a claim on behalf of the individual or corporation that has suffered injury. It should be noted that what is being discussed here is the right to bring claims, and that whether or not a State will actually bring a claim depends on many other considerations, discussion of which are outside the ambit of this book.

8.7.1 Individuals

States may often raise diplomatic protests about the treatment of individuals by foreign States and such protests are not confined to activities involving their own nationals. However, for a State to make specific representation involving claims to reparation and compensation arising from injuries to an individual or group of individuals, or damage to their property, it must be able to show that these individuals are, in fact, its nationals. The basic rule is that the victim must be a national of the plaintiff State at the time the damage was caused and remain so until the claim is decided. This rule was applied by the PCIJ in the *Panevezys-Saldutiskis* case (1939), the court stating that:

> In taking up the case of one of its nationals, by resorting to diplomatic action or international judicial proceedings on his behalf, a State is in reality asserting its own right, the right to ensure in the person of its nationals respect for the rules of international law. This rule is necessarily limited to intervention on behalf of its own nationals, because, in the absence of a special agreement, it is the bond of nationality between the

State and the individual which alone confers upon the State the right of diplomatic protection.

As indicated by the court, the general rule can be waived with the consent of the respondent State.

Problems may arise when the individual concerned has dual nationality. Article 4 of the Hague Convention on Certain Questions Relating to the Conflict of Nationality Laws 1930 provides that a State may not exercise protection in respect of one of its nationals against another State where that person also possesses nationality of that other State. However, State practice has not always accorded with this provision and its utility was doubted when, in 1984, the Iran-US Claims Tribunal had to consider a number of individuals who had dual Iranian-US nationality. Article 4 is probably good law when an individual has equal connections with both States of which he or she is a national. However, tribunals will look to see whether the individual has closer or more effective links with one State when deciding questions of the right to exercise diplomatic protection. A State will be able to bring a claim on behalf of its national even if he or she is a national of the respondent State, provided that the claimant State can establish the closer, more effective links with the individual concerned. This concept of an effective link was approved by the ICJ in the *Nottebohm* case (1955). In that case, the government of Liechtenstein instituted proceedings on the basis that Guatemala had acted unlawfully towards the person and property of Friedrich Nottebohm, a citizen of Liechtenstein. Guatemala disputed Liechtenstein's right to bring the case. Mr Nottebohm had been born in Germany in 1881. In 1905, he had gone to Guatemala and taken up residence there. He continued to travel to Germany and other countries on business and retained his German nationality. He made a few visits to Liechtenstein where his brother lived. While visiting his brother, in 1939, he applied for and obtained Liechtenstein nationality. He subsequently had obtained a Guatemalan visa for his Liechtenstein passport and returned to Guatemala. The essential question for the court was whether the nationality conferred on Nottebohm in 1939 could be relied upon as against Guatemala in justification of the commencement of proceedings. The court acknowledged that the granting of nationality was a matter of municipal law but found that the right to exercise diplomatic protection of nationals was a matter of international law, which the ICJ was entitled to determine. The court stated that:

> According to the practice of States, to arbitral and judicial decisions and to the opinions of writers, nationality is a legal bond having as its basis a social fact of attachment, a genuine connection of existence, interests and sentiments, together with the existence of reciprocal rights and duties. It may be said to constitute the juridical expression of the fact that the individual upon whom it is conferred ... is in fact more closely connected with the population of the State conferring nationality than with that of any other State. Conferred by a State, it only entitles that State to exercise protection vis à vis another State, if it constitutes a translation into juridical

terms of the individual's connection with the State which has made him its national.

The court found that Nottebohm had little real connection with Liechtenstein, whereas he had been settled in Guatemala for 34 years and had an intention to remain there. His connection with Guatemala was therefore far stronger than any connection with Liechtenstein and, consequently, Liechtenstein was not entitled to extend its protection over him vis à vis Guatemala.

In the same year as the *Nottebohm* case, the Italian-US Conciliation Commission considered the *Merge* claim. The claimant had both US and Italian nationality and the tribunal found that:

> The principle, based on the sovereign equality of States, which excludes diplomatic protection in the case of dual nationality, must yield before the principle of effective nationality wherever such nationality is that of the claiming State.

This *dictum* was subsequently approved and found to be an expression of customary international law by the Iran-US Claims Tribunal.

8.7.2 Corporations and their shareholders

Prima facie, a corporation has the nationality of the State where it was incorporated. The problem arises in the fact that companies may be incorporated in States with which they have very little connection. The right of States to bring claims on behalf of shareholders was discussed in the *Barcelona Traction* case (1970). The Barcelona Traction, Light and Power Company was a holding company incorporated in Canada in 1911 to develop and establish an electricity company in Spain. It created three subsidiary companies in Canada (most of the shares of which it owned) and a number of operating and concessionary companies in Spain. The case arose following action taken by Spain, which resulted in the company being declared bankrupt. Belgium sought to bring a claim based upon the allegation that most of Barcelona Traction's shares were owned by Belgian nationals and companies, mainly by a company called Sidro, the principal shareholder of which was another company called Sofina, in which Belgian interests were again predominant. Spain argued that the injury had been done to the company rather than its shareholders and therefore Belgium lacked *locus standi* to bring the claim. The court found that, although shareholders had suffered, it was only as a result of wrongs done to the company. The court adopted the municipal law concept of the corporate veil and the distinction to be drawn between the personality of the company and its individual shareholders. As far as diplomatic protection was concerned, the court stated that:

> The traditional rule attributes the right of diplomatic protection of a corporate entity to the State under the laws of which it is incorporated and

> in whose territory it has its registered office. These two criteria have been confirmed by long practice and by numerous international instruments.

It went on to acknowledge that there were situations where some further degree of connection was necessary but that no absolute test of 'genuine connection' existed in international law. It further suggested that there may be situations where:

> If in a given case it is not possible to apply the general rule that the right of diplomatic protection of a company belongs to its national State, considerations of equity might call for the possibility of protection of the shareholders in question by their own national State.

However, such a situation did not arise in the *Barcelona Traction* case and, therefore, the court rejected the Belgian claim. Such situations may arise where the company itself no longer exists or, more commonly, where it is the national State of the company that actively injures the company.

8.8 Exhaustion of local remedies

An important rule applicable to indirect injuries to States is that a claim will not be admissible on the international plane unless the individual or corporation has exhausted the remedies provided by the local State. The rule is justified by political and practical considerations. It allows the local State to redress any wrong that has been committed before the matter reaches the level of international dispute settlement. In the *Norwegian Loans* case (1957), Judge Lauterpacht commented that:

> The requirement of exhaustion of local remedies is not a purely technical or rigid rule; it is a rule which international tribunals have applied with a considerable degree of elasticity.

In particular, international tribunals are only concerned with effective local remedies. The rule was considered in the *Ambatelios* arbitration (1956), which arose following a contractual dispute between a Greek national and the UK. Mr Ambatelios failed to call a vital witness and also failed to take advantage of the opportunity of taking the case to the Court of Appeal. The Commission of Arbitration found that it was up to the defendant State to prove the existence in its municipal law of effective remedies which have not been used. The commission stated that:

> Local remedies includes not only reference to the courts and tribunals, but also the use of the procedural facilities which municipal law makes available to litigants before such courts and tribunals. It is the whole system of legal protection, as provided by municipal law, which must have been put to the test before a State, as the protector of its nationals, can prosecute the claim on the international plane.

An individual or corporation does not need to exhaust all appeal mechanisms if such appeals are clearly going to prove futile. In the *Finnish Shipowners* arbitration (1934), the UK objected to the Finnish claim on the basis that the Finnish nationals had failed to appeal against a decision of the UK's Admiralty Transport Arbitration Board. The international arbitrator accepted the Finnish argument that, in the particular case, the Court of Appeal would have been unable to overturn the finding of fact made by the Arbitration Board and that an appeal would therefore have made no difference. Finland was therefore within its rights to pursue the claim on the international plane.

It should be emphasised that the requirement of the exhaustion of local remedies only applies to indirect wrongs and is not relevant where the claimant State has suffered direct injury. Thus, the rule did not apply in the *Aerial Incident of 27 July 1955* case (1956), which arose following the shooting down of an Israeli aircraft over Bulgaria. There may be some confusion where a claim arises following injury to nationals which is in breach of treaty provisions. A breach of a treaty obligation would normally be considered to amount to a direct wrong but, where the treaty is invoked on behalf of nationals, the local remedies rule will generally still apply. The point was considered by the ICJ in the *Elettronica Sicula SpA (ELSI)* case (1989). The US brought a claim against Italy following the nationalisation of ELSI, an Italian corporation wholly owned by two US corporations. Italy claimed that local remedies had not been exhausted, while the US argued that the rule did not apply since it was claiming compensation for the two US companies on the basis of the Treaty of Friendship, Commerce and Navigation 1948 between the US and Italy. It therefore sought to argue that the breach of treaty amounted to a direct international wrong. The ICJ found, however, that the principal issue in the case was the injury suffered by the US corporations and it was not possible to separate this from the direct wrong of the breach of treaty. It stated that the parties to treaties could expressly agree that the local remedies rule would or would not apply but, in the absence of any relevant agreement, where a claim was partly based on injury suffered by nationals, the rule would be presumed to apply. Having dealt with the general issues involved, the court then found that, in the particular case, local remedies had been exhausted.

8.9 Defences and justifications

In certain circumstances, a breach of an international obligation imputable to a State may not give rise to international responsibility. Chapter V of the ILC's Draft Articles, Part I, indicates a number of circumstances which will 'preclude wrongfulness' and thus provide a defence to international claims. State responsibility will not arise in the following situations:

(a) where the defendant State was coerced into committing the wrongful act by another State;

(b) where the defendant State had acted with the consent of the harmed State;

(c) where the defendant State was merely taking permissible counter-measures. Actions involving the use of armed force are excluded from this category of defence; and

(d) where the defendant State's officials acted under force majeure or extreme distress and were not wilfully seeking the harm caused. The standard of proof in such cases is high.

The Draft Articles also allow two justifications for wrongful action: necessity and self-defence. Necessity will only justify wrongful action if the act was the only means of safeguarding an essential State interest against a grave and imminent peril, and the act did not seriously impair an essential interest of the State to whom the obligation was owed. For example, in 1967, the Liberian tanker the *Torrey Canyon* went aground off the UK coast, outside territorial waters, spilling large quantities of oil. After several salvage attempts, the UK finally bombed the ship to burn and disperse the oil. The ILC took the view that this action was justified by necessity. Self defence justifies an otherwise wrongful act if the measures adopted in self-defence are taken in conformity with the UN Charter. The topic of self-defence is further discussed in Chapter 12. Neither justification will be available in the case of a violation of a peremptory norm of international law (*jus cogens*).

8.10 Remedies for international wrongs

In the *Chorzow Factory* case (1928), the PCIJ was called upon to consider the consequences of the illegal expropriation by Poland of a factory in Upper Silesia. In the course of its judgment, the court stated that:

> The essential principle contained in the notion of an illegal act – a principle which seems to be established by international practice and in particular the decisions of arbitral tribunals – is that reparation must, as far as possible, wipe out all the consequences of the illegal act and re-establish the situation which would, in all probability, have existed if that act had not been committed.

It seems to be accepted law that the first consideration, following a breach of an international obligation, should be the restoration of the status quo that existed before the wrongful act was committed. Territorial disputes can often readily be settled by means of restitution and, in the *Temple of Preah Vihear* case (1962), Thailand was ordered to return to Cambodia objects it had illegally taken from the temple in Cambodia. Where restitution is not physically possible, or even in cases where it is not politically possible, compensation can be paid. The aim of any monetary compensation should be to wipe out the consequences of the illegal act. Compensation should cover all damage which has flowed from the unlawful act, subject to principles of remoteness.

In some cases, monetary compensation will not be an appropriate remedy. In such cases, reparation can be made by satisfaction, which may involve apologising, acknowledging guilt, or accepting the award of a declaratory judgment. For example, in the *Rainbow Warrior* case, the French government did belatedly apologise to the victims of the sinking of the ship.

It was formerly thought that compensation would only be available for actual injury or damage suffered. This view was largely based on the fact that very often States would accept apologies or acknowledgments of guilt as sufficient reparation where no actual physical damage had been caused. However, it is now believed that compensation can be awarded for non-material damage. In the *I'm Alone* case (1933), the *I'm Alone*, a ship registered in Canada, was sunk by US coastguards. The international tribunal found that the ship was almost wholly owned by US nationals and, therefore, found that no compensation ought to be paid in respect of the loss of the ship or its cargo. However, the US was ordered formally to apologise to the Canadian government and to pay $25,000 compensation as acknowledgement of the wrong done to Canada.

STATE RESPONSIBILITY

A departure point for any discussion of State responsibility is the Draft Articles on State Responsibility prepared by the ILC. Article 1 states:

> Every internationally wrongful act of a State entails the international responsibility of that State.

Such wrongful acts can be divided into two categories: direct and indirect.

Is fault necessary or is liability strict?

The position as to whether fault is necessary or liability strict is not settled and there is support for both the objective and subjective tests. The objective test means that a State is liable for wrongful acts regardless of any question of fault or intention – see the *Caire* claim (1929) and the *Jessie* case (1921). The subjective test involves an element of intention or negligence – see the *Home Missionary Society* claim (1920) and the *Corfu Channel (Merits)* case (1949). The best view is probably that the nature of liability will depend upon the precise nature of the legal obligation in question.

Imputability

A State will only be liable for acts which can be attributed or imputed to it. A State will be liable for its servants and agents, at whatever level, and also for those organisations which exercise elements of governmental authority. A State will be responsible for individuals if they were, in fact, acting on behalf of the State – see the *US Diplomatic and Consular Staff in Tehran* case (1980) and the *Nicaragua (Merits)* case (1986).

The fact that a State official is acting *ultra vires* does not necessarily absolve the State from responsibility. Much will depend on whether the officials have appeared to act within authority – see the *Union Bridge Company* claim (1924) and the *Mallen* claim (1927).

A State will not usually be responsible for the actions of insurrectionaries although, if the insurrectionaries are successful and establish a new government, it will be liable for the actions of the insurrectionaries before they took power – see the *Bolivar Railway Company* claim (1903).

International crimes and international delicts

The ILC Draft Articles provide that wrongful acts resulting from the breach of an international obligation 'so essential for the protection of fundamental interests of the international community' constitute international crimes. All other wrongful acts constitute international delicts. The significance of the distinction lies in the fact that all States have an interest and right to invoke the criminal responsibility of a State, whereas only those States directly affected have an interest and right in pursuing an international delict.

Nationality of claims

Where a State seeks to bring a claim in respect of the treatment of individuals or corporations, the issue of nationality of claims may arise. States may usually only bring claims on behalf of nationals – see the *Panevezys-Saldutiskis* case (1939). Where an individual possesses dual nationality, tribunals will investigate which State has the more genuine and effective link with the individual concerned – see the *Nottebohm* case (1955). Corporations have the nationality of the State of incorporation and tribunals will not entertain claims by other States on behalf of shareholders – see the *Barcelona Traction* case (1970).

Exhaustion of local remedies

Where States have suffered indirect injuries, no claim can be brought on the international plane until all effective local remedies have been exhausted – see the *Norwegian Loans* case (1957).

Defences and justifications

The four principal defences to wrongful action are coercion, consent, countermeasures (not including the use of armed force), and force majeure. There are two justifications for wrongful action: necessity and self-defence.

Remedies

The first consideration following the breach of an international obligation is the restoration of the previous status quo. Where restitution is not possible, compensation may be paid. Often monetary compensation will not be appropriate and reparation may be made by satisfaction, for example, apology or admission of guilt.

CHAPTER 9

THE LAW OF THE SEA

9.1 Introduction

The law of the sea is that law by which States regulate their relations in respect of the marine territory subject to coastal State jurisdiction and those areas of the sea and sea bed beyond any national jurisdiction. The law is an amalgam of treaty and customary rules. It should be noted that the law of the sea is distinct from admiralty or maritime law, which is concerned with relations between private persons involved in the transport of passengers or goods by sea.

The law has developed considerably since the end of the Second World War. The 1950s saw a dramatic rise in the number of claims and disputes involving the sea, and technological advances, together with changes in fishing methods, led to a realisation that there was a need for a clarification of the law. The ILC was requested to work on producing a codification of the law of the sea and their work resulted in the subsequent emergence of four conventions governing much of the law. The four conventions marked the first successful occasion in which the ILC was involved in an attempt to codify an area of international law. Many of the conventions provisions reflected rules of customary international law, although some provisions represented a new development and thus did not bind non-parties. The four conventions were adopted at the first and second Geneva Conferences on the Law of the Sea, in 1958 and 1960 (UNCLOS I and II). The conventions were:

(a) the Convention on the Territorial Sea and the Contiguous Zone (TSC), which entered into force on 10 September 1964;

(b) the Convention on the Continental Shelf (CSC), which entered into force on 10 June 1964;

(c) the Convention on Fishing and the Conservation of the Living Resources of the High Seas (FC), which entered into force on 20 March 1966; and

(d) Convention on the High Seas (HSC), which entered into force on 30 September 1962.

UNCLOS III convened in 1973 to reach agreement on a Law of the Sea Convention which would deal with many new areas of concern, including the Exclusive Economic Zone (EEZ) and the deep sea bed. The conference did not convene to discuss any pre-existing draft convention but had its origins in the Sea Bed Committee which had been established by the UN General Assembly in 1967. Advances in technology during the 1960s opened up for the first time the possibility of exploiting the rich resources of the deep sea bed and discussions about the regime for the deep sea bed took up much of the discussion at UNCLOS III. Because of the big difference in views between developing and developed States, it was thought that there was little use in adopting provisions of a new treaty by majority vote. The success of any new convention would depend upon the acceptance of the major maritime States, who could be outvoted by other participants at the conference. The procedure adopted at UNCLOS III was therefore to look for consensus in an attempt to obtain maximum support for the whole convention. Ultimately, largely as a result of a change in the government of the USA, the final text of the Convention was put to a vote in the traditional way. The outcome of UNCLOS III was the Law of the Sea Convention 1982 (LOSC), which entered into force on 16 November 1994, 12 months after Guyana became the 60th State to ratify it. The Convention has now been ratified by 126 States.

Much of LOSC was uncontroversial and reflected customary international law; however, the provisions relating to the deep sea bed were the site of major disagreement between developed and developing States. The final text of the Convention was unacceptable to many developed States and, for this reason, they did not sign the Convention. The Convention was ratified by many States during the 1980s and early 1990s but the opposition of the developed States continued. However, by the 1990s, the issue of the exploitation of the deep sea bed had become less important than it had seemed in the early 1970s, when UNCLOS III was sitting. During the early 1990s, attempts were made in the UN to reach a compromise and, on 28 July 1994, the Agreement relating to the Implementation of Part XI of the UN Convention on the Law of the Sea of 10 December 1982 (the part dealing with the deep sea bed) was adopted, and it entered into force on 28 July 1996.

Much of the law of the sea is concerned with the rights enjoyed by States in particular maritime zones. The principle zones that can be identified are:

(a) the territorial sea, over which the coastal State enjoys many of the rights which attach to land territory. The regime of the territorial sea is discussed at 9.4;

(b) the Exclusive Economic Zone (EEZ) and the Contiguous Zone, which refers to an area of sea beyond the territorial sea, over which the coastal State enjoys limited rights. The EEZ is discussed at 9.5;

(c) the continental shelf, which refers to the area of sea bed not covered by deep ocean. The continental shelf is discussed at 9.6; and

(d) the high seas, which is constituted by all those areas of sea not included in the territorial sea or EEZ. The regime of the high seas is discussed at 9.8.

9.2 Baselines

In determining the extent of a coastal State's territorial sea and other maritime zones, it is obviously necessary to establish from what line on the coast the outer limits are to be measured. This line is referred to as the baseline. The waters on the landward side of the baseline are internal waters and are an integral part of the territory of the coastal State. None of the provisions of the law of the sea apply to internal waters and a State enjoys full territorial sovereignty over them. The rules for delimiting baselines are to be found in Articles 3–11 and 13 of the TSC and in Articles 4–14 and 16 of the LOSC. The rules there stated are deemed to represent customary international law.

The starting point for drawing the baseline is the low water line along the coast (Article 3 of the TSC and Article 5 of the LOSC) and this will be used wherever the coastline is relatively straight and unindented. Different rules apply to:

(a) coastlines which are heavily indented or fringed with islands;

(b) bays;

(c) river mouths;

(d) harbour works;

(e) low tide elevations;

(f) islands; and

(g) reefs.

There is a general rule that, where States depart from the use of the low water line as a baseline, such departures should be clearly indicated on charts and due publicity should be given to the baseline adopted.

9.2.1 Straight baselines

Where the coastline is heavily indented or fringed with islands, it may be impractical for the baseline to follow exactly the low water mark along the coast. For example, much of the Norwegian coastline is heavily indented by fjords and it is fringed with many small islands and rocky reefs. It would be possible to draw a baseline which followed the low water mark but this would prove difficult and it would mean that ascertaining the outer limit of the territorial sea and other maritime zones would be confusing. Therefore, Norway adopted the practice of drawing straight baselines connecting the outer lying rocks and mouths of fjords along its coast. From the 1930s onwards, the UK protested about this Norwegian practice and, in 1949, the dispute was referred to the ICJ. In the *Anglo-Norwegian Fisheries* case (1951), the ICJ held that the Norwegian system of straight baselines was in conformity with international law. The court made it clear that the coastal State does not have an unfettered discretion as to how to draw the baseline and there was a requirement that such baselines follow the general direction of the coast. If a State does use straight baselines it must indicate that fact on charts and give due publicity to them.

Both Article 4 of the TSC and Article 7 of the LOSC permit the drawing of straight baselines where the coastline is 'deeply indented and cut into, or if there is a fringe of islands along the coast in its immediate vicinity'. Both conventions make it clear that such baselines should not depart from the general direction of the coast and the sea inside the baseline must be sufficiently closely linked to the land domain to be subject to the regime of internal waters. A further condition is that straight baselines cannot be used to cut off the territorial sea of another State from the high seas. There was an attempt at UNCLOS I to introduce a maximum length for a single straight baseline of 15 miles but the proposal did not obtain widespread agreement. In the *Norwegian Fisheries* case, the ICJ approved one baseline which was 44 miles long.

The normal rule remains the drawing of baselines using the low water mark and States are under no obligation to use straight baselines. Both TSC and LOSC make clear that the drawing of straight baselines should be limited to exceptional geographical circumstances. More than 50 States have, in fact, drawn straight baselines along part of their coasts. Not all of these States follow the rules or spirit of the law. For example, Colombia has a straight baseline of 131 miles in length, which encloses a smooth coast with no indentations and Vietnam has connected an island 74 miles from its coast to an islet which is 161 miles away, although it has been objected to by a number of other States. JRV Prescott, who has carried out a survey of State practice has stated ('Straight and archipelagic baselines', in Blake, G (ed), *Maritime Boundaries and Ocean Resources*, 1987, London: Croom Helm, p 50) that:

> It would now be possible to draw a straight baseline along any section of coast in the world and cite an existing straight baseline as a precedent.

However, the fact that a number of States have gone beyond what is permitted by the rules of international law does not mean that new customary rules emerge. As the ICJ stated in the *Norwegian Fisheries* case:

> The delimitation of sea areas has always an international aspect; it cannot be dependent merely upon the will of the coastal State as expressed in its municipal law. Although it is true that the act of delimitation is necessarily a unilateral act, because only the coastal State is competent to undertake it, the validity of the delimitation with regard to other States depends upon international law.

Reference should be made to the discussion of customary international law at 2.3 on the nature of State practice and the effect of objections to it.

9.2.2 Bays

International law has always recognised that bays have a close connection with land and that it is more appropriate for them to be considered internal waters rather than territorial sea. Customary international law therefore has long accepted that straight baselines can be drawn across the mouths of bays. The difficulty was in determining the amount of indentation required for a bay and the maximum length of a closing line. Article 7 of the TSC established clear rules, which are repeated in Article 10 of the LOSC. To establish whether an indentation is a bay, a line should be drawn across the natural entrance points of the indentation. A semicircle should then be drawn with the line forming the diameter. The area of this semicircle should be measured and compared with the area of the total indentation. If the area of water is greater than the semicircle, then the indentation is a bay. A closing line can then be drawn. If the closing line does not exceed 24 miles, it will constitute the baseline. If the closing line is greater than 24 miles, a closing line of 24 miles is drawn to enclose the greatest amount of water possible and the line forms the baseline. With respect to any part of the bay which remains unenclosed, the baseline will be the low water mark. A problem which has remained unresolved is how the natural entrance points to a bay are established. In *Post Office v Estuary Radio* (1968), the UK Court of Appeal had to decide whether the Thames estuary was a bay, in a case involving pirate radio broadcasting. The estuary's status as a bay depended upon where the closing line was drawn. No two points were obviously the entrance points to the estuary, although the Court of Appeal found in favour of the post office's contention that the entrance points could be located at a point which would mean the estuary satisfied the test of a bay set down in TSC.

These rules pertaining to bays do not apply where straight baselines are used, nor do they apply to historic bays. Historic bays are not dealt with in either the TSC or the LOSC but have long been a feature of customary international law, although it is clear that the regime attaching to historic bays depends upon the particular circumstances of each case. In some situations, a State may enjoy full sovereignty over an historic bay whereas, in others, it may only enjoy exclusive fishing rights. In *El Salvador v Nicaragua* (1917), the Central American Court of Justice held that the Gulf of Foncesa, which is surrounded by Nicaragua, Honduras and El Salvador, and which is about 19 miles across at its mouth, was 'an historic bay possessed of the characteristics of a closed sea', over which the three States held joint sovereignty. In 1973, Libya claimed the Gulf of Sidra as an historic bay and drew a closing line across it which is 296 miles in length. Several States objected to Libya's claims and the USA sent a naval squadron into the area, to emphasise the point that it considered the Gulf to constitute high seas. In 1981, the US shot down two Libyan aircraft flying over the Gulf and there seems little evidence that the bay is an historic bay.

The general rules applying to bays do not apply where the bay is bordered by more than one State, for example, Lough Foyle, which is bordered by Ireland and the UK. Such situations will normally be resolved by agreement between the States concerned but the general view seems to be that the baseline follows the low water mark and no closing line is drawn.

9.2.3 River mouths

Both Article 13 of the TSC and Article 9 of the LOSC provide that, if a river flows directly into the sea, the baseline shall be a straight line across the mouth of the river between points on the low water line of its banks. No limit is placed on the length of such a closing line. The rule applies only to rivers which flow directly into the sea. It does not apply to rivers which flow into the sea via estuaries, although this is not always an easy distinction. Estuaries occur where the river valley becomes flooded by the sea and the mouth of the river takes on a characteristic funnel shape. Estuaries are treated as bays, as was seen in *Post Office v Estuary Radio* (1968). Sometimes a river will carry down solid material which, if it cannot be removed by the action of the tides, forms alluvial deposits at the mouth of the river. As the deposits build up, the river will divide and subdivide as it flows into the sea and a delta will be formed. If the river enters the sea via a delta, baselines will be calculated by the low water line or by straight baselines.

9.2.4 Harbour works

Article 8 of the TSC provides that the outermost permanent harbour works, such as piers and breakwaters, which form an integral part of the harbour system, are to be regarded as forming part of the coast and can, therefore, act as the baseline. This provision is repeated in Article 11 of the LOSC, although the LOSC makes it clear that harbour works must be attached to the coast. Offshore installations and artificial islands are not to be considered as harbour works.

9.2.5 Low tide elevations

Article 11(1) of the TSC and Article 13(1) of the LOSC define a low tide elevation as a naturally formed area of land which is surrounded by, and is above, water at low tide but is submerged at high tide. Such elevations are sometimes referred to as drying rocks. Where a low tide elevation is situated wholly or partly at a distance not exceeding the breadth of the territorial sea from the mainland or an island, the low water line on that elevation may be used as the baseline for measuring the breadth of the territorial sea. Where the elevation is situated beyond the limits of the territorial sea, it cannot be used for the purposes of drawing baselines. Low tide elevations are also often used in the drawing of straight baselines.

9.2.6 Islands

Article 10(1) of the TSC and Article 121(1) of the LOSC define an island as a naturally formed area of land which is surrounded by water and which is above water at high tide. There is no condition as to size nor habitation, although, as regards isolated islands which are incapable of sustaining habitation, the rules on acquisition of territory discussed in Chapter 6 may be relevant. The general rules applying to baselines will apply to islands and this clearly poses no problems in the case of large islands, such as Britain. With the development of the regimes of the continental shelf and EEZ, the significance of small islands vastly increased. It is accepted that every island, no matter how small, is capable of possessing a territorial sea but doubts have been expressed as to whether small islands have continental shelves or EEZs.

Article 121(2) of the LOSC provides that islands will possess baselines for all maritime zones, but an exception is made in the case off rocks which are incapable of sustaining human habitation or economic life of their own. Such islands can only serve as the baseline for the territorial sea and contiguous zone and not for the continental shelf and EEZ. In practice, most uninhabitable island rocks lie immediately offshore and will be dealt with under the provisions relating to straight baselines and archipelagic States. Regimes applying to rocks which lie a long way offshore, such as Rockall which lies 240 miles west of the Outer Hebrides, tend to be or have been the subject of specific agreement or dispute resolution.

9.2.7 Reefs

A reef is formed by a ridge of rocks or coral which lies near the surface of the sea. An atoll is a reef which forms in the shape of a horseshoe or ring, usually enclosing an island. Reefs and atolls may be permanently submerged or, if exposed at low tide, may be situated from the mainland at a distance greater than the breadth of the territorial sea. They would, therefore, not come within the definition of low tide elevations and could not, therefore, be used for the purposes of drawing baselines. However, there are strong ecological reasons for holding that the sea on the land side of the reef, the lagoon, has the status of internal waters.

There was discussion about the status of reefs at UNCLOS I but no provisions were included in the TSC. The emergence during the 1960s of many independent States in the Caribbean and the Indian and Pacific Oceans possessing reefs disclosed a need to establish clear rules with respect to reefs and atolls.

Article 6 of the LOSC provides that:

> In the case of islands situated on atolls or of islands having fringing reefs, the baseline for measuring the breadth of the territorial sea is the seaward low water line of the reef.

The provision suggests that the rules will only apply to reefs which are exposed at low tide, although the ILC draft prepared for UNCLOS I provided that 'the edge of the reef as marked on charts should be accepted as the low water line'. It also remains unclear as to whether there is any limit to how far from an island a fringing reef can lie, although most geographical works refer to fringing reefs as lying near the shore of an island, with corals growing out from the shore to a depth of about 50 metres. Fringing reefs are to be distinguished from barrier reefs, which lie at some distance from the shore. Thus, Article 6 would not apply to the Great Barrier Reef, which, in places, is 150 miles from the coast of Australia. The environmental concerns relating to the Great Barrier Reef have partly been dealt with under the World Heritage Convention 1975, which is discussed in Chapter 16.

9.2.8 Archipelagos

'Archipelago' is the term used to refer to a group of islands. A question here arises as to whether the baseline should follow the low water mark of every island, or whether straight baselines can be used to connect the outermost parts of the group of islands to enclose the archipelago. The question was discussed at UNCLOS I but no final agreement was reached, although Article 4 of the TSC did allow the use of straight baselines in the case of coastal archipelagos, that is, groups of islands fringing a coast. In 1957, Indonesia announced that its territorial sea would henceforth be measured from straight baselines drawn between the outermost points on the islands forming the Republic of Indonesia. The waters within the baselines would be regarded as internal waters, although the peaceful passage of foreign vessels through them would be guaranteed. A similar measure was adopted by the Philippines. A number of States protested but the issue was not authoritatively settled. The concern of the major maritime States was that many of the archipelagic States straddled important shipping lanes and they feared that the adoption of straight baselines creating large areas of internal water might lead to a considerable loss of navigational freedom.

During the 1960s, a number of archipelagic States achieved independence and it became clear that there was a need for some agreement on the drawing of baselines in respect of such States. A new regime was introduced in Part IV of the LOSC. The new regime allows straight baselines to be drawn between the outermost points of the islands but would only apply in the case of 'archipelagic States'. An archipelagic State is defined in Article 46 of the LOSC as a State constituted wholly by one or more archipelagos. This definition does not include mainland States with non-coastal archipelagos, for example, Portugal, which possesses the archipelago of the Azores, lying 900 miles west of Lisbon. Nor would it apply to the Azores themselves, since they do not constitute a State on their own. The definition would seem to include States such as the UK and New Zealand, although they would not consider themselves to be archipelagic States. In any event, Article 47 of the LOSC merely provides that archipelagic State may draw straight baselines; it imposes no obligation to do so.

A number of conditions are set down regarding the drawing of straight baselines. They can only be drawn round the archipelago in such a way whereby the ratio of land to water is not more than 1:1 and not less than 1:9. This condition would itself exclude the UK and New Zealand and also the very widely scattered archipelagos. The baselines must not exceed 100 miles in length and must not depart from the general configuration of the archipelago.

9.3 Internal waters

Internal waters are those which lie on the landward side of the baseline from which the territorial sea and other maritime zones are calculated. As has already been seen, internal waters may include bays, estuaries, ports and waters enclosed by straight baselines. Internal waters constitute an integral part of the coastal State and the coastal State enjoys full sovereign rights over them. There is no right of innocent passage through internal waters such as exists through the territorial sea. Two particular aspects of coastal State's sovereignty over internal waters have given rise to much discussion: the right of access to ports and other internal waters; and the exercise of jurisdiction over foreign ships in ports. It should also be noted that a special regime applies to archipelagic waters

9.3.1 Rights of access to ports and other internal waters

The rules of sovereignty over internal waters mean that there is no general right in customary law for foreign ships to enter a coastal State's ports. This point was confirmed by the ICJ in the *Nicaragua* case (1986). Although coastal States will normally allow the entry of foreign merchant ships into their ports, there is no indication that such practice is supported by sufficient *opinio juris* to create a rule of customary international law. The only situation in which a foreign ship would be entitled as of right to enter internal waters would be where it was in distress and seeking safety. Such a situation would give rise to application of the general defences to State responsibility discussed at 9.9. It is clear that there are no general rights of entry to foreign warships.

Normally, States will nominate those of their ports which are open to international trade and will so designate such ports of entry for customs and immigration purposes. Customary international law allows States to close their international ports to protect their vital interests and it is for the State itself to define what constitutes its vital interests. States also have a wide discretion to prescribe conditions for access to their ports. It is usual for States to enter into bilateral treaties, usually known as Treaties of Friendship, Navigation and Commerce (FCN Treaties), which will set down rights and conditions of access to internal waters and ports. Among EU Member States, access to internal waters is governed by the general rules relating to freedom of movement and the free movement of goods.

Questions relating to the access of foreign ships will also arise in respect of navigable rivers and canals which also constitute internal waters. Access here will generally be much more restricted although, as was mentioned at 5.5, most international rivers and canals, that is, those which flow through the territory of more than one State, will be subject to specific international agreement.

9.3.2 Exercise of jurisdiction over foreign ships in internal waters

Since internal waters constitute an integral part of the territory of a State, application of the territorial rules of jurisdiction would imply that a State is entitled to enforce its laws against all ships and those on board within its internal waters, subject to the rules of sovereign and diplomatic immunity. However, since ships are more or less self contained units and are subject to the laws of the flag State at all times, coastal States will usually only enforce their laws in cases where their particular interests are involved. Local jurisdiction will be asserted when the offence affects the peace or good order of the port, for example, in the case of customs or immigration offences.

9.3.3 Archipelagic waters

The concept of archipelagic waters was created at UNCLOS III to deal with the situation arising where archipelagic States made use of straight baselines to enclose the archipelago. Although archipelagic waters form an integral part of the territory of the archipelagic State in the same manner as internal waters, they are subject to certain rights enjoyed by foreign States, which are set out in Articles 51–53 of the LOSC. These Articles provide that existing agreements and traditional rights must be respected and that foreign ships enjoy a right of innocent passage through the archipelagic waters, although the archipelagic State may designate reasonable sea lanes. Within the archipelagic baselines, a State may draw closing lines across river mouths, bays and ports on individual islands and thereby create internal waters.

9.4 Territorial sea

Throughout the history of modern international law, it has been accepted that coastal States enjoy certain rights in the seas adjoining their coasts. A distinction has long been made between the freedom of the high seas, over which no claims to sovereignty could be made, and territorial waters, over which coastal States enjoyed particular rights and undertook certain duties. What was not settled was the question of the breadth of the territorial waters and the precise nature of the rights and duties which existed there. There was also a question as to whether States automatically possessed a territorial sea or whether it had to be specifically and expressly claimed. Debate on these issues continued during the first half of this century and the question did not begin to be settled until the 1950s.

Article 1 of the TSC now provides:

> (1) The sovereignty of a State extends, beyond its land territory and its internal waters, to a belt of sea adjacent to its coast, described as the territorial sea.

Article 2 states:

> The sovereignty of a coastal State extends to the air space over the territorial sea as well as to its bed and subsoil.

These provisions are repeated in Article 2 of the LOSC. Both conventions state that sovereignty over the territorial sea is subject to certain conditions.

9.4.1 The breadth of the territorial sea

The breadth of the territorial sea has been a matter of controversy throughout history. Early writers used criteria of visibility, whilst Grotius and other 17th and 18th century writers suggested that territorial waters extended up to a point at which those waters could be controlled by a shore based cannon. There were differences as to whether this rule meant that territorial sea followed parallel to the coast or only existed where cannon were actually mounted. Towards the end of the 18th century, it was suggested that it made more sense for States to adopt a three mile limit along the whole of the coast, rather than to depend on the existence in particular places of coastal batteries. The three mile limit was chosen as a matter of reasonableness and convenience; contrary to a popular myth, it was not chosen as the actual range of cannon. The three mile rule gained widespread and rapid approval, although it was never unanimously accepted; for example, the Scandinavian countries consistently claimed four miles. During this century, there have been repeated attempts to reach agreement on the breadth of the territorial sea, which have failed. At UNCLOS II, a six mile territorial sea with an additional six mile fishing limit was proposed but failed to be adopted by a single vote. By the time UNCLOS III was convened, many States were claiming territorial seas of 12 miles or more. Article 3 of the LOSC sets the limit of the territorial sea at 12 miles. Since there has been no State which has persistently objected to 12 mile limits and a large number of States, including the UK, have now adopted the 12 mile limit, it would be fair to assume that the 12 mile limit has now been accepted as indicative of customary international law on the matter.

9.4.2 The right of innocent passage

The principle restriction on the exercise of sovereignty by the coastal State over its territorial sea is the customary rule of international law allowing foreign ships the right of innocent passage. The right clearly has two aspects which can be discussed further:

(a) passage

This includes not only actual passage through the territorial sea, but also stopping and anchoring in so far as this is incidental to ordinary navigation or rendered necessary by *force majeure* or distress. This point is reflected in Article 14(3) of the TSC. Article 18 LOSC expressly extends the distress provision to cover cases where one ship seeks to assist another ship, person or aircraft in distress. Apart from permitted stopping and anchoring, passage must be continuous and expeditious and foreign ships have no right to hover or cruise around the territorial sea. All submarines must navigate on the surface; and

(b) innocence

For a long time, the criterion of innocence lacked any clear definition. In 1930, the Hague Conference which was convened to consider codification of the law of the territorial sea adopted a text which read:

> Passage is not innocent when a vessel makes use of the territorial sea of a coastal State for the purpose of doing any act prejudicial to the security, to the public policy or to the fiscal interests of that State.

It was not possible, however, for a convention to be agreed.

The definition of innocent passage received full discussion in the *Corfu Channel* case (1949), which concerned the passage through the Corfu Channel of British warships. The ICJ considered that the manner of passage was the decisive criterion, holding that as long as the passage was conducted in a fashion which presented no threat to the coastal State it was to be regarded as innocent. Innocence itself was regarded as incapable of objective determination.

There was much discussion of various definitions in the lead up to the UNCLOS I and a compromise was reached with Article 14(4) of the TSC, which provides that:

> Passage is innocent so long as it is not prejudicial to the peace, good order or security of the coastal State. Such passage shall take place in conformity with these articles and with other rules of international law.

Article 14(5) goes on to State that:

> Passage of foreign fishing vessels shall not be considered innocent if they do not observe such laws and regulations as the coastal State shall make

and publish in order to prevent these vessels from fishing in the territorial sea.

A more precise definition has been achieved in Article 19 of the LOSC. The provision of Article 14(4) of the TSC is retained, but Article 19(2) goes on to list a number of specific activities that will be considered prejudicial to the peace, good order or security of the coastal State. These include:

(a) weapons practice;

(b) spying;

(c) propaganda;

(d) launching or taking on board aircraft;

(e) wilful and serious pollution;

(f) embarking or disembarking persons or goods contrary to customs, fiscal or immigration or sanitary regulations;

(g) fishing;

(h) research or survey activities;

(i) any threat or use of force in violation of the principles of international law; and

(j) any other activity not having a direct bearing on passage.

The list is not to be regarded as exhaustive and the initial criteria for judging the nature of the passage of foreign ships must remain Article 19(1), which repeats Article 14(4) of the TSC.

One particular issue which has raised controversy has been the extent to which the passage of foreign warships can ever be considered innocent. State practice is inconclusive and, although, in the majority of cases, foreign warships request and are given prior authorisation for passage by the coastal State, it is unclear whether this is a simple act of courtesy or amounts to sufficient *opinio juris* to create a binding rule of customary international law. A related problem arises with regard to nuclear powered vessels and ships carrying hazardous materials. The general rule would seem to be that such vessels do have a right of innocent passage although there are a number of conventions which set down requirements of notification and documentation. This topic is discussed further in Chapter 16.

9.4.3 The right to deny and suspend passage

The territorial sea is subject to the sovereignty of the coastal State, and the only right which foreign ships have, apart from any specific treaty provision, is the right of innocent passage. Consequently, once a ship ceases to be innocent, or steps outside the scope of passage, it may be excluded from the territorial sea. It also follows that a coastal State has the right to suspend or deny passage altogether where the passage of any ship would be prejudicial to peace, good order or security. Coastal States may also require ships to confine their passage to a particular sea lane.

9.4.4 Rights and duties of the coastal State

Article 17 of the TSC provides that:

> Foreign ships exercising the right of innocent passage shall comply with the laws and regulations enacted by the coastal State in conformity with these articles and other rules of international law and, in particular, with such laws and regulations relating to transport and navigation.

LOSC is more explicit, in that it allows the coastal State to legislate with regard to a number of specific issues:

(a) navigation;

(b) cable and pipe laying;

(c) fisheries;

(d) pollution;

(e) scientific research;

(f) customs; and

(g) fiscal, immigration and sanitary regulations.

The coastal State is under a duty to give publicity to such laws. There are some bars on legislation: in particular, it cannot be used to hamper the exercise of the right of innocent passage, nor can such exercise be subject to charge, although charges may be made for specific services, for example, for pilots or the use of rescue services.

The principal duty which is placed on coastal States is to give appropriate publicity to any danger to navigation of which it has knowledge and provide basic navigational services. Such duties can be seen as the necessary corollary of a genuine right of innocent passage.

9.4.5 Straits

A strait is a narrow stretch of water connecting two more extensive areas of sea. It is not defined in any of the law of the sea conventions but reference is made to particular rules which apply in the case of straits. Where straits form part of the high seas, then all States will enjoy freedom of navigation. Problems arise where the strait forms part of the territorial sea. As has already been seen, coastal States are able to suspend innocent passage through their territorial sea in certain situations. If the strait connects two areas of the high seas, such suspension of passage through the strait would affect the freedom of navigation on the high seas. The rule therefore developed, and was reflected in Article 16(4) of the TSC, whereby innocent passage could not be suspended in straits used for international navigation connecting one part of the high seas with another.

By the time of UNCLOS III, the extension of the breadth of the territorial sea in many cases to 12 miles and the creation of other rights for coastal States led to the issue of straits being considered again. The result is to be found in Part III of the LOSC, which concerns straits used for international navigation. The most significant development is the introduction of a new concept of transit passage. Article 38 of the LOSC provides that, in straits used for international navigation:

> All ships and aircraft enjoy the right of transit passage, which shall not be impeded.

The rule does not apply when alternative routes are available. Transit passage is defined in Article 38(2) as the exercise of freedom of navigation and overflight solely for the continuous and expeditious transit of the strait between one area of the high seas and another, or in order to enter or leave a State bordering the strait. There is no criterion of innocence to be satisfied, but ships and planes passing through straits must not act contrary to international law or the principles of the UN Charter. It has been argued by the majority of maritime States, most of whom have not signed the LOSC, that the right of transit passage is now part of customary international law.

The rules on transit passage do not oust those applicable under long standing conventions which regulate passage through particular straits, for example, the Montreux Convention 1936, which concerns the Turkish straits of the Dardanelles and the Bosphorus.

9.5 The exclusive economic zone (EEZ) and the contiguous zone

Following the Second World War, an increasing number of States made claims to extend their authority over ships in waters beyond the territorial sea. Such zones were known as 'contiguous zones 'and the rights within them had to be positively established in each case. In 1958, contiguous zones were given more widespread recognition in Article 24 of the TSC. This allowed States to claim contiguous zones up to a maximum of 12 miles (the territorial sea distance was still generally accepted as 3 miles at this time) for customs, fiscal, immigration and sanitary purposes. With the extension of the territorial sea, the LOSC extended the limits of the contiguous zone to 24 miles and this is generally accepted to be the customary law position.

The contiguous zone has lessened in importance with the development of the exclusive economic zone (EEZ). The concept developed from the view that fishery resources are not inexhaustible and there was widespread concern at the failure to adequately deal with resource management issues at UNCLOS I and II. The Fishing and Conservation of the Living Resources of the High Seas Convention (FC) 1958 had attempted to deal with the conservation of living marine resources but confirmed that all States had the right to engage in fishing on the high seas and only imposed a duty on States to co-operate in adopting such measures as may be necessary for the conservation of resources. The FC set down a procedure for settling disputes and only permitted States to take unilateral action where there was an urgent need for the application of conservation measures. In any event, such unilateral action could not discriminate against foreign fishermen.

In the meantime, many States had been seeking to establish exclusive fishing zones outside their territorial waters. In 1945, US President Truman had issued two declarations, one of which related to the continental shelf which is discussed at para 10.6; the other, the Proclamation with Respect to Coastal Fisheries in Certain Areas of the High Seas, proposed the establishment of fishery conservation zones in waters beyond the US territorial sea. In fact, this proclamation was never applied but a number of other States developed their own fishing limits, and the 12 mile fishing zone was recognised as a rule of customary law by the ICJ in the *Fisheries Jurisdiction* case (1974). Many States were claiming much larger exclusive fishing areas and the ICJ left unanswered in that case whether Iceland's 50 mile claim was legitimate. On the particular facts, it held that Iceland's unilateral extension was contrary to international law.

Negotiation at UNCLOS III led to fairly widespread acceptance of the concept of a maximum 200 mile EEZ and the ICJ, in the *Continental Shelf* case (1985) and the arbitral tribunal in the *Guinea/Guinea-Bissau* case (1985), has indicated that the EEZ now forms part of customary international law.

9.5.1 Rights within the EEZ

Article 57 of the LOSC provides that the EEZ can extend to a distance of up to 200 miles from the baseline. The regime of the EEZ provides that coastal States do not enjoy full sovereign rights but only sovereign rights for the purpose of exploiting, exploring, conserving and managing the natural resources, whether living or non-living, of the sea bed and subsoil and the superjacent waters. So, for example, a coastal State can set fishing quotas within its EEZ with a view to conserving resources. If the coastal State is unable to catch the amount of fish allowed by the quota then other States will be allowed access to take the remaining amount. The coastal State is not the owner, but rather the guardian of the natural resources of the EEZ. Within the EEZ, the coastal State can construct artificial islands and other installations for the purpose of exploring and exploiting the zone which are subject to the coastal State's exclusive jurisdiction. Although such installations are not to be regarded as islands and do not therefore possess territorial seas of their own, it is permissible for the coastal State to establish reasonable safety exclusion zones around them. Other States enjoy the right of free navigation, overflight, pipe laying and cable laying, provided they respect the rights of the coastal State, which is under a duty to ensure the safety of navigation.

It should be noted that the EEZ has to be specifically claimed; it is not inherent in statehood. At the present time, over 80 States have claimed an EEZ. There is further reference to the issue of marine resource management and conservation in Chapter 16.

9.5.2 Straddling stocks

It has been seen how the concept of an exclusive economic zone developed from the idea of fishery conservation zones. The traditional freedoms of the high seas includes the freedom to fish. There is, therefore, the potential for conflict between coastal States wishing to conserve resources within the EEZ and other States wishing to exploit the resources of the high seas. Fish obviously do not recognise the different maritime zones and problems can arise where stocks of fish straddle both EEZ and high seas: conservation regimes could be seriously undermined if overfishing occurred immediately outside the EEZ. Article 63(2) of the LOSC provides that coastal States should try to reach agreement with those States fishing in adjacent areas on necessary measures for the conservation of straddling stocks. However, as the depletion of fish stocks became an ever greater problem it was realised that the provision in LOSC did not go far enough. Accordingly, on 4 August 1995, the UN Agreement for the Implementation of the Provisions of the UNCLOS of 10 December 1982 relating to the Conservation and Management of Straddling Fish Stocks and Highly Migratory Fish Stocks was adopted. The Agreement sets out a number of principles for the conservation and management of fish stocks and establishes that such management must be based on the precautionary principle (discussed further in Chapter 16). The Agreement establishes detailed minimum standards for fish conservation and management. It will enter into force 30 days after the deposit of the 30th instrument of ratification or accession.

9.6 The continental shelf

Strictly speaking, the continental shelf is a geographical term to describe the sea bed, which is covered by shallow water of generally less than 200 metres, projecting from the coast before a relatively steep descent (the continental slope) to the deep sea bed. The breadth of the continental shelf varies enormously: off some parts of the Pacific coast of the USA, the continental shelf extends for less than five miles, while, in contrast, the whole of the North Sea constitutes the continental shelf.

The traditional freedom of the high seas meant that all States enjoyed the rights to explore the sea bed. Disputes began to arise as the oil reserves of the continental shelf became exploitable. In 1945, President Truman claimed exclusive rights to the resources of the contiguous continental shelf in the Proclamation with Respect to the Natural Resources of the Subsoil and Sea bed of the Continental Shelf. No outer limit to the claim was specified in the proclamation, although an accompanying press release indicated that the continental shelf was only considered to exist to a depth of 200 metres. A large number of similar claims followed and it became clear that there was an urgent need for the law to be clarified and settled.

The outcome of discussion in the 1950s was that the Continental Shelf Convention (CSC) was agreed at UNCLOS I in 1958. This provides, in Article 1, a definition of the continental shelf which includes the sea bed and subsoil to a depth of 200 metres or, beyond that limit, to where the depth of superjacent waters admits the possibility of exploitation. Part VI of the LOSC gives an amended definition in terms of maximum distance of 200 miles from the baseline or, exceptionally, to the geophysical limit of the continental shelf, up to a maximum of 350 miles.

9.6.1 Continental shelf rights

Part VI of the LOSC proved to be one of the least controversial sections of the convention and, for the most part, is generally regarded as being a codification of customary international law. This point appeared to be confirmed by the ICJ in the *Continental Shelf* case (1985). The rights of the coastal State over the continental shelf are inherent and, unlike in the case of the EEZ, do not have to be expressly claimed. The coastal State has exclusive rights to the exploitation and exploration of the natural resources of the continental shelf, although it may permit other States to undertake exploitation or exploration. Natural resources are defined in Article 2 of the CSC and Article 77(4) of the LOSC as:

> The mineral and other non-living resources of the sea bed and subsoil together with living organisms belonging to sedentary species, that is to say, organisms which, at the harvestable stage, either are immobile on or under the sea bed or are unable to move except in constant physical contact with the sea bed or the subsoil.

At UNCLOS I, sedentary species were said to include, 'coral, sponges, oysters, including pearl oysters, pearl shell, the sacred chank of India and Ceylon, the trocus and plants'. Disputes have arisen over the status of lobsters and crabs and, in 1963, Brazil raised protests over French fishing of langoustes on the Brazilian continental shelf. Adult langoustes are normally sedentary but will swim if pursued. The dispute was eventually settled by a compromise which allowed the French limited access to the langoustes.

Both the UK and the USA have indicated that they consider lobsters but not crabs to be sedentary species. What are excluded are species generally referred to as fish. Of course, rights to fish are dealt with in the EEZ regime. The rights pertaining to the continental shelf do not affect the status of superjacent waters.

As with the EEZ, the coastal State is permitted to establish artificial islands and other structures on the continental shelf and to authorise and regulate drilling. Safety zones up to a maximum of 5,000 metres can be established around such structures. Article 79 of the LOSC retains the right of all States to lay submarine cables and pipelines on the continental shelf, although they should not impede the coastal State's right to explore and exploit the area and the course of such pipelines and cables requires the consent of the coastal State.

One aspect of Part VI of the LOSC which has proved controversial and does not reflect customary law is Article 82, which provides that the coastal State must make payment to the International Sea bed Authority in respect of exploitation of non-living resources of the continental shelf beyond the 200 mile limit. The role of the International Sea bed Authority and the precise nature of charges is discussed at 9.9.

9.6.2 The status of the Channel Tunnel

Article 7 of the CSC provides that the convention:

> ... shall not prejudice the right of the coastal State to exploit the subsoil by means of tunnelling irrespective of the depth of water above the subsoil.

This provision is repeated in Article 85 of the LOSC, with the consequence that tunnels through the subsoil of the sea bed which begin in the mainland are governed by rules of customary international law. Tunnels which start from above the continental shelf itself will, of course, be subject to the provisions of the conventions. It seems to be widely accepted that the subsoil of the sea bed is capable of acquisition by States, and the right to tunnel beyond the limits of the territorial sea have long been recognised, with the condition that such tunnelling does not affect or endanger the surface of the sea. Where a tunnel connects two States, the delimitation of jurisdiction would have to be made by agreement between the States concerned. When the Channel Tunnel Treaty 1986 between the UK and France was signed, the UK was still only claiming a three mile territorial sea; thus, much of the tunnel was below the high seas. Although both the UK and France now claim 12 mile territorial seas, part of the Channel Tunnel remains under the high seas. The Channel Tunnel Treaty provides that the frontier between the UK and France shall be at the point of delimitation of the continental shelf. The UK Channel Tunnel Act 1987 provides, in s 10, that the tunnel system as far as the frontier constitutes UK territory. As the trains passing through the Tunnel travel at high speed, it is clear that jurisdictional problems could arise in deciding whether offences committed on board were subject to French or UK jurisdiction. Such problems have been resolved by agreement between the two States on such matters as powers of arrest and the siting of customs and immigration offices.

9.7 Delimitation of Maritime Zones

A major cause of disputes between States is the delimitation of maritime boundaries. problems can arise in determining the extent of one State's maritime zones, or disputes may arise between adjacent or opposite States as to how maritime territory is to be apportioned. It is extremely difficult to set down any universally accepted rules, since each case will depend very much on its own particular facts. Very often, maritime boundaries will be settled between neighbouring States in specific bilateral agreements. There are, however, a number of guidelines that can be identified.

In the case of delimitation between opposite States, the normal practice has been to agree upon the median line. Practice in delimiting the boundary between adjacent States has been less consistent. Considerable use has been made of the equidistance principle, which involves drawing a median line outwards from the boundary on the shore. other criteria have been used, for example, by drawing a line perpendicular to the general direction of the coast. Some maritime boundaries follow the line of latitude passing through the point where the land boundaries meet the sea. In all cases, it is possible that special circumstances, such as the presence of offshore islands or the configuration of the coast, or claims based on an historic title, will demand the adopting of some other boundary line by agreement between the States. With regard to the territorial sea, these general principles are reflected in Article 12 of the TSC and Article 15 of the LOSC.

9.7.1 Delimitation of the continental shelf and the EEZ

Given the areas of sea and sea bed involved, it is not uncommon for two or more States, either opposite or adjacent, to share the continental shelf and the EEZ. Many issues of delimitation have been dealt with by agreement but there have been a number of disputes which have required settlement by international tribunal. Through looking at the agreements and the decisions of tribunals, a number of principles governing delimitation can be ascertained.

Under Article 6 of the CSC, delimitation was to be by agreement or, failing that, in the case of opposite States, the boundary should be the median line, every point of which is equidistant from the nearest point of the baselines of each State. This rule could be departed from if there were special circumstances. In the case of adjacent States, in the absence of an agreement, the boundary should be determined by application of the principle of equidistance from the nearest point of the baselines of each State, unless special circumstances justify some other boundary. In the *North Sea Continental Shelf* cases (1969), the ICJ refused to accept that the equidistance principle was a rule of customary international law and, thus, it was not binding on West Germany, which was not at the time a party to the CSC. Instead, the court seemed to favour the application of equitable principles to ensure that each State had a fair allocation of continental shelf which reflected the general configuration and length of the coastlines of the claimant States.

In the *Anglo-French Continental Shelf* arbitration (1979), an *ad hoc* Court of Arbitration was called upon to consider the delimitation of the continental shelf between France and the UK. Both States were parties to the CSC but were unable to reach an agreement. The court accepted that Article 6 formulated a single special circumstances/equidistance rule rather than two separate rules. This meant that there was no requirement to prove special circumstances; the court was only obliged to apply the equidistance principle if no other boundary was justified by special circumstances. The court understood this to require it to ensure an equitable delimitation. It stated that:

> Even under Article 6, it is the geographical and other circumstances of any given case which indicate and justify the use of the equidistance method as the means of achieving an equitable solution rather than the inherent quality of the method as a legal norm of delimitation.

In the both the *Continental Shelf* cases (1982) and (1985) involving Libya, the ICJ stressed the principles of equity and recognised that there should be a reasonable degree of proportionality between the area of shelf appertaining to a State and the length of its coastline. The customary law requirement simply that an equitable result is achieved in delimitation of continental shelf and EEZ boundaries was confirmed in both the *Gulf of Maine* case (1984) and the *Guinea/Guinea-Bissau Maritime Delimitation* case (1985). The most recent case concerning delimitation of the continental shelf and the EEZ involved Denmark and Norway (*Case Concerning Maritime Delimitation in the Area Between Greenland and Jan Mayen* (1993)), where the ICJ again confirmed the need for delimitation to be made according to equitable principles. The case is notable for the separate opinion of Judge Weeramantry, who discussed the role of equity in international law at some length. Article 83 of the LOSC provides that delimitation of the continental shelf between opposite or adjacent States shall be achieved by agreement on the basis of international law in order to achieve equitable principles. If no agreement can be reached, States are required to seek peaceful settlement of the dispute according to Part XV of the convention. It seems, therefore, that the main rule of international law regarding the delimitation of the continental shelf and the EEZ is that an equitable distribution shall be achieved. It therefore follows that each case will depend upon its particular facts, although factors such as length and configuration of coastline will be significant.

9.8 High seas

Traditionally, the high seas were defined as 'all parts of the sea not included in the territorial sea or in the internal waters of a State' (Article 1 of the HSC). With the advent of the EEZ and the concept of archipelagic waters, this definition has had to be modified. Article 86 of the LOSC states that the high seas rules apply to:

> ... all parts of the sea that are not included in the EEZ, in the territorial sea or in the internal waters of a State, or in the archipelagic waters of an archipelagic State.

The dominant principle on the high seas is the presumption of the exclusiveness of flag State jurisdiction. The legal concept of the high seas also extends to the superjacent air space. It used to extend also to the sea bed, but the emergence of special regimes for the continental shelf and the sea bed beyond national jurisdiction has eroded this wider definition.

The high seas are open to all States and no State may validly purport to subject any part of them to its sovereignty (Article 2 of the HSC, Articles 87 and 89 of the LOSC). This is a fundamental rule of customary international law, although it has not always been so. In the 15th and 16th centuries, national claims were made to sovereignty over extensive areas of the oceans. In 1493, for example, Pope Alexander VI divided the Atlantic Ocean between Spain and Portugal. It was during the great period of maritime exploration in the 17th century that the present rules began to emerge. Grotius, in his book *Mare Liberum,* argued for the importance of freedom of navigation and, by the 19th century, it was settled that the high seas were juridically distinct from territorial waters and were not susceptible to appropriation by any State.

9.8.1 Freedom of the high seas

From the rule that no State can subject areas of the high seas to its sovereignty or jurisdiction, it follows that no State has the right to prevent ships of other States from using the high seas for any lawful purpose. Article 2 of the HSC listed the freedoms of navigation, fishing, laying of submarine cables and pipelines and overflight as examples of high seas freedoms but accepted that the list was not exhaustive. All exercise of such freedoms shall be with reasonable regard to the interests of other States; for example, the stringing out of long fishing lines across busy shipping lanes would not be permissible. The exercise of the freedom of the high seas is, of course, subject to the general rules of international law, such as those governing the use of force. The list in Article 2 has been extended by Article 87 of the LOSC to include the freedom to construct artificial islands and other installations and freedom of scientific research. But the LOSC also places greater restrictions on some of the freedoms, particularly in relation to the sea bed and continental shelf. The fact that both conventions give non-exhaustive lists of freedoms means that arguments do ensue over what other freedoms exist. It is generally accepted that some naval manoeuvres and conventional weapons testing may be carried out on the high seas, despite the fact that Article 88 of the LOSC provides that the high seas should be used for peaceful purposes. Mariners are notified of the areas and times at which these take place, and, although they are not usually forbidden to enter the areas and care is taken to avoid busy areas of the sea, there is a clear expectation that foreign vessels should keep out of such areas.

The position with regard to nuclear weapons testing is slightly different. At UNCLOS I, the Soviet Union had proposed that nuclear testing should be expressly prohibited by HSC, but the conference agreed to refer the matter to the UN General Assembly. In 1963, the Nuclear Test Ban Treaty came into force, which expressly prohibits nuclear testing on the high seas. An opportunity to establish whether such testing was contrary to international law was missed in the *Nuclear Tests* cases (1974). France, which was not a party to the Nuclear Test Ban Treaty, had been carrying out tests in the South Pacific, to which New Zealand, Australia and a number of other States objected. New Zealand and Australia sought a declaration from the ICJ that such tests were unlawful but, before the case was heard, France announced it would henceforth cease such tests. The ICJ therefore decided that there was no longer a case to hear. The use of nuclear weapons in armed conflict is discussed in Chapter 13.

9.8.2 Jurisdiction on the high seas

In general, the flag State, the State which has granted to a ship the right to sail under its flag, has the exclusive right to exercise legislative and enforcement jurisdiction over its ships on the high seas (Article 6 of the HSC and Article 92 of the LOSC). The fiction that a ship is a floating piece of territory is not now approved. The exclusiveness of the flag State's jurisdiction is not, however, absolute. It admits of several exceptions, in which other States share legislative or enforcement jurisdiction, or both, with the flag State.

9.8.2.1 The flagging of ships

Traditionally, it has been up to each State to decide itself the grounds on which it will grant a ship the right to fly its flag. The only restriction on this right was that a State could not confer its 'nationality' on a vessel already under the flag of another State, except in consequence of a change of registration. This position was confirmed in Articles 5 and 6 of the HSC. However, in addition to the traditional doctrine, the HSC attempted to impose a requirement that there be a genuine link between ships and the flag State. Article 5(1) of the HSC provides that:

> There must exist a genuine link between the State and the ship; in particular, the State must effectively exercise its jurisdiction and control in administrative, technical and social matters over ships flying its flag.

The requirement of a genuine link was repeated in Article 91 of the LOSC. The practice of States, however, has not always followed the conventions and there is still widespread use of 'flags of convenience', resulting in there being an absence of any genuine link between flag State and ship. The requirement of a genuine link was also questioned during the Iran-Iraq War and the run up to the Gulf War, when the practice of 're-flagging' oil tankers was used to bring the tankers of smaller States under the protection of the US, UK and Soviet navies. Both the HSC and the LOSC require that ships sail under the flag of one State only and ships which sail under more than one flag are considered to be without nationality.

9.8.2.2 Collisions at sea

Collisions at sea may involve two States, each of which considers the collision, and those responsible for it, to be within its jurisdiction. The existence of concurrent jurisdiction was upheld by the PCIJ in the *Lotus* case (1927). The rule was much criticised and the position is now set out in Article 11 of the HSC and Article 97 of the LOSC, which provide that penal and disciplinary jurisdiction in cases of collision or other navigational incidents may only be exercised by authorities of the State in whose ship the defendant served or the State of which he is a national.

9.8.2.3 Exceptions to the flag State's exclusive jurisdiction

- Piracy

  All States have the right and duty to act against piracy (Article 14 of the HSC and Article 100 of the LOSC). Piracy is defined in both conventions (Article 15 of the HSC and Article 101 of the LOSC) as consisting of the following:

  (a) any illegal acts of violence or detention, or any act of depredation, committed for private ends by the crew or the passengers of a private ship or aircraft, and directed:

    (i) on the high seas, against another ship or aircraft, or against persons or property on board such ship or aircraft;

    (ii) against a ship, aircraft, persons or property in a place outside the jurisdiction of any State;

  (b) any act of voluntary participation in the operation of a ship or of an aircraft with knowledge of facts making it a pirate ship or aircraft;

(c) any act of inciting or of intentionally facilitating an act described in sub-paras (a) or (b).

The conventions allow the visiting and boarding of any ship, flying whatever flag, reasonably suspected of being engaged in piracy. If the suspicions prove to be correct, the ship may be seized and those engaged in piracy may be arrested and tried in the courts of the seizing State. If the suspicions of piracy prove to be unfounded and unjustified by any action of the ship, boarded compensation must be paid for any loss or damage that is sustained.

- Unlawful acts against maritime safety

  Following the *Achille Lauro* incident (1985), which is discussed in Chapter 6, the International Maritime Organisation adopted the Convention for the Suppression of Unlawful Acts against the Safety of Maritime Navigation 1988, together with a Protocol for the Suppression of Unlawful Acts against the Safety of Fixed Platforms Located on the Continental Shelf 1988. Both convention and protocol entered into force in 1992. They deal with the issue of acts of violence or detention committed on board ships or oil rigs carried out for non-private ends. Such acts would not come within the definition of piracy and the convention and protocol therefore create the specific offence and provide for the jurisdiction of States other than the flag State.

- Slavery and drug trafficking

  All States are under a duty to suppress the trade and transport of slaves and narcotic and psychotropic drugs, and ships suspected of being engaged in such activities may be visited and boarded but it is the right and responsibility of the flag State to proceed with action against those involved in such activities.

- Unauthorised broadcasting

  Unauthorised broadcasting refers to any radio or television transmission from the high seas which is intended for reception by the general public contrary to international regulations. It is more commonly known as pirate broadcasting. The HSC contained no provisions relating to so called pirate radio broadcasting and there are no clear customary law rules on the subject, although reference should be made to the general rules relating to protective and security jurisdiction discussed at 6.4. Article 109(3)(4) of the LOSC does give wide powers of enforcement jurisdiction over pirate radio stations and allows the flag State, the defendant's State, and any State which can receive transmissions or suffer interference to authorised broadcasts to exercise jurisdiction. This jurisdiction includes the right to prosecute offences together with the right to exercise powers of arrest and seizure.

- Ships of uncertain nationality

  States may visit and enforce their laws against their own ships on the high seas. Consequently, where a ship, though flying a foreign flag, is reasonably suspected of being of the same nationality as a warship, it may be visited and boarded. If the suspicions prove to be unfounded and unjustified by action of the ship boarded, then compensation must be paid.

9.8.3 Hot pursuit

The right of hot pursuit, recognised at customary international law in cases such as the *I'm Alone* case (1933) and in Article 23 of the HSC, allows a coastal State's warships or military aircraft to pursue a foreign ship which has violated the coastal State's laws within internal or territorial waters and to arrest it on the high seas. Pursuit must begin while the foreign ship is within territorial waters (or, in the case of customs, fiscal, immigration or sanitary laws, within the contiguous zone). Article 111 of the LOSC extends the right of hot pursuit to cover offences committed within archipelagic waters and the EEZ. The foreign ship must first be given a visual or auditory signal, within range, to stop. Pursuit must be immediate and continuous upon refusal to stop. Hot pursuit cannot be continued into the foreign ship's own territorial waters or the territorial waters of a third State. The pursuing vessel may use reasonable force to effect the arrest, but compensation is due for unjustifiable hot pursuit.

9.8.4 Safety of shipping

Article 110 of the HSC provides that every State shall take such measures for its vessels as are necessary to ensure safety at sea with regard to communications, the prevention of collisions, crew conditions and seaworthiness of ships. A slightly tougher regime is spelt out in the LOSC. Additionally, there are some specific conventions, mostly the work of the International Maritime Organisation, the principle one being the International Convention for the Safety of Life at Sea (SOLAS) 1974. This convention is the latest version of a line of treaties dating back to the sinking of *The Titanic*. SOLAS lays down minimum crewing standards and deals with such things as provision of life-rafts, fire-fighting equipment, navigational and broadcasting aids. Responsibility for enforcement lies with the flag State, but port States also have some measure of control. The port State is entitled to check that ships in port have a valid certificate, as required by SOLAS. In 1978, a protocol to SOLAS was adopted dealing with tanker safety and pollution prevention (which covers such things as inert gas systems and emergency steering).

In addition to SOLAS, there have been a series of regulations for preventing collisions at sea. The current regulations are annexed to the

Convention on the International Regulations for Preventing Collisions at Sea 1972. The regulations deals with matters of signalling, conduct on the seas, and use of sea lanes.

The issue of marine pollution is discussed in Chapter 16.

9.9 International sea bed

Sovereignty over the deep sea bed, that is to say, the area of the sea bed beyond the continental shelf, has become a topic of conflict as technology has developed. The discovery of important mineral resources in the deep sea bed was made 100 years ago but it has only comparatively recently become technically and commercially viable to exploit such resources. The main resources are the manganese nodules which are composed of high grade metal ores such as manganese, iron, nickel, copper and cobalt. It is only a handful of rich nations who are at present capable of exploiting the resources and such exploitation has the added advantage for the State concerned of lessening dependence on foreign land based deposits. For the mineral exporting countries, the effect could be disastrous; for example, Zaire at present produces over 40% of the world's cobalt and Gabon obtains 20% of its export earnings from its manganese deposits.

Once deep sea mining became a possibility, the few mining States sought legal justification for their actions. Three principle arguments were put forward:

(a) exploitation could be justified on the basis of a continuation of the regime of the continental shelf by defining the continental shelf in terms of the ability to exploit its resources;

(b) exploitation could be justified on the application of the principle of the freedom of the high seas; and

(c) title to the deep sea bed area could be gained by occupation through use.

Many of the potential exploiters of the deep sea bed favoured the second argument. By the late 1960s, many of the newly independent States were expressing concern at the possibility of the exploitation of the resources of the sea bed for the benefit of a few rich nations. In 1969, the General Assembly of the UN passed a resolution by 62 votes to 28, with 28 abstentions, calling for a moratorium on sea bed activities and, in 1970, the Declaration of Principles Governing the Sea Bed and Ocean Floor was passed (108–0, with 14 abstentions), which declared the area to be 'the common heritage of mankind' and therefore not susceptible to any territorial claim. The declaration further proposed the establishment of an international regime to govern all activities in the area. The Group of 77, made up of over 100 States, have argued that this declaration is binding and that it prohibits unilateral sea bed mining. The

Western States have argued that the resolution is merely one of principle. The topic was fully discussed at UNCLOS III and proved to be the major area of disagreement

9.9.1 The LOSC regime

The area of the deep sea bed comprises approximately 60% of the total sea bed area and the LOSC declares the deep sea bed and the resources within it to be part of the common heritage of mankind. As such, the area and its resources are not susceptible to unilateral national appropriation. Rights in the area can only be obtained with the authority of the International Sea Bed Authority (the Authority), which is established by the LOSC with an assembly, council, secretariat and a deep sea mining arm. All activities in the deep sea bed area are to be carried out for the benefit of mankind as a whole.

The LOSC provides that the Authority will carry out its own exploration and exploitation and will also issue licences authorising commercial activity. There is to be a sharing of technology and the Authority charges a licence fee and takes a share of any profits of commercial mining. The calculation of the levy on deep sea bed exploitation is complex and beyond the scope of this book. The LOSC also provides that exploitation of the continental shelf beyond the normal 200 mile limit will be subject to a levy (Article 82). Payment would be due annually after the fifth year of exploitation and would start at a rate of 1% of the production value of any exploitation, rising to 7% per annum by the 12th year of production. There would be an equitable distribution of the profits of the Authority, although States who had previously produced minerals who are seriously affected by deep sea mining would be entitled to specific economic assistance.

In contemplation of the coming into force of the LOSC, a number of Western States have established their own interim regimes to permit and regulate deep sea mining. This system, known as the Reciprocating States Regime, provides that States should adopt similar national laws which will interrelate. In 1981, the UK passed the Deep Sea Bed (Temporary Provisions) Act and similar legislation has been introduced in the USA, France, Germany, Netherlands, Belgium, Italy and Japan. The scheme provides for licensing of deep sea mining, with licensees paying a levy of 3.75% of the value of the nodules recovered (half of what is envisaged under the LOSC).

During the early 1990s, there were concerted attempts at the UN to reach agreement on the deep sea bed regime and so clear the way for widespread acceptance of the LOSC. On 28 July 1994, the Agreement relating to the Implementation of Part XI of the UNCLOS of 10 December 1982 was adopted. It consists of 10 articles and provides that the Agreement and Part XI of the LOSC should be interpreted and applied as a single instrument. In the event of any inconsistency between the two, the provisions of the Agreement shall prevail. The more significant aspects of the Agreement are contained in an annex. The annex deals with such matters as the work of the International Seabed Authority and the Enterprise. The terms of the Agreement are very much more favourable to the developed States than the original provisions of LOSC

9.10 Settlement of Disputes

Part XV of the LOSC contains detailed provisions relating to the settlement of law of the sea disputes. States are under a duty, by virtue of Article 279, to settle any dispute arising out of the Convention by peaceful means and should endeavour to reach a solution by the means indicated in Article 33 of the UN Charter. Article 287 of the LOSC provides that States may choose one of the following means of peaceful settlement: the International Tribunal for the Law of the Sea (ITLOS), the International Court of Justice, an arbitral tribunal under Annex VII of the LOSC, a special arbitral tribunal under Annex VIII of the LOSC (in the case of disputes concerning fisheries, the marine environment, scientific research and navigation). So far, 18 States have made a declaration under Article 287. ITLOS has been established with its seat in Hamburg and received its first case in the autumn of 1997.

THE LAW OF THE SEA

Relevant conventions are:

(a) Convention on the Territorial Sea and the Contiguous Zone 1958;

(b) Convention on the Continental Shelf 1958;

(c) Convention on Fishing and the Conservation of the Living Resources of the High Seas 1958;

(d) Convention on the High Seas 1958; and

(e) Law of the Sea Convention 1982.

Baselines

The baseline is the line from which the outer limits of a State's maritime zones are measured. All waters on the landward side of the baseline constitute internal waters. Where the coastline is straight and unindented the baseline is drawn along the low water line. Different rules apply to a number of specific situations.

- Heavily indented coastlines or coastlines fringed with islands

  Straight baselines may be drawn provided they follow the general direction of the coast and the sea inside the baseline is sufficiently linked to the land to constitute internal waters – see *Anglo-Norwegian Fisheries* case (1951).

- Bays

  Straight baselines can be drawn across bays provided they do not exceed 24 miles.

- River mouths

  The baseline will normally be a straight line across the mouth of the river between points on the low water line of its banks.

- Harbour works

  Outermost permanent harbour works can act as the baseline.

- Low tide elevations

  (Drying Rocks) Land which is submerged by water at high tide but above water at low tide may constitute the baseline if it is situated at a distance not exceeding the breadth of the territorial sea from the mainland or an island.

- Islands

  Baselines will be drawn round islands, no matter how small, in the normal way. Every island is capable of possessing a territorial sea.

- Reefs

  The low water lines of fringing reefs may be used as baselines so that the lagoon has the status of internal waters.

- Archipelagos

  Straight baselines can be used to enclose archipelagic States.

Maritime zones

The various maritime zones can be summarised as follows:

Zone	Breadth	Rights
Internal waters	All water on landward side of baseline	Coastal State has complete sovereignty subject to the right of foreign vessels in distress to seek safety in internal waters.
Territorial sea	Maximum 12 miles	Coastal State has sovereignty subject to the right of innocent passage of foreign ships.
EEZ and contiguous zone	Maximum 200 miles The EEZ must be expressly claimed	Coastal State enjoys sovereign rights for the purpose of exploiting, conserving and managing the natural resources of the sea bed, subsoil and superjacent waters.
Continental shelf	Maximum 200 miles or, exceptionally, 350 miles	Coastal State has exclusive rights to the exploitation and exploration of the natural resources of the sea bed and subsoil.
High seas	All sea not included in the EEZ, territorial sea, or internal waters	All States enjoy freedom of the high seas, jurisdiction is exercised by the flag State, subject to certain exceptions.
International sea bed	Sea bed under the high seas	Constitutes part of the common heritage of mankind.

CHAPTER 10

AIR AND SPACE LAW

10.1 Airspace

Up until the early part of this century, the law relating to airspace was not settled. Certain writers suggested that there should be a territorial airspace above a State's territory with a similar regime to that of the territorial sea. Through the territorial airspace, there would be a right of innocent passage for foreign civilian aircraft and above it there would be freedom of navigation. Another school of thought advocated complete freedom of the air. The law came to be settled during the First World War and the customary law was codified in the Paris Convention on the Regulation of Aerial Navigation 1919. The approach adopted at Paris was that States should have compete and exclusive sovereignty over the airspace above their land and territorial sea. Sovereignty was understood to extend upwards to an unlimited distance. As far as the airspace above the high seas and other areas not subject to national jurisdiction was concerned, it was accepted that there was compete freedom of navigation.

10.2 The Chicago Convention

The present regime concerning aerial navigation was developed at the 1944 Chicago Conference and is reflected in the conventions adopted there. The Chicago Convention on International Civil Aviation (the Chicago Convention) entered into force in January 1945. The Convention recognises the exclusive sovereignty of States over their airspace above their territory, which is deemed to include the territorial sea, but grants a number of rights to the civilian aircraft of foreign States. The Convention does not apply to State aircraft, which are expressed in Article 3 to include military, police and customs aircraft. Underpinning the regime of the Chicago Convention is a distinction between those aircraft which are engaged in scheduled international air services and other civilian aircraft.

Article 5 provides that aircraft not engaged in scheduled international air services shall have the right to make flights into or in transit non-stop across territory and to make stops for non-traffic purposes without the need for prior permission. Contracting States reserve the right to set down prescribed routes. The article goes on to allow such non-scheduled aircraft, if engaged in the carriage of passengers, cargo or mail, to have the privilege to take on or set down passengers, cargo or mail subject to any regulations or limitations imposed by the territorial State. Scheduled air services are subject to Article 6, which only allows such services to operate with special authorisation of the State over whose territory the aircraft is to fly.

In 1952, the International Civil Aviation Organisation (ICAO), a UN body set up at the Chicago Conference, defined a scheduled air service as:

> ... a series of flights that possesses all the following characteristics:
>
> (a) it passes through the airspace over the territory of more than one State;
>
> (b) it is performed by aircraft for the transport of passengers, mail or cargo for remuneration, in such a manner that each flight is open to use by members of the public;
>
> (c) it is operated, so as to serve traffic between the same two or more points, either:
>
> (i) according to a published timetable; or
>
> (ii) with flights so regular and frequent that they constitute a recognisably systematic series.

Over the years since 1952, however, State practice has been such as to indicate that charter flights, although not coming within the ICAO definition of scheduled air services, require prior permission in a manner more in keeping with the provisions of Article 6 than of Article 5.

10.3 The International Civil Aviation Organisation

The ICAO was established by the Chicago Convention and came into existence on 4 April 1947, with its headquarters in Montreal. The ICAO is a specialised agency of the UN and Article 44 of the Chicago Convention provides that its aims and objectives 'are to develop the principles and techniques of international air navigation and to foster the planning and development of international air transport', in a number of particular respects set out in Article 44 and including 'the safe and orderly growth of international civil aviation', and meeting 'the needs of the peoples of the world for safe, regular, efficient and economical air transport'.

The Assembly of the ICAO is made up of representatives of every contracting State. It is convened every three years but has the possibility of meeting in extraordinary session. The main work of the ICAO is carried out by the Council, made up of 36 members elected by the Assembly. The Council adopts International Standards and Recommended Practices (SARPS), which are designated as annexes to the Chicago Convention. There is some debate as to the force of these annexes. The Chicago Convention does allow for Member States to opt out of an annex if it finds it impracticable to comply and this has occurred on a number of occasions. However, if a State does not opt out, the question remains as to whether the international standard is legally binding. ICAO Assembly Resolution A297 seemed to suggest that compliance with standards is compulsory in the absence of any specific opt out. The *travaux preparatories* to the Convention, however, contain a statement that 'the Annexes are given no compulsory force'. In practice, although the annexes may not be formally binding in the manner of treaties, they are highly authoritative and are distinguished in the Chicago Convention from mere recommendations. Their status provides an interesting illustration of the theoretical disputes mentioned in Chapter 1.

It is also useful to note here the existence of the International Air Transport Association (IATA), formed by the commercial airlines of the world and concerned with avoiding 'unreasonable competition'.

10.4 Bilateral Agreements

The Chicago Conference also adopted two further conventions: the Chicago International Air Services Transit Agreement 1944 (known as the Two Freedoms Agreement) and the Chicago International Air Transport Agreement (also known as the Five Freedoms Agreement). Both agreements relate to scheduled air services. The Two Freedoms are:

(a) the privilege to fly across the territory of another contracting State without landing; and

(b) the privilege to land for non-traffic purposes.

A further three freedoms make up the Five Freedoms and they are:

(c) the privilege to put down passengers, mail or cargo taken on in the territory of the State whose nationality the aircraft possesses;

(d) the privilege to take on passengers, mail or cargo destined for the territory of the State whose nationality the aircraft possesses; and

(e) the privilege to take on passengers, mail and cargo destined for the territory of any other contracting State and the privilege to put down passengers, mail and cargo coming from any such territory.

The Two Freedoms Agreement met widespread acceptance and today there are over 100 parties to it, including the UK. The Five Freedoms Agreement proved too ambitious to gain widespread acceptance. It had been proposed by the US, at the time by far the biggest airline operator, but it was thought by many States to give away too much of commercial value. In 1946, the US itself withdrew from the Agreement and today there are just 11 parties, not including the UK. With the failure of the Five Freedoms Agreement, there was resort to widespread bilateral agreement to regulate scheduled air services. One of the first such agreements was the Bermuda Agreement, concluded between the US and the UK in 1946. Initially, it was hoped that the Bermuda Agreement would serve as a model for other bilateral agreements. A number of common principles were found, including the recognition that air transport facilities should bear a close relationship to public needs and that there should be a fair opportunity for the carriers of both States to operate any route between the two States.

However, a dispute between the US and the UK over landing rights for Concord led to British denunciation of the Bermuda Agreement on 22 June 1976. New negotiations followed and Bermuda II was signed on 23 July 1977. The new agreement virtually abolished the fifth of the Five Freedoms and introduced new provisions relating to infrastructure charges and capacities. Increased competition worldwide led to a number of different models for bilateral agreement emerging.

In 1978, the United States moved towards a policy of de-regulation and minimal State interference in civil aviation – often referred to as an open skies policy. The policy was reflected in agreement between the US and the Netherlands in 1978 – airlines were to be given more autonomy in fixing fares and capacity was to be related to customer demand. Since then, there have been a number of other 'open skies' agreements.

As has already been stated, the Chicago Convention does not govern State aircraft and the principle of the exclusive sovereignty of States over their airspace means that there is no general right of such aircraft to overfly the territory of other States. Non-civilian aircraft will therefore always need to point to specific permission to justify flying into any other State's airspace.

10.5 Unauthorised aerial intrusion

A question that flows from the fact that States possess sovereignty over the airspace above their territory is what action can be taken against 'trespassing' aircraft. As far as military aircraft are concerned, the international law position appears to be clear. Unauthorised intrusion by military aircraft (with the exception of military transport aircraft) may be met by the use of force without warning. The most famous example occurred in the *U-2* incident. In May 1960, a U-2 (a US reconnaissance aircraft) was shot down by USSR fighters over Soviet territory. The aircraft had been engaged in the aerial reconnaissance of the Soviet Union. The USSR protested at the flight and the US made no attempt to justify its action in terms of international law or protest at the shooting down or the subsequent trial of the pilot.

The international law position has become more clear following the shooting down of Korean Airlines Flight 007 by Soviet aircraft in 1983. A scheduled flight from Alaska to South Korea had strayed into Soviet airspace and was shot down. All 169 passengers and crew were killed. An ICAO inquiry concluded that the aircraft had strayed off course as a result of the negligence of the crew. They found that the Soviet aircraft had made insufficient efforts to intercept the Boeing 747. It was accepted by all parties that, at the time of the shooting, there was a US military intelligence aircraft in the area but, in spite of this, the inquiry felt that the Soviet aircrew should have made greater effort to establish whether or not the 747 was an intelligence aircraft before shooting it down. As a consequence of the shooting, in 1984, ICAO adopted a new Article 3 *bis* of the Chicago Convention. This new article provides:

> (a) The contracting parties recognise that every State must refrain from resorting to the use of weapons against civil aircraft in flight and that, in case of interception, the lives of persons on board and the safety of aircraft must not be endangered ...
>
> (b) The contracting parties recognise that every State, in the exercise of its sovereignty, is entitled to require the landing ... of a civil aircraft flying above its territory without authority ...
>
> (c) Every civil aircraft shall comply with an order given in conformity with para (b) of this Article ...

The article has yet to come into force, although it has been suggested that it now represents customary international law. The question of responses to unauthorised intrusion is discussed in the context of the right of States to self-defence in Chapter 12.

10.6 Jurisdiction over aircraft

The nationality of civil aircraft is governed by the Chicago Convention, which provides that they shall have the nationality of the State in which they are registered and that they cannot be validly registered in more than one State. The registering State does have a valid claim to exercise jurisdiction while the aircraft is in flight over the high seas or other territory not belonging to any State. As for aircraft within the territory of a State, jurisdiction will be primarily territorial, although the registering State may make express provision for claiming jurisdiction over acts committed on board the aircraft in its own legislation.

10.6.1 Threats to aviation security

The use of hijacking and other acts of terrorism involving aircraft from the early 1960s onwards proved the general rules on jurisdiction inadequate. The nature and situation of the offence meant it was not always easy for the registering State to assert jurisdiction, nor was it always clear over whose territory the offence was committed. Furthermore, even if the offenders could be located, the limitations of extradition treaties meant that it was often not possible to bring them to trial. The Tokyo Convention on Offences Committed on Board Aircraft 1963 was the first convention to deal with:

> ... acts which ... may or do jeopardise the safety of the aircraft or of persons or property therein or which jeopardise good order and discipline on board.

The convention applies to acts committed while the aircraft was in flight, on the surface of the high seas or in any other area outside the territory of any State and provides that the State of registration should have primary jurisdiction. Article 4 provides that non-registering States have the power to interfere with aircraft in flight to exercise criminal jurisdiction only in the following cases, where:

(a) the offence has effect on the territory of such State;

(b) the offence has been committed by or against a national or permanent resident of such State;

(c) the offence is against the security of such State;

(d) the offence consists of a breach of any rules or regulations relating to the flight or manoeuvre of aircraft in force in such State;

(e) the exercise of jurisdiction is necessary to ensure the observance of any obligation of such State under a multilateral international agreement.

The convention also imposes a duty on States to take 'such measures as may be necessary' to establish its jurisdiction over offences committed on board their own registered aircraft. The convention imposed no new extradition obligations in respect of such offences. One of the most important aspects of the Tokyo Convention is the powers that were given to the aircraft's commander. The commander is given particular authority in respect of those on board and contracting parties are under an obligation to assist the commander and ensure the safe continuance of the flight. Article 11 refers to actual seizure of aircraft in flight and provides that contracting States should take 'all appropriate measures' to restore control of the aircraft to its lawful commander.

The principle weakness of the Tokyo Convention is that there is no obligation on States to recognise an offence of unlawful seizure of aircraft. During the later 1960s, the number of hijackings dramatically increased, reaching a peak of 89 separate incidents in 1969. Where hijackers were caught, most States were unable to prosecute for hijacking and, instead, where they had jurisdiction, prosecuted for the constituent acts of assault, etc. The ICAO, concerned at the increase in hijackings and recognising the deficiencies in the Tokyo Convention, called for the reinforcement of the law. The problem was highlighted by the *Dawson's Field* incident.

On 6 September 1970, Palestinian commandos belonging to the Popular Front for the Liberation of Palestine attacked four aircraft; one attack, on an El Al aircraft, took place in London, and three other aircraft, belonging to Pan American, TWA and Swissair, were captured in flight. The Pan American plane was taken to Cairo where, after the passengers were allowed to leave, it was blown up. The TWA and Swissair flight, together with a BOAC plane which had been seized on 9 September, were eventually flown to Dawson's

Field in Jordan and the 400 passengers on board were held hostage while negotiations continued, and US military intervention seemed imminent. As Jordanian troops began attacking Palestinian refugee camps (in what came to be known as *Black September*), the hostages were gradually released in return for the release of a number of Palestinian prisoners held around the world (including Leila Khaled who had led the attack on the El Al plane). The three aircraft were blown up.

The hijackings received worldwide publicity and focused attention on the need to reform the law. On 16 December 1970, the ICAO convened an international conference which resulted in the Hague Convention for the Suppression of Unlawful Seizure of Aircraft 1970. Article 1 provides that:

> Any person who on board an aircraft in flight:
>
> (a) unlawfully, by force or threat thereof, or by any other form of intimidation, seizes, or exercises control of, that aircraft, or attempts to perform any such act; or
>
> (b) is an accomplice of a person who performs or attempts to perform any such act commits an offence.

An aircraft is considered to be in flight from the moment all external doors are closed following embarkation until the doors are opened again for disembarkation. The convention imposes on States an obligation to make the offence punishable by severe penalties and provides that the following States should have jurisdiction:

(a) the registering State of the seized aircraft;

(b) the State in which the aircraft lands with the alleged offender on board;

(c) any State in which an alleged offender is present; and

(d) where the offence is committed on board an aircraft which has been leased without crew, the State where the lessee has his principal place of business or permanent residence.

The State parties also undertook to make the offence an extraditable one and imposed a duty on States in which alleged offenders were found to either prosecute or extradite. The provisions of the Hague Convention were introduced into English law by the Hijacking Act 1971 (since replaced by the Aviation Security Act 1982).

The Hague Convention did not deal with the problem of aircraft sabotage. The ICAO convened a conference in 1971 to remedy this deficiency and the conference adopted the Montreal Convention for the Suppression of Unlawful Acts Against the Safety of Civil Aviation 1971. Following a series of attacks at airports, a protocol to the convention was agreed in 1988: the Montreal Protocol for the Suppression of Unlawful Acts of Violence at Airports Serving International Civil Aviation 1988. The convention makes it an offence to perform an act of violence against a person on board an aircraft in flight where that act is likely to endanger the safety of the aircraft; to destroy an aircraft in service or cause damage that renders it incapable of flight or endangers its safety in flight; to destroy, damage or interfere with the operation of air navigation facilities or to communicate knowingly false information if this is likely to endanger an aircraft in flight. The protocol extended the ambit of the convention to cover acts of violence against a person at an airport serving civil aviation which cause or are likely to cause serious injury or death; destroying or seriously damaging the facilities of such an airport or aircraft not in service located there or disrupting the services of the airport. The convention was given effect in the UK by the Protection of Aircraft Act 1973 (replaced by the Aviation Security Act 1982) and the protocol by the Aviation and Maritime Security Act 1990. The convention and protocol impose an obligation on State parties to make the offences punishable by severe penalties and contain similar jurisdiction provisions to those contained in the Hague Convention, together with confirmation that the State in whose territory the offence is committed has jurisdiction. As with the Hague Convention, there is an obligation to extradite or prosecute.

One of the problems with the conventions on aviation and airport security is that they provide no enforcement measures which can be used against defaulting States. The Bonn Declaration on International Terrorism 1978, which was signed by Canada, France, the Federal Republic of Germany, Italy, Japan, the UK and the US provided that, where a State refused to extradite or prosecute those who have hijacked an aircraft, action should be taken to cease all flights to and from that State and all flights by its airlines. The Tokyo, Hague and Montreal Conventions merely provide that, in the case of a dispute arising over interpretation and application of the conventions, resort should be had to international arbitration and, failing that, to the ICJ.

10.6.2 Lockerbie

On 21 December 1988, Pan American flight PA103 exploded over the Scottish town of Lockerbie and the 259 people on board were killed. Investigations found that the cause of the explosion was a bomb which had been placed on board, allegedly by two Libyan nationals. The offence of placing a bomb on board a plane clearly comes within the ambit of the Montreal Convention, which provides that the UK, as the State, in whose territory the offence was committed, and the USA, as the registering State of the aircraft that was attacked, have jurisdiction. Both States therefore initiated criminal proceedings in their own municipal courts against the alleged offenders.

Both the US and the UK governments alleged that the two accused were in Libya. Repeated demands were made for Libya to surrender the two accused for trial in the US or the UK. The position was complicated by the fact that the UK and the US also alleged that the accused were members of the Libyan security service and that, therefore, Libya itself was internationally responsible for the bombing, and some of the UN Security Council resolutions that have been passed relate to Libya's complicity in and responsibility for acts of terrorism. Security Council Resolution 748 (1992) required Libya to extradite the two accused or suffer sanctions, including the suspension of international flights to and from Libya.

In late 1992, Libya instigated arbitration proceedings under Article 14 of the Montreal Convention, partly arguing that, under the provisions of the convention, it had a choice as to whether to prosecute the accused itself or extradite them and that there was no overwhelming obligation under the convention to extradite. The UK and the US preferred to see the matter resolved by political means through the use of the UN Security Council. Since the US and the UK would not get involved in the arbitration proceedings, Libya applied to the ICJ for interpretation of the obligations owed under the Montreal Convention (*Cases Concerning Questions Arising from the Aerial Incident at Lockerbie* (1992)). Libya asked the court for interim orders to prevent the use of sanctions against it, which raised important issues relating to the relationship between the ICJ and the Security Council, which is discussed in Chapter 11. The court refused to make the interim orders but, in February 1998, the ICJ decided that it had jurisdiction in the case and will now proceed to hear the merits of the case.

10.7 The liability of airline companies

An issue of major importance as far as air law is concerned relates to the liability of civil airline companies for death or injury suffered by passengers. The Warsaw Convention for the Unification of Certain Rules relating to International Carriage by Air 1929 (Warsaw Convention), as amended at the Hague in 1955, establishes upper limits for liability and deals with issues of responsibility and insurance. Article 20 of the convention provides that the airline is not liable if it proves that it and its agents have taken all necessary measures to avoid the damage or that it was impossible to take such measures. Article 22 puts a financial ceiling on compensation available, unless it can be proved that the damage resulted from wilful misconduct of the airline, in which case liability is unlimited. As far as flights flying into and out of the USA are concerned, the position for passengers is much improved by the Montreal Agreement, which was concluded in 1966. But, for all other international flights, the present law is heavily weighted in favour of the airlines and this has resulted in passengers suffering loss or injury suing the manufacturers of the aircraft or the maintenance crew rather than going for the airline itself.

It is worth noting that the question of liability for damage caused by aircraft to persons and property on the surface is covered by the Rome Convention 1952 and the Montreal Protocol 1978. It is the aircraft operator, presumed to be the registered owner, who is responsible for damage caused by an aircraft in flight or by any person or thing falling from it. The convention provides for strict liability but the amount of compensation available in such situations is limited.

10.8 Outer space

New problems of international law have been created by the increase of activity in the upper strata of the atmosphere and beyond. The launching of the first satellite orbiting the earth by the Soviet Union in 1957 heralded the beginning of outer space exploration, which has since rapidly expanded with landings on the moon and other planets and the possibility of permanent space stations all giving rise to territorial and jurisdictional problems.

10.8.1 Definition

It will be remembered that the traditional view of sovereignty over airspace is that extents above the territory of a State without limit. A strict application of this rule would mean that orbiting satellites would require prior authorisation for flight over the territory of foreign States. This would clearly be impractical and thus it has been accepted that satellites may pass above territory, and such overflight does not constitute a violation of airspace sovereignty. It follows from this that national sovereignty ceases at some upper limit. Where that limit is remains uncertain, but what is clear is that outer space constitutes *res communis* and is part of the common heritage of mankind.

There have been a number of attempts to define the boundary between airspace and outer space. There is considerable agreement that it falls somewhere between 10 and 100 miles above the earth's surface – the respective limits of conventional aerodynamic flight and free orbit of spacecraft. In 1979, the USSR proposed a boundary of between 100 and 110 km above sea level but widespread agreement was absent. As well as an absence of a clear boundary between space and outer space, the status of space objects in transit through airspace remains unclear.

10.8.2 International Conventions

In 1958, the UN Committee on the Peaceful Uses of Outer Space was established and it has been responsible for a number of measures adopted regulating outer space activity. All such measures recognise that outer space must be used for peaceful means and is the common heritage of mankind.

The Treaty on Principles Governing the Activities of States in the Exploration and Use of Outer Space including the Moon and other Celestial Bodies (Space Treaty), which was signed in 1967, affirms that space shall be the province of all mankind. No area of space may be appropriated by any

State and exploration is to be conducted according to international law and the principles of the Charter of the UN. Under the Space Treaty, jurisdiction over items launched into space remains with the registering State.

The Space Treaty has been revised and clarified by the Agreement Governing the Activities of States on the Moon and other Celestial Bodies 1979 (Moon Treaty), which provides that the natural resources of the moon and other celestial bodies should be exploited as the common heritage of mankind. The Moon Treaty entered into force in 1984.

The Space Treaty has been further supplemented by two further agreements: the Agreement on the Rescue of Astronauts, the Return of Astronauts and the Return of Objects Launched into Space 1968 (Astronauts Treaty) and the Convention on International Liability for Damages Caused by Space Objects 1972 (Liability Convention). The latter convention is concerned with damage caused by space objects on the surface of the earth or to aircraft in flight. There is a strict liability imposed on the launching State. As regards damage caused in outer space, fault liability applies. The nature of liability for damage caused by space objects was discussed in the *Cosmos 954* claim (1979), which arose after a Soviet satellite, which had a nuclear reactor, disintegrated through Canadian airspace and crashed onto Canadian territory. Canada claimed six million dollars in compensation from the USSR, although the dispute was settled by the Soviet Union making an *ex gratia* payment of three million dollars.

The Registration of Objects Launched into Space Convention 1975 provides that every launch of a space craft must be public and its purpose must be registered on a public register maintained by the UN Secretary General.

10.8.3 Geostationary orbit

On 3 December 1976, Brazil, Colombia, Congo, Ecuador, Indonesia, Kenya, Uganda and Zaire issued a five point declaration about the geostationary orbit (geostationary synchronous orbit). This is the orbit 22,300 miles above the equator, in which satellites orbit at the same speed as the earth rotates. It is therefore possible, using this orbit, for a single satellite to maintain continuous contact with the ground. The eight equatorial States claimed in the declaration that 'the segments of geostationary synchronous orbit are part of the territory over which equatorial States exercise their authority'. Clearly, such a claim conflicts with the provisions of the Space Treaty (to which Brazil, Ecuador and Uganda are parties) and has met with protests from other States. The declaration does, however, indicate a problem which is likely to increase in seriousness as greater use is made of outer space and there emerges a greater need for regulation.

10.8.4 Telecommunication

The major use of outer space has been for telecommunications. The International Telecommunications Union (ITU) has a major role in the development of the law and regulations governing the topic. The ITU has promoted co-ordination between States on such matters as frequency and orbital positioning. The International Telecommunications Satellite Organisation (INTELSAT) is a consortium made up of ITU members, which is run on a commercial basis. INTELSAT agreements have provided the legal framework for the exploitation of outer space for the purposes of telecommunications. As exploitation of outer space has increased, demands for greater regulation have followed. While outer space is not capable of appropriation by States, as Professor Brownlie has pointed out, 'there is a fine line to be drawn between excessive use ... and appropriation' (*Principles of International Law* (5th edn, 1998, Oxford: OUP, p 267). The UN Committee on the Peaceful Use of Outer Space (UNCOPUOS) has been considering further regulation for some time, particularly in the area of remote sensing – the gathering of information by satellites fitted with sensors, for example, for meteorological information – although, so far, no general agreement has been reached.

AIR AND SPACE LAW

Airspace

States have sovereignty over the airspace above their land and territorial sea subject to a number of limited rights enjoyed by foreign civilian aircraft.

- Paris Convention on the Regulation of Aerial Navigation 1919;
- Chicago Convention on International Civil Aviation 1944.

Scheduled air services

A distinction is drawn between scheduled air services, which require prior authorisation, and all other civilian flights, which are allowed over-flight rights and can also make stops for non-traffic purposes and take on and set down passengers, cargo or mail. Scheduled air services are the subject of the Chicago International Air Services Transit Agreement 1944, which grants scheduled flights the privilege to over-fly the territory of another State without landing and the privilege of landing for non-traffic purposes. Further privileges are contained in the Chicago International Air Transport Agreement 1944 but it has obtained little support, and most scheduled air services are now the subject of bilateral agreements.

Unauthorised aerial intrusion

Since States possess sovereignty over their airspace, they have the right to take action against unauthorised airspace but the customary law position today is that States should refrain from using weapons against civilian aircraft in flight and instead are entitled to require unauthorised aircraft to land.

Jurisdiction and aircraft sabotage

Aircraft have the nationality of the State in which they are registered and the registering State has jurisdiction on board an aircraft in flight over the high seas or other territory not belonging to any State. In cases of hijacking and other terrorist action, jurisdiction is often not confined to the registering State.

- Tokyo Convention on Offences Committed on Board Aircraft;
- Hague Convention for the Suppression of Unlawful Seizure of Aircraft 1970;

- Montreal Convention for the Suppression of Unlawful Acts Against the Safety of Civil Aviation 1971;
- Montreal Protocol for the Suppression of Unlawful Acts of Violence at Airports Serving International Civil Aviation 1988;
- *Cases concerning questions arising from the Aerial Incident at Lockerbie* (1992).

Liability of airline companies

Warsaw Convention for the Unification of Certain Rules relating to International Carriage by Air 1929.

Outer space

Outer space constitutes part of the common heritage of mankind and national sovereignty over airspace has some upper limit, although its precise location remains uncertain. Since the serious exploration of outer space began at the end of the 1950s, there have been a number of treaties agreed which have reaffirmed the view that space is the province of all mankind and that its exploration and exploitation should only be carried out for peaceful purposes. Jurisdiction over things launched into space remains with the registering State and the UN Secretary General maintains a public register of the launch and purpose of all space craft under the provisions of the Registration of Objects Launched into Space Convention 1975.

CHAPTER 11

PEACEFUL SETTLEMENT OF DISPUTES

11.1 Introduction

One of the purposes of any effective system of law is the provision of methods and procedures to achieve the peaceful resolution of disputes arising between subjects of the legal system. It is a fundamental principle of international law that States shall settle their disputes by peaceful means and this is reflected in Article 2(3) of the Charter of the United Nations, which provides that:

> All members shall settle their international disputes by peaceful means in such a manner that international peace and security, and justice, are not endangered.

Chapter 6 of the Charter deals specifically with the pacific settlement of disputes, and Article 33(1) provides that:

> The parties to any dispute, the continuance of which is likely to endanger the maintenance of international peace and security, shall, first of all, seek a solution by negotiation, inquiry, mediation, conciliation, arbitration, judicial settlement, resort to regional agencies or arrangements or other peaceful means of their choice.

The obligation on States to achieve peaceful settlement of disputes has been confirmed in a number of other treaties and resolutions, including the UN General Assembly Declaration on Principles of International Law Concerning Friendly Relations and Co-operation among States in Accordance with the Charter of the United Nations 1970 and the Manila Declaration on the Pacific Settlement of International Disputes 1982.

The peaceful methods of international dispute settlement that exist can be divided into diplomatic and legal settlement. Legal settlement refers to modes of dispute settlement which result in binding decisions and will involve either arbitration or judicial settlement. The following can be identified as forms of diplomatic settlement:

(a) negotiation;

(b) good offices;

(c) mediation;

(d) conciliation; and

(e) inquiry.

Of course, States may use a variety of methods. An example of a number of dispute resolution methods being used is provided by the *Chad-Libya Border*

Dispute. In 1973, a dispute arose between Libya and Chad over their joint border and there followed a long period of conflict. On 31 August 1989, the two sides signed a Framework Agreement on the Peaceful Settlement of the Territorial Dispute, in which they undertook to seek a peaceful settlement within one year. In the absence of a political settlement, the parties undertook to refer the matter to the ICJ. Political settlement was not reached and the matter was submitted to the ICJ in 1990. The ICJ gave judgment on 3 February 1994. The Court accepted the Chad argument and the two side concluded an agreement providing for Libyan withdrawal from the disputed Aouzou Strip by 30 May 1994. The agreement provided for UN observers to monitor the withdrawal. The two sides also established a joint team of experts to undertake the delimitation of a common frontier in accordance with the decision of the ICJ. On 4 May 1994, the UN Security Council adopted resolution 915, which established the UN Aouzou Strip Oberserver Group. On 30 May, the two sides signed a Joint Declaration confirming that withdrawal had occurred.

What constitutes an 'international dispute' is a matter for objective determination. In the *Mavrommatis Palestine Concessions (Jurisdiction)* case (1924), the PCIJ stated that a dispute could be regarded as 'a disagreement over a point of law or fact, a conflict of legal views or of interests between two persons'. In the *Interpretation of Peace Treaties* case (1950), the ICJ, in an advisory opinion, confirmed that the existence of an international dispute was a matter of objective determination stating:

> The mere denial of the existence of a dispute does not prove its non-existence ... There has thus arisen a situation in which two sides hold clearly opposite views concerning the question of the performance or non-performance of treaty obligations. Confronted with such a situation, the court must conclude that international disputes have arisen.

11.2 Negotiation

Negotiation is by far the most popular means of dispute settlement and consists of discussions between the interested parties. It is distinguished from other diplomatic means of settlement, in that there is no third party involvement. Negotiations are normally conducted through 'normal diplomatic channels' (foreign ministers, ambassadors, etc), although some States have set up semipermanent 'Mixed Commissions', consisting of an equal number of representatives of both parties which can deal with disputes as and when they arise, for example, the Canadian-US Joint Commission. Negotiation is used to try and prevent disputes arising in the first place and will also often be used at the start of other dispute resolution procedures. In the *Mavrommatis Palestine Concessions (Jurisdiction)* case (1924), the PCIJ indicated that negotiation should be a preliminary to bringing a case before the court in order that the subject matter of a dispute be clearly defined. In the *Free Zones of Upper Savoy* case (1932), the PCIJ stated that:

> Before a dispute can be made the subject of an action at law, its subject matter should have been clearly defined by diplomatic negotiations.

If there is an obligation to negotiate as a result of an existing agreement, attempts at negotiation must be genuine and made in good faith.

11.3 Good offices

Good offices involves the involvement of a third party, with the consent of the States in dispute, to help them establish direct contacts or to take up negotiations. The person providing the 'good offices' will usually be a neutral party who is trusted by both sides. The UN Secretary General is often used in this role to facilitate communication between contending parties and he may, on behalf of a concerned international community, play an active role in encouraging negotiations and promoting a successful outcome.

11.4 Mediation

Whereas, in good offices, the third party is doing little more than providing a channel for communication, in mediation, the third party plays a more active role by offering advice and proposals for a solution of the dispute. In practice, it is often hard to establish a clear distinction between the two. What may begin as provision of good offices may end up as mediation. There are a number of recent examples of US mediation, for example, in Yugoslavia and the Middle East.

11.5 Conciliation

Conciliation also involves the use of third parties, but the third party plays a more detached role. Rather than becoming involved in the negotiations, the conciliator will investigate the dispute and present formal proposals for a solution. Conciliation is often undertaken by a commission of conciliation acting as a formal body. Conciliation became popular in the 1920s and many States concluded bilateral treaties which provided for the use of conciliation in the event of future disputes, although there has been little actual use of conciliation since the Second World War.

11.6 Inquiry

Inquiries prove useful where a dispute is largely concerned with issues of fact. The need for some independent inquiry procedures was illustrated by events leading to the Spanish-American War of 1898. In February 1898, a US warship, at anchor in Cuba, was destroyed by an explosion which killed large numbers of US sailors. Relations between Spain and the US were already strained and the US quickly blamed Spain for the explosion. Spain held a commission of inquiry, which found that the explosion was caused by factors present on the ship, whilst a US inquiry found that the ship had been destroyed by a mine. The conflicting findings of the two inquiries only served to exacerbate the situation.

At the Hague Peace Conference in 1899, the Russians proposed the establishment of international commissions of inquiry, which would be able, impartially, to decide disputes of fact and which would put an end to the type of dispute between the US and Spain. The proposals were accepted and formed the basis for Articles 9–14 of the Hague Convention for the Pacific Settlement of Disputes 1899. In 1904, a Committee of Inquiry, established under the provisions of the Hague Convention, was held to look into the sinking of a number of UK trawlers by Russian warships. The committee consisted of representatives from the UK and Russia and also France, the US and Austro-Hungary. The inquiry made a finding of fact and the dispute between Russia and the UK was settled amicably.

The rules relating to inquiries were further refined by the Hague Convention for the Pacific Settlement of Disputes 1907 (Articles 9–35). However, there has been little use of inquiries as a means of settling disputes since the establishment of a World Court, which can decide questions of both law and fact. The last international inquiry to be held was the *Red Crusader* inquiry (1962), which investigated an incident involving a UK trawler and a Danish fisheries protection vessel. The *Red Crusader* inquiry itself was the first to be held for 40 years.

11.7 Arbitration

Arbitration is defined by the ILC as:

> ... a procedure for the settlement of disputes between States by a binding award on the basis of law and as a result of an undertaking voluntarily accepted.

The essential difference between judicial settlement and arbitration is that, in arbitration, the parties are more active in deciding the law to be applied and the composition of the tribunal. Arbitration can often provide more flexibility for the disputants.

The modern history of international arbitration is traced back to the Treaty of Ghent 1814 between the US and the UK, whereby the two States agreed that certain disputes should be arbitrated by national commissioners with reference to a disinterested third party. The earlier Jay Treaty 1794 between the two States had made provision for arbitration by national commissioners. Throughout the 19th century, arbitration was frequently used, its popularity increasing markedly, following the successful *Alabama Claims* arbitration (1872) between the UK and the US, in which both sides nominated a member of the arbitration tribunal, as did Brazil, Italy and Switzerland.

The Hague Convention for the Pacific Settlement of Disputes 1899 marked the beginning of a new era of arbitration by establishing a Permanent Court of Arbitration (PCA), which began functioning in 1902 and is still in existence. The Permanent Court of Arbitration is a bit of a misnomer, since it is neither a court nor is it permanent. The PCA consists of a panel of 300 members (four nominated by each contracting party to the Hague Conventions 1899 and 1907), from whom each disputant can select one or more arbitrators (normally two, one of whom can be a national). The selected arbitrators then choose an umpire who presides over the arbitration. Decision of the arbitration panel is by majority vote. Of course, it remains that States do not have to use the PCA procedures and can establish *ad hoc* arbitration tribunals of their own, such as the one set up to deal with the *Guinea/Guinea Bissau Maritime Delimitation* case (1985).

Arbitration depends on consent. The law to be applied, the make up of the tribunal and any time limits must all be mutually agreed before the arbitration starts. The mutual agreement under which the parties agree to submit their dispute to arbitration and under which they agree the procedures and rules to be applied is known as the *compromis*. The *compromis* should also provide that the arbitration decision will be binding on the parties. There do exist model rules of procedure, for example, the Model Rules on Arbitral Procedures, which were drawn up by the ILC and adopted by the UN General Assembly in 1958.

Between 1900 and 1932, some 20 disputes went through the PCA procedure but, since then, only three cases have been heard. Arbitration has revived in popularity more recently, especially since the coming into force of the Convention on the Settlement of Investment Disputes 1964, which set up an international arbitration centre in Washington to deal with disputes between States arising out of the expropriation of foreign owned property. Arbitration is most favoured in commercial and technical disputes, in which arbitrators can be appointed who have specialist knowledge. It also has the advantage over judicial settlement, in that it is usually less expensive. The Iran-US Claims Tribunal, which was established in 1981, based at The Hague, is an example of prolonged use of arbitration.

One question which has been raised recently is whether the decision of an arbitration tribunal is capable of review. It has already been seen that the decisions of such tribunals are to be regarded a final and this would seem to rule out the possibility of review or appeal unless there is a clear error of law. However, in *Guinea Bissau v Senegal* (1991), the ICJ was willing to consider whether or not it should declare an arbitration award to be void. Guinea-Bissau alleged that the arbitration tribunal had exceeded its powers, that there was no true majority in favour of the decision, and that the award was based on insufficient reasoning. The court did not uphold Guinea-Bissau's claims but the fact that it was prepared to investigate the claims would indicate that arbitration awards are susceptible to review by the ICJ. The decision has been criticised by a number of writers, on the grounds that it undermines arbitration as a means of achieving final settlement of disputes.

11.8 Judicial settlement

By judicial settlement is meant a settlement brought about by a properly constituted international judicial tribunal, applying rules of law. The most well known of the international judicial tribunals is the International Court of Justice. There are also a number of regional international tribunals and also tribunals with jurisdiction over particular disputes; for example, the Law of the Sea Convention 1982 provides arrangements for the establishment of an International Tribunal for the Law of the Sea and the Sea Bed Disputes Chamber for dealing with disputes arising from the convention. There is no absolute distinction between arbitration and judicial settlement, although judicial settlement generally involves reference of the dispute to a permanent tribunal which applies fixed rules of procedure.

11.8.1 The World Court

The World Court refers to both the Permanent Court of International Justice (PCIJ) and its successor, the International Court of Justice (ICJ).

The PCIJ sat for the first time in the Hague on 15 February 1922 and, between 1922 and 1939, it dealt with 79 cases. The PCIJ was dissolved, together with the League of Nations, in April 1946. It was succeeded by the ICJ, which is the principal judicial organ of the UN. The ICJ is an integral part of the UN, established under Article 92 of the UN Charter. The Statute of the ICJ, which broadly follows the text of the Statute of the PCIJ, contains the basic rules of the court, which are supplemented by the rules of the court adopted by the court under Article 30. The present rules were adopted on 14 April 1978 and represent a major revision of the original 1946 rules. The rules govern the procedure of the court.

11.8.2 Composition of the court

The court is composed of 15 judges nominated by the national groups on the panel of the Permanent Court of Arbitration. No two judges may be of the same nationality. The judges are elected by absolute majority by secret ballot at meetings of the Security Council and General Assembly held simultaneously in an attempt to avoid fixing. In practice, there is much disagreement and political bargaining. Those eligible are persons of high moral character who possess the qualifications required in their country for appointment to high judicial office or, alternatively, are recognised international jurists (Article 2 of the ICJ Statute). Judges are to be elected without regard to nationality although, under a current 'understanding', the regional distribution of judges to be elected is as follows:

Africa	3
Asia	3
Latin America	2
Eastern Europe	2
W Europe & others	5

In general, the five permanent members of the UN Security Council are represented (US, UK, Russia, China, and France). Judges are appointed for a period of nine years, which is renewable. Elections are staggered and five judges are elected every three years. The judges themselves elect a president and vice-president, who serve for a three year term. Presidents and vice-presidents can be re-elected. The most recent elections were held towards the end of 1996. On 6 February 1997, Stephen M Schwebel was elected President and Christopher G Weeramantty became Vice-President.

Although the nationality of judges may be significant in their selection, once appointed, they are expected to be impartial and not subject to control by the States of which they are nationals. A judge is not prohibited from sitting in a case in which his national State is a party, although a president should not act as president in such a case. A party not represented on the bench can be represented by an *ad hoc* judge. This is to provide equality of the parties; the alternative would be to exclude judges from hearing cases about their own national State. Article 17(2) of the Statute provides that no member of the court should participate in the decision of any case in which he has previously acted as a representative for one of the parties, although this rule has not always been observed in practice. For example, in the *Namibia* case (1971), members of the court had previously been involved in UN discussions as national representatives on the Security Council and had played an active part in resolutions directly relevant to the case. South Africa challenged the court's jurisdiction on this basis but the challenge was rejected.

The cases are heard in either English or French and are decided by majority vote. If it is necessary, the president has a casting vote, in addition to his own vote. The court delivers a single judgment, but individual judges can add their own judgment whether or not they are dissenting. The cases can be heard by the full court (the quorum is nine) or by a chamber of three or more for a particular case (Article 26 of the ICJ Statute). The composition of the chamber is decided by the court after the parties have been consulted. In the *Gulf of Maine* case (1982), the US and Canada threatened to withdraw their case if their wishes as to the composition of the chamber were not respected. Since then, a number of other cases have been heard by a chamber of the court and this has led to the expression of some concern on the possible effects on the reputation of the court as a whole. The apparent ability of States to choose the composition of the chamber may have an adverse effect on the court's ability to develop a universally applicable body of international law.

11.8.3 Jurisdiction in contentious cases

Article 34 of the Statute of the Court declares that only States may be parties before the ICJ and the court is open to all members of the UN (who are automatically parties to the Statute). States which are not UN members may become parties to the Statute on conditions set by the UN General Assembly (Article 93 of the UN Charter), and States such as Switzerland and San Marino have taken advantage of this provision. Access to the court is also available to non-parties to the Statute if they lodge a declaration with the court accepting the obligations of the Statute and Article 94 of the UN Charter. Declarations can be particular to a particular dispute, or they can be general.

Article 36(1) of the Statute provides that:

> The jurisdiction of the court comprises all cases which the parties refer to it and all matters specially provided for in the Charter of the United Nations or in treaties or conventions in force.

In contentious cases, in principle, the exercise of the court's jurisdiction is conditional on the consent of the parties to the dispute. This was confirmed in the separate opinion of Judge Lauterpacht given in the *Case Concerning the Application of the Genocide Convention* (1993), where he stated:

> The court can only act in a case if the parties, both applicant and respondent, have conferred jurisdiction upon it by some voluntary act of consent.

He indicated that consent could be given in one of three ways:

(a) under the provisions of a treaty;

(b) by acceptance of the court's compulsory jurisdiction under Article 36(2) of the Statute; or

(c) by acceptance of jurisdiction by the respondent through its conduct following the unilateral initiation of proceedings by the applicant.

A joint decision to make reference to the court will usually be drawn up in a special agreement (*compromis*). A unilateral reference by one State will be sufficient to vest the court with jurisdiction if the other State subsequently consents under the doctrine known as *forum prorogatum*. Such a situation arose in the *Corfu Channel case* (1947). If there is no consent, then the court cannot hear the case. Nor can the court hear a case in the absence of a materially interested State.

The most usual method of conferring jurisdiction under Article 36(1) is by treaty. A treaty may be one providing for the reference of specific disputes, or it may be couched in more general terms. For example, Article 16(1) of the Convention on Unlawful Acts Against Maritime Navigation 1988 provides that:

> Any dispute between two or more State parties concerning the interpretation or application of this convention which cannot be settled through negotiation within a reasonable time shall, at the request of one of them, be submitted to arbitration. If within six months from the date of the request for arbitration, the parties are unable to agree on the organisation of the arbitration any one of those parties may refer the dispute to the International Court of Justice by request in conformity with the Statute of the Court.

In the *US Diplomatic and Consular Staff in Tehran* case (1980), the ICJ founded jurisdiction on Article 1 of the Optional Protocols concerning the Compulsory Settlement of Disputes which accompany both the Vienna Convention on Consular Relations 1963 and the Vienna Convention on Diplomatic Relations 1961.

Although it is true to state that the jurisdiction of the ICJ is conditional on the consent of the parties, matters are slightly confused by Article 36(2) of the Statute, which provides that:

> The State parties to the present statute may at any time declare that they recognise as compulsory *ipso facto* and without special agreement, in relation to any other State accepting the same obligation, the jurisdiction of the court in all legal disputes concerning:
>
> (a) the interpretation of a treaty;
>
> (b) any question of international law;
>
> (c) the existence of any fact which, if established, would constitute a breach of an international obligation;
>
> (d) the nature or extent of the reparation to be made for the breach of an international obligation.

Under this provision, States may make a declaration recognising as compulsory the jurisdiction of the court in a number of defined disputes. Such declarations obviate the need for special agreement. Making the declaration is optional but, once it has been made, acceptance of the court's jurisdiction is compulsory. The effectiveness of Article 36(2) depends on many, if not all, States making such a declaration. So far, less than 50 States have done so. Declarations are lodged with the UN Secretary General and, once a State has made the declaration, it has the right to bring to the court any other State accepting the same obligation, providing the subject matter of the dispute falls within the specified categories. Article 36(3) provides that declarations may be made unconditionally or on condition of reciprocity on the part of several or certain States or for a certain time. Reservations are to be found in most declarations and the court's jurisdiction over a case is restricted to those disputes that States have not excluded from its 'compulsory' jurisdiction.

Declarations can also be made subject to a reservation permitting withdrawal at any time. They may be made indefinitely or for a fixed term of years.

The majority of declarations made according to Article 36(2) operate on the basis of reciprocity. This means that the ICJ will only have jurisdiction to the extent that the two declarations of the parties to the dispute coincide. This point was confirmed by the ICJ in the *Norwegian Loans* case (1957), where France sought to rely on the fact that both it and Norway had made declarations accepting the compulsory jurisdiction of the court. The ICJ found that:

> A comparison between the two declarations shows that the French declaration accepts the court's jurisdiction within narrower limits than the Norwegian declaration; consequently, the common will of the parties, which is the basis of the court's jurisdiction, exists within these narrower limits indicated by the French reservation.

As a result, Norway was entitled to invoke the French reservation and the ICJ found itself without jurisdiction to hear the case.

The type of reservation which was found in the French case, often known as a self-judging or automatic reservation, has caused particular problems. The French reservation was worded as follows:

> This declaration does not apply to differences relating to matters which are essentially within the national jurisdiction as understood by the government of the Republic of France.

Article 36(6) of the Statute provides that it is the ICJ that must ultimately decide any dispute about its jurisdiction and it would therefore appear that such automatic reservations usurp the powers of the court by allowing the reserving State to have the final say as to what constitutes a matter within national jurisdiction. Judge Lauterpacht, in a separate opinion in the *Norwegian Loans* case, stated that the French declaration did conflict with Article 36(6) and was therefore invalid. He went on to consider what the effect of the invalid reservation was. He suggested two alternatives: either the invalid reservation could be severed from the declaration, or the reservation could be regarded as invalidating the entire declaration. Judge Lauterpacht favoured the latter option and was supported in this view by the dissenting opinion of Judge Guerrero. Judge Lauterpacht repeated his view in the *Interhandel* case (1959), where the court was faced with an automatic reservation contained in the US optional declaration. However, in that case, the court itself did not find it necessary to comment on the validity of such reservations. It would seem to be settled that automatic or self-judging reservations are themselves invalid. As to the effect of such invalidity on the rest of the declaration, the position is less clear, although the view preferred by the majority of writers is that the invalid reservation can be severed from the rest of the declaration, thus leaving the amended declaration effective.

States are free to modify and withdraw their declarations and the question of the extent of notice required has created some problems. The declaration made by the USA in 1946 provided for termination after a six month notice period. When it became clear that Nicaragua was going to bring proceedings against it in the ICJ, the US sought to modify, with immediate effect, its declaration so as to exclude the court's jurisdiction. In considering the question of jurisdiction in the *Nicaragua* case (1984), the ICJ held that Nicaragua (whose declaration contained no reservation) was entitled to invoke against the US the six month notice requirement and that this requirement would apply to modifications to the declaration. The US's modification, which was made on 6 April 1984, three days before the court became seised of the case, would therefore only take effect on 6 October 1984, by which time the court would already have begun to hear the case.

A final point to note in respect of reservations to optional declarations made under Article 36(2) is that they only relate to the court's jurisdiction under Article 36(2). Even if a reservation provides an effective bar to Article 36(2) jurisdiction, the court may be able to base jurisdiction on some other manifestation of a common will of the parties. In practice, jurisdiction is based solely on the optional declaration in very few cases.

11.8.4 Incidental jurisdiction

The ICJ may be called upon to exercise an incidental jurisdiction, independently of the main case: hearing preliminary objections, applications to intervene, and taking interim measures.

11.8.4.1 Preliminary objections

Often, before it looks at the merits of the case, the court will be asked to consider objections to jurisdiction. These jurisdictional issues are decided first. As has already been stated, it is the court itself which has authority to settle disputes about jurisdiction by virtue of Article 36(6) of the Statute of the ICJ.

11.8.4.2 Intervention

A State, not a party to the dispute, may intervene under Articles 62 and 63 of the Statute if it considers it has an interest in the case, and it is for the ICJ to decide as a preliminary matter whether or not such an interest exists. In the *Continental Shelf* case (1982), the court rejected Malta's application to intervene. While Malta did have an interest similar to other States in the area in the case in question, the court said that, in order to intervene under Article 62, it had to have an interest of a legal nature which may be affected by the court's decision in the instant case. In the *Land, Island and Maritime Frontier* case (1992), the ICJ gave permission to Nicaragua to intervene in the dispute between Honduras and El Salvador. In doing so, it suggested a number of general principles which would apply with regard to any application to intervene. First, the intervening State has the burden of proving it has an interest of a legal nature which may, rather than will, be affected by the dispute. Secondly, the court can grant permission to intervene even if one or both of the other parties object. Thirdly, if permission is granted, the intervening State does not become a party to the dispute and no binding determination of its rights will occur. The purpose of intervention is to allow the intervening State to remind the court of rights that may be affected by resolution of the dispute between the two parties.

11.8.4.3 Interim measures

Under Article 41 of the Statute, the court may grant provisional measures of protection in order to preserve the respective rights of the parties. These are awarded to assist the court to ensure the integrity of the proceedings and are not to be regarded as judgments on the merits of the case. Interim measures have been awarded in a number of cases but compliance with such orders has been poor. In making interim indications, which are heard first, the court has to be satisfied that there is a *prima facie* basis for jurisdiction. In the *Lockerbie* case (1992), the ICJ refused Libya's requests for interim measures of protection from the use of sanctions and possible use of force against it. The principal ground for refusal was that the sanctions and possible use of force were being effected by a UN Security Council resolution and the court drew back at the interim stage from ruling such a resolution *ultra vires*. The court was therefore unable to find that there was a risk of Libya's interests in the case suffering irreparable damage. The court was also required to consider the effect of a conflict between treaty obligations and Security Council resolutions, and Judge Lachs, in a separate opinion, expressly stated his view that treaty obligations could be overridden by resolutions passed by the Security Council. It seems likely that, when the court considers the merits of the case, it will have to consider the relationship between itself and other organs of the UN and the extent to which it can rule on the validity of resolutions passed under provisions of the UN Charter.

11.8.5 Advisory opinions

In addition to having contentious jurisdiction, Article 65(1) of the Statute allows the ICJ to give advisory opinions on any legal question at the request of any body authorised by, or in accordance with, the UN Charter. The General Assembly and the Security Council are authorised by Article 96 of the UN Charter to request advisory opinions and a large proportion of the specialised agencies of the UN have been authorised in accordance with the Charter. States are not able to request advisory opinions themselves. Although advisory opinions are not binding in law on the requesting body, they have generally been accepted and acted upon by any State concerned. In exercising jurisdiction to give advisory opinions, the ICJ is keen to avoid situations where an answer to a question would have the effect of deciding a specific dispute between two States, since to do so would infringe the general requirement of the consent of States to the resolution of contentious cases. Thus, in the *Eastern Carelia* case (1923), the PCIJ declined to give an opinion which would have directly affected a dispute between Finland and the USSR.

11.8.6 Law applied by the court

It has already been pointed out that a major difference between arbitration and judicial settlement is that with judicial settlement the parties do not have a choice as to the law applied. Article 38(1) of the Statute provides that the ICJ must decide such disputes as are submitted to it in accordance with international law. Article 38(2), however, does provide that, if the parties to a dispute agree, the court can adopt a slightly more flexible approach and decide disputes *ex aequo et bono*.

11.8.7 Effect of judgment

The decision of the ICJ in contentious cases has no binding force except between the parties (Article 59 of the ICJ Statute), although the court does have regard to earlier decisions. According to Article 60, the decision is final and without appeal, although the court can interpret its decision if there is any confusion. Article 61 allows the court to revise its judgment in the light of discovery of some new and decisive fact. Such revision must be requested within 10 years of judgment and the new fact must have been one which could not have been discovered with due diligence at the time of the original case. The rate of compliance with judgments of the court is relatively high. A far greater problem is caused by non-appearance.

11.8.8 Non-appearance

Article 53 of the Statute provides that:

> 1 Whenever one of the parties does not appear before the court, or fails to defend his case, the other party may call upon the court to decide in favour of its claim.
>
> 2 The court must, before doing so, satisfy itself, not only that it has the jurisdiction in accordance with Articles 36 and 37, but also that the claim is well founded in fact and law.

There have been a number of cases in recent years where the court has had to have recourse to Article 53. Its effect is to require the court to advance the legal arguments of the absent party.

11.9 Settlement within the UN

By Article 24 of the UN Charter, the UN Security Council is given primary responsibility for the maintenance of international peace and security, and Member States are under an obligation to carry out the decisions of the Security Council. Chapter VI of the Charter deals with the pacific settlement of disputes. Under Article 34, the Security Council has the power to investigate any dispute or potential dispute and can call upon the parties to seek a peaceful resolution of the dispute. If the parties to the dispute fail to settle it by peaceful means, they should refer it to the Security Council, which can then recommend appropriate action, including terms of settlement. Under Chapter VI, the Security Council can only make non-binding recommendations. However, if the Security Council determines that the continuance of the dispute constitutes a threat to the peace, or that the situation involves a breach of the peace or act of aggression, it can take action under Chapter VII of the Charter. Chapter VII gives the Security Council the power to make decisions which are binding on Member States, once it has determined the existence of a threat to the peace, breach of the peace, or act of aggression. Security Council action under Chapter VII of the Charter is discussed in Chapter 12.

Although the Security Council has primary responsibility for maintaining peace and security, under Article 14 the General Assembly may recommend measures for the peaceful adjustment of any situation which 'it deems likely to impair the general welfare or friendly relations among nations'.

The role of regional organisations in maintaining the peace is recognised by Article 52 of the UN Charter and a number of regional organisations and groupings of States, such as the Organisation of American States and the Conference on Security and Co-operation in Europe, have created their own machinery for the settlement of disputes.

PEACEFUL SETTLEMENT OF DISPUTES

There is an obligation on States to settle their disputes peacefully (Article 2(3) of the Charter of the United Nations).

The peaceful settlement of disputes may be by either legal or diplomatic means. Diplomatic settlement includes:

(a) negotiation;

(b) good offices;

(c) mediation;

(d) conciliation; and

(e) inquiry.

Legal means of settlement refer to arbitration or judicial settlement.The prime distinction between legal and diplomatic settlement is that legal settlement will result in a legally binding resolution of the dispute.

Arbitration

Arbitration is often more flexible than judicial settlement, since the parties will agree on the arbitrator(s) and have some say in the law to be applied – see Hague Convention for the Pacific Settlement of Disputes 1899 and 1907.

Judicial settlement

The best known international judicial tribunal is the International Court of Justice, which sits in The Hague. The ICJ is composed of 15 judges and hears disputes between States. It can also deliver advisory opinions if requested to do so by authorised international organisations. The jurisdiction of the court in contentious cases depends upon the consent of the parties which may be expressed:

(a) in a special agreement;

(b) in the provisions of a treaty;

(c) by conduct following the unilateral initiation of proceedings by the applicant; or

(d) by acceptance of the court's compulsory jurisdiction under Article 36(2) of the Statute of the ICJ (see *Norwegian Loans* case (1957); *Nicaragua* case (1986)).

The ICJ also has an incidental jurisdiction and can hear preliminary objections to jurisdiction, applications to intervene, and issue interim orders – see the *Lockerbie* case (1993).

The final judgment of the ICJ in contentious cases is binding on the parties to the dispute.

CHAPTER 12

THE USE OF FORCE

12.1 Introduction

The corollary of the requirement of any effective legal system to provide a fair and adequate means of peacefully settling disputes is a prohibition on the unlawful use of force. The obligation not to use unlawful force can be said to be one of the most fundamental rules of international law and has the status of *jus cogens*. However, the actual use of force remains one of the most contentious areas of international law. While every State agrees that, *prima facie*, the use of force is impermissible, there is considerable disagreement over the precise definition of force and the circumstances in which it may lawfully be used. It is convenient to divide consideration of the international rules governing the use of force into two main areas:

(a) the unilateral use of force which encompasses the use of force by individual States or groups of States acting on their own initiative; and

(b) the collective use of force which refers to force used by or under the auspices of a competent international organisation.

12.2 The law before 1945

In the early days of international law, the question of a State's right to resort to the use of force was judged in terms of the criteria for the just war. The 16th century writers asserted that war could only be just when used as a defence against attack or for the purpose of righting a great wrong. A State should first try to find a peaceful solution and only if attempts failed could it resort to war, and only then if consideration had been given to whether the war might produce more harm than good. However, with the growth of positivism, international law abandoned efforts to judge right from wrong in this area and, in effect, accepted the use of force as a legitimate instrument of State policy. The use of force was not *per se* prohibited, although the European States recognised the right of the victors of armed conflict to exact reparations from the State judged by the victor to be responsible for causing the war. The main concern of international law at this time was with the actual conduct of hostilities through the development of the laws of war. The laws of war and other armed conflicts are discussed in Chapter 13.

A change in the attitude of international law towards the use of force began with the advent of the League of Nations in 1920. Although the Covenant of the League of Nations did not specifically prohibit the use of force, it did restrict its use, by placing a duty on States to try to reach peaceful settlement first. Article 12 of the covenant required members to observe during a crisis a 'cooling off' period of three months before resorting to war, in order to allow time for peaceful settlement. The provisions contained in the covenant were subsequently reinforced by the Treaty Providing for the Renunciation of War as an Instrument of National Policy 1928 (also known as the Kellogg-Briand Pact and the Pact of Paris). 63 States signed the treaty, which remains in force today. The parties to the treaty renounced war as an instrument of national policy and committed themselves to peaceful settlement of disputes.

Article I of the treaty provides that:

> The high contracting parties solemnly declare in the names of their respective peoples that they condemn recourse to war for the solution of international controversies, and renounce it as an instrument of national policy in their relations with one another.

Article II States that:

> The high contracting parties agree that the settlement or solution of disputes or conflicts of whatever nature or of whatever origin they may be, which may arise among them, shall never be sought except by pacific means.

Two problems arose in relation to the Kellogg-Briand Pact. First, given that, in the international law of the period, 'war' applied only to the legal State existing between nations following an official declaration of war, there was some question whether the parties' undertakings applied also to use of force other than declared war and to the threat of war without actual hostilities. In 1934, the International Law Association, a private organisation of lawyers, suggested that the Pact did cover armed force and threat of war, but such an interpretation was not supported by State practice. Secondly, it was unclear whether the Pact permitted war used in self-defence. The prevailing view was that it did.

12.3 The law after 1945: Article 2(4) of the UN Charter

Those responsible for drafting the UN Charter were much motivated by a desire to correct the inadequacies in the law which events after 1920 had revealed. Consequently, the Charter emphasises in Article 1 that it is a purpose of the United Nations to 'maintain international peace and security', which may involve collective measures to prevent and remove threats to the peace, the suppression of acts of aggression or other breaches of the peace, and the settlement or adjustment of international disputes, or situations which might lead to a breach of the peace, by peaceful means. Article 2(3) obliges members to settle disputes by peaceful means, in such a manner that international peace and security, and justice, are not endangered. The principal prohibition on the use of force is contained in Article 2(4), which states:

> All members shall refrain in their international relations from the threat or use of force against the territorial integrity or political independence of any State, or in any other manner inconsistent with the purposes of the United Nations.

It should be noted that Article 2(4) covers threats as well as the use of force. In the *Legality of the Threat or Use of Nuclear Weapons* Case (1996), the ICJ defined a threat as a signalled intention to use force if certain events occur. It held that the mere possession of nuclear weapons did not constitute a threat under Article 2(4).

It is generally acknowledged that Article 2(4) is declaratory of customary international law. In 1970, the General Assembly adopted by consensus the Declaration on Principles of International Law Concerning Friendly Relations and Co-operation among States in Accordance with the Charter of the United Nations. This declaration reaffirmed the commitment to outlawing the use of force. Further evidence for the customary law prohibition on the use of force is to be found in the ICJ decision in the *Nicaragua* case (1986).

12.4 The definition of force

It can immediately be noted that Article 2(4) is not concerned with outlawing 'war' but prohibits the use of 'force'. The problem is then to define what is meant by 'force'. Use of armed force is certainly covered, but the position as regards threats or action short of actual use of armed force is less clear. There has been dispute as to whether only armed force should be covered or whether the prohibition should extend to economic force. In the *travaux preparatoires* of the UN Charter, Brazil proposed that a prohibition on the use of economic force should be included in Article 2(4). The proposal was rejected, although the significance of the rejection is disputed; some writers argued that it indicated a desire not to outlaw economic force, others suggested that the proposal was rejected because 'force' would encompass all forms of force including economic force. No further definition was provided by the 1970 Declaration, although the section dealing with the prohibition on intervention in the domestic affairs of foreign States provides that:

> No State may use or encourage the use of economic, political or any other type of measures to coerce another State in order to obtain from it the subordination of the exercise of its sovereign rights and to secure from it advantages of any kind.

There is also some argument over whether Article 2(4) is absolute in its prohibition on the use of force or whether it only prohibits force directed against territorial integrity, political independence or force that is contrary to the purposes of the UN. Brownlie argues that territorial integrity and political independence constitute the sum total of legal rights which a State has and, thus, all force is prohibited unless specifically allowed by the UN Charter. This view is often referred to as the restrictive view of force. But others, for example, Bowett, argue for a permissive view of force, suggesting that the use of force which does not result in the loss or permanent occupation of territory, does not compromise a State's ability to make independent decisions and which is not contrary to the purposes of the UN is not unlawful. Bowett points out that, since the phrase is used, 'it must be given its plain meaning' (Bowett, *Self-Defence in International Law*, 1958, Manchester: Manchester UP, p 152). State practice since 1945 would appear to favour the restrictive view and no State has relied solely upon the permissive view to justify its use of force. In the *Corfu Channel* case (1949), the UK sought to argue that its mine-sweeping operation in Albanian territorial waters was not unlawful, since it did not threaten the territorial integrity or political independence of Albania, but the argument was rejected by the ICJ.

12.5 The justifications for the unilateral use of force

Prima facie, the use of force is impermissible, but there are a number of situations in which the use of force may be lawfully justified.

There are three categories of force which may be considered:

(a) retorsion: an unfriendly and harmful act, which is lawful as a method of retaliation, for example, severance of diplomatic relations;

(b) reprisals: unlawful acts done in retaliation. Reprisals involving armed force would contravene Article 2(4); and

(c) self-defence.

12.5.1 Self-defence

Although Article 2(4) of the UN Charter prohibits the use of force, the prohibition has to be read in the light of Article 51, which States that:

> Nothing in the present charter shall impair the inherent right of individual or collective self-defence if an armed attack occurs against a member of the United Nations, until the Security Council has taken measures necessary to maintain international peace and security.

The US Secretary of State, Daniel Webster, gave the classic definition of self-defence in *The Caroline* case (1841), following a British military raid on a US port to seize and destroy a ship, *The Caroline*, which had been used to supply anti-British rebels in Canada. The raid took place at night and without warning; *The Caroline* was set on fire and allowed to drift over the Niagara Falls. Following the attack, the US authorities arrested the British leader of the raid, McLeod, and charged him with murder and arson. The UK sought the release of McLeod, arguing that the action had been one of self-defence. In the course of an exchange of diplomatic notes between the USA and the UK, Webster wrote that such an act could only be justified if there was:

> ... a necessity of self-defence, instant, overwhelming, leaving no choice of means, and no moment for deliberation.

Even if there was such a necessity, there was a requirement of proportionality. The action taken must not be:

> ... unreasonable or excessive, since the act, justified by the necessity of self-defence, must be limited by that necessity, and kept clearly within it.

The test for self-defence proposed by Webster was accepted by the UK and has since been regularly referred to as an articulation of the conditions under which the customary law right of self-defence can be exercised.

Clearly, if a crisis can be avoided by diplomatic representations, or if the 'danger' is so remote as to be nothing more than a feeling or suspicion, self-defence is not justified. Similarly, an attack on a naval vessel cannot be used as an excuse for a full scale occupation of the territory of the offending State, for this would not be a proportionate response. However, if these flexible conditions are satisfied, the customary right of self-defence permits the use of force in any of the following circumstances:

(a) force is lawful in self-defence against an ongoing armed attack against State territory;

(b) force is lawful in anticipatory self-defence, so that a State may strike first, with force, to neutralise an immediate but potential threat to its security;

(c) force is lawful in self-defence in response to an attack (threatened or actual) against State interests, such as territory, nationals, property and rights guaranteed under international law. If any such interests are threatened, then the State may use force to protect them; and

(d) force is lawful in self-defence even if the 'attack' does not itself involve measures of armed force, such as economic aggression and propaganda. All that is required is that there is an instant and overwhelming necessity for forceful action.

It can be seen that the customary right of self-defence is not a narrow exception to the general ban on use of force. It allows the use of force in a variety of situations, so long as there is some element of 'defence' of the 'State'. Importantly, customary self-defence may go beyond the right guaranteed by the Charter and, for this reason, it is important to determine whether customary self-defence has survived the Charter. In many of the recent examples of the use of force, such as the invasion of Grenada in 1983 by the US, the bombing of Libya by the US in 1986, and the destruction of the Iraqi nuclear reactor at Osarik by the Israeli airforce in 1981, the customary right of self-defence has been in part used as a justification by the State resorting to force.

However, under the restrictive approach to the use of force, it is argued that this wide right of self-defence is no longer available. Article 51 stipulates that nothing 'shall impair the inherent right of individual or collective self-defence if an armed attack occurs against a member of the United Nations'. If Article 2(4) prohibits all armed force, then the only right of self-defence available is the right found in article 51. Customary law is superseded and a State may only resort to self-defence 'if an armed attack occurs' but not otherwise. Specifically, the right of anticipatory self-defence is not available and, of the four situations outlined above, only (a) remains lawful.

Many States argue, however, that the customary right of self-defence still exists. It is argued that Article 51 was never intended to be a conclusive statement of the right to self-defence. Indeed, the *travaux preparatoires* of the San Francisco Conference suggest that Article 51 was included in order to clarify the relationship of regional organisations to the Security Council, rather than to define self-defence. Thus, regional organisations may take armed action, without Security Council authorisation, if it is a matter of self-defence and not 'enforcement action' (discussed at 12.6.2). It is also argued that the customary rights are specifically retained by the use of the word 'inherent'. This is taken to mean 'pre-existing in customary law'. It is also pointed out that Article 51 does not say that self-defence is available only if armed attack occurs. This permissive view of self-defence is supported by writers such as Bowett, McDougal and Stone.

One aspect of the right of self-defence which was discussed in the *Nicaragua* case (1986) was the question of what constitutes an 'armed attack'. The ICJ, quoting with approval the Declaration on Principle of International Law 1970, found that it included:

> ... not only action by the regular armed forces of a foreign State across an international border but also 'the sending by or on behalf of a State of armed bands, groups, irregulars, or mercenaries, which carry out acts of armed force against another State of such gravity as to amount to an actual armed attack carried out by regular forces' or its substantial involvement therein.

Writers favouring the restrictive view have argued that 'armed attack' carries a clear and specific meaning which is distinct from a 'use or threat of force' or a 'threat to the peace, breach of the peace or act of aggression' which falls short of actual armed attack.

The major area of controversy surrounding the use of self-defence concerns so-called anticipatory self-defence. Those supporting the restrictive view argue that it no longer exists and they are opposed by advocates of the permissive view. The matter has not been considered by any authoritative international tribunal. In the *Nicaragua* case (1986), the ICJ noted that the issue of a response to an imminent threat of armed attack had not been raised and therefore did not discuss the issue. Judge Schwebel, who gave a dissenting opinion, did express support for the permissive view of self-defence, although some allowance may be made for the fact that he was and is the US judge at the ICJ giving an opinion in a case in which the USA was the defendant. State practice on the issue is divided.

Israel claimed the right of anticipatory self-defence when attacking the Iraqi nuclear reactor in 1981, which it claimed was to be used to produce nuclear weapons that could be used against Israel. In the debate which took place at the UN Security Council following the attack, the majority of delegates condemned the attack and a number discussed the right of anticipatory self-defence in more general terms. Opinion as to whether such a right existed was divided, delegates from Pakistan, Guyana, Syria, Spain and Yugoslavia clearly supporting the restrictive view; delegates from Sierra Leone, Uganda, Malaysia, Niger, and the UK supporting the permissive view. Other examples follow a similar pattern.

It seems to be correct to state that, while there is no consensus among State practice recognising a right of anticipatory self-defence, there is certainly no consensus supporting the restrictive view. Given the general principle that the subjects of international law are free to do everything that is not specifically prohibited, it would seem correct to state that the right of anticipatory self-defence remains, pending the introduction of an authoritative rule prohibiting it.

Two final points should be noted with regard to the right of anticipatory self-defence. First, the general rules applicable to self-defence still apply. In other words, the threat of attack must be imminent and overwhelming and the action taken in self-defence must be proportionate to the perceived threat. This was confirmed by the ICJ in the *Nuclear Weapons* Case (1996). Secondly, it should be noted that an attack may occur before troops actually cross the border, as when a missile is launched or aircraft deployed. Action taken in such circumstances would clearly fall within Article 51.

12.5.2 Invitation and civil wars

In traditional international law, it was quite clear that the principle *volenti non fit injuria* applied, to the effect that a State was free to allow another to use force in any form in its own territory. The question arises as to whether the principle survives the UN Charter. In other words, is consent one of the exceptions to the prohibition on use of force? There seems little doubt from State practice and interpretation of Article 51 that international law permits States to use armed force to assist another State assert its rights to self-defence if an express request is made. Thus, Kuwait was able to ask for assistance from outside States in asserting its rights to self-defence against Iraq. The only rationale for such organisations as NATO is that an attack on one Member State constitutes an attack on all members.

The more problematic area is where armed assistance is requested by a State in the putting down of an internal insurrection. A large number of States have argued that use of armed force is legitimate if requested by a government even if it is to put down an insurrection; for example, in 1958, the UK sent troops to Jordan to assist the Jordanian government in putting down a rebellion. However, a number of writers have argued that international law has been gradually restricting such rights of intervention. First, it was not always easy to be certain that assistance had genuinely been asked for and, secondly, where intervention resulted in armed force being used against an insurrection which had widespread popular support, there were possible conflicts with rights of self-determination. Examples of intervention besides the Jordanian illustration are: USSR interventions in Hungary (1956), Czechoslovakia (1968) and Afghanistan (1979); USA intervention in Lebanon (1958), the Dominican Republic (1965) and Grenada (1983).

Arend and Beck in their study of the use of force (Arend AC and Black, RJ, *International Law and the Use of Force: Beyond the UN Charter Paradigm*,1993, London: Routledge) suggest that the following four types of internal unrest can be identified and distinguished, each of which will give rise to different rights of foreign intervention:

(a) low intensity unrest

This is the least serious form of internal conflict and would be characterised by scattered riots or limited terrorist action. Organised opposition groups may exist but the objectively viewed purpose of such groups would not be the complete overthrow of the State. An example would be the disturbances in China which culminated in the massacre at Tianneman Square;

(b) civil war

A civil war is characterised by the existence of a group or groups that are seeking to overthrow the exiting government and establish themselves in its place. The classic example would be the Spanish Civil War of the 1930s and more recent examples are provided by Afghanistan, Iran and Sri Lanka. In the case of civil wars, a further distinction is often drawn between a State of insurgency and a State of belligerency. The distinction is principally based on the degree of recognition accorded to the rebels. A situation of insurgency exists when the rebels have received little international recognition and becomes a State of belligerency when it is acknowledged that both rebels and government have a similar degree of legitimacy and exercise a similar degree of authority over the population of the territory. Such a situation may well give rise to recognition of separate *de facto* and *de jure* governments;

(c) wars of secession

Such wars occur when a particular ethnic, religious or racial group seeks to break away and form a new separate State. The two main examples of a war of secession are the Biafran War in the late 1960s and the Bangladesh War in 1971. To some extent, recent events in former Yugoslavia have had the characteristics of a war of secession; and

(d) wars of unification

Such wars may be characterised as double wars of secession. They arise where a particular group lays claim to an area of territory which crosses international borders. The particular group wishes to unite to form its own new State. The principal examples of potential wars of unification are provided by the situation of the Kurds (who at present live in Turkey, Iraq and Iran) and the Armenians (who live in Iran and the territory of the former USSR).

In practice, of course, situations do not always neatly fit into one of the four categories. For example, how is the situation with respect to actions taken by the IRA in Northern Ireland and the British mainland to be categorised? Often, the particular categorisation given to a particular situation of internal unrest will depend upon the political allegiance of the one carrying out the categorisation. Nevertheless, the four categories provide some assistance in identifying the degree of foreign intervention that is permitted.

The traditional view was that States had a wide liberty to provide armed assistance to foreign governments but that has been changed with the recognition of the right to self-determination. The use of force to support assertions of self-determination is discussed at 12.5.5. The position with regard to intervention would seem to be as follows: States may now only intervene to assist a foreign government experiencing low level civil strife and only in such situations where the consent of the foreign government is freely given. Subject to the rules relating to self-determination, States may never give assistance to rebels, since to do so would contravene the prohibition on interference in the domestic affairs of another State.

The only discussion of the issue by an international tribunal took place in the *Nicaragua* case (1986). In that case, Nicaragua argued that the US was in breach of international law by providing armed support for the contras. The US argument, although not formally presented to the ICJ, was that it was using force in the collective self-defence of El Salvador, since Nicaragua had previously been providing armed assistance to rebels in El Salvador. The court discussed the principle of non-intervention in the internal affairs of another State and found that customary international law:

> ... forbids all States or groups of States to intervene directly or indirectly in the internal or external affairs of other States. A prohibited intervention must accordingly be one bearing on matters in which each State is permitted, by the principle of State sovereignty, to decide freely. One of these is the choice of political, economic, social and cultural system, and the formulation of foreign policy. Intervention is wrongful when it uses methods of coercion in regard to such choices, which must remain free ones. The element of coercion ... is particularly obvious in the case of intervention which uses force, either in the direct form of military action, or in the indirect form of support for subversive or terrorist armed activities within another State.

It went on to State:

> The court therefore finds that no such general right of intervention in support of an opposition within another State exists in contemporary international law.

The court did, however, recognise a right of third States to intervene where one State has unlawfully intervened in the affairs of another State. The situation was said to be analogous to the right of collective self-defence with the attendant requirement of proportionality.

12.5.3 Protection of nationals and property abroad

On several occasions since the Second World War, States have used armed force without the consent of the territorial State to protect their nationals and property in danger in the foreign territory. One of the earliest examples is the Anglo-French invasion of Egypt in 1956. UK and French troops occupied positions along the Suez Canal. France did not seek to justify its actions on the basis of a right to protect nationals abroad, but the UK government repeatedly asserted that nothing in the UN Charter abrogated the right of governments to use force to protect the lives of nationals abroad. In the debate in the House of Lords that followed the invasion, the Lord Chancellor, Viscount Kilmuir, argued that the right to protect nationals abroad was an extension of the right of self-defence, stating:

> ... self-defence undoubtedly includes a situation in which the lives of a State's nationals abroad are threatened and it is necessary to intervene on that territory for their protection.

Viscount Kilmuir then set down three conditions for the use of such protective action to be legitimate:

(a) the nationals must be in imminent danger of injury;

(b) there must be a failure or inability on the part of the territorial sovereign to protect the nationals in question;

(c) the measures taken must be strictly limited to the object of protecting the nationals against injury.

The invasion was heavily criticised by other States and, in fact, in the UN debates which followed, the UK relied little on a right to protect nationals and instead sought to justify the action on the basis of the need to safeguard international navigation through the canal.

Since 1956, there have been a number of other examples of action taken to protect nationals. In 1960, Belgian paratroopers landed in the Congo, purportedly to protect foreign nationals, on the grounds that the legitimate government of the Congo was no longer capable of affording protection. In fact, Belgium argued it was acting to protect the lives not only of Belgian nationals but of 'human lives in general', which would seem to bring it within the definition of a humanitarian intervention (discussed at para 12.5.4).

In June 1976, Israeli forces landed at Entebbe airport in Uganda to free 96 Israelis who had been taken hostage when the aircraft in which they were flying had been hijacked. The Israelis did not seek the prior approval of Uganda for the action, during the course of which 10 Ugandan military aircraft were destroyed and a number of Ugandan soldiers were killed. The Israeli action was discussed by the UN Security Council, in which Uganda condemned the action and demanded full compensation from Israel. The Israeli delegate argued that Uganda was itself in breach of international law for failing to protect foreign nationals on its territory. Furthermore, he stated:

> The right of a State to take military action to protect its nationals in mortal danger is recognised by all legal authorities in international law.

He quoted with approval a passage from J Brierly's *Law of Nations: An Introduction to the International Law of Peace* (6th edn, 1963, Oxford: OUP), which suggests that, normally, action should be taken by the UN but, where the UN is unable to act in time, unilateral action taken by a State would be legitimate. The reaction of other States was mixed, with only the US positively supporting the right to protect nationals abroad. Interestingly, two years after the Entebbe raid, Egypt intervened at Larnaca airport in Cyprus to protect Egyptian nationals taken hostage by Palestinian commandos. The Egyptians had prior permission from Cyprus to land but they had been forbidden from using force. The Egyptians did use force to free the hostages and, during the fighting, a number of Cypriot nationals were injured. The Cypriot authorities captured and detained the Palestinian commandos and a number of Egyptian soldiers and refused to hand them over to Egypt, claiming a violation of Cypriot sovereignty.

Some of the more recent examples of intervention have involved the US. In April 1980, US forces entered Iran in an unsuccessful attempt to release US nationals held hostage in the US Embassy in Tehran. In 1983, following a coup in Grenada, President Reagan authorised an invasion, partly to protect US nationals who were believed to be at risk. The invasion was also carried out 'to restore democracy' and at the request of the organisation of Eastern Caribbean States. Nevertheless, on 2 November 1983, the UN General Assembly voted 108 to 9 to condemn the US action as a violation of international law. In December 1989, 10,000 US forces entered Panama, following General Noriega's decision to annul the elections which had been held there. The US seized Noriega and he was subsequently charged with drug trafficking offences in the US. US President Bush stated that the action was taken 'to safeguard the lives of Americans, to defend democracy in Panama, to combat drug trafficking and to protect the integrity of the Panama Canal Treaty' and, as such, the US argued, it was consistent with international law. Most other States, however, condemned the invasion as a violation of international law. Finally, the US intervened to protect its nationals in Liberia in August 1990, a day after the rebel leader had ordered the arrest of all foreigners in Monrovia, the capital city.

Contrary to the claim made by the Israeli UN delegate following the Entebbe incident, the majority of writers seem to believe that the use of force to protect nationals abroad is not permissible under present day international law. This view is consistent with statements made by the majority of States and two major UN resolutions: the Declaration on the Inadmissibility of Intervention in the Domestic Affairs of States (1965) and the Declaration of Principles of International Law (1970). However, one point which should be remembered here relates to the formation of customary international law. As was discussed in Chapter 2, in evaluating State practice, 'actions speak louder than words'. The interventions that have taken place have been carried out by those States which have the military power to do so. It might be argued that statements of the law made by States which are unable to mount intervention carry less weight than the actions of States which have the necessary power. This point is stressed by those writers who adhere to the permissive view of the use of force. Writers such as Bowett, McDougal, Reisman and Waldock argue that intervention can be justified by an extension of the right of self-defence, on the basis that an injury to a national in a foreign State which does not or cannot afford adequate protection is tantamount to an injury to the State itself. Such writers accept that use of force to protect nationals abroad is restricted by the three conditions outlined by Viscount Kilmuir following the Suez invasion.

12.5.4 Humanitarian intervention

Humanitarian intervention can be distinguished from action taken to protect nationals, in that it applies to action taken to protect non-nationals. As has already been seen, the distinction is not always a clear one in practice and States often claim to be protecting both their own and other nationals when intervening in foreign States. The topic being discussed here must also be distinguished from humanitarian intervention authorised by the organs of the UN, which is discussed at 13.6.3. What is to be discussed here is the situation where a State or group of States use armed force to protect the inhabitants of the target State from large scale human rights violations.

There are a number of cases where States have partly justified their use of force on the grounds of humanitarian intervention. The most cited example is India's invasion of East Pakistan in December 1971. In elections held in 1970, a party pledged to achieving autonomous status for the region gained the majority of seats in East Pakistan. The Pakistan government responded to the result by imposing martial law and, subsequently, East Pakistan announced its intention to secede from Pakistan. In March 1971, the Pakistan army attacked Dacca, the capital of East Pakistan, and there followed a period of intense fighting, during which the population of East Pakistan was subject to indiscriminate killing and torture. Up to 10 million refugees crossed into India and, in December 1971, Indian forces moved in. After 12 days of fighting, the Pakistan army surrendered and the new State of Bangladesh was recognised. At first, India justified its actions on the basis of humanitarian intervention but subsequently claimed that the invasion was in response to a Pakistan attack on India. Many writers have attached significance to the fact that India changed the basis of its justification and argue that this was because India recognised that no right to humanitarian intervention existed in international law. Some writers have suggested, however, that India changed its argument more on the basis that a claim of humanitarian intervention would be difficult to sustain on the facts, given India's own self-interest in seeing the emergence of an independent Bangladesh.

Indeed, the bulk of State practice seems to deny a right of humanitarian intervention. When Biafra attempted to secede from Nigeria in the late 1960s, the Nigerian army acted with considerable brutality that received worldwide condemnation; yet no State felt it had the right to intervene. In 1979, Tanzania intervened in Uganda, following several years of atrocities committed against the population by the Amin regime; yet Tanzania did not seek to justify its action on the basis of humanitarian intervention but, rather, based its action on somewhat spurious claims to be acting in self-defence. When Vietnam invaded Cambodia in 1979 to overthrow the Pol Pot regime which had been responsible for acts of genocide, the invasion was condemned and little support was found for the right of humanitarian intervention that was asserted by Vietnam.

More recently, military action taken to provide humanitarian assistance has been authorised by the UN. The main examples are the protection of the Kurds in northern Iraq and action taken in Bosnia although, in the case of northern Iraq, the extent of the authority given was not completely clear. It would appear that it is for regional and international organisations to intervene on humanitarian grounds and that no right exists for individual States to act on their own.

12.5.5 Self-determination

The use of force to achieve self-determination and for the assistance of national liberation movements has increasingly been claimed as legitimate in recent years, on the ground that it furthers the principles of the UN Charter.

The issue may arise in three ways. First, may the colonial power use force to suppress self-determination movements? This would seem to be unlawful, being contrary to both customary and charter law. According to the Declaration of Principles of International Law:

> Every State has the duty to refrain from any forcible action which deprives peoples of their right to self-determination and freedom and independence.

Similarly, Article 2(4) prohibits the use of force in any manner inconsistent with the purposes of the UN and this may have been designed to specifically protect peoples who have not yet achieved statehood.

Secondly, may national liberation movements use force to overthrow the colonial power and thereby achieve self-determination? This is more problematic, although many developing countries argue that such a right is implicit in the Declaration on Principles of International Law. Generally speaking, the use of force within a State will remain an internal matter and will thus not be a concern of international law although, as is seen in Chapter 14, there are now rules of international law governing the actual conduct of hostilities in non-international conflicts.

Thirdly, can an established State use force to assist a national liberation movement in its fight for self-determination, as was partly claimed by India in respect of its invasion of East Pakistan? Once again, several States have argued that the obligation in Article 2(4) does not prohibit force for this beneficial purpose and, further, that it is implicitly recognised in a number of UN resolutions. Yet, as has already been seen at 12.5.2 and 12.5.4, if the struggle for self-determination is an internal affair, States are generally under a duty not to intervene.

12.6 Collective use of force

So far, the discussion has been about the use of force by States acting on their own initiative. Force may also be used on behalf of an international organisation, such as the United Nations.

12.6.1 The United Nations: a brief introduction

The term 'United Nations' was first used shortly after the USA entered World War Two in 1941. On 14 August 1941, Churchill and Roosevelt met in mid Atlantic and issued a declaration of common principles known as the Atlantic Charter, on which was based their hopes for a better future for the world. These included the eventual abandoning of the use of force, territorial changes and forms of government to be based on the expressed wishes of the peoples concerned, and economic co-operation between all nations with the object of securing for all improved labour standards, economic advancement and social security. On 1 January 1942, a Declaration by the United Nations was made and adhered to by all those States at war with the Axis Powers. This was followed by the Moscow Declaration of 30 October 1943, in which the USA, the USSR and the UK committed themselves to forming a new world organisation for the maintenance of international peace and security. Proposals for its charter were drawn up in 1944 at Dumbarton Oaks in the USA, by the USA, USSR, UK and China and, in the following year, the three major powers agreed on voting procedures for the Security Council at the

Yalta Conference. The amended Dumbarton Oaks proposals formed the basis of the 50 nation conference held on 25 April in San Francisco and, on 26 June 1945, the Charter of the United Nations was formally signed. It contained 111 Articles, which defined the purposes, principles and methods of the new organisation and set up its structure. The main purposes of the UN are set out in Article 1 and Article 2 sets down the fundamental obligations of Member States. Membership of the UN is open to all peace loving States which accept the obligations contained in the Charter and which, in the opinion of the UN, are able and willing to carry them out.

The UN has six principal organs: the General Assembly, the Security Council, the Economic and Social Council, the Trusteeship Council, the International Court of Justice and the Secretariat. The General Assembly consists of all members of the UN, each of which has equal voting rights. It may discuss any matter within the scope of the Charter, unless it is already under discussion in the Security Council, and it may make recommendations. It has no mandatory powers. Major decisions are taken by a two thirds majority, less important ones by a simple majority. Amendments to the Charter require a two-thirds majority, including the concurrent votes of the five permanent members of the Security Council. The Assembly meets once annually in regular session from September to December. Special sessions and emergency sessions may be called by the Security Council or a majority of members to discuss particular issues. The work of the Assembly continues all year, however, through the special committees and subsidiary organs such as the United Nations Conference on Trade and Development.

The UN Security Council has primary responsibility for maintaining international peace and security. It has five permanent members (the USA, Russia, the UK, China, and France) and 10 non-permanent members who are elected for a two year term (five are elected each year). Decisions of the Security Council must have the affirmative vote of nine members, including the permanent members, except on procedural matters, where voting is by majority. The question of whether something is or is not a procedural matter is itself a non-procedural matter. Any permanent member can therefore veto a decision; abstention, however, is not taken as a veto. According to the Charter, no member should vote on a matter in which it is involved, but this rule is not generally observed in practice.

12.6.2 The UN and collective use of force: the Security Council

Under the UN collective security system as originally envisaged, the Security Council was to be the organ through which international peace and security was to be maintained. It is given specific powers in Chapter VII of the Charter to act on behalf of all States, even if this means using force itself. Resolutions passed under Chapter VII provisions are binding on all States.

Article 39 of the Charter provides that:

> The Security Council shall determine the existence of any threat to the peace, breach of the peace, or act of aggression and shall make recommendations, or decide what measures shall be taken in accordance with arts 41 and 42 to maintain or restore international peace and security.

Under Article 40, the Security Council may indicate provisional measures pending a determination under Article 39. It is therefore important to determine what type of behaviour might fall within Article 39. Article 1 of the General Assembly Resolution on the Definition of Aggression 1974 provides that:

> Aggression is the use of armed force by a State against the sovereignty, territorial integrity or political independence of another State, or in any other manner inconsistent with the Charter of the United Nations, as set out in this definition.

Article 3 sets out the main acts which will qualify as acts of aggression and they are:

(a) the invasion or attack by the armed forces of a State of the territory of another State, or any military occupation, however temporary, resulting from such invasion or attack, or an annexation by the use of force of the territory of another State or any part thereof;

(b) bombardment or the use of any weapons by a State against the territory of another State;

(c) blockade of the ports or coast of a State by the armed forces of another State;

(d) the use of armed forces which are within the territory of another State by agreement in contravention of the conditions of that agreement;

(e) a State allowing its territory to be used by another State to perpetrate acts of aggression against a third State; and

(f) the sending, by or on behalf of a State, armed bands, groups, irregulars or mercenaries which carry out any of the acts listed above.

Article 3 is not intended to be an exhaustive list. It can be seen that aggression will normally depend upon the use or threat of armed force, although some States have argued that it includes economic aggression and, certainly, threats to and breaches of the peace encompasses more than the use or threat of armed force. It is the Security Council which is the final arbiter on whether an Article 39 situation has arisen.

The measures envisaged by Article 41 involve non-military sanctions, such as trade boycotts or arms embargoes. Decisions taken under Article 41 are binding on Member States. In the event of the measures available under Article 41 being considered inadequate, Article 42 enables the Security Council to take such military action as may be necessary to maintain or restore international peace and security. Under the original scheme, the use of force by the Security Council under Article 42 depended upon satisfactory agreements having been concluded under Article 43, which envisaged an organised military force being permanently at the Council's disposal. No such agreements have ever been concluded. There is no indication that Article 42 is dependent upon agreements reached under Article 43, and Article 42 does state that enforcement action 'may include demonstrations, blockade, and other operations by air, sea, or land forces of Members of the UN'.

Enforcement action taken under Chapter VII of the UN Charter must be distinguished from the peace-keeping role exercised by the UN under Chapter VI and often carried out through the use of the so-called 'blue helmets'. This peacekeeping role will be discussed at 12.6.4.

12.6.3 Enforcement action under Chapter VII

In the history of the UN, the Security Council has authorised the use of force under Chapter VII on six occasions and these will be looked at in turn. In addition, the UN has, on a number of occasions, imposed measures falling short of the authorisation of the actual use of force. The use of Chapter VII enforcement action has dramatically increased since the collapse of the former Soviet Union and the ending of the Cold War.

12.6.3.1 Korea 1950

Before World War Two, Korea had been under Japanese control. In 1943, its independence was guaranteed by the allies but, in 1945, Japan surrendered North Korea to the Soviet Union and surrendered South Korea (south of the 38th parallel) to the USA. Deadlock ensued and, in June 1950, North Korean troops crossed the border into South Korea. At that time, the USSR was boycotting meetings of the Security Council in protest against the fact that it was Nationalist China rather than the People's Republic which was the representative of China. The invasion was reported to the Security Council, which determined that the action constituted a breach of the peace and called for an immediate cessation of hostilities. When this call went unheeded, the Council passed a second resolution under Article 39, recommending that all States should provide such assistance to South Korea as was necessary to repel the armed attack and to restore international peace and security to the area. A third resolution established the UN unified command and recommended that Member States should make military force and other assistance available to the unified command under the US. The US provided the commander of such forces and was in overall control. Subsequently, the USSR returned to the Security Council and the matter passed into the hands of the General Assembly, because agreement was no longer possible in the Security Council.

There have been arguments put forward that the Korean action was not legitimate under the UN Charter, on the basis that USSR's absence should not be counted as a concurring vote. A similar argument was mounted against Security Council Resolution 678 (1990), which imposed a deadline on Iraq to withdraw from Kuwait or face military action. In that case, it was China that abstained. The majority of opinion seems to suggest that an abstention should not be considered to be a veto. It was also disputed as to whether the Security Council could instigate the use of armed force outside the Article 42 and Article 43 procedure. The action in Korea has therefore been characterised by some commentators as an example of the collective self-defence of South Korea.

12.6.3.2 Rhodesia 1965

Following the unilateral declaration of independence by Southern Rhodesia in November 1965, the Security Council passed a resolution calling upon all States to refrain from any action which would assist and encourage the illegal regime and, in particular, to desist from providing it with arms, equipment and military material and to do their utmost to break all economic relations with Southern Rhodesia, including an embargo on oil and petroleum products. In April 1966, in Resolution 221, the Security Council made a determination that the situation in Southern Rhodesia constituted a threat to peace and the voluntary sanctions were replaced by mandatory sanctions under Article 41. The resolution passed authorised the UK to use force if necessary to uphold the oil embargo imposed upon Southern Rhodesia. The UK made use of this authority when it threatened to use force against a Greek registered oil tanker in April 1966, although the actual use of force was not necessary.

12.6.3.3 Iraq 1990

On 2 August 1990, Iraqi forces invaded Kuwait, after a period of growing tension between the two States. The invasion was almost universally condemned and the Security Council passed a series of resolutions relating to the situation. On the day of the invasion, the Security Council passed Resolution 660, which determined that the situation constituted a breach of international peace and security and demanded immediate Iraqi withdrawal. Following Iraq's failure to withdraw, Resolution 661 was passed, which imposed comprehensive economic sanctions on Iraq. Resolution 665, passed on 25 August 1990, authorised those Member States co-operating with the government of Kuwait to 'use such measures commensurate to the specific circumstances as may be necessary under the authority of the Security Council' to enforce the sea blockade of Iraq. Colombia and Cuba both questioned whether it was permissible for the Security Council to authorise the use of force without the agreements necessary under Article 43, but no conclusive answer was given. The US and the UK announced that they would use force to uphold the sanctions but their main justification for doing so was based on the right of collective self-defence of Kuwait. The US and the UK continued to maintain that use of force against Iraq was permitted under rights of self-defence, although it was recognised that, politically, it would be better to act under UN authorisation. Accordingly, Security Resolution 678, which was passed by 12 votes to two (with Yemen and China abstaining) on 20 November 1990, authorised Member States 'to use all necessary means' in co-operation with the government of Kuwait to implement Resolution 660, unless Iraq withdrew by 15 January 1991. What was never completely clear was whether the resolution amounted to Chapter VII enforcement action or was merely a recognition of the Kuwaiti right to collective self-defence. The majority of writers seem to support the view that Resolution 678 amounted to enforcement action and, thus, military force was not confined purely to the liberation of Kuwait, as it would have been if restricted by the conditions applicable to self-defence.

12.6.3.4 Somalia, Bosnia and Haiti

Within the last two years, the use of Chapter VII procedures has taken on a new aspect, raising questions of humanitarian intervention by the UN. In both Bosnia and Somalia, the UN Security Council recognised that the situations there constituted a threat to peace and security. However, the main concern in both cases was the provision of humanitarian relief to the local population rather than a response to the use of aggression by another State. In spite of the fact that there was no outside aggressor, the UN Security Council had authorised the use of force in both situations. In the case of Bosnia, Member States were authorised under Security Council resolution 816 (1993) to take 'all necessary measures' to enforce the no-fly zone above the territory of Bosnia-Herzegovina.

Perhaps the greatest extension of UN powers has come in respect of Haiti. Following the overthrow of the democratically elected government of President Aristide, concern was expressed by the organisation of American States at the worsening situation in Haiti. In June 1993, the Security Council determined that the situation constituted a threat to international peace and security, called for the re-instatement of President Aristide, and imposed a number of economic sanctions pending his re-instatement. The sanctions were lifted in August 1993 but stronger sanctions were re-imposed, following a new Article 39 determination in October. In Resolution 875 (1993), the Security Council authorised the use of force to enforce the sanctions. Thus, for the first time, the UN has authorised the use of force in a situation of civil unrest and in an attempt to bring about a return to democracy. While the use of such action in respect of the particular situation in Haiti might be welcomed, the general principle operating gives rise for some concern. If, as seems possible, the ICJ finds in the *Lockerbie* case that it has no power to review the legitimacy of Security Council resolutions, then the use of the Security Council to bring about changes in the government of States is open to considerable abuse.

12.6.4 Peace keeping actions

The Security Council has also been involved in the use of force on other occasions which have not been considered enforcement actions under Chapter VII. In July 1960, the breakdown of law and order following Congo independence brought a request from the Congolese government requesting immediate military assistance. The Security Council passed a resolution authorising the Secretary General to take the necessary steps in consultation with the Congo government to provide such military assistance as was necessary. A multinational force under UN authority was assembled (UN Operation in the Congo (ONUC)) but the authority to use force from the Security Council was given in terms of preventing civil war. The legitimacy of the action was subsequently discussed in the *Expenses* case (1962) and the ICJ concluded that the use of force was not against a State which had committed an act of aggression and that the action did not involve any enforcement measures under Chapter VII. Under chapter VI, the Security Council is given general powers relating to the pacific settlement of disputes. Article 37 States that, once the Council has deemed that a dispute is likely to endanger international peace and security, it shall decide on appropriate measures to be taken. The terms are very wide and, while the general intention is to encourage settlement by arbitration or the ICJ, the words of Articles 36 and 37 do not rule out the creation of a peace keeping force. Such peace keeping forces have been used on a number of occasions but their presence in a State depends upon the consent of that State. It should be noted that, unlike Chapter VII, resolutions passed under the provisions of Chapter VI are not legally binding on States.

12.6.5 The General Assembly's role

The perceived failure of the original system and the widespread use of the veto during the Cold War eventually led the General Assembly to play a more active role in the maintenance of international peace and security. In 1950, the Assembly passed the Uniting for Peace Resolution. This provides that, if the Security Council could not discharge its primary responsibility because of the veto, the General Assembly shall consider the matter immediately with a view to making appropriate recommendations to members for collective measures, including, in the case of a breach of the peace or act of aggression, the use of armed force where necessary to restore peace and security. This resolution has been used on many occasions to justify consideration of cases where force has been used: the resolution was passed in connection with the Korean crisis; it was used in 1956 as the basis for the formation of a multinational force (UN Emergency Force (UNEF)) which operated on Egyptian soil with Egyptian consent after the Suez crisis. Because it was there with Egypt's consent, the ICJ stated in the *Expenses* case that the deployment of the force did not constitute enforcement action and did not, therefore, require the Security Council's authorisation. It is still argued that the Uniting for Peace Resolution does not authorise the General Assembly to carry out enforcement action; that would require a revision of the UN Charter. Multinational forces operating in Lebanon (UN Interim Force in Lebanon (UNIFIL)) and on the Israeli-Syrian border (UN Disengagement Observer Force (UNDOF)) on the basis of General Assembly resolutions do not really operate under the UN Charter; like UNEF, they only remain with the consent of the host State and they have limited powers. Since the ending of the Cold War, the need for the General Assembly to act in a peace keeping role has diminished.

12.6.6 Regional organisations

Under Article 53 of the Charter, the Security Council can utilise regional organisations such as the Organisation of American States (OAS) and the Organisation of African Unity (OAU) for 'enforcement action'. However, it is clearly stated in Article 53 that no enforcement action can be taken without the authorisation of the Security Council. Some States argue that regional organisations can take measures on their own decision to maintain the peace, including use of armed force. For example, the US argued that its invasions of the Dominican Republic in 1965 and Grenada in 1983 were partly justified as actions authorised by the relevant regional organisations taken to restore peace and security in the region. This view has obtained little widespread support and it is thought that action in the name of regional organisations is only legitimate if there has been a request from a sovereign State and the regional force operates within the requesting State or under the doctrine of collective self-defence.

THE USE OF FORCE

It is convenient to consider the rules relating to the unilateral use of force and the rules relating to the collective use of force separately. 'Force' includes all armed force but whether it includes threats or action short of actual use of armed force is less settled.

The unilateral use of force

This encompasses the use of force by individual States or groups of States acting on their own initiative. The principal prohibition is found in Article 2(4) of the UN Charter. The conflicting restrictive and permissive views of force should be noted. State practice seems to support the restrictive view that all force is prohibited, unless specifically permitted by the UN Charter.

Justifications for the unilateral use of force

The UN Charter only refers to one justification for the use of force. Article 51 preserves the inherent right of individual or collective self-defence if an armed attack occurs. This provision has caused debate between those who argue that the sole right of self-defence is that contained in Article 51 and those who claim that Article 51 leaves undisturbed a wider, customary law right of self-defence. The classic definition of self-defence was given in The *Caroline* case (1841). More recent examples are provided by the US invasion of Grenada in 1983, the US bombing of Libya in 1986 and the Israeli bombing of an Iraqi reactor in 1981. There is some discussion of self-defence in the *Nicaragua* case (1986).

In addition to self-defence, a number of other justifications for the use of force have been offered.

- Invitation

  There seems little doubt that it is lawful to use force to assist another State to assert its rights of self-defence if an express request is made. What is less clear is the extent of any right to assist in the suppression of an internal insurrection. While it may be permissible to offer assistance in subduing low intensity unrest, once the unrest becomes a state of insurgency, granting assistance may well contravene principles of non-intervention and the rules relating to self-determination.

- Protection of nationals and property abroad

  States have used force to protect nationals and property abroad, most notably at Entebbe in 1976. The majority of writers deny that there is any right to use force in such situations, although there is a degree of State practice supporting such a right.

- Humanitarian intervention

  This involves the use of force to protect non-nationals abroad. The most cited example is India's intervention in East Pakistan in 1971. The prevailing view is that such intervention must be carried out under the auspices of the UN and there exists no right for individual States to act on their own in such situations.

- Self-determination

  The use of force to suppress self-determination movements would appear to be prohibited, as would the use of force in support of such movements. Although there are international law rules governing the conduct of hostilities in non-international conflicts, the use of force by the self-determination movement is regarded as an internal matter and is therefore not the concern of international law.

The collective use of force

One of the purposes of the United Nations is the maintenance of international peace and security. The Security Council is given specific powers in Chapter VII of the UN Charter and resolutions passed under Chapter VII procedures are binding on all States. Articles 41 and 42 of the Charter provide for enforcement measures, including the use of force. Enforcement measures must be distinguished from the UN's peacekeeping role under Chapter VI of the Charter.

Examples of the use of enforcement action are:

(a) Korea;

(b) Rhodesia;

(c) Iraq;

(d) Somalia;

(e) Bosnia; and

(f) Haiti.

In the event that the Security Council cannot agree upon action to maintain peace and security, the General Assembly can play a role under the Uniting for Peace procedure. The Security Council can also authorise regional organisations to take enforcement action.

CHAPTER 13

THE REGULATION OF ARMED CONFLICT

13.1 Introduction

Traditionally, there has always been a distinction made between the law relating to the resort to war (the *jus ad bellum*) and the law governing the conduct of the war (the *jus in bello*). The law of war in classical international law was the regime that came into operation when the relations of particular countries with each other were no longer governed by the law of peace because a state of declared war existed between them. The law of war dealt with all aspects of the hostile relationship.

The modern development of legal restrictions on the resort to war and the use of armed force has caused a shift in attitude towards the law of war. For example, the traditional view was that treaties were annulled as soon as war broke out. That is now not the case and the position depends much more on the terms of the treaty and the intention of the parties. The law of war is now less regarded as an alternative to the law of peace and more regarded as a device for alleviating the suffering caused by war. Since the end of World War Two, there has been a concerted attempt, led by the International Committee of the Red Cross, to strengthen that branch of the law of war which is now often referred to as international humanitarian law.

Another modern phenomenon has been the reluctance of States to actually admit that they are at war and the absence of international recognition of States of war. For example, in 1982, the UK Prime Minister made it clear that the UK was not at war with Argentina and the hostilities relating to the Falkland Islands were always officially referred to as the Falklands conflict or the Falklands crisis. Similarly, the use of force in 1991 in response to Iraq's continued occupation of Kuwait is usually officially referred to as the Gulf conflict. This reluctance to resort to war, so called, has led to the development of what is known as the law of armed conflict. The scope of the law of armed conflict has been extended over the years to include not only hostilities between States, but also civil wars and other 'non-international' conflicts. This has been necessary because, traditionally, the law of war did not come into operation until there was a recognised state of war.

The definition of war offered by Starke (*International Law*, 11th edn, 1994, London: Butterworths, p 478) is that it is a hostile relationship between two or more States resulting in a contest which is primarily between the armed forces of either side.

There has been some dispute as to whether a formal declaration of war was required before a state of war could exist. Certainly, it is felt that a declaration, even a unilateral one, is sufficient evidence that a state of war exists. But it is now accepted that the question of whether or not a war exists is an objective one and depends on the overall picture. It is also true that, with the development of the law of armed conflict, much of the importance of the distinction has gone.

13.2 The sources of the law of armed conflict

Throughout history, there have been restrictions placed on those using armed force in respect of methods of combat, use of weapons and treatment of civilians and prisoners of war. Up until the middle of the last century, the source of the law governing armed conflict was almost entirely customary law. However, over the last 140 years, a significant number of treaties have been agreed, many of which codify the earlier existing rules of international law. Rules of customary international law still have an enormously important role to play and much of the evidence for specific rules is found in the manuals of military law which most States have promulgated.

One of the first treaties to be concluded was the Paris Declaration Respecting Maritime Law 1856. At the outbreak of the Crimean War in 1854, all belligerents agreed certain rules relating to neutral ships and the capture of property at sea. At the peace conference that ended the war, the seven participants signed the declaration, which has since been acceded to by a large number of States and, strictly speaking, remains in force to this day. In 1864, the Red Cross was established by Henri Dunant and the first of the 'Red Cross' conventions, the Geneva Convention for the Amelioration of the Condition of the Wounded in Armies in the Field 1864, was adopted. Since that time, a large number of treaties have been signed, among the most important of which are:

(a) the Hague Declarations 1899;

(b) the Hague Conventions 1907, in particular, the Hague Convention IV Respecting the Laws and Customs of War on Land 1907 together with the annexed Hague Regulations on the Laws and Customs of War on Land; and

(c) the four Geneva Conventions 1949 and their two additional Protocols 1977.

13.3 Application of the law: international and non-international armed conflicts

As has already been stated, the law regulating armed conflict has developed from the laws of war. War was, by definition, a dispute between States and thus, clearly, within the ambit of international law. As the law was extended to cover situations which could not formally be referred to as war, debate occurred as to whether the law applied to situations of civil war and internal armed conflict. Applying international law to such situations could create problems, in that it might be argued that it contravened the principle of non-interference in the domestic affairs of sovereign States. Historically, internal and civil wars were matters solely for the particular State involved. However, by the 1930s, there existed a number of regional agreements concerned with the regulation of internal conflicts and customary international law had developed to the situation where the laws of war would apply where a recognised situation of belligerency existed. The need for such recognition has diminished since the end of World War Two and a growing acceptance that certain provisions of the law of armed conflict will apply to internal conflict. Article 3, which is repeated in all four Geneva Conventions 1949, provides that, in the case of an armed conflict not of an international character occurring in the territory of one of the parties to the conventions, certain fundamental humanitarian provisions relating to protection of civilians will apply to those participating in the conflict. The law has been further strengthened by the Geneva Protocol II Relating to the Protection of Victims of Non-International Armed Conflicts 1977. The provisions of Protocol II are much less extensive than those which relate to international armed conflicts. Nevertheless, the protocol does provide certain protections for members of the civilian population and the wounded, sick and shipwrecked.

In addition to extending provisions of the law to non-international conflicts, there has also been a broadening of the definition of international conflict to include 'armed conflicts in which peoples are fighting for self-determination against colonial and alien occupation and against racist regimes in the exercise of their rights of self-determination'. This broader definition was first included in General Assembly Resolution 3103 (1973), which was passed by a 82 to 13 vote, with 19 States abstaining. Among those voting against or abstaining were the majority of Western States and the resolution could not be considered to have the status of customary international law at the time. However, the definition was repeated in Article 1(4) of the Geneva Protocol I, to which the majority of States (including the Western States) are parties and it is submitted that it is now correct to include such national liberation struggles within the category of international armed conflict.

Clearly, there remains a large number of actual and potential conflicts which still do not fall into the broader definition and these will be subject to the relatively more restricted provisions contained in Geneva Protocol II. The issue of the nature of the armed conflict has particular relevance in the situation in Bosnia where the status of 'Serbian' troops is critical. At its simplest, the question can be posed thus: were the 'Serbian' forces operating in Bosnia members of the armed forces of the State of Serbia and Montenegro, or were they members of a Bosnian Serb militia? If the former is true, then the conflict must be defined as an international armed conflict, since the armed forces of one State were operating without consent in the territory of another State; if the latter is true, the conflict remained a non-international one. For the civilians who suffered, the question is perhaps purely an academic one, but it has important implications as to the rules of law which apply and, in particular, the degree of responsibility that can attach to those involved in some of the worst atrocities.

13.4 Effect of outbreaks of war and armed conflicts

The outbreak of war has far reaching effects on the relations between the opponent belligerent States. The general rule of international law is that States are free to enact municipal legislation dealing with such matters as trading with the enemy, and provide for seizure of enemy property. This would seem to be true of war and any other armed conflict. As far as individuals are concerned, State practice varies as to the exact nature of test of enemy character, but most States now effectively adopt one based on nationality.

On the outbreak of war, diplomatic relations between the two States will cease although, according to the Vienna Convention on Diplomatic Relations, diplomatic agents must be able to leave. As has already been stated, the effect on treaties remains unsettled and the Vienna Convention on the law of Treaties contains no provision dealing with effect of war.

13.5 Rules on belligerence

Much of the law relating to belligerency has the aim of minimising damage to civilians. Many prohibitions apply to non-military objectives. Military objectives usually means targets which, by their nature, location, purpose or use, make an effective contribution to military action and whose destruction, capture or neutralisation offer a definite military advantage.

13.5.1 Restrictions on weapons

Attempts to prohibit the use of particular types of weapons have been made in various civilisations over a long period of time. In the ancient Hindu codes, there was a prohibition on the use of poisoned arrows. In 1132, the Lateran Council declared that the crossbow was an 'un-Christian weapon'.

When the law of war began to be codified in the 19th century, the prohibition of certain weapons was an early objective. The St Petersburg Declaration 1868 is regarded as the first major international agreement prohibiting the use of particular weapons; in this case, the prohibition of bullets under 400 grammes which exploded on impact – no States objected to exploding shells. Further development of the rules occurred at the Hague Conference in 1899, which resulted in the three Hague Declarations 1899. Declaration 2 prohibits the use of certain asphyxiating gases and Declaration 3 further prohibits the use of exploding bullets. The declaration outlawed the use of so-called 'dum-dum' bullets, which were designed to expand in the body after impact. They were named 'dum-dum' after the place in India where the UK first manufactured them.

A subsequent conference was held in the Hague in 1907, which resulted in a number of treaties relating to war. Hague Convention VIII Relative to the Laying of Automatic Submarine Mines 1907 remains applicable today and regulates the use of naval mines and Hague Convention XIV attempted to regulate the use of bombing from balloons.

More progress was made after World War One and, in 1925, the Geneva Gas Protocol was agreed. The convention deals with the use of poison gas, and biological and chemical weapons, and remains of great relevance today. Its application was discussed in the context of the Iran-Iraq war and, in March 1986, the Security Council issued a statement criticising the use by Iraq of chemical weapons in violation of the Geneva Gas Protocol. It is generally accepted that the protocol now reflects customary international law.

Since the Second World War, there have been a number of attempts to further modify and strengthen the law relating to weapons. However, it has to be sadly admitted that the development of the law is usually one step behind the ingenuity of weapons manufacturers. As particular restrictions are introduced, so States look for ways of evading the new law. An illustration of the problem is provided by examining the law relating to four particular categories of weapons: conventional weapons; weapons of mass destruction; biological and chemical weapons; and environmental weapons.

13.5.2 Conventional weapons

Conventional weapons include all weapons not included in the other three categories. The principal relevant treaty is the UN Convention on Prohibitions or Restrictions of Certain Conventional Weapons that Cause Unnecessary Suffering or Have Indiscriminate Effects 1981 (the Weaponry Convention), together with its three annexed protocols which entered into force in December 1983. It is the protocols which contain the substantive prohibitions. Protocol I prohibits the use of any weapon, the primary effect of which is to injure by fragments which, in the human body, escape detection by X ray. Protocol II deals with land mines, booby traps, and other devices which are designed to kill, injure or maim and which are activated by remote control or after a lapse of time. The protocol prohibits all use of such weapons if they cannot be directed specifically and accurately against a military objective. Protocol III deals with incendiary weapons and prohibits almost all use of any weapon or munition which is primarily designed to set fire to objects or to cause burn injury to persons through action of flame, heat or a combination thereof. Protocol IV prohibits the use of laser weapons 'designed, as their sole combat function or as one of their combat functions, to cause permanent blindness to unenhanced vision, that is, to the naked eye or to the eye with corrective eyesight devices' (Article 1).

13.5.3 Weapons of mass destruction

One of the first decisions taken by the UN General Assembly was made in January 1946 to establish a commission for, *inter alia*, the 'elimination of major weapons adaptable to mass destruction'. The Commission for Conventional Armaments in 1948 defined weapons of mass destruction to include atomic explosive weapons, radioactive material weapons, as well as certain lethal chemical and biological weapons. The General Assembly later expanded the definition to include any weapons developed in the future which have characteristics comparable in destructive effect to those of the atomic bomb.

The main type of weapons of mass destruction are nuclear weapons and the international law on the subject operates on two levels. First, there are restrictions on the production and possession of nuclear weapons, for example, the Treaty on the Non-Proliferation of Nuclear Weapons 1963, which restricts the number of States which can build and possess nuclear weapons. Secondly, there are treaties which prohibit the testing and use of nuclear weapons in particular locations, for example, the Space Treaty 1967 and the Antarctic Treaty 1959. Recently, the Security Council has been concerned with the announcement by North Korea of its intention to withdraw from the Non-Proliferation Treaty and has discussed the possibility of instituting Chapter VII procedures on the basis that such withdrawal could constitute a threat to international peace and security.

The use of nuclear weapons, along with the use of all other weapons, is subject to three basic principles: the necessity to use them; the proportionality of their use; and the obligation not to cause unnecessary suffering. Nuclear weapons cause, by their very nature, indiscriminate suffering and destruction and, as such, it could be argued that their use is contrary to the rules of international law. It has also been argued that the use of nuclear weapons would contravene the Genocide Convention and could also contravene the Hague Regulations which prohibit poisonous weapons. Those who argue in favour of a right to use nuclear weapons have suggested that the rules prohibiting indiscriminate suffering relate to conventional weapons only and that the use of nuclear weapons would be permissible in the absence of any positive law to the contrary. What does seem to be accepted is that the first use of nuclear weapons is unacceptable, although State practice seems to suggest that the possession and production of such weapons is not in itself, providing there is no breach of the Non-Proliferation Treaty, a breach of international law.

A specific aspect of nuclear weapons that has been considered is the use of radiological weapons. Such weapons are designed to utilise the radioactive fallout which follows a nuclear explosion. Radiological weapons fall into two categories: those which use separate radioactive agents which act independently of the nuclear explosion itself, and so-called dirty nuclear weapons, which are designed to maximise the amount of fallout from the nuclear explosion. The use and possession of such weapons has for some time been considered by the UN Conference on Disarmament.

In the *Legality of the Threat or Use of Nuclear Weapons* case (1996), the ICJ gave an advisory opinion at the request of the UN General Assembly. The Court found no rules of customary or conventional international law which specifically authorised the threat or use of nuclear weapons, nor any law which specifically prohibited them. On the President's casting vote, the Court held 'that the threat or use of nuclear weapons would generally be contrary to the rules of international law applicable in armed conflict, and in particular the principles and rules of humanitarian law.' However, the Court continued that it could not 'conclude definitively whether the threat or use of nuclear weapons would be lawful or unlawful in an extreme circumstance of self-defence, in which the very survival of a State would be at stake.'

13.5.4 Biological and chemical weapons

Biological and chemical weapons can be distinguished from other weapons in that they exercise their effect solely on living matter and are aimed at large groups rather than individual soldiers. The use of poisoned weapons is not new. Historically, much use has been made during sieges of the tactic of poisoning water supplies and, in medieval times, plague victims proved effective weapons when thrown over city walls!

The first treaty reference to such weapons appeared in Article 23 of the Hague Regulations Respecting the Laws and Custom of War on Land, which prohibits the use of poison or poisoned weapons. The regulations are generally regarded as constituting customary international law but it remains unclear whether the prohibition on the use of poison covers the use of gas. Gas was used in both World Wars, in Vietnam and in the Iran-Iraq war. The peace treaties concluded after World War One all prohibited the possession by Germany of all 'asphyxiating, poisonous and other gases and analogous liquids, material and devices' but it was unclear whether this prohibition applied to all States. The Geneva Protocol for the Prohibition of the Use in War of Asphyxiating, Poisonous or Other Gases, and of Bacteriological Methods of Warfare 1925 (the Geneva Gas Protocol) expressly recognised that the prohibition of asphyxiating, poisonous and other gases and analogous liquids, materials and devices was part of international law and extended the prohibition to the use in war of bacteriological weapons. However, problems have remained over the interpretation of the Protocol's provisions. In particular, there has been dispute over whether the prohibition covers only lethal weapons or extends to such things as tear gas and other non-lethal materials such as herbicides. The problems is partly caused by the fact that the French text, which is equally authentic to the English text of the protocol, refers to 'similaires' rather than 'other' gases and analogous liquids, etc.

In 1986, a UN Security Council resolution condemned the use by Iraq of chemical weapons, which was stated to be in clear violation of the Geneva Gas Protocol. The prevailing view today seems to be that the provisions of the Protocol have become customary international law and that, consequently, the first use of lethal chemical and biological weapons is prohibited. There is less agreement on the use of non-lethal chemical and biological weapons.

There now exists a Biological Weapons Convention 1972 and a Chemical Weapons Convention 1992, both of which prohibit the production and stockpiling of specific weapons, although they do not deal with the use in armed conflict of such weapons.

13.5.5 Environmental weapons

The widespread use of defoliants by the US during the Vietnam War and growing concern about the environment generally led to calls for regulation of weapons which have a particular effect on the environment. During the Vietnam War, there were press reports that the US was attempting to artificially produce rain in the war zone to flood North Vietnamese supply routes. This provoked international discussions aimed at prohibiting the use of environmental modification techniques as weapons of war. The result of the discussions was the UN Convention on the Prohibition of Military Use of Environmental Modification Techniques 1977. This convention prohibits the hostile use of any technique for changing 'the dynamics, composition or structure of the Earth, including its biota, lithosphere, hydrosphere and atmosphere, or of outer space'. It is arguable that the convention would cover the use of nuclear weapons.

In addition to the 1977 convention, Article 55 of the Geneva Protocol I Additional to the Geneva Conventions of 1949 and Relating to the Protection of Victims of International Armed Conflicts 1977 places an obligation on States in warfare to minimise widespread, long term and sever damage to the natural environment and prohibits the use of weapons and methods of warfare which 'may be expected to cause' such damage and thereby to prejudice the health and survival of the population. It has been suggested that the deliberate spillage by Iraq of quantities of oil into the Persian Gulf during the 1991 Gulf conflict contravened these provisions.

13.5.6 Restrictions on methods of warfare

A basic distinction in the law of armed conflict must be drawn between combatants and civilians. Combatants are those under command, having fixed visible and distinctive emblems, carrying arms openly, and observing the laws of war. The basis of the law of armed conflict is that it is the combatants who fight the war and, if they are captured, they are entitled to prisoner of war (POW) status. The civilian, in turn, should be protected from attack. The distinction between combatant and civilian is crucial to the question of legitimate targets: combatant or military targets are legitimate, civilian targets are not. The rule is one of customary international law, binding on all States. The problem is then one of establishing what is a military target and what is a civilian target. Clearly, some objects can be defined without problem, for example, a tank is a military target, a nursery school is not. However, not all targets can be so clearly distinguished.

An attempt was made at a distinction in the Hague Draft Rules of Aerial Warfare 1923, which were never fully adopted but which are now considered declaratory of customary international law. The draft rules prescribed that attacks from the air would only be permitted if directed against a military objective, the total or partial destruction of which presented a 'distinct military advantage to the attacker'. Article 24 contained a list of targets which were to be classed as military targets:

> ... military forces, military works, military establishments or depots, factories constituting important and well-known centres engaged in the manufacture of arms, ammunition or distinctively military supplies, lines of communication or transportation used for military purposes.

The rules provided that compensation was payable for any breach of the prohibition. As can be seen, the list leaves considerable scope for interpretation and raises problems where targets are used for both military and civilian purposes, for example, railways or roads. The problem was further compounded by the fact that the rules were produced in three languages (French, German and English), all of which were equally authentic and valid and none of which said completely the same thing. The German text, for example, makes more clear reference to radio stations and other news media, and this was not expressly included in the English text 'lines of communication'.

Some writers in the 1930s suggested that a subjective approach should be adopted, based on the dominant purpose. Further development of the definition occurred during and immediately after the Second World War. It became more clear that bombing exclusively directed at civilian population is prohibited. Both the UK and the US governments condemned such bombing in December 1939, in the context of German tactics during the Spanish Civil War and at the beginning of World War Two, and the Charter of the

Nuremberg Tribunal 1946 included such indiscriminate bombing in its definition of war crimes. It has to be noted, however, that UK and US practice, particularly in respect of the 'carpet' bombing of Dresden did not accord with the statements made in 1939. The prohibition on attacks on civilian targets has been re-iterated in a series of UN Resolutions and the most recent example comes from the Iran-Iraq war, when Iraqi bombing of civilian areas in Iran drew widespread condemnation and led to an agreement between the two sides to cease military attacks on purely civilian targets.

The present law can be found in the Geneva Protocol I 1977, which is widely considered to represent a codification of customary international law. The protocol defines military targets as those objects which, by their nature, location, purpose or use, make effective contribution to military action as well as those whose total or partial destruction, capture or neutralisation in the circumstances at the time offers a definite military advantage. Article 52 of the protocol then goes on to outlaw attacks on civilian objects and Article 57 imposes a duty on those planning or deciding upon an attack to take all feasible precautions to verify that the objectives to be attacked are military objectives and to refrain from attack which might cause incidental loss of civilian life which would be excessive in relation to the military advantage gained (the proportionality principle). Part II of the protocol contains provisions relating to the protection of the sick, wounded and shipwrecked, and Article 12 specifically states that medical units shall not be the object of attack. Medical units include any establishment, military or civilian, which is organised for the search for, collection, transportation, diagnosis or treatment of the wounded, sick or shipwrecked. Such units should be clearly identified by the red cross (lion, star or crescent) emblem. Linked to the protection given to medical units is the obligation on States not to site them close to legitimate military targets. During the Gulf conflict in 1991, there were allegations that Iraq had deliberately sited anti-aircraft batteries close to hospitals in Baghdad. Such deliberate siting and the misuse of the red cross emblem will result in the protection given under the Protocol being withdrawn and constitutes a breach of treaty obligations. Part IV of the Protocol deals with the civilian population and States clearly that civil defence installations, such as air raid shelters, shall be protected. However, Article 65 States that the protection shall cease if they are used to commit acts harmful to the enemy. The Chapter goes on to provide that shelters should be identifiable. The internationally recognised symbol for such installations is a blue triangle on an orange background.

The question of legitimate targets was much discussed during the Gulf conflict, specifically in the context of coalition attacks on bridges that were used for both civilian and military transport and one particular attack on a building that Iraq claimed was an air-raid shelter but which the coalition forces argued was being used as a military communications headquarters. The discussions confirmed the existence of binding rules regarding legitimate and non-legitimate targets but showed the immense difficulties encountered in clearly distinguishing between the two in practice. A term which was much used during the war and which has continued to have a high currency is collateral damage. This was used to refer to damage caused to non-legitimate targets during the carrying out of attacks on military targets. Clearly, there is a limit to the amount of collateral damage that can be caused before it becomes wholly disproportionate to the military advantage gained.

13.5.7 Prohibited methods of warfare

In addition to the question of targets of attack, there are four methods of warfare which are specifically prohibited under international law.

13.5.7.1 No quarter

This refers to methods of warfare which admit of no limit. An order to leave no survivors and take no prisoners would amount to no quarter and it has long been prohibited by international law. The Geneva Protocol I specifically forbids such orders given in relation to enemy combatants (Article 40).

13.5.7.2 Starvation

This is the deliberate subjecting of the civilian population to starvation as a means of defeating the enemy. Article 54 of the Geneva Protocol I expressly prohibits the use of starvation as a method of warfare and also prohibits attacks on foodstuffs and other objects and areas indispensable to the survival of the population, for example, drinking water installations. Articles 69–71 further provide protection to those engaged in humanitarian relief operations.

13.5.7.3 Belligerent reprisals

Acts of victimisation or vengeance directed against civilians, POWs or others hors de combat in response to attacks by non-combatants are prohibited by international law.

13.5.7.4 Perfidy

International law draws a distinction, which is not always easy to make in practice, between a general level of deception which is an integral part of warfare and the deliberate use of certain specific acts of treachery and 'impermissible ruses' such as the improper use of the white flag of surrender, the use of false flags, and such things as disguising missile sites as hospitals.

13.6 Humanitarian rules

Humanitarian law in the widest sense concerns the protection of individuals in war or armed conflict. Discussed here are humanitarian rules in a narrower sense, that is to say, those rules which specifically protect the human person, rather than the general rules concerning means and methods of waging warfare. The majority of these humanitarian rules apply to both international and non-international armed conflicts.

13.6.1 Treatment of civilians

Civilians are non-combatants and combatants who are *hors de combat*. Most of the protection afforded to civilians is based on the system laid down in the Geneva Convention IV 1949, as supplemented by Geneva Protocols I and II of 1977. The Protocols actually state that anyone who is not a combatant is presumed to be a civilian. Article 75 of Protocol I includes a catalogue of forbidden practices to which civilians and persons *hors de combat* must not be subjected:

(a) violence to life, health or physical or mental well-being of persons, in particular: murder; torture of all kinds, whether physical or mental; corporal punishment; mutilation;

(b) outrages upon personal dignity, in particular humiliating and degrading treatment, enforced prostitution and any form of indecent assault;

(c) taking of hostages;

(d) collective punishments; and

(e) threats to commit any of the above.

Civilians must not be subjected to any action which causes their physical suffering or their intimidation. Hostages must not be taken and civilians must not be used to protect military targets. These provisions were breached by Iraq during the Gulf Conflict. If civilians are interned, they must be given adequate clothes, light and heat, and must not be subjected to forced mass transfers. There have been many allegations of breaches of these rules during the conflict in former Yugoslavia.

13.6.2 Specially protected groups

Certain categories of persons are afforded specific protection by international law.

13.6.2.1 Wounded, sick and shipwrecked

The protections given to the wounded, sick and shipwrecked apply to both civilians and combatants. They must all be treated humanely and not subjected to murder, torture, or any biological experiments. There is an obligation on captors to search for and collect enemy wounded, sick and shipwrecked and to give them adequate care.

13.6.2.2 Women

Special protection is given to women under Geneva Convention IV, which prescribes that they must not be subjected to attacks on their honour, enforced prostitution, rape or any form of indecent assault. Further protection is given to pregnant women and those with new-born babies.

13.6.2.3 Children under 15

Geneva Convention IV imposes an obligation on belligerents to ensure the safety of those under 15 who have been orphaned or separated from their parents as a result of war.

13.6.2.4 Journalists

War correspondents receive some protection under Geneva Convention III, in that they are to be accorded POW status if captured. They are given further protection under Geneva Protocol I Article 79.

13.6.2.5 Civil defence, medical and religious personnel

Individuals falling within these categories are given extra protection under the Geneva conventions and protocols, in that they must be allowed to carry on their work and medical personnel must not be made POWs.

13.6.2.6 Prisoners of war (POWs)

There was early agreement on rudimentary protection of POWs in the Geneva Convention 1864. The essence of the obligations as far as POWs are concerned is that detaining them does not amount to a sanction or punishment but is purely a precautionary measure. There is an overriding duty to treat POWs humanely. Those who can be accorded POW status are listed in Article 4 of the Geneva Convention III and Protocol I, but there is still some doubt as to the ambit of the protection. There is dispute about the status of those who commit war crimes prior to capture, and the exact status of guerrilla forces is unclear.

As has already been mentioned, POWs must be treated humanely. More specifically, POWs cannot be subjected to summary execution, medical experiments, torture, or interrogation. Article 17 of the Geneva Convention III provides that POWs are only required to give their name, rank and number. POWs are to be given adequate food, clothing and health care and adequate hygiene standards must be observed. Escapees may be disciplined within the limits imposed by Article 89. Non-officers may be compelled to undertake work of a type authorised by the convention. POWs are allowed to receive and send up to two letters and four postcards per month. At the end of hostilities, all POWs must be repatriated and those who are seriously wounded should be repatriated during hostilities.

13.6.2.7 Those living in occupied territories

Section III of the Geneva Convention IV makes detailed provision for situations of belligerent occupation and affords specific protection to those living within the occupied territory.

13.7 Responsibility and enforcement

Violations of the laws of armed conflict involve State responsibility (discussed in Chapter 8) and the duty to make reparation. Yet, as the International Military Tribunal at Nuremberg stated:

> Crimes against international law are committed by men, not abstract entities, and only by punishing individuals who commit such crimes can the provisions of international law be enforced.

The problem for international law has therefore been to identify the individuals responsible for breaches of the laws of armed conflict and to ensure that they are effectively punished. The issue of enforcement has often shown up weaknesses in international law. This has partly been because of the procedural difficulties encountered in bringing to trial those responsible for breaches but, more particularly, it is because the enforcement of the law has usually been seen as little more than the application of the principle of *vae victis*: it only ever appears to be members of the defeated side that bear responsibility for breaches of the law. The legitimacy of war criminal trials is always adversely effected by the fact that the tribunal itself is seen as having a major interest in the result since, generally, it is made up of representatives of the victorious States. The alternative is for trials to take place within the municipal courts of the defendant's State. The drawback with this option is that the defendant's State often has little interest in pursuing the trial with any real conviction.

One aspect of individual responsibility that was established at Nuremberg that should be noted is that the fact that an individual was acting pursuant to the orders of his or her government or of a superior does not automatically absolve him or her from responsibility. It may only be considered in mitigation of punishment. This seemed to confirm a view that had been held for some time that 'superior orders' does not constitute a defence to breaches of the laws of armed conflict. The one exception to this is where it can be shown that the subordinate individual could not reasonably have been expected to be aware of the illegality of the superior orders given. Of course, in such a situation, the individual giving the order will bear responsibility for the action carried out.

Following the end of the First World War, the Allied Commission upon the Responsibility of the Authors of the War and on the Enforcement of Penalties prepared a list of 896 alleged war criminals, including the German Kaiser Wilhelm II, and the intention was to try the leading members before an international tribunal. However, difficulties in actually bringing any of the principal defendants to trial and criticism that the whole process was motivated by a spirit of vindictiveness led to the proposals' failure. In 1920, an Advisory Commission of Jurists investigated the possibilities of establishing an international criminal court with powers to try crimes constituting a breach of international public order or against the universal law of nations. The League of Nations rejected the proposal on the grounds that there was not sufficient agreement among nations on the content of an international penal code.

The events of World War Two led to repeated demands for the trial of those responsible for war crimes and crimes against peace. By 1943, there were discussions among the allies as to what to do with the leaders of the Axis powers at the end of the war. The American Secretary of State proposed that they should be hanged after a summary trial or court martial. However, Churchill, Roosevelt and Eden favoured an international trial. Subsequent discussion led to the London Conference in August 1945, at which basic agreement was reached on a trial of German leaders by an international military tribunal. There remained considerable differences of opinion, not least because of different conceptions of criminal justice between those used to an Anglo-American system and those used to the Continental system. The Charter of the International Military Tribunal 1945 that was agreed by the USA, UK, USSR and France therefore represents a considerable compromise. The Charter established the International Military Tribunal, although it was not a truly international tribunal, since the four allies were acting in the capacity of occupying powers in place of the dissolved Nazi regime in Germany. There have therefore been arguments that the tribunal operated in some way as a municipal court under the authority of the national government of occupation. This would deal with the difficulty posed by the fact that, certainly at the time, individuals could not be considered the subjects of international law and could not, therefore, come within the jurisdiction of true international tribunals. Article 6 of the Charter gave the tribunal jurisdiction over three types of offence:

(a) crimes against peace: planning, preparation, initiation, or waging a war of aggression, or a war in violation of international treaties, or conspiracy to commit the foregoing;

(b) war crimes: violations of the laws or customs of war, including murder, ill-treatment of civilian population, plunder of public or private property, wanton destruction of cities, towns or villages, or devastation not justified by military necessity; and

(c) crimes against humanity: namely, murder, extermination, enslavement, deportation or other inhumane acts committed against any civilian population before or during a war and genocide, whether or not in violation of the domestic law of the country where perpetrated.

The Tribunal began its proceedings in November 1945. A similar charter was agreed with respect to Japanese War Criminals and an International Military Tribunal for the Far East sat in Tokyo. The judgment of the Nuremberg tribunal in 1946 and of the Tokyo tribunal in 1948 affirmed the principle of direct individual responsibility in international law.

The ILC subsequently drew up a Draft Code of Principles Recognised in the Tribunal's judgment which was the start of attempts to establish an international criminal law. The code reiterated the principle of individual responsibility which is repeated in the Genocide Convention. The ILC has since drawn up a draft statute for an International Criminal Court which would sit at the Hague. The proposed court would have jurisdiction over, *inter alia*, aggression, war crimes, unlawful use and possession of certain weapons, crimes against humanity and genocide. The draft statute is now being considered by a diplomatic conference in Rome. The question of the establishment of an international criminal court is linked to the concept of international crimes, which is discussed in Chapter 8 (at 8.4).

The definition of war crimes has implications for the individual jurisdiction of States and may involve application of the universality principle (discussed in Chapter 6 at 6.7). A number of serious violations of the laws of armed conflict were identified in the Charter of the International Military Tribunal as constituting war crimes but the list contained in Article 6 was not intended to be exhaustive. The Geneva Conventions 1949 referred to certain 'grave breaches' of the provisions of the conventions which would constitute war crimes and imposed a duty on States 'to provide effective penal sanctions for persons committing, or ordering to be committed, any grave breaches of the Convention'. Every State party to the conventions was further obliged to search for offenders and to bring them, irrespective of their nationality, to trial before its municipal courts or to hand them over for trial in the courts of another contracting party. The definition of grave breaches is further extended in Protocol I, which repeats the obligation on States to bring offenders to trial but, in addition, places an obligation on States to take 'all measures necessary' for the suppression of all acts contrary to the conventions and protocols other than grave breaches. Protocol I also provides for the establishment of an International Fact Finding Commission to investigate grave breaches of the Conventions or the Protocol.

13.7.1 Events in former Yugoslavia and Rwanda

Following the end of the Gulf conflict, there were calls for the establishment of an international tribunal to try Saddam Hussein for war crimes. Such a tribunal was not established and doubts were expressed at the time about the precise motives of those arguing for such a trial, since there was the possibility that it would be seen as yet another example of the victors punishing the defeated. The situation in former Yugoslavia where there have been allegations of a considerable number of serious breaches of the law of armed conflict has raised the issue of an international tribunal again. On this occasion, there is a major difference from previous cases, in that those who have called for the establishment of a tribunal are not limited to those involved in the fighting.

The requests for the establishment of such a tribunal were answered by Security Council Resolution 827 (1993), which agreed to the setting up of an international tribunal 'for the sole purpose of prosecuting persons responsible for serious violations of international humanitarian law committed in the territory of former Yugoslavia between 1 January 1991 and a date to be determined by the Security Council upon the restoration of peace and security'. The tribunal has been established at the Hague with 12 judges, currently presided over by the American Gabrielle Kirk McDonald. As at the 18 June 1998, 21 indictments had been issued against 60 individuals. Five trials are on-going and there have been two guilty verdicts.

Under Resolution 955 (1994) of 8 November 1994, a similar International Tribunal for Rwanda was established and it sits in Arusha, Tanzania.

THE REGULATION OF ARMED CONFLICT

Up until the mid-19th century, the rules governing armed conflict were almost entirely contained in customary law but, since that time, a considerable number of treaties have come into force. Among the most important are:

(a) the Hague Conventions 1907 together with the Hague Regulations;

(b) four Geneva Conventions 1949; and

(b) two Geneva Protocols 1977.

It is important to recognise the distinction between international and non-international armed conflict, since the rules relating to the latter are less extensive – Geneva Protocol II 1977.

The main aim of the law relating to armed conflict is the minimisation of damage and injury to civilians. Much of the law draws a distinction between combatants and non-combatants and between military and non-military objectives. The law is also concerned to prevent unnecessary suffering.

Restrictions on weapons

The main rules can be divided into four categories (a) conventional weapons; (b) weapons of mass destruction; (c) chemical and biological weapons; (d) environmental modification.

- Weaponry Convention 1981
- Non-Proliferation Treaty 1963
- Geneva Gas Protocol 1925
- Biological Weapons Convention 1972
- Chemical Weapons Convention 1992
- Environmental Modification Convention 1977

Restrictions on methods of warfare

Note the distinction between combatants and civilians and the definition of legitimate targets – see Hague Draft Rules on Aerial Warfare 1923 and Geneva Protocol I 1977. Note, also, the four specifically prohibited methods of warfare:

(a) no quarter;

(b) starvation;

(c) belligerent reprisals; and

(d) perfidy.

Humanitarian rules

Particular protection is granted to civilians – Geneva Convention IV and Geneva Protocols I and II

Violations of the laws of armed conflict give rise to State responsibility but there is also the possibility of individuals being held responsible for particular breaches – see Charter of the International Military Tribunal 1945 and Security Council Resolution 827 (1993) and Resolution 955 (1994).

CHAPTER 14

HUMAN RIGHTS

14.1 Introduction

As was stated in Chapter 1, the present system of international law has developed from the law of nations that governed the relations between sovereign States. Prior to World War One, it was a clear principle of international law that a State's treatment of its own nationals was a matter exclusively within its domestic jurisdiction. The only exception to this was the concept of humanitarian intervention to prevent large scale atrocities but, as was shown in Chapter 12, the concept is one of dubious legality. As has already been noted in Chapter 8, the mistreatment of aliens can give rise to State responsibility.

Following World War One, and with the establishment of the League of Nations, widespread concern was expressed about the protection of 'minorities'. The mandate system obliged the mandatory powers to ensure the just treatment of the native populations of the mandate territories and a number of specific arrangements dealt with the position of racial linguistic and religious minorities in Eastern Europe and the Balkans. The League of Nations Council was given the task of monitoring the rights of minorities and there was also a right of petition procedure by minorities to the League of Nations. However, such protections only applied to the minorities expressly mentioned and there was no attempt at the creation of any binding obligations of general application.

The atrocities committed before and during World War Two exposed the need for some comprehensive system of protection of fundamental human rights and this was recognised in the preamble to the Charter of the United Nations, which States:

> We the peoples of the United Nations determined to save succeeding generations from the scourge of war ... and to reaffirm faith in fundamental human rights, in the dignity and worth of the human person, in the equal rights of men and women and of nations large and small ... have resolved to combine our efforts to accomplish these aims.

Article 1(3) of the Charter pledged Member States to achieve international co-operation in promoting and encouraging respect for 'human rights and for fundamental freedoms for all without distinction as to race, sex, language, or religion'. The obligation to promote respect for and observance of human rights and fundamental freedoms is made express in Articles 55 and 56 of the Charter.

Since 1945, a considerable number of rules of international law, both customary and treaty, have been developed with the aim of protecting human rights and fundamental freedoms. Of course, the effectiveness of such rules is open to doubt. The mere existence of rules does not ensure observance of them and, over the years, it has proved far easier to identify particular rights than to provide effective enforcement mechanisms. More has been achieved on a regional basis than at a global level and many human rights experts look to developments regionally as the way forward rather than hoping for great things on the global plane. It is worth noting, however, that the mere existence of human rights agreements can have a beneficial role by giving publicity to abuses and by raising expectations and standards of behaviour and treatment. The role of publicity in the sphere of human rights enforcement should not be underestimated.

It is clearly beyond the scope of a book of this nature to discuss in great detail the nature of all the rights protected and the enforcement machinery available. Instead, this chapter will concentrate on providing an introduction to the subject by looking at the global and regional frameworks which exist.

One final introductory point can be made. Human 'rights' are extremely difficult to define. Generally speaking, they are regarded as those fundamental and inalienable rights which are essential for life as a human being. Put another way, they are those rights which are inherent, in that they exist by virtue of the human condition. However, the view of what specific rights exist and more importantly the interpretation of the extent of such rights may well differ according to the particular economic, social and cultural society in which they are being defined. Thus, while it may be comparatively easy to obtain global agreement that human rights are 'a good thing' the task of reaching consensus on the articulation of particular rights has proved, and is still proving, far more difficult.

14.2 The sources of the law

International human rights law is a combination of customary international law and treaty law. The treaties may be global or regional and general or specialised.

14.2.1 General international agreements

At the inaugural conference of the United Nations held in San Francisco in April 1946, the representatives of Cuba, Mexico and Panama had proposed that the conference should adopt a Declaration on the Essential Rights of Man. However, there was insufficient time available to discuss the proposal and so, at the first session of the UN General Assembly, Panama submitted a Draft Declaration on Fundamental Human Rights and Freedoms. On 11 December 1946, the General Assembly decided to refer the draft to the Economic and Social Council (ECOSOC) for detailed consideration by its Commission on Human Rights. The commission had been established by ECOSOC under

Article 68 of the UN Charter and it spent two years working on a draft International Bill of Rights with the instructions that the bill should be acceptable to all, short, simple and easy to understand. The draft bill was presented to the third session of the UN General Assembly and, on 10 December 1948, resolution 217A was adopted: the Universal Declaration of Human Rights (UDHR). There was no opposition to the resolution, although eight States did abstain, primarily because of the effect that such obligations could have on State sovereignty. The Declaration contains a list of economic, social, cultural and political rights. Since it was only a resolution of the General Assembly, it could not create binding legal obligations, nor was it intended to do so. Rather, the UDHR serves to provide a guideline of standards for States. The precise effect of the resolution was to urge States to establish procedures for the future protection of human rights. The declaration has, however, provided the impetus for the development of customary law (which is discussed at 15.2.4). Commitment to the provisions of the UDHR and other instruments relating to human rights was recently reaffirmed in the Vienna Declaration and Programme of Action 1993 made by States at the UN World Conference on Human Rights held in Vienna in June 1993.

As far as substantive rights are concerned, Articles 1–21 of the UDHR deal with the civil and political rights, Articles 22–27 deal with economic, social and cultural rights, and Articles 28–30 recognise that everyone is entitled to a social and international order in which these rights and freedoms may be realised and stress the duties and responsibilities which the individual owes to the community.

Following the adoption of the UDHR, the UN Commission on Human Rights began work on drafting two international covenants on human rights: one on economic, social and cultural rights and one on civil and political rights. Initially, a single treaty had been envisaged but, in consequence of continued revision and debate, the commission requested that two separate instruments should be prepared. The two conventions, the International Covenant on Civil and Political Rights and the International Covenant on Economic, Social and Cultural Rights, were completed by the mid 1950s and they were adopted by the UN General Assembly and opened for signature in 1966. The two conventions recognise different sets of rights but they do contain some common provisions. However, the machinery for enforcement differs between the two documents and will be discussed at 14.4.1.

The International Covenant on Civil and Political Rights (ICPR) 1966 entered into force in January 1976 and, at present, there are over 100 States party to it, including the UK. The ICPR is a treaty binding on the parties and each State is obliged to give effect to the provisions. In particular, each State should adopt legislative measures to give effect to the covenant and provide effective remedies for violations. The covenant establishes a code of civil and political rights similar to those found in the UDHR. Derogation in times of emergency is allowed with respect to some rights, but not with respect to those rights expressed to be fundamental, such as the right to life (Article 6) and the right to freedom from torture (Article 7).

The International Covenant on Economic, Social and Cultural Rights 1966 entered into force in March 1976 and there are now over 100 State that are party to it, including the UK. Obligations under the ICESCR are less specific than those under the ICPR and the tone of the whole covenant is more promotional than mandatory. Whereas Article 2 of the ICPR provides that:

> Each State party to the present covenant undertakes to respect and to ensure to all individuals within its territory and subject to its jurisdiction the rights recognised in the present covenant

Article 2 of the ICESCR provides that:

> Each State party to the present covenant undertakes to take steps, individually and through international assistance and co-operation, especially economic and technical, to the maximum of its available resources, with a view to achieving progressively the full realisation of the rights recognised in the present covenant by all appropriate means, including particularly the adoption of legislative measures.

14.2.2 Specialised international agreements

The two covenants adopted in 1966 set down a number of general rights which apply equally to all human beings. In addition to these two general agreements, there exists an increasing number of specialised agreements, either directed to the protection of particular rights or particular categories of individual. The specialised conventions have often been the work of the specialised agencies of the UN. For example, the International Labour Organisation has played an important role in addressing the issue of workers' rights and employment conditions and has been responsible for the adoption of a number of conventions dealing with such things as freedom of association.

One of the earliest specialised agreements actually pre-dates the UDHR. The Slavery Convention 1926 outlaws slavery and the slave trade and makes such activities subject to the universal jurisdiction of States. The Slavery Convention was followed by the Forced Labour Convention 1930. Since 1948, there have been a considerable number of specialised agreements among the most significant of which are:

(a) the Genocide Convention 1949 (which was the first human rights treaty to be adopted under the auspices of the UN);

(b) the Convention on the Status of Refugees 1951;

(c) the Convention on the Suppression and Punishment of the Crime of Apartheid 1973;

(d) the Convention against Torture and Other Cruel Inhuman or Degrading Treatment or Punishment 1984; and

(e) the Convention on the Rights of the Child 1989.

With regard to discrimination on grounds of sex, ECOSOC established a Commission on the Status of Women in 1946, which was largely responsible for the adoption of the Convention on the Political Rights of Women 1952 and the Convention on Elimination of all forms of Discrimination against Women 1979. The convention establishes a UN Committee on the Elimination of Discrimination against Women which is charged with monitoring the observance and implementation of the conventions provisions.

As far as racial discrimination is concerned, the Convention on the Elimination of all Forms of Racial Discrimination 1966 entered into force in 1969 and prohibits States from engaging in acts or practices which involve the 'distinction, exclusion, restriction or preference based on race, colour, descent, or national or ethnic origin' and which have the purpose or effect 'of nullifying or impairing the recognition, enjoyment or exercise, on an equal footing, of human rights and fundamental freedoms in the political, economic, social, cultural or any other field of public life'. The Convention does not refer to discrimination on grounds of religion or nationality, which have been the subject of UN resolutions but in relation to which there is no specific treaty. Article 1(4) of the Convention expressly permits action taken to advance the interests of particular groups in order to secure their equal rights and would cover instances of so called 'affirmative action' or 'positive discrimination'. There exists a UN Committee on the Elimination of Racial Discrimination which monitors observance of the convention.

14.2.3 Regional agreements

It has already been stated that human rights may be more effectively protected on a regional basis and there are a number of regional agreements which set down rights and provide enforcement machinery.

14.2.3.1 European agreements

The first regional agreement pertaining to the protection of human rights was the European Convention for the Protection of Human Rights and Fundamental Freedoms (ECHR) 1950, which was signed by the Member States of the Council of Europe at Rome on 4 November 1950 and which entered into force in 1953. The rights and freedoms protected in the convention are those which are generally called civil and political rights. The convention guarantees the right to life, freedom from torture, inhuman or degrading treatment and punishment, freedom from slavery and forced labour, the right to liberty and security of the person, the right to justice, respect for privacy and family life, the right to freedom of thought and conscience and religion, the right to freedom of expression and opinion, peaceful assembly and association, and the right to marry and found a family. Since the convention was drawn up, new rights and obligations have been added in a number of protocols. The rights and freedoms guaranteed by the convention are not enjoyed absolutely. The majority may be restricted in particular circumstances, provided that such restrictions can be justified on grounds of public order, public security and the need to protect the rights and freedoms of others.

The ECHR went far beyond the UDHR, in that it imposed binding obligations on the parties to provide effective domestic remedies with regard to a number of rights, and it refined the definition of such rights. It also established the European Commission of Human Rights to investigate and report on violations of human rights at the instigation of State parties, or, with the express prior consent of individual States, upon petition of any person, non-governmental organisation (NGO) or group of individuals within that State's jurisdiction. The convention also provides for a European Court of Human Rights with compulsory jurisdiction. This was set up in 1959, after eight States had accepted its compulsory jurisdiction.

The ECHR was followed later by the European Social Charter 1961, which entered into force in 1965. The Social Charter deals with the social, economic and cultural rights including the right to work, the right to fair remuneration, the right to bargain collectively and the right to social security. The Social Charter puts claims rather than restrictions on States and the enforcement machinery is very different from that created under ECHR. The European Social Charter 1961 must be distinguished from the Social Chapter of the Treaty on European Union (the Maastricht Treaty).

More recently, the Member States of the Council of Europe adopted the European Convention for the Prevention of Torture and Inhuman or Degrading Treatment or Punishment 1987, which entered into force in 1989. The convention establishes a European Committee for the Prevention of Torture, which is charged with monitoring the treatment of those deprived of their liberty and envisages a system of inspections of prisons and other places of detention. The convention aims to encourage observance of its provisions rather than to provide formal enforcement mechanisms. Torture and other forms of degrading or inhuman treatment are already prohibited under Article 3 of the ECHR.

14.2.3.2 Other regional agreements

A number of other regional organisations have adopted conventions relating to human rights: the American Declaration of the Rights and Duties of Man of 1948, which was closely modelled on the UDHR, was followed by the Protocol to the Charter of the Organisation of American States 1967, which established the Inter-American Commission on Human Rights as a principal organ of the Organisation of American States with the function of promoting respect for human rights. Two years later, the Inter-American Convention on Human Rights 1969 was adopted, which details the rights to be observed and provides for an Inter-American Court of Human Rights.

The Organisation of African Unity has adopted the African Charter on Human and Peoples' Rights 1981. State parties are placed under an obligation to adopt measures to give effect to the rights contained in the charter rather than a strict obligation to observe the rights contained. The substantive provisions of this charter differ from other general human rights treaties, in that far greater emphasis is placed on peoples' rights. The Charter establishes an African Commission on Human and Peoples' Rights which is given responsibility for the promotion of such rights.

Discussions have also taken place with a view to establishing other regional agreements, for example, among the members of the Arab League and within the region of South Asia.

It is also worth noting here certain provisions of the Helsinki Declaration 1975 adopted by the Conference on Security and Co-operation in Europe, although, as has previously been stated, this declaration was expressed to be non-legally binding. Part VII of the declaration pledged respect for fundamental freedoms and human rights. Certain human rights are also dealt with in other more general treaties, for example, the Treaty of Rome 1957.

14.2.4 Customary rules

A significant number of the provisions contained in the various human rights treaties are now considered to be rules of customary international law. In particular, many of the provisions of UDHR, which, as a UN resolution, is not binding *per se*, have come to be regarded as expressing customary rules. An important case in this respect is *Filartiga v Pena-Irala* (1980), which was heard by a US court. The defendant in the case was a former chief of police in Asuncion, Paraguay, and the case was brought by two Paraguayan nationals who alleged that Pena-Irala had tortured to death a member of their family. In the course of giving judgment, the court had cause to consider whether the torture violated customary international law and it cited with approval the view that UDHR had become, *in toto*, a part of binding, international customary law. The Third Restatement of US Foreign Relations Law (1987), which commands considerable respect as a statement of general international law, indicates in paragraph 702 that the following practices, where carried out by or on behalf of States, constitute a violation of customary international law:

(a) genocide;

(b) slavery;

(c) murder or causing the disappearance of individuals (this would not include executions imposed following a fair trial);

(d) torture and other cruel, inhuman or degrading treatment;

(e) prolonged arbitrary detention; and

(f) systematic racial discrimination.

It is suggested that such violations should be considered as breaches of *jus cogens* and that the customary rules protecting human rights are binding *erga omnes*. Some support for this view is found in the judgment of the ICJ in the *Barcelona Traction* case (1970), in which the court indicated that certain obligations deriving from the outlawing of acts of aggression and genocide and 'from the principles and rules concerning basic rights of the human person including protection from slavery and racial discrimination' were owed to the international community as a whole and could be considered obligations *erga omnes*. In addition, the restatement suggests that consistent gross violations of other generally recognised human rights would be contrary to customary international law, even if isolated violations of such rights were not prohibited except by treaty. The restatement suggests that a gross violation is one which is particularly shocking given its particular context.

14.3 Third generation human rights

It has already been indicated that international law distinguishes between civil and political rights and economic, social and cultural rights. The former are often referred to as first generation rights and the latter as second generation rights. According to the classical justification of human rights, which argued that such rights as existed were inherent in the existence of a human being, any rights belonging to entities other than human beings could not be considered as 'human rights' and their justification would have to be found elsewhere. However, with the development of rights such as those of assembly and association which are possessed by individuals but which can only be asserted by collections of individuals, it has become clear that collective rights are recognised by the international community. From this, the idea of peoples' rights has followed. Such rights are seen as belonging to peoples rather than individuals and the principal two such rights are the right to self-determination and the right to development. These rights are often referred to in the literature as 'third generation rights'. The right to development is discussed in Chapter 16 in the context of the international law governing economic relations. In this chapter, discussion will be limited to the right of self-determination. In addition to these peoples' rights, there is also a growing argument about the existence and nature of a right to a decent, viable, healthy and sustainable environment, and such argument is discussed in Chapter 16.

14.3.1 The right to self-determination

Although the principle of self-determination has long been recognised as a political concept, it has only assumed the status of a legal right since 1945. It remains controversial because it is not always easy to clearly identify who possesses the right nor what implementation of the right entails. The UN Charter refers to the principle of 'equal rights and self-determination of peoples' in Article 1(2) but the UDHR make no specific mention of self-determination, although Article 21 provides that:

> (1) Everyone has the right to take part in the government of his country, directly or through freely chosen representatives;
>
> ...
>
> (3) The will of the people shall be the basis of the authority of government ...

Events during the 1950s in colonial territories brought the issue of self-determination to the forefront of discussion and, in 1960, a UN General Assembly, now including a number of newly independent States, adopted the Declaration on the Granting of Independence to Colonial Territories and Peoples, which States that:

> 1 The subjection of peoples to alien subjugation, domination and exploitation constitutes a denial of fundamental human rights is contrary to the Charter of the United Nations and is an impediment to the promotion of world peace and co-operation;
>
> 2 All peoples have the right to self-determination; by virtue of that right they freely determine their political status and freely pursue their economic, social and cultural development.

The provisions of the second paragraph were contained in the common Article 1 of both the ICPR and the ICESCR and, since 1966, recognition of the right of peoples to self-determination has been repeated in a number of resolutions and treaties. In the *Western Sahara* case (1975), the ICJ confirmed that the right was one recognised by international law.

The principle of self-determination certainly now seems to be a part of international law but the problem remains as to who or what constitutes a people capable of possessing and asserting the right. The legal concept was developed during the period of de-colonisation, when it was easier to identify peoples who did not enjoy full rights to determine their own economic, social and cultural development because of the presence of the colonial government. From the 1970s onwards, the right has been asserted by groups wishing to establish a State in part of the territory of an existing State or States and this has created problems which have yet to be resolved. Article 27 of the ICPR provides that:

> In those States in which ethnic, religious or linguistic minorities exist persons belonging to such minorities shall not be denied the right, in community with the other members of their group, to enjoy their own culture, to profess and practise their own religion, or to use their own language.

This article certainly appears to recognise a peoples' right and echoes some of the minority protection measures that were adopted after World War One, but it does not provide a full blown right of self-determination.

The question of the existence of such a right in a non-colonial situation was considered by the Badinter Arbitration Committee, which was established by the European Union in August 1991 to consider various questions of law arising from events in former Yugoslavia. One of the questions presented was whether the Serbs living in Bosnia and Croatia had the right to self-determination. The Arbitration Committee, after making a study of the international law regarding the issue, came to four main conclusions:

(a) the right to self-determination must not involve changes to existing frontiers at the time of independence, except where the States concerned agree otherwise;

(b) where there are two or more groups within a State constituting one or more ethnic, religious or language communities, they have the right to recognition of their identity under international law;

(c) Article 1 of the two 1966 covenants establishes that the principle of the right of self-determination serves to safeguard human rights. By virtue of that right, every individual may choose to belong to whatever ethnic, religious or language community he or she wishes; and

(d) the Serbian population in Croatia and Bosnia is entitled to the rights accorded minorities and such rights must be protected by the governments of Croatia and Bosnia.

The decision is important as it is one of the few, if not the only, occasions in which an international tribunal has been called upon to consider whether a particular group has a right of self-determination and the consequence of that right. It would appear that, although all peoples have the right to self-determination, this should not be understood as a right to independent statehood. Where a identifiable group lives in an existing independent State, it is clear that they are entitled to minority rights but it could be argued that 'the right to recognition of their identity' goes beyond this and suggests that such a group is entitled to some measure of autonomy as well. Certainly, many of the peace proposals that have been made with regard to Bosnia have included recommendations that the Serbian population in Bosnia would possess powers in respect of their own government. However, such an interpretation of a limited right of self-determination in a non-colonial situation is not supported by the provisions of the Vienna Declaration 1993 adopted at the

UN World Conference on Human Rights. Paragraph 2 re-affirms the right of all peoples to self-determination but continues by stating that:

> This shall not be construed as authorising or encouraging any action which would dismember or impair, totally or in part, the territorial integrity or political unity of sovereign and independent State conducting themselves in compliance with the principle of equal rights and self-determination of peoples and thus possessed of a government representing the whole people belonging to the territory without distinction of any kind.

The extent to which this is applied within the recognised sovereign and independent State of Bosnia remains to be seen.

14.4 Enforcement

A survey of the implementation of international human rights law throughout the world could easily give the impression that the law is honoured more in its breach than its observance and that international agreements on human rights law are of little practical use. Such a view, it is submitted, would be wrong, since the very existence of international human rights law can serve to acknowledge abuses are occurring and can set standards for future behaviour. A number of the conventions contain specific provision for their enforcement and, of course, as treaties, they are subject to the usual rules of observance discussed in Chapter 4. But, any discussion of the enforcement of human rights law cannot ignore the prominent role played by publicity both of abuses which occur and of the existence of the rights themselves. A number of organisations exist to monitor human rights violations, either in specific regions or States or throughout the world. A number of States also have introduced a formal system of monitoring, relying on information provided by their embassies abroad; for example, the US Congress prepares a fairly comprehensive annual report on the State of human rights throughout the world, which can have an important role to play in foreign policy decisions which are taken by the executive.

14.4.1 UN mechanisms

Both the ICPR and the ICESCR establish enforcement machinery, although neither have proved to be extremely effective. Under Article 40 of the ICPR, every State party is bound to submit periodic reports to a Human Rights Committee, which is established under part VI of the covenant. The committee is made up of 18 members elected by the parties. Reports should indicate measures that have been taken to implement the covenant and the committee can ask further questions about the report. The committee itself produces a report on the State of human rights but it has proved reluctant or unable to criticise States, and the reports submitted by individual States are unlikely to admit serious human rights violations.

Article 41 of the ICPR establishes a procedure for inter-State complaints, whereby a party may declare, at its option, and on the basis of reciprocity, that it recognises the competence of the Human Rights Committee to receive complaints from other States, subject to the requirement of exhaustion of local remedies. If an inter-State complaint is referred to the committee, it will attempt to mediate and, if necessary, refer the matter to an *ad hoc* Conciliation Commission – but the final report of such a commission is not binding on States. A limited number of States have made optional declarations under Article 41.

In addition, the optional protocol to the ICPR provides for the possibility of individual complaints to the Human Rights Committee, which can then carry out an investigation. The report of the committee is not binding, although its publication may shame a State into action.

Enforcement mechanisms are much less strong under the ICESCR. Under its provisions, parties must submit periodic reports to a Group of Experts established by ECOSOC. The Group of Experts tends to be more open to political influence than the Human Rights Committee. There is also an 18 member Committee on Economic, Social and Cultural Rights, set up by ECOSOC to assist in the implementation of rights.

Aside from the provisions of the two covenants, the Human Rights Commission established by ECOSOC has an important role to play. The commission is composed of 53 members representing their States and, since 1967, it has had jurisdiction to investigate allegations of widespread human rights violations and can establish independent working groups if necessary; for example, a special *rapporteur* has responsibility for monitoring the situation of human rights in Iraq.

Since 1971, the UN Human Rights Commission has debated complaints submitted to it by the Sub-Commission on the Prevention of Discrimination and Protection of Minorities, which was authorised in 1970 to examine individual petitions relating to violations of human rights received by the Secretary General and reported to the Sub-Commission, where they have revealed a consistent pattern of gross violation of human rights. It should be noted that the Sub-Commission has been subjected to immense political pressures and so has lacked effectiveness.

Recognising the problems of enforcement and realisation of human rights, the UN Conference on Human Rights at Vienna recommended a number of new measures, in particular, the creation of the office of UN High Commissioner for Human Rights. The recommendation was acted upon by the UN General Assembly in December 1993, when it voted in favour of creating such a post. In February 1994, Jose Ayala Lasso from Ecuador was appointed the first UN High Commissioner for Human Rights. He was succeeded in September 1997 by Mary Robinson, former President of Ireland. The High Commissioner has responsibility for co-ordinating UN human rights activities and for promoting and protecting human rights.

14.4.2 European mechanisms

As has already been stated, the ECHR was the first human rights treaty to provide mechanisms for enforcement and, to some extent, it has served as a model for other regional agreements. In recent years, the system established under the ECHR has been subject to considerable criticism, much of it related to the cost and time involved in bringing cases to conclusion. The Council of Europe has been debating changes and, in May 1994, the then 32 members of the Council of Europe signed Draft Protocol 11. The Protocol replaces Articles 19–56 of the ECHR and establishes a new permanent European Court of Human Rights.

Protocol 11 came into force on 1 November 1998. The new Court replaces the two existing, part time bodies, the European Court and the Commission of Human Rights. Under Protocol 11, the jurisdiction of the Court is compulsory, whereas, under the previous system, acceptance of both the right of individual petition to the Commission and of the Court's jurisdiction was optional. Another feature of the previous system that has disappeared is the adjudicative role of the Committee of Ministers of the Council of Europe, which, at present, determines complaints in cases declared admissible by the Commission but not subsequently referred to the Court. The Committee of Ministers will, however, retain its present responsibility for supervising the execution of the Court's judgments.

The new Court is composed of a number of judges equal to the number of Contracting Parties (39). The Court's seat is, like its predecessor's, at the Human Rights Building in Strasbourg. For the examination of cases, it will sit in committees of three members, which may reject cases unanimously where such a decision can be taken without further examination, in Chambers of seven and in a Grand Chamber of 17. The Chambers will decide on the admissibility and merits of cases which cannot be dealt with by a committee but they may relinquish jurisdiction in favour of the Grand Chamber when a case raises a serious question affecting the interpretation of the Convention or the Protocols, or when the resolution of a question before the Chamber might have a result inconsistent with a judgment previously delivered by the Court. The parties may, however, object to the relinquishment of jurisdiction by a Chamber.

HUMAN RIGHTS

International law rules protecting human rights have been developed since the end of World War Two. In December 1948, the UN General Assembly adopted the Universal Declaration of Human Rights, which pledged Member States to strive to protect a list of economic, social, cultural and civil and political rights. Civil and political rights are often referred to as first generation rights, with economic, social and cultural rights constituting second generation rights. More recently, a number of third generation rights have been identified; such rights are seen as belonging to peoples rather than individuals and include rights such as self-determination, development and the right to a decent and sustainable environment

Human rights law can be found in a number of global conventions, regional conventions and rules of customary international law.

Global conventions

Among the important global conventions are:

(a) International Covenant on Civil and Political Rights 1966;

(b) International Covenant on Economic, Social and Cultural Rights 1966;

(c) Slavery Convention 1926;

(d) Genocide Convention 1949;

(e) Refugee Convention 1951;

(f) Convention on the Elimination of Racial Discrimination 1966;

(g) Convention on the Elimination of Discrimination against Women 1979;

(h) Torture Convention 1984; and

(i) Convention on the Rights of the Child 1989.

Regional conventions

In many respects, regional protection has proved to be more effective and there now exists a number of regional agreements, notably:

(a) European Convention for the Protection of Human Rights and Fundamental Freedoms 1950;

(b) European Social Charter 1961;

(c) Protocol to the Charter of the Organisation of American States 1967; and

(d) African Charter on Human and Peoples' Rights 1981.

Customary law

Many of the provisions of the UDHR are now regarded as rules of customary international law (see *Filartiga v Pena-Irala* (1980)).

The right to self-determination.

Many international agreements refer to the right of self-determination, although it remains controversial because it is not always easy to identify who possesses the right, nor what implementation of the right involves. There appears to be a distinction in the operation of the right in colonial and non-colonial situations (see Badinter Arbitration Committee 1991).

Enforcement

Convention	Enforcement machinery	Right of individual petition?
UN Charter	43 member Human Rights Commission established by ECOSOC has jurisdiction to investigate widespread abuses. UN High Commissioner on Human Rights appointed in 1994.	No
ICPR	Periodic reports submitted to Human Rights Committee (Article 40). Inter-State complaints submitted to Human Rights Committee (Article 41). Human Rights Committee produces non-binding reports.	Yes, under optional protocol
ICESCR	Periodic reports submitted to Group of Experts established by ECOSOC. Committee on Economic, Social and Cultural Rights assists in implementation of ICESR.	No
ECHR	European Commission of Human Rights and European Court of Human Rights – Nb Protocol 11 establishes Permanent Court of Human Rights to replace previous Court and Commission.	Yes, under Protocol 11, individual right is guaranteed.

CHAPTER 15

ECONOMIC RELATIONS

15.1 Introduction

International economic law has tended to be marginalised in general works in English on public international law. Clearly, any discussion of the law of the sea will need to consider the economic aspects of the management of the sea's resources and discussion of State responsibility will usually consider the issue of expropriation of foreign owned property. But it is rare to find a chapter devoted solely to economic law. This is not to say that it is not a valid subject of study, nor should it be taken to suggest that there is no coherent body of international economic law. On the contrary, any effective legal system needs to provide some framework for the conduct of economic relations. If, as was suggested in Chapter 5, the majority of wars have had as their cause a dispute over territory, the desire to acquire territory has usually had an economic motive. With the realisation that the world's physical resources are not infinite, there has developed a need for the existence of rules governing the exploitation and trade in such resources and the products of such resources. The attempts made by international law to conserve and manage the world's natural resources will be discussed in Chapter 16. This chapter will consider the rules of international law which pertain to trade and development. It will not refer to developments that have occurred within the European Union, which can be studied in the textbooks of European law.

The rules regulating economic relations are of comparatively recent origin. During the 19th century, most States operated a *laissez faire* policy towards their internal economies and, accordingly, there was little, if not no, control of commercial and financial transactions involving foreigners. Such controls as existed were contained in provisions of municipal law and were largely confined to customs and import restrictions. A major impetus for change came with the emergence of the USSR in 1917 and its adoption of economic policies based on the State ownership of the means of production. Implementation of such policies involved the expropriation of foreign owned property and, at the Brussels Conference on Russia in 1921, a resolution was passed, which stated that:

> The forcible expropriations and nationalisations without compensation or remuneration of property in which foreigners are interested is totally at variance with the practice of civilised States. Where such expropriation has taken place, a claim arises for compensation against the government of the country.

The current position regarding expropriation of foreign owned property is discussed at 15.6.

An important aspect of international economic law is the emphasis placed on the need for free trade. During the 19th century, many States had swung between policies of free trade and polices of protectionism depending upon estimations of the relative strength of their own economies. Following the end of World War Two, with many economies in ruins, the USA saw the opportunity to expand its own economy by foreign investment. Such foreign investment undoubtedly helped in the recovery of local economies but, to facilitate such investment, it was necessary to keep trade barriers to a minimum. The international community also accepted the importance of international monetary stability. It was widely recognised that the extremely high inflation in Germany during the late 1920s and early 1930s had been one of the contributory factors in Hitler's rise to power. To assist in the maintenance of currency stability and the encouragement of free trade, three international institutions were established. In July 1944, an international conference was held at Bretton Woods in the USA, at which was established the International Monetary Fund (IMF) and the International Bank for Reconstruction and Development (IBRD). In 1947, 53 States met in Cuba and adopted the Havana Charter 1947, which established the International Trade Organisation (ITO). However, the Charter was not signed by the US and the ITO did not come into existence. Instead, as a temporary measure, the General Agreement on Tariffs and Trade 1947 (GATT) was signed. In 1954, following the Uruguay round (one of a series of regular negotiations) of the GATT, the World Trade Organisation was established. The role of these institutions will be discussed at 15.3 and 15.4.

The emergence of a large number of new independent States during the 1950s and 1960s resulted in new problems for international economic law. In particular, the new States argued for the recognition of a right to economic development which was not always compatible with the rules established through the work of the IMF, World Bank and GATT, and the principle of free trade conflicted with the new States' desire to protect their own fledgling economies. In addition, a number of the new States had strong reservations about foreign companies having control of important local industries and therefore adopted policies involving expropriation. In 1964, the first UN Conference on Trade and Development (UNCTAD) was attended by the overwhelming majority of States. The conference adopted a number of resolutions, which set down guiding principles which should govern the law relating to economic development. The General Assembly subsequently established UNCTAD as one of its permanent institutions, with a secretariat and executive body (the Trade and Development Board). The conference has met on a regular basis since then. The international law of development will be discussed at 15.5.

15.2 The sources of international economic law

The international law governing economic relations differs from many other areas of law, in that customary rules play a far more limited role. Although the majority of States may practise a capitalist form of economics and, in varying degrees, support the idea of a free market and free trade, there are a number of States that vehemently oppose such views. Even among the capitalist States there can exist considerable differences of view as to the rules that should be imposed. The bulk of the rules are contained in bilateral agreements made between States to regulate such things as import and export trade, shipping, foreign investment and banking. Many of these bilateral treaties display common characteristics but their nature has not given rise to a body of State practice and *opinio juris* sufficient to create binding customary rules. There are also a number of important multilateral treaties, for example, the Articles of Agreement of the International Monetary Fund 1944, the General Agreement on Tariffs and Trade 1947 and the various international commodity agreements. A third category of treaties relevant to the international economy would include those treaties which establish a regional body with powers relating to the economy, the best known example being the Treaty of Rome 1957.

In addition to treaty law, there is an ever growing body of resolutions and declarations which, while not constituting formal sources of law, do have an enormous impact on the economic behaviour of States. The importance of such resolutions has led to arguments that they should be considered to constitute a body of *quasi* law, not binding in themselves but representing a firm plan for future legal developments. Such *quasi* law is generally referred to as soft law. Among the resolutions which constitute soft law are the UN General Assembly's Declaration on the Establishment of a New International Economic Order 1974 and the Charter of Economic Rights and Duties of States 1974. Additionally, the declarations of institutions such as the Organisation for Economic Co-operation and Development (OECD) have an important role to play in the development of the law. The Organisation for European Economic Co-operation (OEEC) was established in 1948 to help implement the Marshall aid plan for European economic recovery and to provide a forum for the harmonisation of economic policies and the exchange of information, and operates through the holding of regular meetings of government ministers. In 1961, the European members of OEEC were joined by the US, Canada and Japan, and the OECD was created.

15.3 Free Trade and the World Trade Organisation

The emergence at the end of World War Two of the US as the world's most economically powerful State had the consequence that there was enormous pressure on international law to adopt and reflect principles of capitalist economics. Since US economists stressed the need for a free market at home, it is not surprising that free trade should become the guiding principle for the international economy. The institution principally charged with the development and encouragement of free trade has been GATT. In fact, as has already been indicated, GATT was not created as an international organisation and it was only agreed after the failure to establish an international trade organisation. The abbreviation, GATT, is used in two senses: to indicate the actual treaty which was drafted in 1947, and to indicate the Geneva based institution which administers the agreement. In the latter sense, GATT is hard to distinguish from an international organisation, although it is one without a separate international legal personality of its own. Over 100 States are now contracting parties to the agreement and their combined trade represents 80% of total world trade. The agreement provides a framework for developing rules governing international trade as well as setting down certain fundamental principles. GATT established a framework for discussion and set down a number of important guiding principles. The work of GATT is overseen by the GATT council and there exists a procedure for settling trade disputes between States and the possibility of imposing sanctions on those State parties who do not abide by GATT rules. The agreement contains six principal obligations:

(a) commitment to most-favoured-nation trade;

(b) reduction of tariff barriers;

(c) non-discrimination between imported and domestic goods;

(d) elimination of import quotas;

(e) anti-dumping; and

(f) restriction on export subsidies.

Most of the significant work of GATT has been achieved at the regular, and sometimes protracted, negotiations that are held between the parties to the agreement. In December 1993, the Uruguay round was concluded. The Uruguay round achieved a number of important breakthroughs in the development of international law. The GATT rules were extended to several new areas of trade, including agriculture, film and broadcasting, and intellectual property rights. In addition, it was agreed to extend the life of the Multifibre Agreement (MFA), which regulates certain aspects of the international trade in textiles and clothing. Significantly, the 117 participants at the concluding session agreed to establish the World Trade Organisation (WTO) as a true international organisation with a General Council and bi-annual ministerial meetings. The main functions of the WTO are:

(a) administering and implementing the multilateral and plurilateral trade agreements which together make up the WTO;

(b) acting as a forum for multilateral trade negotiations;

(c) seeking to resolve trade disputes;

(d) overseeing national trade policies; and

(e) co-operating with other international institutions in global economic policy making.

The highest authority of the WTO is the Ministerial Conference, which meets every two years – most recently in Singapore in December 1996. The day to day work of the WTO is carried out by the General Council, which also convene as the Dispute Settlement Body and the Trade Policy Review Body. The General Council delegates responsibility to three other major bodies – the Council for Trade in Goods; the Council for Trade in Services; and the Council for Trade Related Aspects of Intellectual Property Rights. In addition, there are three other bodies which report to the General Council: the Committee on Trade and Development, the Committee on Balance of Payments and the Committee on Budget, Finance and Administration.

15.3.1 Commitment to most-favoured-nation trade

A guiding principle of GATT is non-discrimination. Accordingly, Article I of the agreement provides that:

> Any advantage, favour, privilege, or immunity granted by any other contracting party to any product originating in or destined for any other country shall be accorded immediately and unconditionally to the like product originating in or destined for the territories of all other contracting parties.

In the late 19th century, it was common for bilateral trade agreements to include a most-favoured-nation clause, which committed each party to grant to the other all the trading rights and benefits that it accorded to the third State it treated best, in other words, the States agreed to treat each other as well as their most-favoured-nations. Article I amounts to a most-favoured-nation (MFN) clause binding on, and between, all parties to the agreement. MFN treatment governs all import and export trade and applies to import and export customs duties and similar charges, to all rules and formalities connected with import and export and to internal taxes or charges of any kind in excess of those applied to like domestic products. The commitment to immediate and unconditional MFN trade means that, whenever a State party to GATT extends some privilege or right to one of its trading partners, it will automatically extend to all other State parties. An important aspect of the unconditional nature of the rule is that it does not require reciprocity: if State A agrees to impose a reduced tariff on particular goods imported from State B, that reduction will apply to State C and all other parties to GATT, irrespective of whether State C and the other parties reduce tariffs on imports from State A. For this reason, MFN status does not ensure that all GATT members trade on the basis of equality, although the multilateral and reciprocal basis of most trade agreements does help to avoid extreme imbalances.

15.3.2 Reduction of tariff barriers

Article II of GATT commits the parties to co-operate on the lowering of tariffs. This is to be done through the tariff concession, whereby a party promises to levy a tariff on a stated product no higher than that level agreed to at trade negotiations. GATT establishes the framework for regular negotiations between States to set tariff levels. These regular negotiations are known as 'rounds' and there have been eight such rounds. The early rounds tended to be conducted on a bilateral basis but, gradually, it became clear that more would be achieved by holding multilateral talks. The Kennedy round (1962–67) resulted in a considerable lowering of tariffs and, by the mid 1970s, tariffs had been lowered to such an extent that they were no longer seen as the major barrier to international trade. Instead, attention was turned to non-tariff barriers and a number of codes of practice were adopted at the Tokyo round, for example, the GATT Agreement on Technical Barriers to Trade, which has the aim of harmonising product standards.

15.3.3 Non-discrimination

Article III of GATT requires States to treat imported goods in the same way as domestically produced goods. Specifically, imported goods cannot be regulated or taxed in a manner different to that applying to domestic products. Article III(4) provides that:

> The products ... imported into the territory of any other contracting party shall be accorded treatment no less favourable than that accorded to like products of national origin in respect of all laws, regulations, and requirements affecting their internal sale.

Article VII does allow charges to be imposed on imports where they reflect services provided to the importer, for example, charging for the use of port facilities or for product inspection is permitted, provided that it is reasonable and based on actual costs. Such charges cannot be used as an indirect import duty.

15.3.4 Import quotas

There is clearly little point in reducing import tariffs if States impose harsh restrictions on the number of imports allowed. Article XI of GATT therefore prohibits States from imposing any restriction on imports other than duties, taxes and other charges. This prohibition is subject to a number of exceptions. Article XII allows States to impose import quotas where they are considered necessary to correct a severe balance of payments deficit which is resulting in the imminent threat or actual occurrence of 'a serious decline in its monetary reserves'.

15.3.5 Anti-dumping

Underlying GATT is the belief that everyone benefits from the existence of free trade and that obstacles to such trade should be kept to a minimum. However, this belief relies on trade being fair. Just as imposing high duties on imports is unfair to the importing country and adversely affects the flow of trade, so artificially reducing the price of exports is unfair to the importing country and can have a devastating effect on its economy. Dumping refers to the practice of selling goods in a foreign country for less than the price charged for the same goods in the producer's domestic market. Article VI of GATT provides that, where such a situation causes or threatens material injury to domestic industry, or retards the development of such an industry, the importing State may impose an additional duty which reflects the difference between the price being charged for the goods and the price of the goods, or comparable goods, in the exporter's home market. Thus, for example, if a Japanese company were to market a machine in the UK at a price of £400 while the same machine was marketed at £800 in Japan, then the UK would be entitled to impose a £400 anti-dumping duty on the imported Japanese machine. The usual motivation behind the practice of dumping is an intention to drive competing companies in the importing State out of business. However, the intention of the exporter is not relevant to the imposition of anti-dumping duties. In 1979, the GATT Anti-Dumping Code was adopted in an attempt to further clarify Article VI. The code sets down a procedure for dealing with disputes arising out of allegations of dumping and establishes the Committee on Anti-Dumping Practices, which is responsible for assisting in the settlement of such disputes

15.3.6 Export subsidies

Just as dumping may distort international trade, so can subsidies granted to exports since they too can make a product less expensive in the importing country which is likely to be to the detriment of foreign competitors. Export subsidies may take the form of export credit guarantees, favourable tax rates for income earned from export trade, or foreign exchange risk guarantees. Article XVI restricts the right of States to grant export subsidies where such subsidies threaten or cause material injury to an industry in the importing State. In such a situation, if export subsidies have been imposed, the importing State is entitled to offset the effect of the subsidies by imposing an additional tariff (countervailing duty). In 1979, GATT adopted the Subsidies

Code, which further refines the law and provides a mechanism for the settlement of disputes. One such dispute arose out of the development, manufacture and export of the European Airbus. Germany provided currency stabilisation guarantees to assist in the sale of the planes in the US. The US alleged that such guarantees violated the GATT code by threatening and causing injury to the American aviation industry. In 1992, a GATT panel of experts upheld the US complaint.

15.4 Financial stability

At the end of World War Two, the international community was faced with two major problems relating to international finance. An immediate problem concerned the need to finance the rebuilding of domestic economies devastated by six years of war. It was also recognised that there was a need to provide some system of regulation of currency exchange to help prevent the violent exchange rate fluctuations and associated hyper-inflation that had occurred during the 1920s and 1930s. These problems were addressed at the international conference held at Bretton Woods in 1944, which resulted in the establishment of the IMF and the International Bank for Reconstruction and Development.

15.4.1 The International Monetary Fund

The IMF was established to promote international monetary co-operation, to facilitate the growth of international trade and to promote foreign exchange stability. The IMF has a board of governors, 22 executive directors and a managing director. The Articles of Agreement of the IMF place a number of obligations on Member States. Originally, the currency of each member was assigned a par value expressed in terms of gold, and members were under a duty to maintain this value. Changes in par value could only be made to correct serious balance of payment crises and required the agreement of the IMF. By the late 1960s, the fixed exchange rates were becoming increasingly difficult to maintain and, in 1973, the Articles of Agreement were amended to allow for floating exchange rates. The IMF is financed through subscription by its members. Each member is allocated a subscription quota, which is based on a number of criteria relating to the strength of its economy. The size of a State's quota affects its voting rights at meetings of the IMF. The IMF operates a system of weighted voting, which gives those States with the strongest economies the biggest voice. As a result, the IMF, which now has over 150 members, has always been heavily influenced by the Western industrialised nations. The size of the quota also influences a State's 'special drawing rights'. The special drawing rights allow Member States to draw currency from the IMF to correct temporary balance of payments problems. It amounts to a sort of overdraft facility for members. It was envisaged that the provision of special drawing rights would remove the need for States to resort to protectionism in times of economic crisis. For the first 30 years of the IMF, currency transactions and payments into the fund were calculated by reference to the official price of gold. In 1978, the Articles of Agreement were amended with the effect of abolishing this gold standard and, since that time, transactions have been valued on the basis of a 'weighted basket' of the five principal currencies (US dollar, Deutschmark, Japanese yen, French franc, and pound sterling).

15.4.2 The International Bank for Reconstruction and Development

Traditionally, States wishing to raise capital resorted to the private financial markets or borrowed from other States. As far as the private markets were concerned, investors did not always see an adequate rate of return and also ran the risk that such investment might be wiped out by nationalisation or other measures adopted by the borrowing State. Borrowing from other States often led to problems involving the lending State interfering in the domestic affairs of the borrowing State. With the need for a massive injection of capital into the economies of many States after World War Two, and with the desire to avoid some of the problems that had been encountered with the traditional methods, the Bretton Woods conference agreed to establish the International Bank for Reconstruction and Development (IBRD). Membership of the bank is the same as that of the IMF and the two organisations work closely together. The capital of the bank is contributed by the members in proportion to their relative economic strength. Like the IMF, voting is weighted according to contribution. The bank exists to lend money to States or to private enterprises where such loans are guaranteed by the government in whose territory the loan is to be used. Although initially the bank provided money to finance immediate post-war reconstruction, loans are now given only for projects which will enhance economic growth. Before any loan is made, the bank will carry out a thorough investigation. Money is not lent for high risk projects and the loans are generally provided on market terms

It was soon realised that the IBRD's policies were aimed largely at industrialised nations experiencing short term problems and were not really appropriate to the situation of a newly independent State attempting to establish its own economy. Developing States argued that a UN fund for development should be established but the Western States felt that this would not be in their own interests. As some sort of compromise, the IBRD established the International Finance Corporation (IFC) in 1956. The aim of the IFC is to promote private investment in developing countries and to supplement such investment with its own funds. In 1960, the bank established the International Development Association (IDA). The IDA provides long term low cost finance for the establishment of basic economic infrastructure, such as power supply and communications. The voting rights in the IDA are very heavily weighted in favour of the Western States, which has led to criticisms of the organisation by a number of developing or under-developed States.

Together, the IBRD, IFC and IDA are generally referred to as the World Bank.

15.5 Development

A fundamental principle of international law is the sovereign equality of States. Sovereign equality is, however, largely dependent upon economic equality and the question therefore arises of the extent to which rules of international law should positively encourage the achievement of such economic equality. Article 55 of the UN Charter provides that the UN shall promote:

> (a) higher standards of living, full employment, and conditions of economic and social progress and development ...

and, under Article 56, all Member States pledge themselves to take joint and separate action for the achievement of this aim. The 1950s saw the granting of independence to many former colonies and with it came a realisation that political independence would amount to very little without the economic independence which would come from the development of local industry. In the early 1950s, the UN established various bodies charged with providing technical assistance and, as has already been seen, provision was made for limited financial assistance through the IMF and World Bank. However, by the 1960s, the newly independent States were becoming more forceful in their criticism of the provisions; in particular, they objected to the fact that they did not have equal voting rights at the IMF or World Bank. They also felt that the international economic system that was in place favoured the rich nations and was resulting in the poor nations becoming poorer. Arguments started to be put forward for a new international economic order (NIEO). The first development was the establishment of the UN Conference on Trade and Development (UNCTAD) in 1964. In 1965, the UN Development Programme was established and, in 1966, the UN Industrial Development Organisation (UNIDO) was created with the objective of promoting and accelerating industrial development in the developing countries.

Probably the greatest single factor in the emergence of a law of development was the Arab-Israeli War 1973 and the oil boycott imposed on the industrialised States. For the first time, developing States were able to assert real power against the industrialised States and it was felt that what had been achieved with oil might also be possible with other raw materials, the bulk of which were possessed by the developing States. Since 1972, UNCTAD had been working on a draft charter of economic rights and duties of States and, in 1974, the UN General Assembly discussed the draft together with a number of other resolutions relating to the economic order. By consensus, the General Assembly adopted the Declaration on the Establishment of a New International Economic Order and a Programme of Action on the Establishment of the NIEO. Both resolutions set down objectives to be achieved rather than any standards of behaviour. However, the Charter of Economic Rights and Duties of States was drafted in similar terms to the various human rights conventions. The Charter was adopted by the General Assembly, although a few Western States voted against it and a number of others abstained. As a result, the Charter cannot be considered to be a declaration of existing rules of international law, although some of its provisions, particularly those relating to the expropriation of foreign owned property, have been claimed as binding law.

A major concern of the developing States is with the activities of multinational or transnational companies, which can often achieve a position of dominance within the local economy without contributing to the positive development of that local economy. The UN has established the Commission on Transnational Corporations which has developed a draft Code of Conduct for Transnational Corporations 1988. The code is designed 'to maximise the contributions of transnational corporations to economic development and growth and to minimise the negative effects of the activities of these corporations'. So far, however, the code has not been accepted by the western industrialised States.

Alongside these specific activities, there has also been a continued call for the recognition of a right to development. The idea of promoting such a right is to link the call for an NIEO to more general questions of human rights and to recognise the duty of the richer States to assist in the realisation of the right to development of the poorer States. Whilst the concept of a right to development has had political significance, it is not capable of being sufficiently precisely defined for it to become a binding rule of international law.

15.6 Expropriation of foreign owned property

Interference with foreign owned property has assumed major importance since World War Two. Injury to foreign nationals or damage to their property by the organs or officials of a State has always been considered a *prima facie* breach of international law. Even prior to the war, certain rules had been developed to deal with seizures of foreign owned property:

(a) discrimination against an individual alien or aliens in general was contrary to international law, irrespective of whether compensation had been paid or not;

(b) there was support for the view that seizure of foreign owned property was *prima facie* illegal, even if compensation was offered, if the seizure was not part of a programme of public utility; and

(c) in cases where nationalisation was permissible, prompt, adequate and effective compensation had to be paid.

In the *German Interests in Polish Upper Silesia* case (1928), the PCIJ had held that the expropriation of a German owned factory at Chorzow was contrary to a treaty between Germany and Poland. In the subsequent *Chorzow Factory (Merits)* case (1928), the court pointed to the significant difference between an expropriation without justification under international law, and one that, although justifiable, was not accompanied by satisfactory compensation. In the latter case, the wrongful act could be remedied by the payment of the appropriate compensation with interest from the date of the nationalisation. In the former situation, however, the amount of reparation was not limited to the value of the property but should also include a sum representing the fact that no right to take over the property existed at all.

The widespread nationalisations that followed World War Two, and the emergence of new States in Africa and Asia resentful of the economic interests of the former colonial powers, resulted in demands for a change in the law. It was soon accepted that States did have an inherent right to adopt economic policies involving nationalisation. This was confirmed by the arbitrator in *Texaco Overseas Petroleum Company v Libyan Arab Republic* (1977), and the arbitrator in *LIAMCO v Libyan Arab Republic* (1977) confirmed that the motives of a State in nationalising property were no concern of international law. The main area of dispute then became the issue of compensation.

The question of compensation was discussed in the UK memorial submitted in the *Anglo-Iranian Oil* case (1952), in which the UK claimed that international law imposed a duty on States to provide prompt, adequate and effective compensation. By 'adequate' was understood an amount equal to the value of the property or undertaking at the time expropriation occurs plus interest up until the day of judgment. In 1962, the UN General Assembly adopted Resolution 1803 (XVII), the Declaration on Permanent Sovereignty over Natural Resources, which recognises the rights of States to expropriate foreign owned property on grounds of public utility, security or the national interest (consideration of which must be an internal matter for the State concerned) and further provides that, in cases of expropriation:

> The owner shall be paid appropriate compensation in accordance with the rules in force in the State taking such measures in the exercise of its sovereignty and in accordance with international law.

The resolution is widely accepted as reflecting customary international law, although its provisions relating to compensation are clearly ambiguous. The

Charter of Economic Rights and Duties of States favours the developing States' view regarding compensation, since it provides, in Article 2(2)(c), that:

> Appropriate compensation should be paid by the [nationalising] State ..., taking into account its relevant laws and regulations and all the circumstances that the State considers pertinent. In any case where the question of compensation gives rise to a controversy, it shall be settled under the domestic law of the nationalising States and its tribunals ...

As has already been seen, the Charter was not accepted by the majority of Western States, and the arbitrator in the *Texaco Overseas Petroleum* case (1977) viewed Article 2(2)(c) as having the nature of *de lege ferenda* rather than constituting a rule of customary international law. Decisions of international tribunals since then have confirmed the view that the assessment of compensation is not exclusively a matter within a State's domestic jurisdiction. These decisions, such as the one given in the *Aminoil* case (1982), suggest that the amount of compensation payable should be determined by a balancing process taking into account the investment made by the foreign company and taxes and royalties legitimately due to the nationalising State. The aim of the process should be the achievement of an equitable result. More recently, there has been a tendency for States involved in foreign investment to include clauses relating to compensation in the initial agreement which sets up the investment.

[illegible] against [illegible] the [illegible] ICSID [illegible]

> A prominent [illegible] the need for the [illegible] including the following [illegible] relevant laws and regulations and additional [illegible] that the State [illegible] question of [illegible] controversy [illegible]

As has already occurred in the [illegible] accepted by the majority of [illegible] 1977 [illegible] Article 26 [illegible] The [illegible] international law [illegible] international tribunal [illegible] that the [illegible] the [illegible] investment made by the [illegible] company and [illegible] the [illegible] State. The [illegible] investment [illegible] to the [illegible]

[illegible]

[illegible]

ECONOMIC RELATIONS

Sources of international economic law

The bulk of the rules are contained in bilateral, although there are a number of important multilateral treaties:

(a) Articles of Agreement of the International Monetary Fund 1944;

(b) General Agreement on Tariffs and Trade 1947; and

(c) Various commodity agreements.

In addition, there is an important body of soft law, including the Charter of Economic Rights and Duties of States 1974 and the Declaration on the Establishment of a New International Economic Order 1974.

GATT and WTO

The underlying philosophy of international economic law is the promotion of free trade. In furtherance of this, GATT contains six principal obligations:

(a) commitment to most-favoured-nation trade;

(b) reduction of tariff barriers;

(c) non-discrimination;

(d) elimination of import quotas;

(e) anti-dumping; and

(f) restrictions on export subsidies.

The most significant work of GATT has been achieved at the regular negotiation rounds, the most recent of which was the Uruguay round, which concluded in December 1993 and resulted in the establishment of the World Trade Organisation, a new international organisation which will take over the organisational role of GATT.

The World Bank

In addition to the regulation of international trade, there have also been moves to stabilise international currency exchange. The main body responsible for this is the IMF, which provides overdraft facilities for Member States. The IBRD, which works closely with the IMF, facilitates loans for industrial development, and the IFC and IDA exist to promote private investment in developing States.

Development

The UN Charter commits States to promoting higher standards of living and to create conditions of economic development. During the late 1950s and 1960s, arguments were put forward in favour of establishing a new international economic order, which would allow the economies of the newly independent States to grow and compete with western economies. In 1964, UNCTAD was established and it was followed by the UN Development Programme and the UN Industrial Development Organisation. In 1974, discussions at UNCTAD resulted in the Declaration on the Establishment of a New International Economic Order and the Charter of Economic Rights and Duties of States. In the mid 1980s, attention began to focus on the activities of the multinational companies and, in 1988, the Code of Conduct for Transnational Corporations was drawn up, although it has met with little acceptance from western States.

Expropriation of foreign owned property

- *German Interests in Polish Upper Silesia* case (1928)
- *Chorzow Factory* case (1928)
- *Anglo-Iranian Oil Co* case (1952)
- *Texaco Overseas Petroleum Company v Libyan Arab Republic* (1977)
- *LIAMCO v Libyan Arab Republic* (1977)
- *Aminoil* case (1982)
- Declaration on Permanent Sovereignty over Natural Resources 1962
- Charter of Economic Rights and Duties of States 1974

CHAPTER 16

ENVIRONMENTAL PROTECTION

16.1 Introduction

The sovereignty possessed by States over their own territory has long been limited by the obligation not to interfere in the rights of other States. States are under a duty not to act within their own territory in such a way as to cause harm in the territory of other States. Thus, in the *Trail Smelter* arbitration (1941), Canada was held liable for damage caused in the USA by sulphur dioxide emitted from a smelter in Canada. The arbitration tribunal found that, under the principles of international law:

> No State has the right to use or permit the use of its territory in such a manner as to cause injury by fumes in or to the territory of another State or the properties or persons therein, when the case is of serious consequence and the injury is established by clear and convincing evidence.

Provided that a State did not cause harm in or to the territory of another State, it was free to act as it wished, even if this resulted in serious damage to the environment within the State. Since World War Two, there has been a growing realisation that the world's resources are not infinite and that the nature of industrial and agricultural practices adopted can have serious implications for future generations. The international community has come to accept that there is a need for common action to help sustain life, in all its forms, on this planet and that this need cannot always be met within an approach based on territorial sovereignty of States. Just as human rights law has developed to the extent that States are no longer free to act with regard to their nationals as they alone see fit, so too, a body of rules has developed to suggest that there are now restrictions on the way States behave towards their immediate environment. As will be discussed at 16.5, there is some overlap between international environmental law and human rights law in discussion of whether or not there exists a right to a decent environment.

16.2 The nature of the obligations

One particular question that has been raised about international environmental law concerns the nature of the obligations imposed. Several writers have argued that the general obligation to preserve the environment constitutes a norm of *jus cogens* and that it is binding *erga omnes*. In the *Nuclear Tests* case (1974), the ICJ doubted whether rights relating to the high seas could be enforced as *erga omnes* obligations, although the reasoning of the court has been criticised by some writers and conflicts with the ILC Draft Articles on State Responsibility 1980. Article 19(3)(d) provides that:

> A serious breach of an international obligation of essential importance for the safeguarding and preservation of the human environment, such as those prohibiting massive pollution of the atmosphere or of the seas

constitutes an international crime and therefore is the concern of all States and not just those suffering injury. The repetition of the obligation on States to safeguard and preserve the human environment in numerous international resolutions, including the declaration made at the Rio Conference on the Environment and Development 1992, would seem to support the view that the obligation is indeed now one of *jus cogens*. The full extent of the obligation, however, remains to be clearly enunciated.

16.3 Sources

The bulk of international environmental law is contained in multilateral treaties and the important ones will be discussed in the subsequent sections. Such treaties may be designed to apply globally, such as the Convention on Long-Range Transboundary Air Pollution 1979, or may be concerned with protection of a specific region, for example, the Antarctic Treaty 1959 and the Convention on Protection of the Mediterranean Sea 1976. In addition, there are a number of treaties which, while not concerned exclusively with environmental matters, nevertheless contain some provisions which have significance for the environment, for example, the Law of the Sea Convention 1982.

Besides treaty law, there are also some important rules of customary international law affecting the environment. For example, reference has already been made to the prohibition on causing harm in or to the territory of another State. However, although States often make statements in support of environmental protection, these statements are not always adhered to in practice. Furthermore, it has often been difficult to prove the necessary accompanying *opinio juris* to be able to assert a binding rule of customary international law. Therefore, writers on international environmental law have made considerable use of the concept of soft law. It is often the case that States are unwilling to agree to legally binding obligations in particular areas of environmental protection because of the unavailability of relevant scientific information or knowledge. The concept of soft law allows there to be a statement of principle and intention and the soft law can gradually harden as scientific knowledge expands. Much of the soft environmental law is to be found in the resolutions of various international organisations concerned with environmental matters, such as the World Heath Organisation, the International Atomic Energy Agency, the International Maritime Organisation and the Food and Agriculture Organisation. In 1972, a UN Conference on the

Human Environment was held at Stockholm, Sweden. The conference adopted the Stockholm Declaration on the Human Environment 1972 (the Stockholm Declaration), which has had an important role in developing the law. It also established the UN Environment Programme (UNEP), based in Nairobi and consisting of 58 members elected by the UN General Assembly, with a Governing Council and Secretariat. UNEP has since adopted a number of codes of practice and recommendations, many of which could be considered soft law.

16.4 The Stockholm Conference

During the 1960s, concern grew about the State of the human environment and manifested itself in Resolution 2398 (XXIII), which was passed by the General Assembly of the United Nations on 3 December 1968. The resolution noted that there was 'an urgent need for intensified action at national and international level to limit and, where possible, to eliminate the impairment of the human environment' and convened an international Conference on the Human Environment to be held under the auspices of the United Nations. The Conference met in June 1972 in Stockholm and was attended by 113 States. At the end of the Conference, agreement had been reached on four major areas of policy:

(a) an Action Plan for environmental policy was agreed, consisting of 106 recommendations, including the establishment of Earthwatch, which was charged with monitoring and providing information on the State of the environment;

(b) an Environment Fund would be created, funded by voluntary contributions from States;

(c) the establishment of the UN Environment Programme (UNEP) with a Governing Council and Secretariat. UNEP is based in Nairobi, Kenya, and has adopted a number of codes of practice and recommendations, many of which could be considered soft law; and

(d) a declaration of principles on the human environment which would provide a focus for future binding rules of international law in a manner analogous to the Universal Declaration of Human Rights.

16.5 The environment and development

Although concern about the environment was growing, during the 1960s, the priority at the United Nations was economic development. The resolution on Permanent Sovereignty over Natural Resources adopted in 1962 made no reference to conservation of resources or other environmental concerns and, during the 1960s, there were few voices in support of linking economic development issues to the environment. In fact, among developing States there was a significant number of people who viewed environmental concern with suspicion, fearing that measures taken to protect and conserve the environment were simply a Western capitalist plot to prevent Third World development. Patricia Birnie ('The UN and the environment' in Roberts, A and Kingsbury, B (eds) *United Nations, Divided World*, 1993, Oxford: OUP, p 338) identifies the preparations for the Stockholm Conference as marking a change in attitudes:

> A catalytic event, facilitating the success of UNCHE [UN Conference on the Human Environment, Stockholm 1972], was the convening of a meeting at Founex, Switzerland, in 1971, to consider a study (instigated by the UNCHE Prepcom) on environment and development. The study group brought together representatives of international development agencies and governments, including economists, bankers, planners, social scientists, and ecologists. its conclusion that 'the kind of environmental problems that are of importance in developing countries are those that can be overcome by the process of development itself' reassured developing countries, which were wavering in their support for the conference. Twenty five guidelines were laid down aimed at protecting their interests. This articulation of the symbiosis of environment and development was thus from the beginning central to the UN's work in the environmental field.

The Stockholm Declaration acknowledged the link between the protection and improvement of the human environment and economic development, although the emphasis of the Charter of Economic Rights and Duties of States, adopted two years after the Stockholm Conference, was on optimum use of resources and full economic development, with limited acknowledgement of environmental concerns. It was not until 1983 that the link between environment and development started to attain practical significance. In that year, the World Commission on Environment and Development (WCED) was created as a consequence of General Assembly Resolution 38/161, adopted at the 38th Session of the UN in December 1983. That resolution called upon the Secretary General to appoint the Chairman and Vice-Chairman of the Commission and, in turn, directed them jointly to appoint the remaining members, at least half of whom were to be selected from the developing world. The Secretary General appointed Mrs Brundtland, then leader of the Norwegian Labour Party, as Chairman and Dr Mansour Khalid, the former minister of Foreign Affairs from Sudan, as Vice-Chairman. The WCED functioned as an independent body and its members served the Commission in their individual capacities, not as State representatives. Its brief was to investigate the major environmental and development problems that faced the world and to formulate realistic proposals for their solution. The WCED reported back to the 42nd session of the General Assembly in the autumn of 1987. In her foreword to the report, Mrs Brundtland wrote:

> The environment does not exist as a sphere separate from human actions, ambitions and needs, and attempts to defend it in isolation from human concerns have given the very word 'environment' a connotation of naivety in some political circles. The word 'development' has also been narrowed by some into a very limited focus, along the lines of 'what poor nations should do to become richer', and thus again is automatically dismissed by many in the international arena as being a concern of specialists, of those involved in questions of 'development assistance'.
>
> But the 'environment' is where we all live; and 'development' is what we all do in attempting to improve our lot within that abode. The two are inseparable.

The Report itself acknowledged the important role that international law needed to play in protecting the environment.

16.6 The 1992 Earth Summit

In June 1992, 176 States met in Rio de Janeiro for the United Nations Conference on Environment and Development. The preparatory debates for the Conference revealed that there was still considerable dispute as to the where the emphasis was to be put: on environment or on development. Although the Conference had, as its backdrop, the ending of the Cold War, the recent successful international action against Iraq and President Bush's calls for the establishment of a new international order, the divisions between North and South on environmental and developmental issues were still very much apparent. Nonetheless, the Conference succeeded in producing five major documents:

(a) *Agenda 21*, which is an 800 page document setting out an action plan for managing the various sectors of the environment in the 21st century;

(b) the Climate Change Convention;

(c) the Biological Diversity Convention;

(d) a non-binding statement of Consensus on Forest Principles; and

(e) a Declaration on Environment and Development.

The Rio Declaration was adopted by consensus of those 176 States attending the conference and, although not formally binding, is of major legal significance and can be seen as an example of soft law. In the preamble to the Declaration, the Conference reaffirmed the Stockholm Declaration and expressed the desire to build upon it.

16.7 General principles

It should already be clear that it is not possible to maintain an absolute notion of territorial sovereignty. The freedom of States to act is necessarily constrained by the duty to have regard to the rights of other States and the environment in general. The principle of 'good neighbourliness' is a feature of international law. In the sphere of environmental law, this extremely general principle has been developed further and a number of more specific governing principles can be identified.

16.7.1 The duty to prevent, reduce and control environmental harm

Reference has already been made to the *Trail Smelter* Arbitration, in which the tribunal made it clear that States are under a duty not to use or permit the use of their territory in such a manner as to cause injury in or to the territory of another State. Similarly, in the *Corfu Channel* case, the International Court made reference to 'every State's obligation not to allow knowingly its territory to be used for acts contrary to the rights of other States'. Principle 21 of the Stockholm Declaration, while affirming the sovereign right of States to exploit their own resources, re-affirms the duty incumbent on States 'to ensure that activities within their jurisdiction or control do not cause damage to the environment of other States or to areas beyond the limits of national jurisdiction'. A number of States made clear at the Stockholm Conference that they felt Principle 21 to be declaratory of existing customary international law. Its use in numerous conventions, declarations and resolutions since then only strengthens the view that it is indeed a rule of international law.

It should be noted that the principle involves more than the need to make reparation for damage caused. States are under a duty to prevent future harm occurring. This duty is often expressed as the need for States to exercise 'due diligence'. In deciding whether due diligence has been exercised, it is legitimate to take into account a States resources and capabilities, the effectiveness of territorial control and the nature of the specific activities under consideration. The more inherently dangerous the activity undertaken, the greater the amount of diligence required. Of course, such a formulation does not clearly provide what specific action is required of a State and there have been attempts to provide a more detailed minimum standard of care. Alternatively, a number of conventions have used the formulation of 'best available technology' or 'best practicable means'. Increasingly, reference is made to the 'precautionary principle', according to which, States have a duty to undertake assessment of the likely consequences for the environment of planned activities and to take preventive measures where appropriate. However, the principle should be used with care:

> Despite its attractions, the great variety of interpretations given to the precautionary principle, and the novel and far-reaching effects of some

> applications suggest that it is not yet a principle of international law. Difficult questions concerning the point at which it becomes applicable to any given activity remain unanswered and seriously undermine its normative character and practical utility, although support for it does indicate a policy of greater prudence on the part of those States willing to accept it. [Boyle, A and Birnie, P, *International Law and the Environment*, 1992, Oxford: OUP, p 98.]

16.7.2 Consultation, co-operation and communication

An increasingly common provision in international conventions on the environment requires States to co-operate with other States likely to suffer environmental risks from proposed activities. In the *Lac Lanoux* Arbitration (1957), Spain complained that France had violated a treaty by diverting a river which flowed through the territory of both States. Although the tribunal found no treaty violation, it affirmed the requirement of prior notice and consultation:

> ... a State which is liable to suffer repercussions from work undertaken by a neighbouring State is the sole judge of its interests and if the neighbouring State has not taken the initiative the other State cannot be denied the right to insist on notification of works or concessions which are the object of a scheme.

The tribunal made clear that consultations between the two States must be genuine and conducted in good faith.

Principle 24 of the Stockholm declaration re-affirms the need for co-operation, and the duty to notify and consult has been repeated in a number of conventions and draft conventions dealing with shared natural resources. It is generally accepted that States are under a duty to give timely notification to States at risk following environmental accidents and emergencies. Thus, it can be seen that, while States are under a duty to prevent accidents, should an accident or emergency occur, they have a continuing obligation to minimise its effects.

16.7.3 The polluter pays principle

A guiding principle that has found growing support in various measures taken to prevent pollution is that the polluter pays. The principle was endorsed by the OECD States in 1972 and adopted by the First Environmental Action Programme 1973 of the European Union. Article 25 of the Single European Act 1986 provides that action taken by the EU relating to the environment shall be based on the principles 'that environmental damage should as a priority be rectified at source and that the polluter should pay'. The principle was again endorsed, this time by the Conference on Security and Co-operation in Europe, in 1990. For a long time, it was argued that the principle was only supported by the industrial States, but Principle 16 of the Declaration on Environment and Development 1992 calls for national authorities to endeavour to internalise environmental costs by making the polluter 'in principle' bear the cost of pollution.

16.8 Pollution

Although the *Trail Smelter* arbitration illustrates that the discharge of toxic or other harmful substances in such a way as to cause harm on or to neighbouring States would give rise to international liability, until the 1970s, there was no real attempt to control pollution in other situations. In 1968, the UN General Assembly had recognised that there was an urgent need of action to limit and, if possible, eliminate 'the impairment of the human environment' and the decision was taken to convene an international conference to discuss possible action. The UN Conference on the Human Environment met in Stockholm in 1972. Among the concerns of the conference was the issue of pollution, and Principle 6 of the Stockholm Declaration States that:

> The discharge of toxic substances or of other substances and the release of heat, in such quantities or concentrations as to exceed the capacity of the environment to render them harmless, must be halted in order to ensure that serious or irreversible damage is not inflicted upon ecosystems. The just struggle of the peoples of all countries against pollution should be supported.

Principle 6 specifically deals with marine pollution. Principle 21 recognises the sovereign right of States to exploit their own resources but imposes an obligation on States to ensure that activities within their jurisdiction or control do not cause damage to the environment of other States or of areas beyond the limits of national jurisdiction. This extends the principle applied in the *Trail Smelter* arbitration, which was concerned only with damage done to other States. The provisions of Principle 21 were broadly repeated in Article 30 of the Charter of Economic Rights and Duties of States 1974. After the conference, UNEP, along with other concerned organisations, began investigating more specific measures that could be adopted to control pollution.

One difficulty that was encountered early on was how best to define the level of pollution that would give rise to international responsibility. In 1974, the OECD adopted a definition of pollution that referred to:

> ... the introduction by man, directly or indirectly, of substances or energy into the environment resulting in deleterious effects of such a nature as to endanger human health, harm living resources and ecosystems, and impair or interfere with amenities and other legitimate uses of the environment.

This definition was subsequently included in Article 1 of the Convention on Long-Range Transboundary Air Pollution 1979 and has been used in a number of other conventions. The definition has two main implications. First, the term is confined to the introduction of substances or energy by man into the environment and, thus, overuse of resources (however harmful it might be) will not constitute, in itself, pollution. Secondly, the issue is raised of how harmful pollution needs to be before it will give rise to liability. Many conventions refer to harmful or deleterious effects, not just to property, but also to living resources and ecosystems. It would appear that some injury is necessary to establish responsibility subject to *de minimis* principles. Often, the question of degree of harm is linked to the need to act with due diligence. Very often, the allocation of responsibility will involve a balancing exercise between the harm caused and the practicable, available means to prevent such harm.

16.8.1 Marine pollution

The biggest area of the world not subject to any one State's jurisdiction is the high seas. Concern about the effects of marine pollution have been expressed for a long time. In 1926, a draft convention on pollution from ships was drawn up, although it was never signed. By the late 1960s, it was clear that action needed to be taken to preserve the marine environment and reduce the level of pollution. In particular, the increase in the number of high tonnage oil tankers posed a particular risk of devastating environmental damage. In April 1967, the Liberian tanker, *The Torrey Canyon*, broke up off the coast of the UK, spilling thousands of gallons of crude oil into the sea, and the publicity surrounding the disaster provided further ammunition to those calling for new laws. At the same time, it was discovered that mercury emissions from a Japanese factory were poisoning fish and it was realised that marine pollution was possible not only from ships but also from land sources.

The *Torrey Canyon* disaster had an immediate effect on the law relating to liability for the effects of pollution. The International Convention on Civil Liability for Oil Pollution Damage 1969 (the Civil Liability Convention) and the International Convention on the Establishment of an International Fund for Compensation for Oil Pollution Damage 1971 (the Fund Convention) impose obligations on the shipowner to pay for pollution damage and the cost of any preventive measures taken. The Fund Convention establishes an International Oil Pollution Compensation Fund, which will compensate victims in the event that the shipowner is not liable. The Fund is financed by a levy on oil imports. In addition to these measures, two private schemes were adopted: the Tanker Owners' Voluntary Agreement Concerning Liability for Oil Pollution (TOVALOP) and the Contract Regarding an Interim Supplement to Tanker Liability for Oil Pollution (CRISTAL). These private schemes mirror the provisions of the conventions and are still of relevance to those States that are not parties to the conventions.

Aside from the question of compensation arrangements, it was recognised that there was a need also for stricter controls on pollution. This was recognised at the Stockholm Conference and it was resolved that new controls would be introduced. In the same year as the conference, the Convention on the Prevention of Marine Pollution by Dumping of Wastes and Other Matters 1972 (the London Dumping Convention) was signed. Dumping is defined as the deliberate disposal of waste and the convention prohibits the dumping of specific categories of waste. The Convention for the Prevention of Marine Pollution by Dumping from Ships and Aircraft 1972 (the Oslo Dumping Convention) imposes stricter rules in respect of the north-east Atlantic and the North Sea. There have since been a number of other similar regional conventions. The year after the adoption of the London and Oslo conventions, the International Convention for the Prevention of Pollution by Ships 1973 (MARPOL) was signed. Marine pollution was a major concern at UNCLOS III, and the Law of the Sea Convention 1982 (LOSC) has a number of significant provisions relating to marine pollution. Most importantly, the LOSC gives the coastal State rights to make and enforce regulations protecting its territorial sea and the EEZ and Continental Shelf. More recently, such regulations have been co-ordinated by regional agreements between neighbouring States and this can be particularly effective where the continental shelf and EEZs cover the major shipping lanes.

Attention has not only been focused on pollution occurring at sea. A number of treaties and resolutions deal with pollution from sea bed activities, for example, Articles 208–14 of the LOSC. There have also been a number of regional treaties dealing with marine pollution from land sources, which is estimated to account for over 80% of all marine pollution

16.8.2 Atmospheric pollution

The municipal laws of industrialised States have long shown a concern with air pollution and have endeavoured to minimise the emission of noxious or other harmful gases. Unfortunately, one of the methods often used to reduce the risk to the local population is to ensure that emissions are sent high into the atmosphere to disperse. It gradually came to be recognised that such actions did not irradicate the pollution altogether but were merely postponing the harmful effects. Today, the major source of air pollution is the burning of fossil fuels in the course of energy production. Advances in scientific knowledge have meant that it has become more possible to track the spread of gases such as sulphur dioxide and nitrogen oxide to be able to establish both the source of the pollution and the location of its harmful effects. During the 1980s, there was growing concern about the phenomena of acid rain, caused by the reaction of sulphur and nitrogen with water vapour in the air, and global warming. In addition, the discovery was made that the ozone layer, which protects the earth from the sun's ultraviolet radiation, was being damaged by the release of high levels of chlorine based substances.

One aspect of the law relating to air pollution has been the question of sovereign rights to airspace (discussed in Chapter 10). It is accepted that, for the purposes of control of pollution, the transient physical characteristics of the atmosphere must be recognised. As a result, there has been a tendency to treat the atmosphere as a shared resource for the purposes of pollution and other environmental protection. This approach was adopted by the Geneva Convention on Long-Range Transboundary Air Pollution 1979, which governs issues of air pollution within Europe and North America. The convention is largely an expression of broad principles and the parties agree to 'endeavour to limit' and gradually reduce air pollution. The important provisions relate to information exchange and the need to give notification of significant risks.

Another major treaty dealing with atmospheric matters is the Vienna Convention for the Protection of the Ozone Layer 1985, which was largely the work of UNEP. The convention is supplemented by the Montreal Protocol on Substances that Deplete the Ozone Layer 1987, which sets targets for the gradual elimination of CFCs and other substances that have a deleterious effect on the ozone layer. In some ways linked to the question of depletion of the ozone layer, is the issue of climatic change and, in particular, global warming and the so called greenhouse effect. Partly because of the limitations of universally accepted scientific knowledge in the area, and also because of the strong economic interests that are connected with practices which are alleged to adversely affect the climate, it has proved difficult to obtain agreement on rules relating to climatic change. However, at the Rio Conference in 1992, the Convention on Global Climate Change 1992 was adopted. The Convention, which entered into force in March 1994, has been criticised for not going far enough to protect the global climate but it is at least a start from which further refinements may follow.

16.8.3 Nuclear energy

The risks connected with nuclear energy have long been recognised and the accident at Chernobyl in 1986 showed that the risks apply not only to those States which use nuclear energy but, potentially, to all other States. When the possibility of nuclear power first became a reality, it was believed that it would provide an answer to many of the world's economic problems. In 1956, the International Atomic Energy Agency (IAEA) was established, with the objective of encouraging the use of nuclear power. By the early 1970s, however, it was increasingly recognised that nuclear power carried with it great risks. The Stockholm Conference 1972 indicated particular concern about nuclear waste and the dumping of radioactive waste at sea was outlawed by the London Dumping Convention 1972. Gradually too, the IAEA was given strongly enhanced powers with regard to the safety of nuclear installations, including the right to carry out inspections. The basis of the legal regime pertaining to nuclear power is the requirement of publicity and notification, especially of significant risks, but also to encourage the spread of best practices with regard to safety. Following the Chernobyl accident, when, for some considerable time, it was impossible to know exactly the extent of the disaster, the Convention on Assistance in cases of Nuclear Emergency 1986 and the Convention on Early Notification of Nuclear Accidents 1986 were signed, setting down some important provisions applicable should an accident or emergency occur.

16.9 Conservation of natural resources

An important attribute of statehood is sovereignty over the natural resources within the State's own territory. The basic principle has been recognised in a number of UN resolutions, including the Charter of Economic Rights and Duties of States 1974 and the Stockholm Declaration 1972. Traditionally, sovereignty over resources was regarded as subject to the requirement not to act in a way harmful to the interests of other States; however, increasingly, rules of law are emerging which subject such sovereignty to a duty to conserve resources. International law has always recognised that there are areas of land, sea and air which do not fall, or are not capable, of falling under the jurisdiction of any State. For example, the high seas have long been considered to be the common property of all States. Such areas of common property have gradually come to be governed by rules that stress the need for conservation and this is reflected in the recognition of such common areas as forming the common heritage of mankind. More recently, there have been a number of treaties which attempt to place restrictions on the freedom of States to exploit their natural living resources. As yet, there is no duty imposed on States to conserve non-living natural resources, although the manner of exploitation may be affected by rules relating to pollution.

16.9.1 Sustainable development

A concept which has had a growing importance in the area of conservation is sustainable development. The need to safeguard the natural resources of the earth for the benefit of present and future generations was recognised in Principle 2 of the Stockholm Declaration, and endorsement of the concept of sustainable development has been made in a number of international resolutions. Sustainable development recognises the need for economic growth and development but indicates that such growth shall not involve the use of resources in excess of their capacity for regeneration. Attempts have been made to spell out in more detail what sustainable development entails and draft articles on sustainable development were included in the principles adopted at the Rio Conference in 1992. The concept finds specific application in a number of treaties which deal with conservation matters, most recently in the Convention on Biological Diversity 1992, which entered into force in December 1993.

16.9.2 Conservation of migratory and land based species

An ever increasing number of treaties, both global and regional, attempt to provide protection for species of non-marine living natural resources. Some treaties refer to specific species, for example, the Agreement on the Conservation of Polar Bears 1973, while others impose rules of more general application. In addition, there are a number of bilateral agreements relating to conservation. There are four multilateral treaties which are regarded as being particularly significant:

(a) Convention on Wetlands of International Importance 1971 (Ramsar Convention);

(b) Convention for the Protection of the World Cultural and Natural Heritage 1972 (the World Heritage Convention);

(c) Convention on International Trade in Endangered Species of Wild Fauna and Flora 1973 (CITES); and

(d) Convention on the Conservation of Migratory Species of Wild Animals 1980 (Bonn Convention).

All four treaties adopt different approaches to the problem of conservation. The Ramsar Convention and the Bonn Convention make provision for the protection of habitats and the Ramsar Convention refers to sustainable utilisation of wetland areas. The World Heritage Convention is concerned with identifying natural sites of particular importance and imposing specific obligations in respect of such sites. The convention also establishes a trust fund to be administered through UNESCO for assisting in the protection of such sites. The Bonn Convention, in addition to providing habitat protection, also seeks to protect migratory species during the course of their migration. The convention is particularly concerned to encourage co-operation between States for the protection of migratory species. CITES has been the most successful of the four conventions and attempts to encourage conservation by outlawing commercial trade in endangered species, the view being that the ending of commercial trade will result in the ending of the endangered status of many species. The convention lists two categories of endangered species: those seriously threatened with extinction, in which all trade is prohibited, and those who are not yet threatened with extinction but which may become so if trade continues uncontrolled. Trade in the latter category is permitted but is subject to stringent controls.

16.9.3 Conservation of marine resources

The conservation regime governing living marine resources has a slightly different history, since it has largely developed as an integral part of the law of the sea and the main concern has been with fishing rights and the need to avoid over-fishing. The first treaties regulating fishing rights were agreed before World War One and, since that time, there have been a number of treaties governing such things as fishing quotas and fishing rights. The UN Food and Agriculture Organisation has had an important role in encouraging co-operation between coastal States. Many groups of coastal States have made agreements setting a 'total allowable catch' and, very often, attempting to exclude other States from fishing grounds. The first truly global attempt to regulate the conservation of marine resources was the Convention on Fishing and Conservation of the Living resources of the High Seas 1958, which imposes only limited duties of conservation. Conservation provisions are considerably strengthen in LOSC, although concerns continue to be expressed about the extent to which such provisions will prove effective.

In addition to the general rules relating to marine resources, there are a number of specific agreements which relate to single species or groups of species, the best known of which is probably the International Convention for the Regulation of Whaling 1946.

16.9.4 Antarctica

Antarctica constitutes the largest area of land not subject to the jurisdiction of a single State. The special nature of the region has meant that it has been the subject of specific attention by international law. The region is important from an environmental point of view but it also has an economic importance since the discovery in the 1980s of significant quantities of manganese nodules. Historically, Antarctica had been the subject of competing claims to sovereignty by a number of different States. However, in the late 1950s, pressure from the scientific community resulted in the suspension of such claims and the signing of the Antarctic Treaty 1959 by the main claimant States. The treaty provides that the region shall only be used for peaceful purposes. Subsequently, the Convention for the Conservation of Antarctic Seals 1972 and the Convention on the Conservation of Antarctic Marine Living Resources 1980 were signed. The discovery of the manganese deposits led to renewed discussions and a 50 year ban on mining was agreed in April 1991. In the same year, a protocol to the Antarctic Treaty, the Protocol on Environmental Protection 1991, was signed. The Protocol has the effect of establishing Antarctica as a world park, thus putting a permanent end to the individual claims of sovereignty, and significantly strengthening the conservation provisions of the Antarctic regime.

16.10 A right to a decent environment

As was discussed in Chapter 1, traditionally, international law was only concerned with the rights and obligations of States. It has already been seen in Chapter 14 that significant changes occurred with the establishment of rules governing human rights. Arguments have since been raised about the existence of people's rights additional to, and different from, the rights of individual human beings. The growth of environmental law has now led to discussion about whether there exists a right to a decent environment. Such a right might not only be possessed by individuals and peoples but raises the connected question of whether future generations, animals or even the environment itself have recognisable rights. Clearly, much depends on the concept of 'rights' that is employed. Some would argue that rights which are not capable of legal enforcement should not properly be called rights. Jeremy Bentham expressed such a view when he referred to claims of the existence of rights as 'nonsense on stilts'. Others argue that no right can exist without a corresponding clearly defined duty.

It seems clear that the existence of recognised human rights has implications for environmental law. For example, the right to life must in some part be dependent on the existence of an environment capable of sustaining life. Principle 1 of the Stockholm Declaration provides that:

> Man has the fundamental right to freedom, equality and adequate conditions of life, in an environment of a quality that permits a life of dignity and well being ...

and imposes a corresponding duty to protect and improve the environment for present and future generations. Article 24 of the African Charter on Human and Peoples' Rights 1981 contains a similar provision, although the right is a collective rather than an individual one. No other treaty appears to expressly recognise an individual right to a decent environment and it is submitted that the right operates at the level of a general principle, in a manner similar to the right of self determination, rather than as a individually enforceable human right.

As far as the rights of future generations, animals and the environment itself are concerned, much depends on the view one takes as to the basis of environmental protections. Certainly, if one adopts the view that environmental protection measures are taken, not purely in the long term interests of man, but also for the intrinsic value of the environment, then the better argument seems to be that there exists something in the nature of a fiduciary duty on States to respect and protect the environment. Whatever view one takes, it is clear that the system of international law at the end of the 20th century is very different from that existing in 1900.

ENVIRONMENTAL PROTECTION

International law has always limited the territorial sovereignty of States by imposing a duty on States not to act within their own territory in such a way as to cause harm in the territory of other States – *Trail Smelter* arbitration (1941). Since 1945, there has been a growing realisation of the need to provide further and better protection for the environment.

The bulk of international environmental law is contained in treaties. In addition, there is a considerable body of soft law relating to environmental matters, particularly in the form of recommendations adopted by the UN Environment Programme and also the Stockholm Declaration 1972 and the Rio Declaration 1992.

Two important principles relating to environmental law are:

(a) the polluter pays; and

(b) the need for sustainable development.

Marine pollution

- Civil Liability Convention 1969;
- Fund Convention 1971;
- TOVALOP;
- CRISTAL;
- London Dumping Convention 1972;
- MARPOL 1973; and
- LOSC 1982.

Note, also, the growing number of regional agreements.

Atmospheric pollution

- Geneva Convention on Long-Rang Transboundary Pollution 1979;
- Vienna Convention for the Protection of the Ozone Layer 1985; and
- Convention on Global Climate Change 1992.

Nuclear energy

Note the role of the International Atomic Energy Agency.

- Convention on Assistance in cases of Nuclear Emergency 1986; and
- Convention on Early Notification of Nuclear Accidents 1986.

Conservation

- Convention on Biological Diversity 1992;
- Ramsar Convention 1971;
- World Heritage Convention 1972;
- CITES 1973;
- Bonn Convention 1980;
- Antarctic Treaty 1959;
- Convention on the Conservation of Antarctic Marine Living Resources 1980; and
- Protocol on Environmental Protection 1991.

A right to a decent environment

Considerable discussion has taken place recently as to whether there exists a right to a decent environment. A major question is who would possess such a right and how and against whom could it be enforced?

CHAPTER 17

THE RELATIONSHIP BETWEEN MUNICIPAL LAW AND INTERNATIONAL LAW

17.1 Introduction

This chapter is concerned with the relationship that exists between international law and municipal law. That relationship gives rise to two main areas of discussion:

(a) the theoretical question as to whether international law and municipal law are part of a universal legal order (monism) or whether they form two distinct systems of law (dualism); and

(b) the practical issue of what rules govern the situation where there appears to be a conflict between the rules of international law and the rules of municipal law; this may occur either:

- before an international court; or
- before a municipal court.

17.2 The theoretical issue

Historically, there have been two main schools of thought: monism and dualism. Their ideas are outlined here but it should be noted that many modern writers doubt the utility of the monism/dualism dichotomy. Furthermore, courts faced with practical problems involving potential conflicts between the rules of international law and municipal law rarely refer to the theoretical issues. The ninth edition of *Oppenheim's International Law* (Jennings, R (Sir) and Watts, A (Sir) (eds), 9th edn, 1992, Harlow: Longman, p 53 suggests that:

> ... the doctrinal dispute is largely without practical consequences, for the main practical questions which arise – how do States, within the framework of their internal legal order, apply the rules of international law, and how is a conflict between a rule of international law and a national rule of law to be resolved? – are answered not by reference to doctrine but by looking at what the rules of various national laws and of international law prescribe.

It is, however, instructive when considering actual court decisions to question their theoretical underpinnings.

17.2.1 Monism

Monism considers international law and municipal law to be both part of the same body of knowledge – law. They both operate in the same sphere of influence and are concerned with the same subject matter and, thus, can come into conflict. If there is a conflict, it is international law that prevails. Some, like Kelsen, argue that this is because international law is a higher law, from which the State derives its authority and, thus, its ability to make municipal laws. Kelsen, in *General Theory of Law and the State* (1945, Cambridge, Mass: Harvard UP, pp 367–68) wrote:

> Since the basic norms of the national legal orders are determined by a norm of international law, they are basic norms only in a relative sense. It is the basic norm of the international legal order which is the ultimate reason of validity of the national legal orders too.

Others, including Lauterpacht, argue on natural law grounds that international law prevails because it protects individuals, and the State itself is only a collection of individuals; it is supported by the natural law doctrine that authority and legal duty are both subject to the universality of natural law. A recent articulation of this view is to be found in the writing of Philip Allott in *Eunomia: New Order for a New World* (1990, Oxford: OUP, p 308):

> Every legal power in every society in the world is connected with every other legal power in every other society in the world through the international law of the international society, the society of all societies, from which all law making power is delegated.

17.2.2 Dualism

The dualist doctrine developed in the 19th century, partly because of the development of theories about the absolute sovereignty of States and partly alongside the development of legal positivism. Dualist doctrine considers international law and municipal law to be two separate legal orders operating and existing independently of one another. International law is the law applicable between sovereign States and is dependent on the common will of States for its authority; municipal law applies within the State regulating the activities of its citizens and has as the source of its authority the will of the State itself. On this basis, neither system has the power to create nor alter the rules of the other. Since both systems may deal with the same subject matter, it is possible for conflicts between the two systems to arise. Where there is a conflict between the two systems, a municipal court following the dualist doctrine would apply municipal law. This might lead to a State being in breach of its international obligations, but that would be a matter for an international tribunal.

17.2.3 A third way?

Both monism and dualism take the view that international law and municipal law can deal with the same subject matter. A third school of thought can be identified which, while subscribing to the dualist concept of two separate legal orders, argues that the two orders deal with different subject matters.

Foremost among the advocates of this doctrine are two former judges at the World Court: Sir Gerald Fitzmaurice and Dionisio Anzilotti. In an opinion given in *The Electricity Company of Sofia and Bulgaria* (1939), Anzilotti stated:

> It is clear that, in the same legal system, there cannot at the same time exist two rules relating to the same facts and attaching to these facts contradictory consequences ... In cases of this kind, either the contradiction is only apparent and the two rules are really co-ordinated so that each has its own sphere of application and does not encroach on the sphere of application of the other, or else one prevails over the other, that is, is applicable to the exclusion of the other.

Anzilotti seemed to support the view that the two sets of rules, international law and municipal law, each had their own sphere of application. In an earlier case (*Certain German Interests in Polish Upper Silesia* (1928)), he had indicated how international tribunals should deal with rules of municipal law:

> From the standpoint of international law and of the court which is its organ, municipal laws are merely facts which express the will and constitute the activities of States, in the same manner as do legal decisions or administrative measures.

In a lecture to the Hague Academy of International Law ('The general principles of international law considered from the standpoint of the rule of law' (1957) 92 Hague Recueil 70), G Fitzmaurice made the point even more forcefully:

> A radical view of the whole subject may be propounded to the effect that the entire monist-dualist controversy is unreal, artificial and strictly beside the point, because it assumes something that has to exist for there to be any controversy at all – and which in fact does not exist – namely a common field in which the two legal orders have their spheres of activity.

Fitzmaurice continues by discussing the relationship between English and French laws and arguing that, even though the two systems do come into conflict in a certain sense, such conflicts are dealt with by the municipal rules of private international law. On this basis, he argues that there cannot be any real conflict between the two systems in the domestic field because any apparent conflict is settled by domestic conflict rules. Fitzmaurice argues that the same must apply to the relationship between international law and municipal law. The two systems of law can never formally come into conflict because they deal with different subject matters; apparent conflicts are dealt with by the conflict of law rules of the particular forum.

17.3 The practical issue

Although it may be possible to argue that as a matter of legal theory there can be no formal conflict between international law and municipal law, the potential for conflict is very real and courts, both municipal and international, have often been faced with the problem of resolving a perceived conflict.

17.3.1 Municipal law before international tribunals

There is ample judicial and arbitral authority for the rule that a State cannot rely upon the provisions or deficiencies of its municipal law to avoid its obligations under international law. One of the earliest authorities is the decision in the *Alabama Claims* arbitration (1872). During the American Civil War, a number of ships were built in England for private buyers. The vessels were unarmed when they left England but it was generally known that they were to be fitted out by the Confederates in order to attack Union shipping. They were so fitted and caused considerable damage to American shipping. The US sought to make the UK liable for these losses on the basis that it had breached its international obligations as a 'neutral' during the war. The UK argued that, under English law as it stood, there was no way in which it could prevent the sailing of the vessels. The arbitrator rejected the UK argument and had no hesitation in upholding the supremacy of international law. Similar rulings were made by the PCIJ in the *Serbian Loans* case (1929). In the Draft Declaration on the Rights and Duties of States 1949, prepared by the International Law Commission, Article 13 States:

> Every State has the duty to carry out in good faith its obligations arising from treaties and other sources of international law, and it may not invoke provisions in its constitution or its laws as an excuse for failure to perform this duty.

Similarly, Article 27 of the Vienna Convention on the Law of Treaties 1969 provides:

> A party may not invoke the provisions of its internal law as justification for its failure to perform a treaty.

Although international tribunals will uphold the supremacy of international law over municipal law, this should not be taken to mean that municipal law is of no relevance. Municipal law, and in particular domestic legislation, has an important role to play. Very often, an international tribunal will have cause to examine domestic legislation closely to discern the practice of States. For example, one of the main ways of establishing a State's position on the boundaries of the territorial sea will be to look at the relevant domestic legislation. Another manner in which municipal law may be of importance in a case before an international tribunal arises from the doctrine of opposability. This doctrine allows one State to invoke against, or 'oppose' to, another State a rule of its own municipal law. As a general principle, provided that the rule of municipal law is not contrary to rules of international law, it may be legitimately opposed in order to defeat the international claims of the other State. Thus, in the *Anglo-Norwegian Fisheries* case (1951), the ICJ held that a Norwegian law delimiting an exclusive fishery zone along almost 1,000 miles of coastline was not contrary to international law and therefore could be successfully opposed to defeat British claims to fish in the disputed waters.

17.3.2 International law before municipal tribunals: transformation and incorporation

Before considering a number of examples of the treatment of international law by municipal courts, it is necessary to explain briefly the concepts of transformation and incorporation. If, as the dualist theory maintains, international law and municipal law constitute two distinct legal systems, a practical consequence is that, before any rule of international law can have effect within domestic jurisdiction, it requires express and specific 'transformation' into municipal law by the use of the appropriate constitutional machinery, such as a municipal statute. A different view, and one reflecting the monist position, is that that rules of international law automatically become part of municipal law as a result of the doctrine of 'incorporation'.

Put at its simplest, transformation doctrine views rules of international law as being excluded from municipal law unless specifically included; incorporation doctrine holds that rules of international law are included as part of municipal law unless they are specifically excluded.

17.3.3 Customary international law and British practice

As far as the rules of customary international law are concerned, the English courts have generally adopted the doctrine of incorporation. Provided that they are not inconsistent with Acts of Parliament or prior authoritative judicial decisions, then rules of customary international law automatically form part of English law – customary international law is incorporated into English law. The 18th century lawyer Blackstone wrote in his *Commentaries* (Vol IV, Chapter 5):

> The law of nations, wherever any question arises which is properly the object of its jurisdiction, is here adopted in its full extent by the common law, and it is held to be a part of the law of the land.

In *Buvot v Barbuit* (1737), Lord Talbot declared that 'the law of nations in its full extent was part of the law of England'. Lord Talbot's statement was followed in a series of 18th and early 19th century cases. Cynics may suggest that the reason for this view was that at the time the international community was small and Britain had a major impact on the formation of customary international law.

Some doubt was thrown on the incorporation doctrine by the decision in *R v Keyn (The Franconia)* (1876). *The Franconia*, a German ship, collided with a British ship in the English Channel, three miles off the British coast. The defendant was prosecuted for manslaughter of a passenger on board the English ship, who drowned as a result of the collision, and was found guilty. However, the question of whether an English court had jurisdiction to hear the case was reserved for the Court of Crown Cases Reserved, which decided, by a 7–6 majority, that it did not. Cockburn CJ found that, under international law, events occurring on board a foreign ship while it was on the high seas were governed by the law of the foreign State. It was only when the foreign ship came into the ports or waters of another State that the ship and those on board become subject to the local law. Unless, therefore, the defendant at the time of the offence was on British territory or on board a British ship, an English court would have no jurisdiction. The question for the court was whether the collision had occurred in British territory. It found that, according to English law, the three mile belt of sea surrounding Great Britain was not British territory. The court could also not find any clear rule of international law stipulating jurisdictional rights over a three mile territorial sea and therefore found that there was no basis for jurisdiction over Keyn. The case led to the passing of the Territorial Waters Jurisdiction Act 1878, which gave the English courts jurisdiction over the territorial sea.

Some have argued that the judgment of Lord Cockburn supports the transformation doctrine. In the course of his judgment, he discussed what the position would have been had the court been able to discern a clear rule of international law recognising a three mile territorial sea. He argued that, even if unanimity could be found among States on the adoption of a three mile territorial sea, it would amount to a new law and the courts were not able to usurp the role of Parliament in creating new law. However, other writers have confined the case to its particular facts and argued that the decision was only concerned with the existence or not of any jurisdiction over the territorial sea and did not amount to a rejection of the rule that international law is part of the law of England.

The confusion was not resolved in the case of *West Rand Central Gold Mining Co v R* (1905). Lord Alverstone CJ stated that whatever had received the common consent of civilised nations must also have received the assent of Great Britain and may properly be called international law. As such, it would be applied by the municipal tribunals. This might be considered a straightforward application of the incorporation doctrine but Lord Alverstone went on to qualify it by saying:

> ... [the rule] that the law of nations forms part of the law of England ought not to be construed so as to include as part of the law of England opinions of text-writers upon a question as to which there is no evidence that Great Britain has ever assented, *a fortiori* if they are contrary to the principles of her laws as declared by her courts. The cases of *Wolff v Oxholm* (1817) and *R v Keyn* are only illustrations of the same rule – namely, that questions of international law may arise, and may have to be considered in connection with the administration of municipal law.

The incorporation doctrine was further qualified by the Privy Council in *Chung Chi Cheung v The King* (1939), where Lord Atkin stated:

> It must always be remembered that, so far, at any rate, as the courts of this country are concerned, international law has no validity save in so far as

> its principles are accepted and adopted by our own domestic law. There is no external power that imposes its rule upon our own code of substantive law or procedure.
>
> The courts acknowledge the existence of a body of rules which nations accept amongst themselves. On any judicial issue they seek to ascertain what the relevant rule is and, having found it, they will treat it as incorporated into the domestic law, so far as it is not inconsistent with rules enacted by statutes or finally declared by their tribunals.

The issue of the relationship of customary international law and English law was raised again in the important case of *Trendtex Trading Corporation v Central Bank of Nigeria* (1977). The case concerned issues of State immunity, which were discussed in Chapter 8. In the course of their judgments, all three members of the Court of Appeal accepted the incorporation doctrine, Shaw LJ stating 'What is immutable is the principle of English law that the law of nations ... must be applied in the courts of England'. The case also raised the question of the relationship between the doctrine of precedent and customary international law. The court had to consider whether *stare decisis* applies to rules of UK law that incorporate rules of customary international law so that a change in international law can only be recognised within the limits of that doctrine. Earlier cases seemed to suggest that the doctrine of precedent prevailed and that the courts could not recognise a change in the rules of customary international law if it conflicted with an earlier decision of the English courts. The majority in *Trendtex* rejected this view, Lord Denning stating:

> ... a decision of this court – as to what was the ruling of international law 50 or 60 years ago – is not binding on this court today. International law knows no rule of *stare decisis*. If this court today is satisfied that the rule of international law on a subject has changed from what it was 50 or 60 years ago, it can give effect to that change – and apply the change in our English law – without waiting for the House of Lords to do it.

Confirmation of the incorporation doctrine applying to customary international law is to be found in the Court of Appeal judgments in *Maclaine Watson v Department of Trade* (1989). Their view was not contradicted in the House of Lords (1990), although their lordships found that the case concerned the application of treaty rights rather than of rules of customary international law.

Taken as a whole, the authorities would seem to support the incorporation doctrine and, thus, it can be said that customary international law will be applied by the English courts, subject to two main conditions:

(a) if there is a conflict between customary international law and an Act of Parliament, the Act of Parliament prevails. It should be noted that, as a general rule of statutory interpretation, the courts will try to interpret statutes so as to avoid a conflict with international law – this does not, of course, apply if the statute is clear and unambiguous; and

(b) if there is a conflict between customary international law and a binding judicial precedent laying down a rule of English law, the judicial precedent prevails. But, following the *Trendtex* case, the English courts may now depart from earlier judicial precedent which lays down a rule of international law if the international law has changed in the meantime.

One final point about the incorporation doctrine is that, since customary international law is considered to be part of English law, it does not need to be proved as fact by expert evidence, unlike the position with regard to rules of foreign municipal law. The British courts will take judicial notice of international rules, and may, of their own volition, refer to textbooks and other sources for evidence thereof.

17.3.4 Treaties and British practice

The British practice regarding treaties is different from that regarding customary law. The main reason for this is that the conclusion and ratification of treaties is a matter for the executive, coming as it does under the scope of the prerogative. Parliament has no say in the making of treaties. If they were to have direct effect, the Crown could alter the law without recourse to Parliament; therefore, it is established that treaties only become part of English law if an enabling Act of Parliament has been passed. This point has been reiterated by the courts in a number of cases and should be familiar to those who have studied the doctrine of parliamentary supremacy and the effect of British membership of the European Union.

Discussion of the place of treaties in English law took place in the House of Lords in *Department of Trade v Maclaine Watson* (1990). The question for the courts was whether a Member State of an international organisation could be sued directly for the liabilities of the organisation. As has already been stated, the Court of Appeal saw the matter as raising issues of customary international law. The House of Lords viewed the matter differently – they saw it as an issue of treaty rights and explicitly confirmed that a treaty to which the UK is a party cannot automatically alter the laws of the UK. Only if a treaty is transformed into UK law by statute can it be enforced by the courts in this country – hence the need for the European Communities Act 1972 to transform the Treaty of Rome.

The usual way in which treaties are transformed into English law is by the passing of an enabling Act, to which a schedule is attached containing the provisions of the treaty to be enacted. For example, the Diplomatic Privileges Act 1964 enacts the Vienna Convention on Diplomatic Relations 1961. Where the treaty is contained in a schedule, it is an integral part of the Act and any interpretation of the statute will involve interpretation of provisions of the treaty. Full discussion of the international law rules on treaty interpretation is to be found in Chapter 3. The issue here is the rules of interpretation that the

English courts use when considering the provisions of a treaty. The leading case is *Fothergill v Monarch Airlines Ltd* (1980). In that case, the House of Lords was called upon to interpret the provisions of the Warsaw Convention for the Unification of Certain Regulations Concerning International Air Travel 1929 which formed part of the Carriage by Air Act 1961. The House of Lords held that it was entitled to use the rules of treaty interpretation found in the Vienna Convention on the Law of Treaties 1969, even though such rules conflicted with the English rules of statutory interpretation.

On some occasions, Parliament may pass legislation to give effect to the terms of a treaty without enacting the treaty itself in a schedule. In such cases, the question arises as to the extent to which the courts can have regard to the treaty in interpreting the statute. The leading case here is *Salomon v Commissioners of Customs and Excise* (1967), in which the Court of Appeal had to interpret the Customs and Excise Act 1952. The Act was intended to give effect to the Convention on Valuation of Goods for Customs Services 1950, although no specific mention was made of the Convention in the Act. The court set down three principles to be applied in such cases:

(a) first, if the terms of the statute are clear and unambiguous, the court must give effect to them, even if they conflict with the treaty provisions;

(b) secondly, if the provisions of the statute are not clear and are capable of more than one meaning, the treaty can be used as an aid to interpretation and a presumption operates that Parliament cannot have intended to legislate contrary to international law; and

(c) thirdly, the court may refer to the treaty in such cases even if there is no reference to it anywhere in the statute. Extrinsic evidence can be brought to show that the statute was intended to give effect to the treaty.

It must be noted that the rules regarding European law are different and reference should be made to the House of Lords decision in *R v Secretary of State for Transport ex p Factortame (No 2)* (1990) for a discussion of the relationship between English statute and European law.

Finally, there is the situation where an Act of Parliament, while not intended to give effect to any specific treaty, deals with the same subject matter as a treaty to which the UK is a party. Again, it should be noted that there are specific rules dealing with the position of European law and reference should be made to textbooks on constitutional law and European law for the position with regard to conflict between statute and law derived from the Treaty of Rome. In other situations, the rules are fairly straightforward. The courts will always give effect to clear and unambiguous words contained in a statute, even if they conflict with a treaty to which the UK is a party. Therefore, in *R v Secretary of State for the Home Department ex p Brind* (1991), the House of Lords upheld the broadcasting ban on certain 'terrorist' organisations introduced under the provisions of the Broadcasting Act 1981, even though it was argued that it breached provisions of the

European Convention on Human Rights 1950, to which the UK is a party. However, where there is some ambiguity in the statute, the courts will endeavour to interpret it so as to conform with UK's international obligations. Similarly, if the common law is uncertain, the courts should approach the issue on the basis that any decision should be in conformity with international obligations. Thus, in *Derbyshire County Council v Times Newspapers* Ltd (1992), the Court of Appeal was asked to decide whether a local authority could sue for libel. The court held that it could not and, in the course of his judgment, Balcombe LJ expressed the view that, since the domestic law was uncertain, the court could take into account the provisions of Article 10 of the European Convention on Human Rights. Clearly, the law and the position of the English courts in relation to the European Convention on Human Rights will change on the coming into force of the Human Rights Bill currently before Parliament.

17.3.5 The practice of other States

It is impossible to discern any uniform practice among States, although a number of similarities in approach can be identified. The majority of States with a common law system adopt an approach similar to that in Britain. Those States which have a written constitution do have the opportunity to make the situation clear by making specific reference to the status of international law. For example, although US practice concerning customary law is similar to Britain, the US Constitution (s 2 of Article VI) provides:

> ... all treaties made or which shall be made with the authority of the United States, shall be the supreme law of the land and the judges in every State shall be bound thereby, anything in the Constitution or law of any State to the contrary notwithstanding.

To mitigate the effects of this rule, the US courts have distinguished 'self-executing treaties', which automatically become law, and 'non-self-executing treaties', which require legislation by Congress to become law. Discussion of the distinction between self-executing and non-self-executing treaties has taken up much American court time and the implication of the various cases is that the distinction depends on the political content of the treaty. Where a treaty involves political questions, the issue should be left to Congress but, where a treaty contains provisions which are capable of enforcement as between private parties, then it will be regarded as self-executing. Treaties in conflict with the US Constitution are not regarded as binding.

The constitutions of Austria, Germany and Italy all declare that the generally recognised rules of international law form part of the domestic system. For example, Article 25 of the Basic Law of Germany states:

> ... the general rules of public international law are an integral part of federal law. They shall take precedence over the laws and shall create rights and duties for the inhabitants of the federal territory.

The courts in all three States have found that, while such provision may apply to customary international law, the provisions of treaties do not automatically become part of municipal law. A different approach is taken by the Dutch Constitution, which provides that international treaties to which the Netherlands is a party become part of municipal law and prevail over incompatible provisions of Dutch law. No mention is made of the rules of customary international law and the Dutch courts have not considered international custom to be automatically part of Dutch law. As a general observation, it can be said that few municipal courts have upheld the priority of international law over municipal law.

17.3.6 The relationship between international law and European law

An area of developing interest is the relationship between European law and international law, although it has not yet been subject to the same degree of analysis as that given to the relationship between international law and municipal law. It is generally accepted that the European Union has a separate legal personality under international law and that European law constitutes a distinct legal order. Article 177 of the Treaty of Rome allows the European Court of Justice to rule on questions of the validity of European law and this can involve discussion of the relationship between it and international law. According to Article 228 of the Treaty of Rome, treaties concluded by the EU are binding on its institutions and on Member States. They are regarded as forming an integral part of European law. Rules of customary international law will be upheld and applied by the European Court, provided they are not incompatible with provisions of European law. A particular point which arises in respect of the EU is the extent to which a Member State can rely on a rule of international law as a defence against it failing to fulfil obligations under European law. Article 234 of the Treaty of Rome provides that Community law leaves unaffected the treaty rights and obligations entered into between Member States and non-Member States if the conclusion of such agreements predates Community competence. The provision was considered in *Commission v UK* (1991), which concerned Britain's decision to extend its territorial sea and restrict fishing rights. The European Court held that European law could not compel Member States to violate international law and, in such cases, a defence based on international law could succeed to defeat provisions of European law. However, in the present case, the court found that international law did not force the UK to act in the way it did but only provided the possibility of action. The court therefore found that the defence failed.

17.3.7 The relationship between regional international law and universal international law

Since 1945, particularly in the areas of human rights and environmental protection, there has been a growth in the number of treaties setting down rules applicable to particular regions of the world. Specific treaties are discussed in earlier chapters but it is worth highlighting here the potential problems which have yet to be fully resolved. In the event of a conflict between the regional rule and the rule of universal application, which rule is to prevail? As has been seen in Chapter 3, the problem may be resolved by use of one of the principles: *lex posterior derogat priori* (a later law repeals an earlier law); *lex posterior generalis non derogat priori speciali* (a later law, general in character, does not derogate from an earlier law which is special in character); or the principle *lex specialis derogat generali* (a special law prevails over a general law). However, such principles are not always easily applicable to specific circumstances and it is not always clear which is the special law and which is the general law. It will only be as State practice builds up that it will be possible to state with any degree of certainty the relationship between rules of international law of limited regional application and those rules which have universal, global application.

THE RELATIONSHIP BETWEEN MUNICIPAL LAW AND INTERNATIONAL LAW

The theoretical issue

The main question is whether international law and municipal law are part of a universal legal order or whether they form two distinct systems of law. Historically, there have been two schools of thought.

Monism considers international law and municipal law to be part of a universal legal order. Since they operate in the same sphere of influence and are concerned with the same subject matter, they come into conflict. Where a conflict does arise, it is international law that prevails.

Dualism considers international law and municipal law to constitute two separate legal orders which exist independently of one another. Conflicts between the two systems may arise and the manner in which the conflict is resolved depends upon the forum in which it arises. In international tribunals, it is international law which will prevail, whereas municipal courts will apply in municipal law.

Some writers have suggested that the monism/dualism dichotomy is unhelpful and instead argue that, since international law and municipal law constitute separate legal orders governing different subject matters, no real conflict can arise and apparent conflicts are dealt with by the conflict of law rules of the particular forum.

Municipal law before international tribunals

The practice of international tribunals has been to uphold international law, even where it is in conflict with provisions of municipal law – see the *Alabama Claims Arbitration* (1872). It remains a fundamental rule of international law that a State may not invoke provisions of its municipal law to excuse breaches of international law. However, municipal law remains of relevance to international tribunals, particularly as a result of the doctrine of opposability. This allows a State to invoke against another State a rule of its own municipal law provided that it is not contrary to a rule of international law – see the *Anglo-Norwegian Fisheries* case (1951).

International law before domestic tribunals

State practice is characterised by the adoption of either the transformation or incorporation doctrine, or a combination of the two.

Transformation refers to the express and specific adoption of a rule of international law by the municipal law system. Transformation will usually be carried out by the enactment of a municipal statute. The transformation doctrine provides that no rule of international law will become part of municipal law unless it is specifically included.

Incorporation avoids the need for new legislation, since it denotes the view that rules of international law are automatically incorporated into municipal law. The incorporation doctrine provides that all rules of international law will automatically become part of municipal law unless they are specifically excluded.

Those States which have written constitutions will often make specific reference to the manner in which international law is to be treated by the municipal courts.

The UK courts have generally adopted an incorporation approach as far as rules of customary international law are concerned. The most recent confirmation of this view is to be found in the Court of Appeal judgment in *Maclaine Watson v Department of Trade* (1989). Customary international law is part of English law to the extent that it does not conflict with acts of parliament or judicial precedent. Where a judicial decision itself sets down a rule of international law, the courts may depart from the decision if the rule of international law has changed – see *Trendtex Trading Corporation v Central Bank of Nigeria* (1977).

British practice

As far as rules of international law created by treaties are concerned, the courts adopt the transformation doctrine. Treaty rules will only become part of English law if specifically adopted by an Act of Parliament.

There is a general rule of statutory interpretation, whereby the courts will always endeavour to construe a statute so as to avoid conflict with rules of international law. However, the courts will give effect to clear and unambiguous words, even if it results in the UK being in breach of international obligations.

The relationship between international law and European law

European law constitutes a distinct legal order and there is therefore the potential for conflicts to arise between its rules and those of international law. In general, the EU adheres to the incorporation doctrine. Rules of customary international law are regarded as being an integral part of European law to the extent that they are not incompatible with provisions of European law. As a general rule, it would seem that member States cannot rely on provisions of international law as a defence to breaches of European law, although this point has yet to be subject to detailed consideration – see *Commission v UK* (1991).

FURTHER READING

Akehurst, M, 'Custom as a source of international law' (1974–75) 47 BYIL 1

Akehurst, M, 'Equity and general principles of law' (1976) 25 ICLQ 801

Akehurst, M, 'Jurisdiction in international law' (1972–73) 46 BYIL 145

Alexidze, A, 'Legal nature of *jus cogens* in contemporary international law' (1981) 172 Hague Recueil

Allot, P, 'State responsibility and the unmasking of international law', 1995, 29 Harvard International LJ 1

Allott, P, *et al*, *Theory and International Law: An Introduction,* 1991, London: BIICL

Alston, P, *The United Nations and Human Rights* , 1992, Oxford: Clarendon

Arend, A and Beck, R, *International Law and the Use of Force,* 1993, London: Routledge

Attard, D, *The Exclusive Economic Zone in International Law*, 1987,Oxford: OUP

Badr, GM, *State Immunity: An Analytical and Prognostic View,* 1984, The Hague: M Nijhoff

Bassiouni, MC, *The Law of the International Criminal Tribunal for the Former Yugoslavia*, 1996, New York: Transnational

Baxter, R, 'Multilateral treaties as evidence of customary international law' (1965) BYIL 275

Baxter, RR, 'International law in "her infinite variety"' (1980) 29 ICLQ 549

Bowett, D, 'Contemporary developments in legal techniques in the settlement of disputes' (1983) 180 Hague Recueil 169

Bowett, D, 'The State Immunity Act 1978' (1978) 37 CLJ 193

Bowett, D, *Self Defence in International Law*, 1958, Manchester: Manchester UP

Bowett, D, *The Law of International Organisations*, 1982, London: Stevens

Boyle, A and Birnie, P, *International Law and the Environment*, 1992, Oxford: OUP

Brandon, M, 'The validity of non-registered treaties' (1952) 29 BYIL 186

Brown, J, 'Diplomatic immunity: State practice under the Vienna Convention on Diplomatic Relations' 37 ICLQ 53

Brownlie, I, 'Reality and efficacy of international law' (1982) 53 BYIL 1

Brownlie, I, *International Law and the Use of Force by States*, 1963, Oxford: OUP

Brownlie, I, *Principles of Public International Law*, 5th edn, 1998, Oxford: OUP

Brownlie, I, *System of the Law of Nations: State Responsibility*, 1983, Oxford: OUP

Carty, A, 'Critical international law' (1991) 2 EJIL 66

Carty, A, *The Decay of International Law*, 1986, Manchester: Manchester UP

Cassese, A, (1985) 192 Hague Recueil 331

Cassese, A, *International Law in a Divided World*, 1989, Oxford: Clarendon

Cassese, A, *The Current Legal Regulation of the Use of Force*, 1986, Dordrecht: Nijhoff

Charlesworth, H, Chinkin, C and Wright, S, 'Feminist approaches to international law' (1991) 85 AJIL

Charney, J, 'The persistent objector rule and the development of customary International Law' (1985) 56 BYIL 1

Cheng, B, 'UN resolutions on outer space: instant customary law', in Cheng, B (ed), *International Law: Practice and Teaching*, 1982, London: Stevens

Cheng, B, *General Principles of Law as Applied by International Courts and Tribunals*, 1987, London: Stevens

Cheng, B, *The International Law of Air Transport*, 1962, London: Stevens.

Chinkin, CM, 'The challenge of soft law: development and change in international law' (1989) 38 ICLQ 850

Christenson, G, 'The world court and *jus cogens*' (1987) 81 AJIL 93

Churchill, R and Lowe, A, *The Law of the Sea*, 2nd edn, 1988, Manchester: Manchester UP

Collier, J, 'Is international law really part of the law of England?' (1989) 38 ICLQ 924

Crawford, J, *The Creation of States in International Law*, 1988, Oxford: Clarendon

Crawford, J, *The Rights of Peoples*, 1988, Oxford: Clarendon

Czaplinski, W, 'Sources of law in the *Nicaragua* case' (1989) 38 ICLQ 15

D'Amato, A, 'Is international law really "law?"' (1985) 79 Northwestern UL Rev 1301

D'Amato, A, *International Law: Process and Prospects*, 2nd edn, 1995, Irvington, NY: Transnational

D'Amato, A, *The Concept of Custom in International Law*, 1971, New York: Cornell UP

Dannilenko, GM, 'International *jus cogens*: issues of law making' (1991) 2 EJIL 42

De Arechaga, J, 'The work of the ICJ' (1987) 58 BYIL 1

De Lupis, I, *The Law of War*, 1989, Cambridge: CUP

Denza, E, *Diplomatic Law: Commentary on the Vienna Convention on Diplomatic Relations*, 1976, Dobbs Ferry, New York: Oceana

Dinstein, *War, Aggression and Self-Defence*, 2nd edn, 1994, Cambridge: Grotius

Eide, A, *et al*, *The Universal Declaration of Human Rights: A Commentary*, 1992, Oslo: Scandinavian UP

Elias, T, *The Modern Law of Treaties*, 1974, Dobbs Ferry, New York: Oceana

Falk, R, *The Status of Law in International Society*, 1970 Princeton: Princeton University Center of International Studies

Fastenrath, J, 'Relative normativity in international law' (1993) 4 EJIL 305

Fawcett, J, *Outer Space*, 1984, Manchester: Manchester UP

Fitzmaurice, G, 'Some problems regarding the formal sources of international law' [1958] Symbolae Verzijl 153

Fitzmaurice, G, 'The general principles of international law considered from the standpoint of the rule of law' (1957) 92 Hague Recueil 70

Fitzmaurice, G, 'The foundations of the authority of international law and the problem of enforcement' (1956) 19 MLR 1

Franck, TM, *The Power of Legitimacy among Nations*, 1990, New York: OUP

Gaja, G, '*Jus cogens* beyond the Vienna Convention' (1981) 172 Hague Recueil

Gianviti, F, 'The IMF and external debt' (1989) 215 Hague Recueil 205

Gilbert, G, 'Crimes sans frontieres: jurisdictional problems in English law' (1992) 63 BYIL 415

Gold, J, 'Developments in the international monetary system' (1982) 174 Hague Recueil 107

Goodwin-Gill, G, *The Refugee in International Law*, 2nd edn, 1996, Oxford: OUP

Gray, C, *Judicial Remedies in International Law*, 1992, Oxford: Clarendon

Hannum, H, *Guide to Human Rights Practice*, 2nd edn, 1993, Pennsylvania: Pennsylvania UP

Hossain, K, *Legal Aspects of the New International Economic Order*, 1980, London: Pinter

Jackson, JH and Davey, WJ, *Legal Problems of International Economic Relations*, 3rd edn, 1995, St Paul: West

Jacobs, F and Roberts, S (eds), *The Effect of Treaties in Domestic Law*, 1987, London: Sweet & Maxwell

Jennings, R, 'Extraterritorial jurisdiction and the US antitrust laws' (1957) 33 BYIL 146

Jennings, R, 'The internal practice of the ICJ' (1988) 59 BYIL 31

Jennings, R, *The Acquisition of Territory in International Law*, 1963, Manchester: Manchester UP

Kelsen, H, *Principles of International Law*, 2nd edn, revised and edited by RW Tucker, 1966, New York: Holt, Rinehart and Winston

Kennedy, D, *International Legal Structures*, 1987, Baden Baden: Nomos

Kennedy, D, 'The sources of international law' [1987] 2 American University Journal of International Law and Policy 1

Kiss, A and Shelton, D, *International Environmental Law*, 1991, London: Graham and Trotman

Koskenniemi, M (ed), *International Law (International Library of Essays in Law and Legal Theory)*, 1992, Aldershot: Dartmouth

Lauterpacht, E (ed), *International Law*, 1970, Cambridge:CUP

Lauterpacht, H, *Recognition in International Law*, 1947, Cambridge: CUP

Lee, L, *Consular Law and Practice*, 2nd edn, 1991, Oxford: Clarendon

Lewis, CJ, *State and Diplomatic Immunity*, 3rd edn, 1990, London: LLP

Lillich, RB, *International Law of State Responsibility for Injuries to Aliens*, 1983, Charlottesville: Virginia UP

Lillich, RB, *The Human Rights of Aliens in Contemporary International Law*, 1984, Manchester: Manchester UP

Lowe, V (ed), *Extraterritorial Jurisdiction*, 1983, Cambridge: Grotius

Lyster, S, *International Wildlife Law*, 1985, Cambridge: Cambridge UP

Mann, FA, 'The consequences of an international wrong' (1975–76) 49 BYIL 1

Mann, FA, 'The doctrine of *jus cogens* in international law', in Mann, FA, *Further Studies in International Law*, 1990, Oxford: OUP

Mann, FA, 'The protection of shareholders' interests in the light of the *Barcelona Traction* case' (1973) 67 AJIL 259

Mann, FA, 'Inviolability and other problems of the Vienna Convention on Diplomatic Relations', in Mann, FA, *Further Studies in International Law*, 1990, Oxford: OUP

Mann, FA, 'The doctrine of international jurisdiction revisited after 20 years' (1984) 186 Hague Recueil

Mann, FA, 'The State Immunity Act 1978' (1979) 50 BYIL 43

Mann, FA, *Foreign Affairs in English Courts*, 1986, Oxford: OUP

McClanahan, GV, *Diplomatic Immunity*, 1989, London: Hurst

McCoubrey, H, *International Humanitarian Law*, 1990, Aldershot: Dartmouth

McDougal, M and Reisman, NM, *International Law in Contemporary Perspective*, 1981, Mineola: Foundation

McDougal, M and Myres, S, 'International law, power and policy: a contemporary conception' (1953) 82 Hague Recueil 133

McGovern, E, *International Trade Regulation*, 1995, Exeter: Globefield

McNair, AD, *The Law of Treaties*, 1961, Oxford: Clarendon

McRae, M, 'The legal effects of interpretative declarations' (1978) 49 BYIL 155

Mendelsohn, M, 'Practice, propaganda and principle in international law' [1990] CLP 3

Meron, T, *Human Rights and Humanitarian Norms as Customary Law*, 1989, Oxford: OUP

Merrills, J, *International Dispute Settlement*, 2nd edn, 1991, Cambridge: Grotius

Meuwissen, T, 'The relationship between international law and municipal law and fundamental rights' (1977) 24 Netherlands International L Rev 192

O'Connel, DP, *The International Law of the Sea*, 1982, Oxford: OUP

Palmer, T, 'New ways to make international environmental law' (1992) 86 AJIL 259

Parry, C, *The Sources and Evidences of International Law*, 1965, Manchester: Manchester UP

Reuter, P, *Introduction to the Law of treaties*, 1995, London: Kegan Paul

Roberts, A and Guelff, R, *Documents on the Laws of War*, 2nd edn, 1989, Oxford: Clarendon

Robertson, A and Merrills, J, *Human Rights in the World*, 3rd edn, 1989, New York: Manchester UP

Rosenne, S, *The Law and Practice of the International Court*, 3rd edn, 1997, The Hague: Nijhoff

Sahovic, M and Bishop, WW, 'The Authority of the State', in Sorensen, M (ed), *Manual of International Law*, 1968, London: Macmillan

Sands, P, *The International Liability for Transboundary Oil Pollution*, 1989, Cambridge: Grotius

Schachter, O, 'Resolution of the General Assembly as evidence of law' (1982) 178 Hague Recueil 114

Schachter, O, 'The twilight existence of non-binding international agreements (1977) 71 AJIL 296

Schmidt, MG, *Common Heritage or Burden?*, 1989, Oxford: Clarendon

Schreuer, CH, 'The waning of the sovereign State: towards a new paradigm in international law' (1993) 4 EJIL 441

Schreuer, CH, *State Immunity: Some Recent Developments*, 1988, Cambridge: Grotius

Scobie, I, 'Towards the elimination of international law: some radical scepticism about radical scepticism' (1990) 61 BYIL 339

Seidl-Hohenveldern, I, 'International economic law' (1986) 198 Hague Recueil 198

Seidl-Hohenveldern, I, 'International economic soft law' (1979) 163 Hague Recueil 68

Sharma, *International Boundary Disputes and International Law*, 1976, the Hague: Nijhoff

Shaw, M, 'Territory in international law' (1982) 13 Netherlands Yearbook of International Law 62

Shaw, M, *Title to Territory in Africa*, 1984, Oxford: OUP

Shawcross, CN and Beaumont, A, 1995, *Air Law*, London: Butterworth

Shubber, S, *Jurisdiction over Crimes Committed on Board Aircraft*, 1973, The Hague: Nijhoff

Sieghart, P, *Human Rights in International Law*, 1984, Oxford: OUP

Sieghart, P, *The International Law of Human Rights*, 1984, Oxford: OUP

Sieghart, P, *The Lawful Rights of Mankind*, 1985, Oxford: Clarendon

Sinclair, I, 'The Law of Sovereign Immunity: Recent Developments' (1980-II) 167 Hague Recueil 113

Sinclair, I, *The Vienna Convention on the Law of Treaties*, 1984, Manchester: Manchester UP

Skubiszewski, K, 'Use of force by States', in Sorensen (ed), *Manual of International Law*, 1968, London: Macmillan

Sloan, B, 'General Assembly resolutions revisited' (1987) 58 BYIL 93

Snyder, F and Slinn, P, *International Law of Development*, 1987, Abingdon: Professional

Sohn, L, 'The Stockholm Declaration on the Human Environment' (1973) 14 Harvard International LJ 423

Stanbrook, I and Stanbrook, C, *The Law and Practice of Extradition*, 1980, Chichester: Rose

Starke, JG, 'Monism and dualism in the theory of international law' (1936) 17 BYIL 66

Starke, JG, 'The acquisition of territory by newly emerged States' (1965–66) 41 BYIL 411

Sucharitkul, S, *State Immunities and Trading Activities in International Law*, 1959, London: Stevens

Symmons, CR, 'United Kingdom abolition of the doctrine of recognition of governments: a rose by another name?' [1981] PL 249

Sztucki, J, *Jus Cogens and the Vienna Convention on the Law of Treaties*, 1974, New York: Springer-Verlag

Talmon, S, 'Recognition of governments: an analysis of the new British policy and practice' (1992) 63 BYIL 231

Thirlway, HWA, 'The law and procedure of the ICJ' (1989) 60 BYIL; (1990) 61 BYIL

Thirlway, HWA, *International Customary Law and Codification*, 1972, Leiden: AW Sijthoff

Thornberry, P, *International Law and the Rights of Minorities*, 1991, Oxford: OUP

Tunkin, GI, 'Remarks on the juridical nature of customary norms of international law' (1961) 49 California L Rev 419

Tunkin, GI, 'Is general international law customary law only?' (1993) 4 EJIL 534

United Nations, *Handbook on the Peaceful Settlement of Disputes between States*, 1992, New York: United Nations

Vali, FA, *Servitudes in International Law*, 1958, London: Stevens

Van Hoof, GJH, *Re-thinking the Sources of International Law*, 1983, Dordrecht: Kluwer

Villiger, ME, *Customary International Law and Treaties*, 2nd edn, 1997, Dordrecht: Kluwer

Virally, M, 'The sources of international law', in Sorensen (ed) *Manual of International Law*, 1968, London: Macmillan

Volker, ELM and Steenbergen, J, *Leading Cases and Materials on the External Relations of the EC*, 1985, Dordrecht: Kluwer

Watson, H, 'A realistic jurisprudence of international law' (1980) 34 Yearbook of World Affairs 265

White, ND, 'The State Immunity Act 1978' (1979) 42 MLR 72

Whomersley, C, 'Some reflections on immunity of individuals for official acts' (1992) 41 ICLQ 848

Wilson, HA, *International Law and the Use of Force by National Liberation Movements*, 1988, Oxford: Clarendon

INDEX

Index